D0875713

PRAISING IT NEW

PRAISING
THE BEST OF THE
IT NEW
NEW CRITICISM

Edited by Garrick Davis

Foreword by William Logan

Swallow Press / Ohio University Press • Athens, Ohio

Swallow Press / Ohio University Press, Athens, Ohio 45701
www.ohioswallow.com

© 2008 by Swallow Press / Ohio University Press
"Forward into the Past: Reading the New Critics" © 2008 by William Logan

Printed in the United States of America

Swallow Press / Ohio University Press books are printed on acid-free paper ⊗ ™

16 15 14 13 12 11 10 09 08   5 4 3 2 1

Library of Congress Cataloging-in-Publication Data

Praising it new : the best of the New Criticism / edited by Garrick Davis ; foreword by William Logan.
    p. cm.
  Anthology of New Criticism, edited with an introduction, notes, biographies, and selected bibliographies.
  Includes bibliographical references.
  ISBN-13: 978-0-8040-1108-2 (alk. paper)
  ISBN-10: 0-8040-1108-7 (alk. paper)
  ISBN-13: 978-0-8040-1109-9 (pbk. : alk. paper)
  ISBN-10: 0-8040-1109-5 (pbk. : alk. paper)
  1. New Criticism—United States. 2. American poetry—History and criticism—Theory, etc. 3. English poetry—History and criticism—Theory, etc. I. Davis, Garrick.
  PS79.P73 2008
  801'.950973—dc22

2008004301

CONTENTS

FOREWORD

Forward into the Past: Reading the New Critics

WILLIAM LOGAN

Great poetry is not a matter of memorable snippets and gobbets—but without snippets worth remembering, poetry does not exist. The critic must give meaning to memory; yet there has long been an argument about what that job of work requires. If you walk into college classrooms now, you'll meet two armed camps of critics. In a poetry workshop, discussion turns on the poem's meaning and how meaning becomes lodged through metaphor, image, meter, symbol, allusion, argument (what Pound called the *"art of getting meaning into words"*). In a literature class, the poem will be analyzed, often as not, as a "text" that mirrors the world of its making, as if it had been written not by a poet but by Sir History or Dame Sociology. The professor will employ the cryptic jargon of methods that to their promoters reveal hidden tensions in language, but to their detractors tar and feather poems for the sins of another day and force very different poets to sing the same tune. To the Marxists, the sins remain those of class; to the feminists, gender; to the scholars of ethnic literature, race—they wave over poems, mere poems, a Geiger counter that detects the decaying radioactivity of racism, sexism, and class hatred. "Sir!" says the critic, accusingly. "I have discovered a swarm of phonemes in your poems." "Aye, sir," the poet replies, "the damned lines are infested with 'em."

Perhaps there was a prelapsarian era, before the flood of "theory," as it is so unhappily called, when men were men and women were women and critics were critics. There may also have been an exact hour in the seventeenth century when, as Eliot declared, a "dissociation of sensibility set in" or a specific day, "in or about December 1910," when Virginia Woolf noticed that "human character changed." My quarrelsome reading of history, however, suggests that men were never simply men, women never simply women, and critics never simply critics.

There did exist, however, a golden age of modern literary criticism, roughly from the early essays of Eliot and Pound to the end of the heyday of *Partisan Review.* Call it fifty years when a reader could pick up certain magazines and be gratified, provoked, or happily infuriated by the discussion of poems (of course it didn't seem a golden age then—it never does at the time). We are rarely so stimulated or flabbergasted today (when infuriated now, we're not happy about it)—if readers have grown no less intelligent, the time must no longer be ripe for critics. One of the ways a time is not right is if it falls after an age of such criticism.

I've known poets who kept runs of the old *Partisan* or *Hudson* or *Kenyon Review* at arm's reach, just to browse the stray essays of an Empson or a Blackmur. I'm speaking of criticism proper, not reviewing—for reviewing is always its own fashion, its pleasure the Force-9 gales of the reviewers themselves, whether George Bernard Shaw and Bernard Haggin on music, James Agee and Pauline Kael on film, Mary McCarthy on fiction, Randall Jarrell on poetry, or Robert Hughes on art. A good reviewer is both of his time and beyond his time—we can read his charities and condemnations with delight, even if we haven't the faintest notion of the book or play or painting judged. A good *critic*, however, must say something, not just about a particular work of art, but about the structures of the art itself; and to understand him you need to know the work criticized.

Great critics have a long afterlife, but sometimes a long beforelife. When Matthew Arnold at last gave them a name, "touchstones" had lain ready for a millennium or two in the teaching of schoolboys—among ancient grammarians a similar idea rescued lines from the lost plays of Athenian drama. It's good to be reminded of exactly what Arnold wrote:

> Indeed there can be no more useful help for discovering what poetry belongs to the class of the truly excellent, and can therefore do us most good, than to have always in one's mind lines and expressions of the great masters, and to apply them as a touchstone to other poetry.

Arnold was not without subtlety, for he went on:

> Of course we are not to require this other poetry to resemble them; it may be very dissimilar. But if we have any tact we shall find them, when we have lodged them well in our minds, an infallible touchstone for detecting the presence or absence of high poetic quality, and also the degree of this quality, in all other poetry which we may place beside them.

Behind Pound's gists and piths and Eliot's vaunted gift for quotation lies the touchstone. Though Arnold has often been disparaged, I caught a critic recently referring to the touchstone with approval; and a century or two from now it will not be dead to critics yet. We think of criticism as transient, as *à la mode* and all too soon outmoded; but the name and nature of criticism have sometimes proved more durable than what was criticized. (Though I hesitate to accept it, the reviewers of one day may inherit the outmoded critical practice of the day before—reviewers are often conservative in their technique, even when radical in their tastes.)

Criticism never starts over; yet sometimes it suffers a forgetfulness, an ill nature, an ignorance of its soundings. There's no going back, but there is a going forward that does not fear looking back. The complaint about "theory" is that it treats literature with the dispatch of a meat grinder—if you know the method, long before the poem has been dragged in by the tail you can predict whether the butcher will sell you the sausages of Derrida, or Foucault, or Lacan. It's disheartening to see a poem raided for evidence of sins long defunct or treated with a forensics kit, as if it were a crime scene. I therefore find it hard to work up enthusiasm for the latest announcement of racism in *Oliver Twist* or *Huckleberry Finn* (there are scholars who would ban both books, and gladly), or elitism in Shakespeare, or sexism in, well, in just about everything. There have been sophisticated and revealing studies on these subjects, but in the classroom what you tend to get is a professor who counts penis symbols—this reduces criticism to something like trainspotting. If even teaching Shakespeare is elitist, what of the professor who uses a jargon so pompous, tortured, and harrowingly opaque the man on the street would stand scratching his head about it for a month of Sundays?

Seventy or eighty years ago, what we now call criticism was forbidden in literature classes—English professors clerkishly confined their studies to literary history or philology. John Crowe Ransom recalled the head of graduate English studies at a prestigious university telling a student, "This is a place for exact scholarship, and you want to do criticism. Well, we don't allow criticism here, because that is something which anybody can do." (Ransom remarked that it was easy for a professor of literature "to spend a lifetime in compiling the data of literature and yet rarely or never commit himself to a literary judgment.") What passed for "criticism," where it existed at all, was an amateur course in appreciation, the instructor like some hereditary retainer rambling the halls of a stately home, pointing out the heroic cast of a rusty suit of armor or the haunted eye of some time-darkened portrait, as well as the cupful of finger bones dubiously from the Battle of Towton—the professor, in his own house of literature, repeated the plot; muttered respectfully over artistic touches of language; and enthused, if not on the nobility of character, then on its iniquity.

New Criticism was created by a divided and often embattled group of American poets (they were almost all poets) born between 1888 and 1907—John Crowe Ransom, Allen Tate, Robert Penn Warren, Cleanth Brooks, W. K. Wimsatt, R. P. Blackmur, Yvor Winters, and Kenneth

Burke, less a close-knit family than a quarrel of cousins and perfect strangers. To them may be added their precursors and influences, the expatriate poets Ezra Pound and T. S. Eliot, the English literary critic I. A. Richards, and Richards's brilliant student William Empson. The age in which they practiced most fruitfully, from about 1913 to 1963, was an age newly scientific, the age of Einstein's relativity and Bohr's quantum mechanics (the equations of Maxwell half a century earlier came from a ruder mechanic age). New Criticism grew up partly to justify modernist literature—the novel's novel disruption of voice or narrative and the rejection of meter in *vers libre* were the literary correlatives of the repudiation of figure in painting and sculpture (English use of *avant garde* for art rather than armies dates only to 1910). The tension between Eliot's resistance, in "The Perfect Critic," to the "vague suggestion of the scientific vocabulary" in criticism and his wish to cultivate an Aristotelian intelligence that might "see the object as it really is" dramatized the ambivalence toward science in much of the New Criticism. (When Ransom writes that "criticism must become more scientific," he means "precise and systematic," not something using beakers and Bunsen burners.)

The New Critics reacted violently against the impressionistic criticism of the previous generation, which favored books like Palgrave's *The Golden Treasury* and *A Thousand and One Gems of English Poetry*—such criticism longed for the moral suasion of art. (The moral appeal has been smuggled back into literature in the self-righteousness of the "poetry of witness.") The comprehensions of art a century later live within the climate that reaction established; even when our arts are more conservative, or at least tolerant of conservation (figure has returned to painting, fiction has abandoned experiment in wholesale fashion, meter occasionally worms its way back into poetry), they are created on the foundations of the moderns, and often with the moderns in mind—in fiction the sense of belatedness is especially demanding.

According to René Wellek, there were four major objections to New Criticism: that it was (1) merely aestheticism by another name; (2) a method profoundly unhistorical; (3) an attempt to make criticism a science; and (4) a deracinated imitation of the French schoolboy's *explication de texte*. In the American volume of *A History of Modern Criticism, 1750–1950*, he vigorously refutes these accusations. Even so, if a shiver of suspicion regarding history or the whiff of aestheticism infects New Criticism (any criticism so fond of literature must have some taste for the aesthetic), the bill of complaint betrays the prejudice of critics at times dubious in their own practice of history and flagrantly hostile to aesthetic concern—which has meant, among other things, hostile to the notion that some poems are better than others. As Winters wrote some seventy years ago, "The professor of English Literature, who believes that taste is relative yet who endeavors to convince his students that *Hamlet* is more worthy of their attention than some currently popular novel, is in a serious predicament." The resolution to this dilemma is that the professor has stopped trying.

Critics cannot be blamed for every wrong turn taken by art; but a less frantic approval of the modish and "original," of gesture over craft, of idea over execution might have spared visual art in the past half century from fashions dizzying in their rapid and rabid succession. (This is not to deny that an artist as rich in character as Richard Serra may emerge from a sometimes trivial movement; but the rage for novelty that produced the broken crockery of Julian Schnabel, now almost forgotten as a painter, has replaced it with the formaldehyde-drenched sharks of Damien Hirst.) To look back at the New Critics is to indulge in a nostalgia for the days when books were books and not "texts" (when critics natter on about "dialogic intertextuality" in *Batman*, my eyes glaze over). Beyond the holy trinity of race, class, and gender; beyond the murder of the author (hardly the death of him); beyond jargon-ridden, vatic, riddling "methodologies" fond of sophomoric wordplay and genial mystification (recall how Pound despised "critics who use vague terms to *conceal* their meaning"), contemporary theory remains largely inoculated against the way poems work. In the end, it is a very dull way to look at poetry.

Despite its pretense of dispassion, theory—which often lies in a fog of unfinished philosophy—turns out to be surprisingly judgmental, for behind the mask of tolerance, the love of the "free play of the signifier" and respect for the "other," the "valorization" of relative values, it wallows in the age's prejudice: for female over male, black over white, poor over rich, gay over straight, Palestinian over Jew, colonist over empire, native over colonist, anarchy over order. It little matters where one's sympathies lie in such oppositions, if they require sympathies at all (rather than, say, curiosity); but you can't pretend to moral relativity, as theorists do, and embrace such prejudices. Theory often mingles, in a way Orwell would have noticed, the language of revolutionaries with that of prison guards—who will "subvert" these subversives or "interrogate" these interrogators? For a criticism that prizes nonconformity and "difference," theory proves alarmingly fond of orthodoxy. (In the classrooms of theory, all readings are tolerated, except the wrong ones—the morally absolute masquerades here as the morally relative and manages to be high-minded about it, too. Kafka would have smiled in recognition.) Having deprived the author of "agency," reduced him to the victim or weathervane of his time, the smug discriminations of theory are exactly those New Criticism set out to disturb. To the New Critics, the poem struggles to escape its time; the interest lies in the rare poem that succeeds, not the mass that do not. (The importance of some poems, especially in the modern period—*Howl*, for example—may *be* largely sociological. That is their failure.)

Poets become poets by making sense of the poets who came before them. As literature classes were slowly dyed in the blood of theory, New Criticism retreated to writing workshops. Like all schools of criticism, the New Critics have been derided by their successors; but they retain an extraordinary influence on the daily practice of criticism (this division between practice and theory is more than peculiar just now). It's not surprising that the close reading of poetry has remained the method of choice in workshops, which are—lamentably, no doubt—more concerned with craft than capitalism. They still believe, with Allen Tate, that "literature is neither religion nor social engineering." The New Critics developed a mechanics of poetry that any poet would love—by attending to the words. Such critics did not treat poems in ignorance of what literary history or biography reveal, but these became the means of criticism, not the end. This turned topsy-turvy the academic study of the day—it would be no less radical now.

Wellek reminds us that close reading was a late development in New Criticism—it was not the point but the tool developed to prove the point. The method was secured by the textbook *Understanding Poetry* (1938), which became a mainstay of college classrooms for two generations. The editors, Cleanth Brooks and Robert Penn Warren, tried to dissect what a poem said, not reveal the poet as a dolt, a closet racist, a chauvinist, a snob, or a prig. New Criticism takes as its task to understand how meaning and feeling are invented in language (theory flinches as much from the neural itch of feeling as from aesthetics) and to judge if some poems are better than others—not simply better at kowtowing to the mores and manners of our day, but better in aesthetic terms. If New Criticism seems a bit like a hen house built by foxes, the foxes sometimes walked and talked like hens themselves, out of respect—or because they *were* secretly hens themselves.

T. S. Eliot is often accused of writing the criticism necessary to read his own poetry (this is like a man rich in nails inventing the hammer); and his taste for Donne and antipathy to Milton did clear-cut a few square miles of metaphysics for *The Waste Land*. (It might be more accurate to say he was working out in prose the apprehensions about his predecessors that animated his verse line.) Many of Eliot's insights, however, apply to poetry generally and can be read against his notions of taste. Taste is always more narrow than criticism, at least if it is at all interesting *as* taste. However much Ezra Pound's promotion of the troubadours licensed his poems in pseudo-medieval English (he labored like a man trying to drag Edwardian England back to a world of sack-buts and krummhorns), in the end Provençal lyrics have proved one of the standards against which his poems are measured. Meanwhile, it did not harm the troubadours to be dragged to the century's attention. Pound's later drum-beating for Li Po, the Anglo-Saxons, Chaucer, and Dante opened a few dusty parlors for *The Cantos* in the House of Fame; but, judged against such poetry, *The Cantos* look less than dominating. The tastes have endured, but criticism abides even when taste goes astray—criticism creates values, taste often vices, though that is no reason not to have taste.

What happened to New Criticism? Even the best critical method may run out of things to say, may become arthritic in its response to new work, may reduce itself merely to choreography. (Though New Critics analyzed some kinds of poetry more brilliantly than others, any universal criticism might be universally suspect. New Criticism works well for a poetry of logical and defensible meaning, even modernist work where ambiguities have been strained to the limit—but there *is* a limit.) By the sixties, a sense of routine and exhaustion had set in—most of the New Critics still alive had stopped writing criticism (though Empson was scribbling combative reviews until the end), and younger critics were not, most of them, nearly so talented, nor were they poets. (The poets—Jarrell, Berryman, Lowell—made better reviewers than they did writers of critical essays.) The founders, a cleverer lot than their followers, grew old in their understandings; but discoverers always claim the richest land in *terra incognita*. New Criticism did, eventually, grow tired of it-self; its legacy lies in the craft revealed and the clarity gained.

Most contemporary poetry is written in a tradition, a tradition more susceptible to New Critical readings than to any criticism that has fol-lowed. New Criticism remains our basic critical language—the reader schooled there is best placed to return to Matthew Arnold, or David Masson, or Coleridge, or Dr. Johnson, and extract the most from them. (I suspect the New Criticism was largely founded on the footnotes of editors of Shakespeare, beginning with Johnson, if not before.) The good doctor says little in *The Lives of the Poets* about how poems actu-ally work; but he illustrates the value to the critic of generous knowledge, a robust sensibility, and a style like a battery of cannon.

If I have been unfair to the natural disaster of theory, I have grown weary of hearing my students complain that their professors don't like literature very much—indeed, seem to prefer truffle-hunting the sins of the authors. (Of course I'm interested in the effect of his time upon the poet, and vice versa—but I'm not interested only in that.) Theory has reduced literature largely to what Winters calls the didactic function— but the poems, in their poor, poetic way, serve almost entirely as a store- house of negative examples. A generation of students, having chosen English because they love books, has graduated bemused that anyone would read such debauched and offensive trash—the brightest wonder why studying literature seems no different from political indoctrination and why their professors have turned into grim-faced, razor-beaked theocrats. (It's past time to launch a new *Dunciad*—where is Pope when you need him?)

I used to think things would get better; but young PhD's now learn no way but theory's way of discussing poetry, if they discuss poetry at all (they also know little about grammar and less about meter, but those are complaints for another hour). We might instead think of what was lost when the New Critics were cast into the shadows and, as Eliot said of the metaphysical poets, "consider whether their virtue was not something permanently valuable, which subsequently disappeared, but ought not to have disappeared." It might be time to rehearse arguments about poetry won almost a century ago, arguments worth winning once more. By bringing together the essential texts of New Criticism in *Praising It New*, Garrick Davis has done a new generation of students a great service.

ACKNOWLEDGMENTS

My gratitude must first be expressed to Erika Koss, who assisted me in the editing of this anthology, and to David Sanders, who provided encouragement and advice in the planning of this masochistic endeavor.

Thanks must also be given to David Lynn, John Pickard, and especially Marlene Landefeld at the *Kenyon Review* for their help and research regarding permissions requests. Leigh Ann Couch at *Sewanee Review* also heroically tracked down permissions.

Joseph Frank generously permitted the reprinting of work by R. P. Blackmur, while John M. Walsh provided the same for Cleanth Brooks.

Also, thanks to Neil Otte at *New Directions*, Mack McCormick at the University Press of Kentucky, Stacey Hayes at the University of Georgia Press, and Habiba Alcindor at the *Nation* for their swift and thoughtful work.

No gratitude should be expressed to Harcourt Brace, which required fees for the reprinting of R. P. Blackmur that were so exorbitant I briefly considered excluding him altogether. (The rights for many important works by T. S. Eliot, Cleanth Brooks, Kenneth Burke, and I. A. Richards are also retained by the firm.) Oddly, Harcourt Brace does not seem interested in keeping Blackmur's books in print, and the combination of these two grotesque practices may leave him (and other important New Critics) inaccessible to future generations of readers.

Garrick Davis

A NOTE ON THE EDITOR'S METHOD
OF SELECTION

Many readers will notice that such important New Critics as I. A. Richards, William Empson, and F. R. Leavis are absent from these pages. For reasons of space, only American critics have been included here (with the sole exception of Canadian Hugh Kenner). Obviously, the British contributors to the New Criticism deserve their own book—which should appear as a companion to this volume in due time.

In addition, such notable American critics of that time as Edmund Wilson, Lionel Trilling, F. O. Matthiessen, and Alfred Kazin have been deliberately excluded since they were never considered New Critics. Likewise, the neo-Aristotelians (also known as the Chicago school) led by the scholar R. S. Crane have been left out. Also, there are no female writers included here because there were no female New Critics in America. The arguable exception would be Marianne Moore—but though she was certainly a supporter of the New Criticism, her own critical prose (so perceptive and aphoristic in its typical brevity) does not place her meaningfully within the camp.

Randall Jarrell and Delmore Schwartz have been included because, though they did not consider themselves part of the movement, they inherited and inhabited the earlier generation's ideas. Both men wrote compulsively on their immediate ancestors, reviewed their books assiduously, and ultimately praised more than they repudiated. (This cannot be said, for example, of their contemporary Karl Shapiro, who wrote an interesting antimodernist diatribe, *In Praise of Ignorance*.) As for Hugh Kenner, he was included in this volume because so much of his teaching and writing life was spent in America, and so much of his mind was preoccupied with explicating American masters such as Pound and Eliot— he would also have probably disliked being placed among the British (as those who have read his study *A Sinking Island* can attest).

Finally, British spellings have been altered to accord with our American ways.

INTRODUCTION

The Golden Age of Poetry Criticism

> I do not believe there has been another age in which so much
> extraordinarily good criticism of poetry has been written.
> —Randall Jarrell

A renaissance begins, if it begins at all, in the unlikeliest of places. It was in the cramped London offices of one Methuen & Co. Ltd., for instance, as the printers finished binding a collection of essays entitled *The Sacred Wood* in 1920, that the Golden Age of Poetry Criticism dawned. Methuen & Company Limited—the name conjures up the very archetype of the tiny English press, now long extinct. And the author of the collection? Once an unfamiliar name as well, now rather famous, belonging to an American living in England: Thomas Stearns Eliot.

Now, a renaissance is not born in one place and, to be effective, is not the product of one man. Dates can be quibbled with, and other books chosen. Two years before, the first collection of another expatriate American's prose had been issued in New York: *Pavannes and Divisions* by Ezra Pound. That poet's criticism was to be just as influential, in its way, as Eliot's—but the two were close friends and collaborators, so it is not particularly enlightening to investigate who came first. They both helped create the "current of ideas" that produced so much of what is admirable in the poetry and criticism of the twentieth century.

The Sacred Wood, then, has been preferred because it contains many passages in which that current was shaped into its most durable and influential forms. Of what was this current of ideas composed? In the preface to the 1928 edition of his book, Eliot offered the following summation of its intent: "It is an artificial simplification, and to be taken only with caution, when I say that the problem appearing in these essays, which gives them what coherence they have, is the problem of the integrity of poetry, with the repeated assertion that when we are considering poetry we must consider it primarily as poetry and not another thing." Out of this rather drab statement, almost a banality, sprang the New Criticism.

To understand why this should be so would require a catalog of the faults and errors committed by the literary ancestors of Eliot's generation. And in the first forty-six pages of his book, evaluating figures as diverse as Aristotle, Arthur Symons, and Charles Whibley, the author provided just such an examination. In these pages we are told: "Hence, in criticizing poetry, we are right if we begin, with what sensibility and what knowledge of other poetry we possess, with poetry as excellent words in excellent arrangement and excellent meter. That is what is called the technique of verse."

The outline of a new approach to poetry criticism was contained in these lines. Poetry was to be criticized *as poetry*, and not some other thing, which meant "as excellent words in excellent arrangement and excellent meter." It was to be studied as a definite genre of writing—with its own history and practices—and not for the sake of its philological origins, its political aims, or its social content. It was to be studied by comparing the present object under scrutiny with the best samples drawn from foreign and ancient languages—the great procedure of comparative literature. It was an art form that critics could study as seriously as any of the classical subjects, and that some had taken as seriously as life itself.

Eliot's approach to—or attitude toward—criticism had an enormous influence on his contemporaries, of course, but it made even greater demands. It assumed that the critic approached his task with the demeanor of the professional—poetry being such an essentially serious matter that it rewarded one's lifelong study and devotion. It assumed that the critic would exceed the scholar's narrow specializations and be intimate with the finest poetry of many periods and literatures. The attitude, in other words, assumed *perfection*—or the disinterested pursuit of it. But who would care to commit to such a profession? Who would study with such devotion?

And what was the purpose of such cultivation—criticism being itself such a tenuous and disposable form of writing? The ages remembered their artists—but their book reviewers? Eliot, considering why the criticism of artists should so often prove durable, remarked:

> The writer of the present essay once committed himself to the statement that "The poetic critic is criticizing poetry in order to create poetry." He is now inclined to believe that the "historical" and the "philosophical" critics had better be called historians and philosophers quite simply. As for the rest, there are merely various degrees of intelligence. It is fatuous to say that criticism is for the sake of "creation" or creation for the sake of criticism. It is also fatuous to assume that there are ages of criticism and ages of creativeness,

as if by plunging ourselves into intellectual darkness we were in better hopes of finding spiritual light. The two directions of sensibility are complementary; and as sensibility is rare, unpopular, and desirable, it is to be expected that the critic and the creative artist should frequently be the same person.

And so Eliot dispensed with the old division of labor between the artist and critic. For it remains a perpetual heresy that the critic who is not an artist must be the more dependable judge simply because he does not engage in "creative activity"—he is impartial and thus objective—whereas the artist's engagement must alter his views, making them partisan. The creative and critical faculties were not mutually exclusive, Eliot averred. In fact, "When one creative mind is better than another, the reason often is that the better is the more critical."

This, then, was the impetus and justification for the rise of the poet-critics. Of those associated with the New Criticism—in the American South (John Crowe Ransom, Allen Tate, Cleanth Brooks, and Robert Penn Warren), in England (I. A. Richards, William Empson, and F. R. Leavis), and elsewhere (Yvor Winters, R. P. Blackmur, Kenneth Burke, and William K. Wimsatt)—all but Wimsatt and Brooks were published poets. And if we include those mavericks who came a generation later—like Randall Jarrell and W. H. Auden—then we shall immediately see just how various and how great this golden age was.

Nor should it surprise us that the greatest age of poetry criticism was also one of the great ages of poetry in English, if we take Eliot's comments for truth. When the poets of the first half of the twentieth century began to write criticism seriously—that is, as an examination of themselves, and of their contemporaries and masters *undertaken as a necessity for their own development*—their own poetry matured as a matter of course. Here is at least one reason our poetry enjoyed such a renaissance in that half century: never before, or since, has the discussion of the techniques of poetry been so varied or so astute.

These poets brought about a great revolution in criticism in their day, a revolution that overturned the practices of nineteenth-century literary scholarship. Of course, to fully understand this we must first understand the previous regime they conquered and replaced.

•   •   •

In that earlier era, the university student who wished to study poetry could do so—for the sake of its word origins, or its historical and social implications. What he could *not* do was study poetry for the sake of writing it himself. The study of literature was conducted, in other words, only for purposes ulterior to literature, while scholarship had become an end in itself.

It was this brand of academic scholarship that was denounced by the poet-critics, who labeled it the *historical method*. In the most brilliant denunciation of this approach—or antipathy—to literature ever written, entitled "Miss Emily and the Bibliographer," Allen Tate complained: "It was—and still is—a situation in which it is virtually impossible for a young man to get a critical, literary education. If he goes to a graduate school he comes out incapacitated for criticism. . . . He cannot discuss the literary object in terms of its specific form; all that he can do is to give you its history or tell you how he feels about it."

Now the reason why young men interested in literature became incapacitated for criticism, became either historians who "amassed irrelevant information" or journalists "for whom intensity of feeling was the sole critical standard," was their inability to "discern the objectivity of the forms of literature." They were *expressionists*, who saw no essential difference between the genres of literature—between poetry, plays, and prose.

When *Paradise Lost, Othello*, and *Huckleberry Finn* are lumped together in one genre, what is left to discuss but the content or the history of the particular work? To the expressionist, "the subject matter alone has objective status, the specific form of the work being external and mechanical—mere technique." Tate added: "The historical method will not permit us to develop a critical instrument for dealing with works of literature as existent objects; we see them as expressive of substances beyond themselves. At the historical level the work expresses its place and time, or the author's personality, but if the scholar goes further and says anything about the work, he is expressing himself. Expressionism is here a sentiment, forbidding us to think and permitting us to feel as we please."

Tate's argument demonstrated that, within the critical terms of the historical method, criticism was impossible. The literary historian and the journalist, the learned academic scholar and the ignorant book reviewer, wrote incoherently for the same reason: they had abandoned the very categories that would allow the formation of a critical judgment. So the revolution that overturned nineteenth-century academic scholarship returned, first, to the categories such scholarship had dismissed: *form* and *technique*.

It must be said, in passing, that *revolution* is not a romantic but, rather, a precise term—indicative, as it is, of warfare and great social change—and that the literary historian and the book reviewer perceived the threat to themselves and fought vigorously against a superior force. Eliot had robbed them of the traditional sanction of their office, while Tate had destroyed their philosophy, but they were not about to abdicate their department chairs or their assignments. As Yvor Winters testified:

> I am proud of my part in this revolution, but my part was not an easy one. Of the four gentleman who have been head of the department of English at Stanford in my time, the second, the late Professor A. G. Kennedy, told me that criticism and scholarship do not mix, that if I wanted to become a serious scholar I should give up criticism. And he added that my publications were a disgrace to the department. Fortunately for myself, he was the only one of the four department heads to hold these views, but one was almost enough. And he was far from an exception so far as the profession as a whole was concerned.

This was the state of affairs that confronted the poet-critics, and which Irving Babbitt had been the first to excoriate in *Literature and the American College* (1908). Only with great difficulty did such brilliant teachers as Winters and Leavis gain tenure. In 1941, Randall Jarrell despaired of the situation:

> The last twenty-five years have seen part of a great change in taste, a reevaluation of most English poetry—I do not believe there is a good critic living who shares the taste of the scholars. So the scholar, who already looks down on the critic in theory, is able in practice to condemn him, even more severely and sincerely, for the immense disparity in all their judgments. Today there is not merely a division between scholars and critics, but open war; and since scholars are a thousand to one, and occupy every important position in the colleges, there is not much hope for the critic.

By 1955 all of this had changed so dramatically that the English critic A. Alvarez complained, in an essay that year, about the number of poets teaching at universities. What had happened in the space of those fourteen years? I am tempted to say that by the sheer force of its analytical brilliance, and by the eloquence of its proponents—a number of whom are counted among the great teachers of the century—the New Criticism simply replaced the old academic scholarship in the universities. And this is certainly true, but not the whole truth either—in that victory was sown the defeat of the New Criticism. It became a victim of its own success.

For the scholars never went away, nor could they remain silent. Tenure demanded that they produce articles. If scholarship had been soundly defeated by criticism, then the scholars would simply do the unthinkable: they would switch sides and become critics too. Rather than collect facts, they would analyze the structure of poems; rather than sift clues concerning Keats's love life, they would sift through the verbs of "Hyperion."

This had been the hope of more than one New Critic. In 1938, John Crowe Ransom had called on the professors of English to make "the erection of intelligent standards" in literature their collective business. That same year, Cleanth Brooks and Robert Penn Warren published their textbook, *Understanding Poetry*, which soon became the standard classroom guide for a generation. But this was the Indian summer of our golden age. As Robert Lowell remarked, "Somehow in the next generation the great analytical and philosophical project turned to wood, the formidable inertia of the pedagogue, the follow-up man."

The New Criticism was boiled down to a method by these imitators, who promptly produced analysis every bit as dull as their hastily abandoned scholarship. Alvarez explained: "Perhaps this was inevitable; the pressures of academic life sooner or later bring everything down to plain method. For method is impersonal, almost an abstraction. It reduces to clear teachable elements the huge complexity of disciplined response and choice which the reader otherwise needs to re-create for himself each poem. Method, of whatever brand, is always easier to teach than discrimination." So the New Criticism became institutionalized, with the usual results.

• • •

What has been traced here is the rise and fall of the New Criticism *as an academic movement*. Its influence in the universities was immense: it was responsible for the introduction of close reading and the verbal analysis of the rhetorical structures of poetry as the central method of criticism, and that contribution remains vital to this day. That is not, however, the main concern of this essay. We must, instead, discover what is worthy of retrieval from that former time; what principles led these critics to issue such lasting judgments; what examples may serve to guide us through the bewildering present.

The main point that must be made is that there was nothing new about the New Criticism. What Eliot found in Aristotle, and Tate in Longinus, was a criticism of permanence rendered so because it "looked solely and steadfastly at the object." Ransom called such criticism *ontological*, while Brooks preferred the term *formalist*; the latter enjoyed a wide circulation, and was eventually preferred as the group name for the New Critics and their followers. It was given a better title by R. P. Blackmur, who called it *technical* criticism: it would focus on the techniques and forms of poetry, not on its uses as social comment, political statement, or historical document.

That poetry criticism should concern itself primarily with "the technique of poetry" appears, at first sight, to be an obvious point and self-evident: it is not. There are temptations that distract critics, always, away from the poem. The temptation to make poetry the crude vehicle of some purpose greater than itself is perennial, and has overwhelmed the least among us (like the Marxist critics of the 1930s and the academic theorists of the 1980s) as well as a few of the greatest (witness Plato and the elderly Tolstoy). The temptation to moralize is greater still.

It has often been remarked that the New Critics do not hold together as a group, sharing as they do such disparate aims. Yet they were all united against certain deplorable tendencies in their time: principally, the use of such extra-literary criteria in the judgment of poetry. Of course, this was sometimes honored more in the breach than in the letter—Yvor Winters, for example, was a tireless moralizer. Yet his morality was no simple affair of interrogating a poem's subject matter for heresies, but rather weighing how every metrical variation, "no matter how slight, is exactly perceptible and as a result can be given exact meaning as an act of moral perception." Even this most moral-minded of New Critics argued for the indivisibility of form and content, so that the distance of his insights from the comparable blushings of Victorian prudery at, say, Swinburne's verse simply cannot be measured.

Such distinctions were lost on a subsequent generation of readers who preferred their ideas to be simplistic. Academic taste, in particular, ridiculed the New Critics for half a century as either insufficiently political or politically unsound. Randall Jarrell anticipated the pointless objections of these detractors and called it "a fool's game." The poet-critic Stephen Burt has been even more unsparing: "It is a grim irony that people who argued for the independence of literary art from instrumental political ends should now be impeached or dismissed for their politics; it makes an even harsher irony that people who insisted on fine distinctions now get lumped together as reactionaries."

Since those who objected to the New Criticism most categorically have left us with little criticism of any value, we may conclude that envy animated more than a few.

And what of the ironies of our own day? When poets occupy all the important positions at the universities and scholars have all but disappeared, it seems inconceivable that criticism has become a neglected art once more. Yet *technique* has, again, become a suspect word. The graduates of our writing programs produce derivative work, and negligible scholarship, and receive polite applause for their errors. Doggerel is festooned with laurel. There seems, at the moment, little hope for the critic. It is at such a time that the directions of Ezra Pound become prescient once more: "The first step of a renaissance, or awakening, is the importation of models for painting, sculpture, or writing. . . . We must learn what we can from the past, we must learn what other nations have done successfully under similar circumstances, we must think how they did it."

This is the spirit that brought about a golden age—and will again, when the poets are ready.

PART 1 — WHERE TO BEGIN?

THOUGH THE FOUNDERS OF THE NEW CRITICISM, T. S. ELIOT AND EZRA POUND, were the greatest poet-critics of the twentieth century and appear to us *sui generis* several generations later, they both had important intellectual forebears. Yet the literary culture of the United States was largely sterile in the early 1900s. Eliot has written that, for young poets in 1908, "the question was still: where do we go from Swinburne? And the answer appeared to be, nowhere." Meanwhile, the study of English literature did not exist as an academic discipline at all, while literary works were considered primarily as source documents for the more important fields of philology and history. Literary criticism, such as it was, hardly interested anyone outside the universities (with a few brilliant exceptions such as the epicurean journalist James Huneker). There were only a few popular magazines that deigned to print literature, and no little magazines devoted to it.

At Harvard University, Eliot studied under Irving Babbitt and George Santayana. According to Yvor Winters in *The Function of Criticism* (1957), the revolution in the teaching of literature in American colleges "was initiated, doubtless, by Babbitt," who was feared by his colleagues because "he was a critic and had defended criticism as an academic discipline and had attacked the colleges and universities for neglecting it." The cosmopolitan philosopher-poet George Santayana was also influential, with his students (who included Wallace Stevens and Gertrude Stein) and his books (such as *Interpretations of Poetry and Religion,* 1900). In addition, while at Harvard Eliot discovered Arthur Symons's *The Symbolist Movement in Literature,* which introduced his generation to such French poets as Jules Laforgue and Villiers de l'Isle Adam.

Ezra Pound, meanwhile, studied the latest philological methods of what would later be called comparative literature at the University of Pennsylvania, and then promptly produced a book of scholarship on medieval Romance-language poetry (*The Spirit of Romance*) and a long article ("I

Gather the Limbs of Osiris") that marked the opening of his distinguished career as a poet and polemicist of various poetic schools (modernism, imagism, vorticism). Having moved to England in 1908, Pound became acquainted with William Butler Yeats, Ford Madox Ford, and the philosopher T. E. Hulme. (Hulme's *Speculations* was an important book for the modernist poets, particularly its chapter on romanticism and classicism.) Pound also admired the work of the French poet-critic Remy de Gourmont, and he even translated some of his works into English.

A year after Eliot moved to London in 1914, he was introduced to Ezra Pound through a mutual friend, Conrad Aiken. Pound and Eliot soon became lifelong friends and literary allies. Together, their early works of criticism clearly signaled a new direction in literature that was enthusiastically embraced by a number of British and American disciples who extended and codified their ideas into the New Criticism (though both Eliot and Pound ignored, or quibbled with, that name and some of their disciples).

In the arc of these essays, the reader can also trace the history of the New Criticism as a critical movement in the American universities: it begins with one of the founding documents, the introduction to T. S. Eliot's *The Sacred Wood*, and then continues on from Allen Tate's destruction of the historical method of the old guard to John Crowe Ransom's highly influential call to professors and scholars, "Criticism, Inc."

Suggested Further Reading

The Symbolist Movement in Literature, by Arthur Symons (1895)
Interpretations of Poetry and Religion, by George Santayana (1900)
Literature and the American College, by Irving Babbitt (1908)
The Spirit of Romance, by Ezra Pound (1910)
The Pathos of Distance, by James Huneker (1912)
America's Coming-of-Age, by Van Wyck Brooks (1915)
Speculations, by T. E. Hulme (1924)
Remy de Gourmont, translated and edited by Richard Aldington (2 vols.; 1929)
Axel's Castle, by Edmund Wilson (1931)
The Pound Era, by Hugh Kenner (1972)

THE IDEAL APPROACH TO CRITICISM

Introduction to *The Sacred Wood*

T. S. ELIOT

Published in 1920, The Sacred Wood *was T. S. Eliot's first collection of critical essays and quite possibly the most influential book of poetry criticism of the twentieth century. Here, he outlines a new direction in poetry criticism: the study of poetry for itself and not as social commentary, political statement, or historical documentation.*

To anyone who is at all capable of experiencing the pleasures of justice, it is gratifying to be able to make amends to a writer whom one has vaguely depreciated for some years. The faults and foibles of Matthew Arnold are no less evident to me now than twelve years ago, after my first admiration for him; but I hope that now, on re-reading some of his prose with more care, I can better appreciate his position. And what makes Arnold seem all the more remarkable is, that if he were our exact contemporary, he would find all his labor to perform again. A moderate number of persons have engaged in what is called "critical" writing, but no conclusion is any more solidly established than it was in 1865. In the first essay in the first *Essays in Criticism* we read that

> it has long seemed to me that the burst of creative activity in our literature, through the first quarter of this century, had about it in fact something premature; and that from this cause its productions are doomed, most of them, in spite of the sanguine hopes which accompanied and do still accompany them, to prove hardly more lasting than the productions of far less splendid epochs. And this prematureness comes from its having proceeded without having its proper data, without sufficient material to work with. In other words, the English poetry of the first quarter of this century, with plenty of energy, plenty of creative force, did not know enough. This makes Byron so empty of matter, Shelley so incoherent, Wordsworth even, profound as he is, yet so wanting in completeness and variety.

This judgment of the Romantic Generation has not, so far as I know, ever been successfully controverted; and it has not, so far as I know, ever made very much impression on popular opinion. Once a poet is accepted, his reputation is seldom disturbed, for better or worse. So little impression has Arnold's opinion made, that his statement will probably be as true of the first quarter of the twentieth century as it was of the nineteenth. A few sentences later, Arnold articulates the nature of the malady:

> In the Greece of Pindar and Sophocles, in the England of Shakespeare, the poet lived in a current of ideas in the highest degree animating and nourishing to the creative power; society was, in the fullest measure, permeated by fresh thought, intelligent and alive; and this state of things is the true basis for the creative power's exercise, in this it finds its data, its materials, truly ready for its hand; all the books and reading in the world are only valuable as they are helps to this.

At this point Arnold is indicating the center of interest and activity of the critical intelligence; and it is at this perception, we may almost say, that Arnold's critical activity stopped. In a society in which the arts were seriously studied, in which the art of writing was respected, Arnold might have become a critic. How astonishing it would be, if a man like Arnold had concerned himself with the art of the novel, had compared Thackeray with Flaubert, had analyzed the work of Dickens, had shown his contemporaries exactly why the author of *Amos Barton* is a more *serious* writer than Dickens, and why the author of *La Chartreuse de Parme* is more serious than either? In *Culture and Anarchy*, in *Literature and Dogma*, Arnold was not occupied so much in establishing a criticism as in attacking the uncritical. The difference is that while in constructive work something can be done, destructive work must incessantly be repeated; and furthermore Arnold, in his destruction, went for game outside of the literary preserve altogether, much of it political game untouched and inviolable by ideas. This activity of Arnold's we must regret; it might perhaps have been carried on as effectively, if not quite so neatly, by some disciple (had there been one) in an editorial position on a newspaper. Arnold is not to be blamed: he wasted his strength, as men of superior ability sometimes do, because he saw something to be done and no one else to do it. The temptation, to any man who is interested in ideas and primarily in literature, to put literature into the corner until he cleaned up the whole country first, is almost irresistible. Some persons, like Mr. Wells and Mr. Chesterton, have succeeded so well in this latter profession of setting the house in order, and have attracted so much more attention than Arnold, that we must conclude that it is indeed their proper rôle, and that they have done well for themselves in laying literature aside.

Not only is the critic tempted outside of criticism. The criticism proper betrays such poverty of ideas and such atrophy of sensibility that men who ought to preserve their critical ability for the improvement of their own creative work are tempted into criticism. I do not intend from this the usually silly inference that the "Creative" gift is "higher" than the critical. When one creative mind is better than another, the reason often is that the better is the more critical. But the great bulk of the work of criticism could be done by minds of the second order, and it is just these minds of the second order that are difficult to find. They are necessary for the rapid circulation of ideas. The periodical press—the ideal literary periodical—is an instrument of transport; and the literary periodical press is dependent upon the existence of a sufficient number of second-order (I do not say "second-rate," the word is too derogatory) minds to supply its material. These minds are necessary for that "current of ideas," that "society permeated by fresh thought," of which Arnold speaks.

It is a perpetual heresy of English culture to believe that only the first-order mind, the Genius, the Great Man, matters; that he is solitary, and produced best in the least favorable environment, perhaps the Public School; and that it is most likely a sign of inferiority that Paris can show so many minds of the second order. If too much bad verse is published in London, it does not occur to us to raise our standards, to do anything to educate the poetasters; the remedy is, Kill them off. I quote from Mr. Edmund Gosse:[1]

> Unless something is done to stem this flood of poetastry the art of verse will become not merely superfluous, but ridiculous. Poetry is not a formula which a thousand flappers and hobbledehoys ought to be able to master in a week without any training, and the mere fact that it seems to be now practiced with such universal ease is enough to prove that something has gone amiss with our standards. . . . This is all wrong, and will lead us down into the abyss like so many Gadarene swine unless we resist it.

We quite agree that poetry is not a formula. But what does Mr. Gosse propose to do about it? If Mr. Gosse had found himself in the flood of poetastry in the reign of Elizabeth, what would he have done about it? would he have stemmed it? What exactly is this abyss? and if something "has gone amiss with our standards," is it wholly the fault of the younger generation that it is aware of no authority that it must respect? It is part of the business of the critic to preserve tradition—where a good tradition exists. It is part of his business to see literature steadily and to see it whole; and this is eminently to see it *not* as consecrated by time, but to see it beyond time; to see the best work of our time and the best work of twenty-five hundred years ago with the same eyes.[2] It is part of his business to help the poetaster to understand his own limitations. The poetaster who understands his own limitations will be one of our useful second-order minds; a good minor poet (something which is very rare) or another good critic. As for the first-order minds, when they happen, they will be none the worse off for a "current of ideas"; the solitude with which they will always and everywhere be invested is a very different thing from isolation, or a monarchy of death.

NOTE.—I may commend as a model to critics who desire to correct some of the poetical vagaries of the present age, the following passage from a writer who cannot be accused of flaccid leniency, and the justice of whose criticism must be acknowledged even by those who feel a strong partiality toward the school of poets criticized:—

"Yet great labor, directed by great abilities, is never wholly lost; if they frequently threw away their wit upon false conceits, they likewise sometimes struck out unexpected truth: if their conceits were far-fetched, they were often worth the carriage. To write on their plan, it was at least necessary to read and think. No man could be born a metaphysical poet, nor assume the dignity of a writer, by descriptions copied from descriptions, by imitations borrowed from imitations, by traditional imagery, and hereditary similes, by readiness of rhyme, and volubility of syllables.

"In perusing the works of this race of authors, the mind is exercised either by recollection or inquiry: something already learned is to be retrieved, or something new is to be examined. If their greatness seldom elevates, their acuteness often surprises; if the imagination is not always gratified, at least the powers of reflection and comparison are employed; and in the mass of materials which ingenious absurdity has thrown together, genuine wit and useful knowledge may be sometimes found buried perhaps in grossness of expression, but useful to those who know their value; and such as, when they are expanded to perspicuity, and polished to elegance, may give lustre to works which have more propriety though less copiousness of sentiment."—JOHNSON, *Life of Cowley*

1. *Sunday Times*, May 30, 1920.
2. Arnold, it must be admitted, gives us often the impression of seeing the masters, whom he quotes, as canonical literature, rather than masters.

The Perfect Critic

T. S. ELIOT

In this essay from The Sacred Wood, *Eliot examines the defects of the greatest literary critics, and explains why artists are themselves often the best critics. Here too is found Eliot's famous dictum that, where criticism is concerned, "there is no method except to be very intelligent."*

"Eriger en lois ses impressions personnelles, c'est le grand effort d'un homme s'il est sincère."

—*Lettres à l'Amazone*

Coleridge was perhaps the greatest of English critics, and in a sense the last. After Coleridge we have Matthew Arnold; but Arnold—I think it will be conceded—was rather a propagandist for criticism than a critic, a popularizer rather than a creator of ideas. So long as this island remains an island (and we are no nearer the Continent than were Arnold's contemporaries) the work of Arnold will be important; it is still a bridge across the Channel, and it will always have been good sense. Since Arnold's attempt to correct his countrymen, English criticism has followed two directions. When a distinguished critic observed recently, in a newspaper article, that "poetry is the most highly organized form of intellectual activity," we were conscious that we were reading neither Coleridge nor Arnold. Not only have the words "organized" and "activity," occurring together in this phrase, that familiar vague suggestion of the scientific vocabulary which is characteristic of modern writing, but one asked questions which Coleridge and Arnold would not have permitted one to ask. How is it, for instance, that poetry is more "highly organized" than astronomy, physics, or pure mathematics, which we imagine to be, in relation to the scientist who practices them, "intellectual activity" of a pretty highly organized type? "Mere strings of words," our critic continues with felicity and truth, "flung like dabs of paint across a blank canvas, may awaken surprise . . . but have no significance whatever in the history of literature." The phrases by which Arnold is best known may be inadequate, they may assemble more doubts than they dispel, but they usually have some meaning. And if a phrase like "the most highly organized form of intellectual activity" is the highest organization of thought of which contemporary criticism, in a distinguished representative, is capable, then, we conclude, modern criticism is degenerate.

The verbal disease above noticed may be reserved for diagnosis by and by. It is not a disease from which Mr. Arthur Symons (for the quotation was, of course, not from Mr. Symons) notably suffers. Mr. Symons represents the other tendency; he is a representative of what is always called "aesthetic criticism" or "impressionistic criticism." And it is this form of criticism which I propose to examine at once. Mr. Symons, the critical successor of Pater, and partly of Swinburne (I fancy that the phrase "sick or sorry" is the common property of all three), *is* the "impressionistic critic." He, if anyone, would be said to expose a sensitive and cultivated mind—cultivated, that is, by the accumulation of a considerable variety of impressions from all the arts and several languages—before an "object"; and his criticism, if anyone's, would be said to exhibit to us, like the plate, the faithful record of the impressions, more numerous or more refined than our own, upon a mind more sensitive than our own. A record, we observe, which is also an interpretation, a translation; for it must itself impose impressions upon us, and these impressions are as much created as transmitted by the criticism. I do not say at once that this is Mr. Symons; but it is the "impressionistic" critic, and the impressionistic critic is supposed to be Mr. Symons.

At hand is a volume which we may test.[1] Ten of these thirteen essays deal with single plays of Shakespeare, and it is therefore fair to take one of these ten as a specimen of the book:

> *Antony and Cleopatra* is the most wonderful, I think, of all Shakespeare's plays . . .

and Mr. Symons reflects that Cleopatra is the most wonderful of all women:

> The queen who ends the dynasty of the Ptolemies has been the star of poets, a malign star shedding baleful light, from Horace and Propertius down to Victor Hugo; and it is not to poets only . . .

What, we ask, is this for? as a page on Cleopatra, and on her possible origin in the dark lady of the Sonnets, unfolds itself. And we find, gradually, that this is not an essay on a work of art or a work of intellect; but that Mr. Symons is living through the play as one might live it through in the theatre; recounting, commenting:

> In her last days Cleopatra touches a certain elevation . . . she would die a thousand times, rather than live to be a mockery and a scorn in men's mouths . . . she is a woman to the last . . . so she dies . . . the plays ends with a touch of grave pity . . .

Presented in this rather unfair way, torn apart like the leaves of an artichoke, the impressions of Mr. Symons come to resemble a common type of popular literary lecture, in which the stories of plays or novels are retold, the motives of the characters set forth, and the work of art therefore made easier for the beginner. But this is not Mr. Symons's reason for writing. The reason why we find a similarity between his essay and this form of education is that *Antony and Cleopatra* is a play with which we are pretty well acquainted, and of which we have, therefore, our own impressions. We can please ourselves with our own impressions of the characters and their emotions; and we do not find the impressions of another person, however sensitive, very significant. But if we can recall the time when we were ignorant of the French symbolists, and met with *The Symbolist Movement in Literature*, we remember that book as an introduction to wholly new feelings, as a revelation. After we have read Verlaine and Laforgue and Rimbaud and return to Mr. Symons's book, we may find that our own impressions dissent from his. The book has not, perhaps, a permanent value for the one reader, but it has led to results of permanent importance for him.

The question is not whether Mr. Symons's impressions are "true" or "false." So far as you can isolate the "impression," the pure feeling, it is, of course, neither true nor false. The point is that you never rest at the pure feeling; you react in one of two ways, or, as I believe Mr. Symons does, in a mixture of the two ways. The moment you try to put the impressions into words, you either begin to analyze and construct, to "ériger en lois," or you begin to create something else. It is significant that Swinburne, by whose poetry Mr. Symons may at one time have been influenced, is one man in his poetry and a different man in his criticism; to this extent and in this respect only, that he is satisfying a different impulse; he is criticizing, expounding, arranging. You may say this is not the criticism of a critic, that it is emotional, not intellectual—though of this there are two opinions, but it is in the direction of analysis and construction, a beginning to "ériger en lois," and not in the direction of creation. So I infer that Swinburne found an adequate outlet for the creative impulse in his poetry; and none of it was forced back and out through his critical prose. The style of the latter is essentially a prose style; and Mr. Symons's prose is much more like Swinburne's poetry than it is like his prose. I imagine—though here one's thought is moving in almost complete darkness—that Mr. Symons is far more disturbed, far more profoundly affected, by his reading than was Swinburne, who responded rather by a violent and immediate and comprehensive burst of admiration which may have left him internally unchanged. The disturbance in Mr. Symons is almost, but not quite, to the point of creating; the reading sometimes fecundates his emotions to produce something new which is not criticism, but is not the expulsion, the ejection, the birth of creativeness.

The type is not uncommon, although Mr. Symons is far superior to most of the type. Some writers are essentially of the type that reacts in excess of the stimulus, making something new out of the impressions, but suffer from a defect of vitality or an obscure obstruction which prevents nature from taking its course. Their sensibility alters the object, but never transforms it. Their reaction is that of the ordinary emotional person developed to an exceptional degree. For this ordinary emotional person, experiencing a work of art, has a mixed critical and creative reaction. It is made up of comment and opinion, and also new emotions which are vaguely applied to his own life. The sentimental person, in whom a work of art arouses all sorts of emotions which have nothing to do with that work of art whatever, but are accidents of personal association, is an incomplete artist. For in an artist these suggestions made by a work of art, which are purely personal, become fused with a multitude of other suggestions from multitudinous experience, and result in the production of a new object which is no longer purely personal, because it is a work of art itself.

It would be rash to speculate, and is perhaps impossible to determine, what is unfulfilled in Mr. Symons's charming verse that overflows into his critical prose. Certainly we may say that in Swinburne's verse the circuit of impression and expression is complete; and Swinburne was therefore able, in his criticism, to be more a critic than Mr. Symons. This gives us an intimation why the artist is—each within his own limitations—oftenest to be depended upon as a critic; his criticism will be criticism, and not the satisfaction of a suppressed creative wish—which, in most other persons, is apt to interfere fatally.

Before considering what the proper critical reaction of artistic sensibility is, how far criticism is "feeling" and how far "thought," and what sort of "thought" is permitted, it may be instructive to prod a little into that other temperament, so different from Mr. Symons's, which issues in generalities such as that quoted near the beginning of this article.

II

"L'écrivain de style abstrait est presque toujours un sentimental, du moins un sensitif. L'écrivain artiste n'est presque jamais un sentimental, et très rarement un sensitif."

—*Le Problème du Style*

The statement already quoted, that "poetry is the most highly organized form of intellectual activity," may be taken as a specimen of the abstract style in criticism. The confused distinction which exists in most heads between "abstract" and "concrete" is due not so much to a manifest fact of the existence of two types of mind, an abstract and a concrete, as to the existence of another type of mind, the verbal, or philosophic. I, of course, do not imply any general condemnation of philosophy; I am, for the moment, using the word "philosophic" to cover the unscientific ingredients of philosophy; to cover, in fact, the greater part of the philosophic output of the last hundred years. There are two ways in which a word may be "abstract." It may have (the word "activity," for example) a meaning which cannot be grasped by appeal to any of the senses; its apprehension may require a deliberate suppression of analogies of visual or muscular experience, which is none the less an effort of imagination. "Activity" will mean for the trained scientist, if he employ the term, either nothing at all or something still more exact than anything it suggests to us. If we are allowed to accept certain remarks of Pascal and Mr. Bertrand Russell about mathematics, we believe that the mathematician deals with objects—if he will permit us to call them objects—which directly affect his sensibility. And during a good part of history the philosopher endeavored to deal with objects which he believed to be of the same exactness as the mathematician's. Finally Hegel arrived, and if not perhaps the first, he was certainly the most prodigious exponent of emotional systematization, dealing with his emotions as if they were definite objects which had aroused those emotions. His followers have as a rule taken for granted that words have definite meanings, overlooking the tendency of words to become indefinite emotions. (No one who had not witnessed the event could imagine the conviction in the tone of Professor Eucken as he pounded the table and exclaimed *Was ist Geist? Geist ist . . .*) If verbalism were confined to professional philosophers, no harm would be done. But their corruption has extended very far. Compare a mediaeval theologian or mystic, compare a seventeenth-century preacher, with any "liberal" sermon since Schleiermacher, and you will observe that words have changed their meanings. What they have lost is definite, and what they have gained is indefinite.

The vast accumulations of knowledge—or at least of information— deposited by the nineteenth century have been responsible for an equally vast ignorance. When there is so much to be known, when there are so many fields of knowledge in which the same words are used with different meanings, when every one knows a little about a great many things, it becomes increasingly difficult for anyone to know whether he knows what he is talking about or not. And when we do not know, or when we do not know enough, we tend always to substitute emotions for thoughts. The sentence so frequently quoted in this essay will serve for an example of this process as well as any, and may be profitably contrasted with the opening phrases of the *Posterior Analytics*. Not only all knowledge, but all feeling, is in perception. The inventor of poetry as the most highly organized form of intellectual activity was not engaged in perceiving when he composed this definition; he had nothing to be aware of except his own emotion about "poetry." He was, in fact, absorbed in a very different "activity" not only from that of Mr. Symons, but from that of Aristotle.

Aristotle is a person who has suffered from the adherence of persons who must be regarded less as his disciples than as his sectaries. One must be firmly distrustful of accepting Aristotle in a canonical spirit; this is to lose the whole living force of him. He was primarily a man of not only remarkable but universal intelligence; and universal intelligence means that he could apply his intelligence to anything. The ordinary intelligence is good only for certain classes of objects; a brilliant man of science, if he is interested in poetry at all, may conceive grotesque judgments: like one poet because he reminds him of himself, or another because he expresses emotions which he admires; he may use art, in fact, as the outlet for the egotism which is suppressed in his own speciality. But Aristotle had none of these impure desires to satisfy; in whatever sphere of interest, he looked solely and steadfastly at the object; in his short and broken treatise he provides an eternal example—not of laws, or even of method, for there is no method except to be very intelligent, but of intelligence itself swiftly operating the analysis of sensation to the point of principle and definition.

It is far less Aristotle than Horace who has been the model for criticism up to the nineteenth century. A precept, such as Horace, or Boileau gives us, is merely an unfinished analysis. It appears as a law, a rule, because it does not appear in its most general form; it is empirical. When we understand necessity, as Spinoza knew, we are free because we assent. The dogmatic critic, who lays down a rule, who affirms a value, has left his labor incomplete. Such statements may often be justifiable as a saving of time; but in matters of great importance the critic must not coerce, and he must not make judgments of worse and better. He must simply elucidate: the reader will form the correct judgment for himself.

And again, the purely "technical" critic—the critic, that is, who writes to expound some novelty or impart some lesson to practitioners of an art—can be called a critic only in a narrow sense. He may be analyzing perceptions and the means for arousing perceptions, but his aim is limited and is not the disinterested exercise of intelligence. The narrowness of the aim makes easier the detection of the merit or feebleness of the work; even of these writers there are very few—so that their "criticism" is of great importance within its limits. So much suffices for Campion. Dryden is far more disinterested; he displays much free intelligence; and yet even Dryden—or any *literary* critic of the seventeenth century—is not quite a free mind, compared, for instance, with such a mind as Rochefoucauld's. There is always a tendency to legislate rather than to inquire, to revise accepted laws, even to overturn, but to reconstruct out of the same material. And the free intelligence is that which is wholly devoted to inquiry.

Coleridge, again, whose natural abilities, and some of whose performances, are probably more remarkable than those of any other modern critic, cannot be estimated as an intelligence completely free. The nature of the restraint in his case is quite different from that which limited the seventeenth-century critics, and is much more personal. Coleridge's metaphysical interest was quite genuine, and was, like most metaphysical interest, an affair of his emotions. But a literary critic should have no emotions except those immediately provoked by a work of art—and these (as I have already hinted) are, when valid, perhaps not to be called emotions at all. Coleridge is apt to take leave of the data of criticism, and arouse the suspicion that he has been diverted into a metaphysical hare-and-hounds. His end does not always appear to be the return to the work of art with improved perception and intensified, because more conscious, enjoyment; his center of interest changes, his feelings are impure. In the derogatory sense he is more "philosophic" than Aristotle. For everything that Aristotle says illuminates the literature which is the occasion for saying it; but Coleridge only now and then. It is one more instance of the pernicious effect of emotion.

Aristotle had what is called the scientific mind—a mind which, as it is rarely found among scientists except in fragments, might better be called the intelligent mind. For there is no other intelligence than this, and so far as artists and men of letters are intelligent (we may doubt whether the level of intelligence among men of letters is as high as among men of science) their intelligence is of this kind. Sainte-Beuve was a physiologist by training; but it is probable that his mind, like that of the ordinary scientific specialist, was limited in its interest, and that this was not, primarily, an interest in art. If he was a critic, there is no doubt that he was a very good one; but we may conclude that he earned some other name. Of all modern critics, perhaps Remy de Gourmont had most of the general intelligence of Aristotle. An amateur, though an excessively able amateur, in physiology, he combined to a remarkable degree sensitiveness, erudition, sense of fact and sense of history, and generalizing power.

We assume the gift of a superior sensibility. And for sensibility wide and profound reading does not mean merely a more extended pasture. There is not merely an increase of understanding, leaving the original acute impression unchanged. The new impressions modify the impressions received from the objects already known. An impression needs to be constantly refreshed by new impressions in order that it may persist at all; it needs to take its place in a system of impressions. And this system tends to become articulate in a generalized statement of literary beauty.

There are, for instance, many scattered lines and tercets in the *Divine Comedy* which are capable of transporting even a quite uninitiated reader, just sufficiently acquainted with the roots of the language to decipher the meaning, to an impression of overpowering beauty. This impression may be so deep that no subsequent study and understanding will intensify it. But at this point the impression is emotional; the reader in the ignorance which we postulate is unable to distinguish the poetry from an emotional state aroused in himself by the poetry, a state which may be merely an indulgence of his own emotions. The poetry may be an accidental stimulus. The end of the enjoyment of poetry is a pure contemplation from which all the accidents of personal emotion are removed; thus we aim to see the object as it really is and find a meaning for the words of Arnold. And without a labor which is largely a labor of the intelligence, we are unable to attain that stage of vision *amor intellectualis Dei.*

Such considerations, cast in this general form, may appear commonplaces. But I believe that it is always opportune to call attention to the torpid superstition that appreciation is one thing, and "intellectual" criticism something else. Appreciation in popular psychology is one faculty, and criticism another, an arid cleverness building theoretical scaffolds upon one's own perceptions or those of others. On the contrary, the true generalization is not something superposed upon an accumulation of perceptions; the perceptions do not, in a really appreciative mind, accumulate as a mass, but form themselves as a structure; and criticism is the statement in language of this structure; it is a development of sensibility. The bad criticism, on the other hand, is that which is nothing but an expression of emotion. And emotional people—such as stockbrokers, politicians, men of science—and a few people who pride themselves on being unemotional—detest or applaud great writers such as Spinoza or Stendhal because of their "frigidity."

The writer of the present essay once committed himself to the statement that "The poetic critic is criticizing poetry in order to create poetry." He is now inclined to believe that the "historical" and the "philosophi-

cal" critics had better be called historians and philosophers quite simply. As for the rest, there are merely various degrees of intelligence. It is
fatuous to say that criticism is for the sake of "creation" or creation for
the sake of criticism. It is also fatuous to assume that there are ages of
criticism and ages of creativeness, as if by plunging ourselves into intellectual darkness we were in better hopes of finding spiritual light. The
two directions of sensibility are complementary; and as sensibility is
rare, unpopular, and desirable, it is to be expected that the critic and the
creative artist should frequently be the same person.

1. *Studies in Elizabethan Drama*, by Arthur Symons.

How to Read

EZRA POUND

One of the truly indispensable essays of the twentieth century, this essay appeared in the New York Herald Tribune *in 1929. It not only provides a definition of the function of literature but also presents Pound's three famous categories of poetry, as well as a severe accounting of all the great poets from Homer to Heine. This is the syllabus of modernist poetry.*

Part One: Introduction

Largely Autobiographical, Touching the Present, and More or Less Immediately Past, "State of Affairs."

Literary instruction in our "institutions of learning"[1] was, at the beginning of this century, cumbrous and inefficient. I dare say it still is. Certain more or less mildly exceptional professors were affected by the "beauties" of various authors (usually deceased), but the system, as a whole, lacked sense and co-ordination. I dare say it still does. When studying physics we are not asked to investigate the biographies of all the disciples of Newton who showed interest in science, but who failed to make any discovery. Neither are their unrewarded gropings, hopes, passions, laundry bills, or erotic experiences thrust on the hurried student or considered germane to the subject.

The general contempt of "scholarship," especially any part of it connected with subjects included in university "Arts" courses; the shrinking of people in general from any book supposed to be "good"; and, in another mode, the flamboyant advertisements telling "how to seem to know it when you don't," might long since have indicated to the sensitive that there is something defective in the contemporary methods of purveying letters.

As the general reader has but a vague idea of what these methods are at the "center," i.e. for the specialist who is expected to serve the general reader, I shall lapse or plunge into autobiography.

• • •

In my university I found various men interested (or uninterested) in their subjects, but, I think, no man with a view of literature as a whole, or with any idea whatsoever of the relation of the part he himself taught to any other part.

Those professors who regarded their "subject" as a drill manual rose most rapidly to positions of executive responsibility (one case is now a provost). Those professors who had some natural aptitude for comprehending their authors and for communicating a general sense of comfort in the presence of literary masterwork remained obscurely in their less exalted positions.

A professor of Romanics admitted that the *Chanson de Roland* was inferior to the *Odyssey*, but then the Middle Ages were expected to present themselves with apologies, and this was, if I remember rightly, an isolated exception. English novelists were not compared with the French. "Sources" were discussed; forty versions of a Chaucerian anecdote were "compared," but not on points of respective literary merit. The whole field was full of redundance. I mean that what one had learned in one class, in the study of one literature, one was told again in some other.

One was asked to remember what some critic (deceased) had said, scarcely to consider whether his views were still valid, or ever had been very intelligent.

In defense of this dead and uncorrelated system, it may be urged that authors like Spengler, who attempt a synthesis, often do so before they have attained sufficient knowledge of detail: that they stuff expandable and compressible objects into rubber-bag categories, and that they limit their reference and interest by supposing that the pedagogic follies which they have themselves encountered, constitute an error universally distributed, and encountered by every one else. In extenuation of their miscalculations we may admit that any error or clumsiness of method that has sunk into, or been hammered into one man, over a period of years, probably continues as an error—not merely passively, but as an error still being propagated, consciously or unconsciously, by a number of educators, from laziness, from habits, or from natural cussedness.

"Comparative literature" sometimes figures in university curricula, but very few people know what they mean by the term, or approach it with a considered conscious method.

To tranquillize the low-brow reader, let me say at once that I do not wish to muddle him by making him read more books, but to allow him to read fewer with greater result. (I am willing to discuss this privately with the book trade.) I have been accused of wanting to make people read all the classics; which is not so. I have been accused of wishing to provide a "portable substitute for the British Museum," which I would do, like a shot, were it possible. It isn't.

American "taste" is less official than English taste, but more derivative. When I arrived in England (A.D. 1908), I found a greater darkness in the British "serious press" than had obtained on the banks of the Schuylkill. Already in my young and ignorant years they considered me "learned." It was impossible, at first, to see why and whence the current opinion of British weeklies. It was incredible that literate men—men literate enough, that is, to write the orderly paragraphs that they did write constantly in their papers—believed the stupidities that appeared there with such regularity. (Later, for two years, we ran fortnightly in the *Egoist*, the sort of fool-column that the French call a *sottisier*, needing nothing for it but quotations from the *Times Literary Supplement*. Two issues of the *Supplement* yielding, easily, one page of the *Egoist*.) For years I awaited enlightenment. One winter I had lodgings in Sussex. On the mantelpiece of the humble country cottage I found books of an earlier era, among them an anthology printed in 1830, and yet another dated 1795, and there, there by the sox of Jehosaphat was the British taste of this century, 1910, 1915, and even the present, A.D. 1931.

I had read Stendhal's remark that it takes eighty years for anything to reach the general public, and looking out on the waste heath, under the December drizzle, I believed him. But that is not all of the story. Embedded in that naïve innocence that does, to their credit, pervade our universities, I ascribed the delay to mere time. I still thought: With the attrition of decades, ah, yes, in another seventy, in another, perhaps, ninety years, they will admit that . . . etc.

I mean that I thought they wanted to, but were hindered.

Later it struck me that the best history of painting in London was the National Gallery, and that the best history of literature, more particularly of poetry, would be a twelve-volume anthology in which each poem was chosen not merely because it was a nice poem or a poem Aunt Hepsy liked, but because it contained an invention, a definite contribution to the art of verbal expression. With this in mind, I approached a respected agent. He was courteous, he was even openly amazed at the list of three hundred items which I offered as an indication of outline. No autochthonous Briton had ever, to his professed belief, displayed such familiarity with so vast a range, but he was too indolent to recast my introductory letter into a form suited to commerce. He, as they say, "repaired" to an equally august and long-established publishing house (which had already served his and my interest). In two days came a hasty summons: would I see him in person. I found him awed, as if one had killed a cat in the sacristy. Did I know what I had said in my letter? I did. Yes, but about Palgrave? I did. I had said: "It is time we had something to replace that doddard Palgrave." "But don't you know," came the awestruck tones, "that the whole fortune of X & Co. is founded on Palgrave's *Golden Treasury?*"

From that day onward no book of mine received a British imprimatur until the appearance of Eliot's castrated edition of my poems.

I perceived that there were thousands of pounds sterling invested in electro-plate, and the least change in the public taste, let alone swift, catastrophic changes, would depreciate the value of those electros (of Hemans, let us say, or of Collins, Cowper, and of Churchill, who wrote the satiric verses, and of later less blatant cases, touched with a slighter flavor of mustiness).

I sought the banks of the Seine. Against ignorance one might struggle, and even against organic stupidity, but against a so vast vested interest the lone odds were too heavy.

Two years later a still more august academic press reopened the question. *They* had ventured to challenge Palgrave: they had been "interested"—would I send back my prospectus? I did. They found the plan "too ambitious." They said they might do "something," but that if they did it would be "more in the nature of gems."

For a Method

Nevertheless, the method I had proposed was simple, it is perhaps the only one that can give a man an orderly arrangement of his perception in the matter of letters. In opposition to it, there are the forces of superstition, of hang-over. People regard literature as something vastly more flabby and floating and complicated and indefinite than, let us say, mathematics. Its subject-matter, the human consciousness, is more complicated than are number and space. It is not, however, more complicated than biology, and no one ever supposed that it was. We apply a loose-leaf system to book-keeping so as to have the live items separated from the dead ones. In the study of physics we begin with simple mechanisms, wedge, lever and fulcrum, pulley and inclined plane, all of them still as useful as when they were first invented. We proceed by a study of discoveries. We are not asked to memorize a list of the parts of a side-wheeler engine.

And we could, presumably, apply to the study of literature a little of the common sense that we currently apply to physics or to biology. In poetry there are simple procedures, and there are known discoveries, clearly marked. As I have said in various places in my unorganized and fragmentary volumes: in each age one or two men of genius find something, and express it. It may be in only a line or in two lines, or in some quality of a cadence; and thereafter two dozen, or two hundred, or two or more thousand followers repeat and dilute and modify.

And if the instructor would select his specimens from works that contain these discoveries and solely on the basis of discovery—which may lie in the dimension of depth, not merely of some novelty on the surface—he would aid his student far more than by presenting his authors at random, and talking about them *in toto*.

Needless to say, this presentation would be entirely independent of consideration as to whether the given passages tended to make the student a better republican, monarchist, monist, duality, rotarian, or other sectarian. To avoid confusion, one should state at once that such method has nothing to do with those allegedly scientific methods which approach literature as if it were something *not literature*, or with scientists' attempts to sub-divide the elements in literature according to some non-literary categoric division.

You do not divide physics or chemistry according to racial or religious categories. You do not put discoveries by Methodists and Germans into one category, and discoveries by Episcopalians or Americans or Italians into another.

Defective Relativities

It is said that in America nothing is ever consciously related to anything else. I have cited as an exception the forty versions of the Chaucerian anecdote; they and the great edition of Horace with the careful list and parallel display of Greek sources for such line or such paragraph, show how the associative faculty can be side-tracked. Or at any rate they indicate the first gropings of association. Let us grant that some bits of literature have been, in special cases, displayed in relation to some other bits; usually some verbose gentleman writes a trilogy of essays, on three grandiose figures, comparing their "philosophy" or personal habits.

Let us by all means glance at "philology" and the "germanic system." Speaking as an historian, "we" may say that this system was designed to inhibit thought. After 1848 it was, in Germany, observed that some people thought. It was necessary to curtail this pernicious activity, the thinkists were given a china egg labeled scholarship, and were gradually unfitted for active life, or for any contact with life in general. Literature was permitted as a subject of study. And its study was so designed as to draw the mind of the student away from literature into inanity.

Why Books?

I

This simple first question was never asked.

The study of literature, or more probably of morphology, verb-roots, etc., was permitted the German professor in, let us say 1880–1905, to keep his mind off life in general, and off public life in particular.

In America it was permitted from precedent; it was known to be permitted in Germany; Germany had a "great university tradition," which it behooved America to equal and perhaps to surpass.

This study, or some weaker variety of it, was also known to be permitted at Oxford, and supposed to have a refining influence on the student.

II

The practice of literary composition in private has been permitted since "age immemorial," like knitting, crocheting, etc. It occupies the practitioner, and, so long as he keeps it to himself, *ne nuit pas aux autres,* it does not transgress the definition of liberty which we find in the declaration of the *Droits de l'Homme*: Liberty is the right to do anything which harms not others. All of which is rather negative and unsatisfactory.

III

It appears to me quite tenable that the function of literature as a generated prize-worthy force is precisely that it does incite humanity to continue living; that it eases the mind of strain, and feeds it, I mean definitely as *nutrition of impulse.*

This idea may worry lovers of order. Just as good literature does often worry them. They regard it as dangerous, chaotic, subversive. They try every idiotic and degrading wheeze to tame it down. They try to make a bog, a marasmus, a great putridity in place of a sane and active ebullience. And they do this from sheer simian and pig-like stupidity, and from their failure to understand the function of letters.

IV

Has literature a function in the state, in the aggregation of humans, in the republic, in the *res publica*, which ought to mean the public convenience (despite the slime of bureaucracy, and the execrable taste of the populace in selecting its rulers)? It has.

And this function is *not* the coercing or emotionally persuading, or bullying or suppressing people into the acceptance of any one set or any six sets of opinions as opposed to any other one set or half-dozen sets of opinions.

It has to do with the clarity and vigor of "any and every" thought and opinion. It has to do with maintaining the very cleanliness of the tools, the health of the very matter of thought itself. Save in the rare and limited instances of invention in the plastic arts, or in mathematics, the individual cannot think and communicate his thought, the governor and legislator cannot act effectively or frame his laws, without words, and the solidity and validity of these words is in the care of the damned and despised *litterati*. When their work goes rotten—by that I do not mean when they express indecorous thoughts—but when their very medium, the very essence of their work, the application of word to thing goes rotten, i.e. becomes slushy and inexact, or excessive or bloated, the whole machinery of social and of individual thought and order goes to pot. This is a lesson of history, and a lesson not yet half learned.

The great writers need no debunking.

The pap is not in them, and doesn't need to be squeezed out. They do not lend themselves to imperial and sentimental exploitations. A civilization was founded on Homer, civilization not a mere bloated empire. The Macedonian domination rose and grew after the sophists. It also subsided.

It is not only a question of rhetoric, of loose expression, but also of the loose use of individual words. What the renaissance gained in direct examination of natural phenomena, it in part lost in losing the feel and desire for exact descriptive terms. I mean that the medieval mind had little but words to deal with, and it was more careful in its definitions and verbiage. It did not define a gun in terms that would just as well define an explosion, nor explosions in terms that would define triggers.

Misquoting Confucius, one might say: It does not matter whether the author desire the good of the race or acts merely from personal vanity. The thing is mechanical in action. In proportion as his work is exact, i.e., true to human consciousness and to the nature of man, as it is exact in formulation of desire, so is it durable and so is it "useful"; I mean it maintains the precision and clarity of thought, not merely for the benefit of a few dilettantes and "lovers of literature," but maintains the health of thought outside literary circles and in non-literary existence, in general individual and communal life.

Or "*dans ce genre on n'émeut que par la clarté.*" One "moves" the reader only by clarity. In depicting the motions of the "human heart" the durability of the writing depends on the exactitude. It is the thing that is true and stays true that keeps fresh for the new reader.

With this general view in mind, and subsequent to the events already set forth in this narrative, I proposed (from the left bank of the Seine, and to an American publishing house), not the twelve volume anthology, but a short guide to the subject. That was after a few years of "pause and reflection." The subject was pleasantly received and considered with amity, but the house finally decided that it would pay neither them to print nor me to write the book, because we "weren't in the text-book ring." For the thing would have been a text-book, its circulation would have depended on educators, and educators have been defined as "men with no intellectual interests."

Hence, after a lapse of four years, this essay, dedicated to Mr. Glenn Frank, and other starters of ideal universities, though not with any great hope that it will rouse them.

Part II: Or What May Be an Introduction to Method

It is as important for the purpose of thought to keep language efficient as it is in surgery to keep tetanus bacilli out of one's bandages.

In introducing a person to literature one would do well to have him examine works where language is efficiently used; to devise a system for getting directly and expeditiously at such works, despite the smokescreens erected by half-knowing and half-thinking critics. To get at them, despite the mass of dead matter that these people have heaped up and conserved round about them in the proportion: one barrel of sawdust to each half-bunch of grapes.

Great literature is simply language charged with meaning to the utmost possible degree. When we set about examining it we find that this charging has been done by several clearly definable sorts of people, and by a periphery of less determinate sorts.

(a) *The inventors*, discoverers of a particular process or of more than one mode and process. Sometimes these people are known, or discoverable; for example, we know, with reasonable certitude, that Arnaut Daniel introduced certain methods of rhyming, and we know that certain finenesses of perception appeared first in such a troubadour or in G. Cavalcanti. We do not know, and are not likely to know, anything definite about the precursors of Homer.

(b) *The masters.* This is a very small class, and there are very few real ones. The term is properly applied to inventors who, apart from their own inventions, are able to assimilate and co-ordinate a large number of preceding inventions. I mean to say they either start with a core of their own and accumulate adjuncts, or they digest a vast mass of subject-matter, apply a number of known modes of expression, and succeed in pervading the whole with some special quality or some special character of their own, and bring the whole to a state of homogeneous fullness.

(*c*) *The diluters*, these who follow either the inventors or the "great writers," and who produce something of lower intensity, some flabbier variant, some diffuseness or tumidity in the wake of the valid.

(*d*) (And this class produces the great bulk of all writing.) The men who do more or less good work in the more or less good style of a period. Of these the delightful anthologies, the song books, are full, and choice among them is the matter of taste, for you prefer Wyatt to Donne, Donne to Herrick, Drummond of Hawthornden to Browne, in response to some purely personal sympathy, these people add but some slight personal flavor, some minor variant of a mode, without affecting the main course of the story.

At their faintest "*Ils n'existent pas, leur ambiance leur confert une existence.*" They do not exist: their ambience confers existence upon them. When they are most prolific they produce dubious cases like Virgil and Petrarch, who probably pass, among the less exigent, for colossi.

(*e*) *Belles Lettres.* Longus, Prévost, Benjamin Constant, who are not exactly "great masters," who can hardly be said to have originated a form, but who have nevertheless brought some mode to a very high development.

(*f*) And there is a supplementary or sixth class of writers, the starters of crazes, the Ossianic McPhersons, the Gongoras[2] whose wave of fashion flows over writing for a few centuries or a few decades, and then subsides, leaving things as they were.

It will be seen that the first two classes are the more sharply defined: that the difficulty of classification for particular lesser authors increases as one descends the list, save for the last class, which is again fairly clear.

The point is, that if a man knows the facts about the first two categories, he can evaluate almost any unfamiliar book at first sight. I mean he can form a just estimate of its worth, and see how and where it belongs in this schema.

As to crazes, the number of possible diseases in literature is perhaps not very great, the same afflictions crop up in widely separated countries without any previous communication. The good physician will recognize a known malady, even if the manifestation be superficially different.

The fact that six different critics will each have a different view concerning what author belongs in which of the categories here given, does not in the least invalidate the categories. When a man knows the facts about the first two categories, the reading of work in the other categories will not greatly change his opinion about those in the first two.

Language

Obviously this knowledge cannot be acquired without knowledge of various tongues. The same discoveries have served a number of races. If a man has not time to learn different languages he can at least, and with very little delay, be told what the discoveries were. If he wishes to be a good critic he will have to look for himself.

Bad critics have prolonged the use of demoded terminology, usually a terminology originally invented to describe what had been done before 300 B.C., and to describe it in a rather exterior fashion. Writers of second order have often tried to produce works to fit some category or term not yet occupied in their own local literature. If we chuck out the classifications which apply to the outer shape of the work, or to its occasion, and if we look at what actually happens, in, let us say, poetry, we will find that the language is charged or energized in various manners.

That is to say, there are three "kinds of poetry":

MELOPŒIA, wherein the words are charged, over and above their plain meaning, with some musical property, which directs the bearing or trend of that meaning.

PHANOPŒIA, which is a casting of images upon the visual imagination.

LOGOPŒIA, "the dance of the intellect among words," that is to say, it employs words not only for their direct meaning, but it takes count in a special way of habits of usage, of the context we *expect* to find with the word, its usual concomitants, of its known acceptances, and of ironical play. It holds the aesthetic content which is peculiarly the domain of verbal manifestation, and cannot possibly be contained in plastic or in music. It is the latest come, and perhaps most tricky and undependable mode.

The *melopœia* can be appreciated by a foreigner with a sensitive ear, even though he be ignorant of the language in which the poem is written. It is practically impossible to transfer or translate it from one language to another, save perhaps by divine accident, and for half a line at a time.

Phanopœia can, on the other hand, be translated almost, or wholly, intact. When it is good enough, it is practically impossible for the translator to destroy it save by very crass bungling and the neglect of perfectly well-known and formulative rules.

Logopœia, does not translate; though the attitude of mind it expresses may pass through a paraphrase. Or one might say, you can *not* translate it "locally," but having determined the original author's state of mind, you may or may not be able to find a derivative or an equivalent.

Prose

The language of prose is much less highly charged, that is perhaps the only availing distinction between prose and poesy. Prose permits greater factual presentation, explicitness, but a much greater amount of language is needed. During the last century or century and a half, prose has, perhaps for the first time, perhaps for the second or third time, arisen to challenge the poetic pre-eminence. That is to say, *Cœur Simple*, by Flaubert, is probably more important than Théophile Gautier's *Carmen*, etc.

The total charge in certain nineteenth-century prose works possibly surpasses the total charge found in individual poems of that period; but that merely indicates that the author has been able to get his effect cumulatively, by a greater heaping up of factual data; imagined fact, if you will, but nevertheless expressed in factual manner.

By using several hundred pages of prose, Flaubert, by force of architectonics, manages to attain an intensity comparable to that in Villon's *Heaulmière*, or his prayer for his mother. This does not invalidate my dissociation of the two terms: poetry, prose.

In *phanopœia* we find the greatest drive toward utter precision of word; this art exists almost exclusively by it.

In *melopœia* we find a contrary current, a force tending often to lull, or to distract the reader from the exact sense of the language. It is poetry on the borders of music and music is perhaps the bridge between consciousness and the unthinking sentient or even insentient universe.

All writing is built up of these three elements, plus "architectonics" or "the form of the whole," and to know anything about the relative efficiency of various works one must have some knowledge of the maximum already attained by various authors, irrespective of where and when.[3]

It is not enough to know that the Greeks attained to the greatest skill in melopœia, or even that the Provençaux added certain diverse developments and that some quite minor, nineteenth-century Frenchmen achieved certain elaborations.

It is not quite enough to have the general idea that the Chinese (more particularly Rihaku and Omakitsu) attained the known maximum of *phanopœia*, due perhaps to the nature of their written ideograph, or to wonder whether Rimbaud is, at rare moments, their equal. One wants one's knowledge in more definite terms.

It is an error to think that vast reading will automatically produce any such knowledge or understanding. Neither Chaucer with his forty books, nor Shakespeare with perhaps half a dozen, in folio, can be considered illiterate. A man can learn more music by working on a Bach fugue until he can take it apart and put it together, than by playing through ten dozen heterogeneous albums.

You may say that for twenty-seven years I have thought consciously about this particular matter, and read or read at a great many books, and that with the subject never really out of my mind, I don't yet know half there is to know about *melopœia*.

There are, on the other hand, a few books that I still keep on my desk, and a great number that I shall never open again. But the books that a man needs to know in order to "get his bearings," in order to have a sound judgment of any bit of writing that may come before him, are very few. The list is so short, indeed, that one wonders that people, professional writers in particular, are willing to leave them ignored and to continue dangling in mid-chaos emitting the most imbecile estimates, and often vitiating their whole lifetime's production.

Limiting ourselves to the authors who actually invented something, or who are the "first known examples" of the process in working order, we find:

OF THE GREEKS: Homer, Sappho. (The "great dramatists" decline from Homer, and depend immensely on him for their effects; their "charge," at its highest potential, depends so often, and so greatly on their being able to count on their audience's knowledge of the *Iliad*. Even Æschylus is rhetorical.)

OF THE ROMANS: As we have lost Philetas, and most of Callimachus, we may suppose that the Romans added a certain sophistication; at any rate, Catullus, Ovid, Propertius, all give us something we cannot find now in Greek authors.

A specialist may read Horace if he is interested in learning the precise demarcation between what can be learned about writing, and what cannot. I mean that Horace is the perfect example of a man who acquired all that is acquirable, without having the root. I beg the reader to observe that I am being exceedingly iconoclastic, that I am omitting thirty established names for every two I include. I am chucking out Pindar, and Virgil, without the slightest compunction. I do not suggest a "course" in Greek or Latin literature, I name a few isolated writers; five or six pages of Sappho. One can throw out at least one-third of Ovid. That is to say, I am omitting the authors who can teach us no new or no more effective method of "charging" words.

OF THE MIDDLE AGES: The Anglo-Saxon *Seafarer*, and some more cursory notice of some medieval narrative, it does not so greatly matter what narrative, possibly the *Beowulf*, the *Poema del Cid*, and the sagas of *Grettir* and *Burnt Nial*. And then, in contrast, troubadours, perhaps thirty poems in Provençal, and for comparison with them a few songs by Von Morungen, or Wolfram von Essenbach, and von der Vogelweide; and then Bion's *Death of Adonis*.

From which mixture, taken in this order, the reader will get his bearings on the art of poetry made to be sung; for there are three kinds of *melopœia*: (1) that made to be sung to a tune; (2) that made to be intoned or sung to a sort of chant; and (3) that made to be spoken; and the art of joining words in each of these kinds is different, and cannot be clearly understood until the reader knows that there are three different objectives.

OF THE ITALIANS: Guido Cavalcanti and Dante; perhaps a dozen and a half poems of Guido's, and a dozen poems by his contemporaries, and the *Divina Commedia*.

In Italy, around the year 1300, there were new values established, things said that had not been said in Greece, or in Rome or elsewhere.

VILLON: After Villon and for several centuries, poetry can be considered as *fioritura*, as an efflorescence, almost an effervescence, and without any new roots. Chaucer is an enrichment, one might say a more creamy version of the "matter of France," and he in some measure preceded the verbal richness of the classic revival, but beginning with the Italians after Dante, coming through the Latin writers of the Renaissance, French, Spanish, English, Tasso, Ariosto, etc., the Italians always a little in the lead, the whole is elaboration, medieval basis, and wash after wash of Roman or Hellenic influence. I mean one need not read any particular part of it for purpose of learning one's comparative values.

If one were studying history and not poetry, one might discover the medieval mind more directly in the opening of Mussato's *Ecerinus* than even in Dante. The culture of Chaucer is the same as that which went contemporaneously into Ferrara, with the tongue called "*francoveneto.*"

One must emphasize one's contrasts in the quattrocento. One can take Villon as pivot for understanding them. After Villon, and having begun before his time, we find this *fioritura*, and for centuries we find little else. Even in Marlowe and Shakespeare there is this embroidery of language, this talk about the matter, rather than presentation. I doubt if anyone ever acquired discrimination in studying "The Elizabethans." You have grace, richness of language, abundance, but you have probably nothing that isn't replaceable by something else, no ornament that wouldn't have done just as well in some other connection, or for which some other figure of rhetoric couldn't have served, or which couldn't have been distilled from literary antecedents.

The "language" had not been heard on the London stage, but it had been heard in the Italian law courts, etc.; there were local attempts, all over Europe, to teach the public (in Spain, Italy, England) Latin diction. "Poetry" was considered to be (as it still is considered by a great number of driveling imbeciles) synonymous with "lofty and flowery language."

One Elizabethan specialist has suggested that Shakespeare, disgusted with his efforts, or at least despairing of success, as a poet, took to the stage. The drama is a mixed art; it does not rely on the charge that can be put into the word, but calls on gesture and mimicry and "impersonation" for assistance. The actor must do a good half of the work. One does no favor to drama by muddling the two sets of problems.

Apologists for the drama are continually telling us in one way or another that drama either cannot use at all, or can make but a very limited use of words charged to their highest potential. This is perfectly true. Let us try to keep our minds on the problem we started with, i.e., the art of writing, the art of "charging" language with meaning.

After 1450 we have the age of *fioritura*; after Marlowe and Shakespeare came what was called a "classic" movement, a movement that restrained without inventing. Anything that happens to mind in England has usually happened somewhere else first. Someone invents something, then someone develops, or some dozens develop a frothy or at any rate creamy enthusiasm or over-abundance, then someone tries to tidy things up. For example, the estimable Pleiad emasculating the French tongue, and the French classicists, and the English classicists, etc., all of which things should be relegated to the subsidiary zone: period interest, historical interest, bric-à-brac for museums.

At this point someone says: "O, but the ballads." All right, I will allow the voracious peruser a half-hour for ballads (English and Spanish, or Scottish, Border, and Spanish). There is nothing easier than to be distracted from one's point, or from the main drive of one's subject by a desire for utterly flawless equity and omniscience.

Let us say, but directly in parenthesis, that there was a very limited sort of *logopœia* in seventeenth- and eighteenth-century satire. And that Rochester and Dorset may have introduced a new note, or more probably re-introduced an old one, that reappears later in Heine.

Let us also cut loose from minor details and minor exceptions: the main fact is that we "have come" or that "humanity came" to a point where verse-writing can or could no longer be clearly understood without the study of prose-writing.

Say, for the sake of argument, that after the slump of the Middle Ages, prose "came to" again in Machiavelli; admit that various sorts of prose had existed, in fact nearly all sorts had existed. Herodotus wrote history that is literature. Thucydides was a journalist. (It is a modern folly to suppose that vulgarity and cheapness have the merit of novelty; they have always existed, and are of no interest in themselves.)

There have been bombast, oratory, legal speech, balanced sentences, Ciceronian impressiveness; Petronius had written a satiric novel, Longus had written a delicate nouvelle. The prose of the Renaissance leaves us Rabelais, Brantôme, Montaigne. A determined specialist can dig interesting passages, or sumptuous passages, or even subtle passages out of Pico, the medieval mystics, scholastics, platonists, none of which will be the least use to a man trying to learn the art of "charging language."

I mean to say that from the beginning of literature up to A.D. 1750 poetry was the superior art, and was so considered to be, and if we read books written before that date we find the number of interesting books in verse at least equal to the number of prose books still readable; and the poetry contains the quintessence. When we want to know what people were like before 1750, when we want to know that they had blood and bones like ourselves, we go to the poetry of the period.

But, as I have said, the "*fioritura* business" set in. And one morning Monsieur Stendhal, not thinking of Homer, or Villon, or Catullus, but having a very keen sense of actuality, noticed that "poetry," *la poésie*, as the term was then understood, the stuff written by his French contemporaries, or sonorously rolled at him from the French stage, was a damn nuisance. And he remarked that poetry, with its bagwigs and its bobwigs, and its padded calves and its periwigs, its "fustian à la Louis XIV," was greatly inferior to prose for conveying a clear idea of the diverse states of our consciousness (les mouvements du cœur).

And at that moment the serious art of writing "went over to prose," and for some time the important developments of language as means of expression were the developments of prose. And a man cannot clearly understand or justly judge the value of verse, modern verse, any verse, unless he has grasped this.

Part III: Conclusions, Exceptions, Curricula

Before Stendhal there is probably nothing in prose that does not also exist in verse or that can't be done by verse just as well as by prose. Even the method of annihilating imbecility employed by Voltaire, Bayle, and Lorenzo Valla can be managed quite as well in rhymed couplets.

Beginning with the Renaissance, or perhaps with Boccaccio, we have prose that is quite necessary to the clear comprehension of things in general: with Rabelais, Brantôme, Montaigne, Fielding, Sterne, we begin to find prose recording states of consciousness that their verse-writing contemporaries scamp. And this fuller consciousness, in more delicate modes, appears in l'Abbé Prévost, Benjamin Constant, Jane Austen. So that Stendhal had already "something back of him" when he made his remarks about the inferiority of "*La Poésie*."

During the nineteenth century the superiority, if temporary, is at any rate obvious, and to such degree that I believe no man can now write really good verse unless he knows Stendhal and Flaubert. Or, let us say, *Le Rouge et le Noir*, the first half of *La Chartreuse*, *Madame Bovary*, *L'Education*, *Les Trois Contes*, *Bouvard et Pécuchet*. To put it perhaps more strongly, he will learn more about the art of charging words from Flaubert than he will from the floribund sixteenth-century dramatists.

The main expression of nineteenth-century consciousness is in prose. The art continues in Maupassant, who slicked up the Flaubertian mode. The art of popular success lies simply in never putting more on any one page than the most ordinary reader can lick off it in his normally rapid, half-attentive skim-over. The Goncourts struggled with praiseworthy sobriety, noble, but sometimes dull. Henry James was the first person to add anything to the art of the nineteenth-century novel not already known to the French.

Thought was churned up by Darwin, by science, by industrial machines. Nietzsche made a temporary commotion, but these things are extraneous to our subject, which is the *art of getting meaning into words*. There is an "influence of Ibsen," all for the good, but now exploited by cheap-jacks. Fabre and Frazer are both essential to contemporary clear thinking. I am not talking about the books that have poured something into the general consciousness, but of books that show *how* the pouring is done or display the implements, newly discovered, by which one can pour.

The nineteenth-century novel is such an implement. The Ibsen play is, or perhaps we must say was, such an implement.

It is for us to think whether these implements are more effective than poetry: *(a)* as known before 1800; *(b)* as known during the nineteenth century and up to the present.

France

The decline of England began on the day when Landor packed his trunks and departed to Tuscany. Up till then England had been able to contain her best authors; after that we see Shelley, Keats, Byron, Beddoes on the Continent, and still later observe the edifying spectacle of Browning in Italy and Tennyson in Buckingham Palace.

In France, as the novel developed, spurred on, shall we say, by the activity in the prose-media, the versifiers were not idle.

Departing from *Albertus*, Gautier developed the medium we find in the *Emaux et Camées*. England in the 'nineties had got no further than the method of the *Albertus*. If Corbière invented no process he at any rate restored French verse to the vigor of Villon and to an intensity that no Frenchman had touched during the intervening four centuries.

Unless I am right in discovering *logopœia* in Propertius (which means unless the academic teaching of Latin displays crass insensitivity as it probably does), we must almost say that Laforgue invented *logopœia* observing that there had been a very limited range of *logopœia* in all satire, and that Heine occasionally employs something like it, together with dash of bitters, such as can (though he may not have known it) be found in a few verses of Dorset and Rochester. At any rate Laforgue found or refound *logopœia*. And Rimbaud brought back to *phanopœia* its clarity and directness.

All four of these poets, Gautier, Corbière, Laforgue, Rimbaud, redeem poetry from Stendhal's condemnation. There is in Corbière something one finds nowhere before him, unless in Villon.

Laforgue is not like any preceding poet. He is not ubiquitously like Propertius.

In Rimbaud the image stands clean, unencumbered by nonfunctioning words; to get anything like this directness of presentation one must go back to Catullus, perhaps to the poem which contains *dentes habet*.

If a man is too lazy to read the brief works of these poets, he cannot hope to understand writing, verse writing, prose writing, any writing.

England

Against this serious action England can offer only Robert Browning. He has no French or European parallel. He has, indubitably, grave limitations, but *The Ring and the Book* is serious experimentation. He is a better poet than Landor, who was perhaps the only complete and serious man of letters ever born in these islands.

We are so encumbered by having British literature in our foreground that even in this brief survey one must speak of it in disproportion. It was kept alive during the last century by a series of exotic injections. Swinburne read Greek and took English metric in hand; Rossetti brought in the Italian primitives; FitzGerald made the only good poem of the time that has gone to the people; it is called, and is to a great extent, a trans- or mistrans-lation.

There was a faint waft of early French influence. Morris translated sagas, the Irish took over the business for a few years; Henry James led, or rather preceded, the novelists, and then the Britons resigned *en bloc*; the language is now in the keeping of the Irish (Yeats and Joyce); apart from Yeats, since the death of Hardy, poetry is being written by Americans. All the developments in English verse since 1910 are due almost wholly to Americans, In fact, there is no longer any reason to call it English verse, and there is no present reason to think of England at all.

We speak a language that was English. When Richard Coeur de Lion first heard Turkish he said: "He spik lak a fole Britain." From which orthography one judges that Richard himself probably spoke like a French-Canadian.

It is a magnificent language, and there is no need of, or advantage in, minimizing the debt we owe to Englishmen who died before 1620. Neither is there any point in studying the "History of English Literature" as taught. Curiously enough, the histories of Spanish and Italian literature always take count of translators. Histories of English literature always slide over translation—I suppose it is inferiority complex—yet some of the best books in English are translations. This is important for two reasons. First, the reader who has been appalled by the preceding parts and said, "Oh, but I can't learn all these languages," may in measure be comforted. He can learn the art of writing precisely where so many great local lights learned it; if not from the definite poems I have listed, at least from the men who learned it from those poems in the first place.

We may count the *Seafarer*, the *Beowulf*, and the remaining Anglo-Saxon fragments as indigenous art; at least, they dealt with a native subject, and by an art not newly borrowed. Whether alliterative meter owes anything to Latin hexameter is a question open to debate; we have no present means of tracing the debt. Landor suggests the problem in his dialogue of Ovid and the Prince of the Gaetae.

After this period English literature lives on translation, it is fed by translation; every new exuberance, every new heave is stimulated by translation, every allegedly great age of translations, beginning with Geoffrey Chaucer, Le Grand Translateur, translator of the *Romaunt of the Rose*, paraphraser of Virgil and Ovid, condenser of old stories he had found in Latin, French, and Italian.

After him even the ballads that tell a local tale tell it in art indebted to Europe. It is the natural spreading ripple that moves from the civilized Mediterranean center out through the half-civilized and into the barbarous peoples.

The Britons never have shed barbarism; they are proud to tell you that Tacitus said the last word about Germans. When Mary Queen of Scots went to Edinburgh she bewailed going out among savages, and she herself went from a sixteenth-century court that held but a barbarous, or rather a driveling and idiotic and superficial travesty of the Italian culture as it had been before the débâcle of 1527. The men who tried to civilize these shaggy and uncouth marginalians by bringing them news of civilization have left a certain number of translations that are better reading today than are the works of the ignorant islanders who were too proud to translate. After Chaucer we have Gavin Douglas's *Eneados*, better than the original, as Douglas had heard the sea. Golding's *Metamorphoses*, from which Shakespeare learned so much of his trade. Marlowe's translation of Ovid's *Amores*. We have no satisfactory translation of any Greek author. Chapman and Pope have left Iliads that are of interest to specialists; so far as I know, the only translation of Homer that one can read with continued pleasure is in early French by Hugues Salel; he, at least, was intent on telling the story, and not wholly muddled with accessories. I have discussed the merits of these translators elsewhere. I am now trying to tell the reader what he can learn of comparative literature through translations that are in themselves better reading than the "original verse" of their periods. He can study the whole local development, or, we had better say, the sequence of local fashion in British verse by studying the translations of Horace that have poured in uninterrupted sequence from the British Press since 1650. That is work for a specialist, an historian, not for a man who wants simply to establish his axes of reference by knowing *the best of each kind* of written thing; as he would establish his axes of reference for painting by knowing a few pictures by Cimabue, Giotto, Piero della Francesca, Ambrogio de Predis, etc.; Velasquez, Goya, etc.

It is one thing to be able to spot the best painting and quite another and far less vital thing to know just where some secondary or tertiary painter learned certain defects.

Apart from these early translations, a man may enlarge his view of international poetry by looking at Swinburne's Greek adaptations. The Greeks stimulated Swinburne; if he had defects, let us remember that, apart from Homer, the Greeks often were rather Swinburnian. Catullus wasn't, or was but seldom. From which one may learn the nature of the Latin, non-Greek contribution to the art of expression.[4]

Swinburne's Villon is not Villon very exactly, but it is perhaps the best Swinburne we have. Rossetti's translations were perhaps better than Rossetti, and his *Vita Nuova* and early Italian poets guide one to originals, which he has now and again improved. Our contact with Oriental poetry begins with FitzGerald's Rubáiyát. Fenollosa's essay on the Chinese written character opens a door that the earlier students had, if not "howled without," at least been unable to open.

In mentioning these translations, I don't in the least admit or imply that any man in our time can think with only one language. He may be able to invent a new carburetor, or even work effectively in a biological laboratory, but he probably won't even try to do the latter without study of a least one foreign tongue. Modern science has always been multilingual. A good scientist simply would not be bothered to limit himself to one language and be held up for news of discoveries. The writer or reader who is content with such ignorance simply admits that his particular mind is of less importance than his kidneys or his automobile. The French who know no English are as fragmentary as the Americans who know no French. One simply leaves half of one's thought untouched in their company.

Different languages—I mean the actual vocabularies, the idioms— have worked out certain mechanisms of communication and registration. No one language is complete. A master may be continually expanding his own tongue, rendering it fit to bear some charge hitherto borne only by some other alien tongue, but the process does not stop with any one man. While Proust is learning Henry James, preparatory to breaking through certain French paste-board partitions, the whole American speech is churning and chugging, and every other tongue doing likewise.

To be "possible" in mentally active company the American has to learn French, the Frenchman has to learn English or American. The Italian has for some time learned French. The man who does not know the Italian of the duocento and trecento has in him a painful lacuna, not necessarily painful to himself, but there are simply certain things he don't know, and can't; it is as if he were blind to some part of the spectrum. Because of the determined attempt of the patriotic Latinists of Italy in the renaissance to "conquer" Greek by putting every Greek author effectively into Latin it is now possible to get a good deal of Greek through Latin cribs. The disuse of Latin cribs in Greek study, beginning, I suppose, about 1820, has caused no end of damage to the general distribution of "classic culture."

Another point miscomprehended by people who are clumsy at languages is that one does not need to learn a whole language in order to understand some one or some dozen poems. It is often enough to understand thoroughly the poem, and every one of the few dozen or few hundred words that compose it.

This is what we start to do as small children when we memorize some lyric of Goethe or Heine. Incidentally, this process leaves us for life with a measuring rod *(a)* for a certain type of lyric, *(b)* for the German language, so that, however bored we may be by the *Grundriss von Groeber*, we never wholly forget the feel of the language.

Vaccine

Do I suggest a remedy? I do. I suggest several remedies. I suggest that we throw out all critics who use vague general terms. Not merely those who use vague terms because they are too ignorant to have a meaning; but the critics who use vague terms to *conceal* their meaning, and all critics who use terms so vaguely that the reader can think he agrees with them or assents to their statements when he doesn't.

The first credential we should demand of a critic is *his* ideograph of the good; of what he considers valid writing, and indeed of all his general terms. Then we know where he is. He cannot simply stay in London writing of French pictures that his readers have not seen. He must begin by stating that such and such *particular* works seem to him "good," "best," "indifferent," "valid," "non-valid." I suggest a definite curriculum in place of the present *émiettements*, of breaking the subject up into crumbs quickly dryable. A curriculum for instructors, for obstreperous students who wish to annoy dull instructors, for men who haven't had time for systematized college courses. Call it the minimum basis for a sound and liberal education in letters (with French and English "aids" in parentheses).

CONFUCIUS—In full (there being no complete and intelligent English version, one would have either to learn Chinese or make use of the French version by Pauthier).

HOMER—in full (Latin cribs, Hugues Salel in French, no satisfactory English, though Chapman can be used as reference).

OVID—And the Latin "personal" poets, Catullus and Propertius. (Golding's *Metamorphoses*, Marlowe's *Amores*. There is no useful English version of Catullus.)

A PROVENÇAL SONG BOOK—With cross reference to Minnesingers, and to Bion, perhaps thirty poems in all.

DANTE—"And his circle"; that is to say Dante, and thirty poems by his contemporaries, mostly by Guido Cavalcanti.

VILLON—

PARENTHETICALLY—Some other medieval matter might be added, and some general outline of history of thought through the Renaissance.

VOLTAIRE—That is to say, some incursion into his critical writings, not into his attempts at fiction and drama, and some dip into his contemporaries (prose).

STENDHAL—(At least a book and half).

FLAUBERT (omitting *Salammbô* and the *Tentation*)—And the Goncourts.

GAUTIER, CORBIÈRE, RIMBAUD.

This would not overburden the three- or four-year student. After this inoculation he could be "with safety exposed" to modernity or anything else in literature. I mean he wouldn't lose his head or ascribe ridiculous values to works of secondary intensity. He would have axes of reference and would, I think, find them dependable.

For the purposes of general education we could omit all study of monistic totemism and voodoo for at least fifty years and study of Shakespeare for thirty on the ground that acquaintance with these subjects is already very widely diffused, and that one absorbs quite enough knowledge of them from boring circumjacent conversation.

This list does not, obviously, contain the names of every author who has ever written a good poem or a good octave or sestet. It is the result of twenty-seven years' thought on the subject and a résumé of conclusions. That may be a reason for giving it some consideration. It is not a reason for accepting it as a finality. Swallowed whole it is useless. For practical class work the instructor should try, and incite his students to try, to pry out some element that I have included and to substitute for it something more valid. The intelligent lay reader will instinctively try to do this for himself.

I merely insist that *without* this minimum the critic has almost no chance of sound judgment. Judgment will gain one more chance of soundness if he can be persuaded to consider Fenollosa's essay or some other, and to me unknown but equally effective, elucidation of the Chinese written character.

Before I die I hope to see at least a few of the best Chinese works printed bilingually, in the form that Mori and Ariga prepared certain texts for Fenollosa, a "crib," the picture of each letter accompanied by a full explanation.

For practical contact with all past poetry that was actually *sung* in its own day I suggest that each dozen universities combine in employing a couple of singers who understand the meaning of words. Men like Yves Tinayre and Robert Maitland are available. A half-dozen hours spent in listening to the lyrics actually performed would give the student more knowledge of that sort of *melopœia* than a year's work in philology. The Kennedy-Frazers have dug up music that fits the *Beowulf*. It was being used for heroic song in the Hebrides. There is other available music, plenty of it, from at least the time of Faidit (A.D. 1190).

I cannot repeat too often or too forcibly my caution against so-called critics who talk "all around the matter," and who do not define their terms, and who won't say frankly that certain authors are demnition bores. Make a man tell you *first* and specially what writers he thinks are good writers, after that you can listen to his explanation.

Naturally, certain professors who have invested all their intellectual capital, i.e., spent a lot of time on some perfectly dead period, don't like to admit they've been sold, and they haven't often the courage to cut a loss. There is no use in following them into the shadows.

In the above list I take full responsibility for my omissions. I have omitted "the Rhooshuns." All right. Let a man judge them after he has encountered Charles Bovary; he will read them with better balance. I have omitted practically all the fustian included in curricula of French literature in American universities (Bossuet, Corneille, etc.) and in so doing I have not committed an oversight. I have touched German in what most of you will consider an insufficient degree. All right. I have done it. I rest my case.

If one finds it convenient to think in chronological cycles, and wants to "relate literature to history," I suggest the three convenient "breaks" or collapses. The fall of Alexander's Macedonian empire; the fall of the Roman empire; the collapse of Italy after 1500, the fall of Lodovico Moro, and the sack of Rome. That is to say, human lucidity appears to have approached several times a sort of maximum, and then suffered a set-back.

The great break in the use of language occurs, however, with the change from inflected to uninflected speech. It can't be too clearly understood that certain procedures are good for a language in which every word has a little final tag telling what part of speech it is, and what case it is in, and whether it is a subject, or an object or an accessory; and that these procedures are not good in English or French. Milton got into a mess tying to write English as if it were Latin. Lack of this dissociation is largely responsible for late renaissance floridity. One cannot at this point study all the maladies and all their variations. The study of misguided Latinization needs a treatise to itself.

1. Foot-note a few decades later: The proper definition would be "Institutions for the obstruction of learning."

2. One should perhaps apologize, or express a doubt as to the origin of Gongorism, or redefine it or start blaming it on some other Spaniard.

3. Lacuna at this point to be corrected in criticism of Hindemith's "Schwanendreher." E.P. Sept. 1938.

4. To be measured against the Sophoklean economy.

Miss Emily and the Bibliographer[1]

ALLEN TATE

Randall Jarrell described this essay (originally published in 1941 in
Reason in Madness) as "the most brilliant attack on scholarship of
the PMLA variety I have ever read." Tate's defense of the objectivity
of literature is matchless; his destruction of the "naturalist" literary
historians comprehensive: "The scholar who tells us that he under-
stands Dryden but makes nothing of Hopkins or Yeats is telling us
that he does not understand Dryden." Indeed.

The scene is a seminar room at a large American university. It is the
first meeting of the year. The eager young man asks the professor a question. "What," he says, "is the ultimate purpose of graduate research in
English literature?" The professor, whose special field is English bibliography of the decade 1840–1850, does not hesitate. "To lay the foundations of literacy criticism," he replies. The eager young man is pleased
because secretly and discreetly he hopes that some day he may hope to
be a critic. A month later the bibliographer assigns the group a paper.
"Gentlemen," he says, "we must maintain in these papers the graduate
point of view. There must be no impressionism. There must be no literary criticism. Anybody can write that."

I came upon this tale about a year ago but a year before that I had
read one like it in an essay written by Mr. John Crowe Ransom some
time before the incident that I relate occurred. I began to wonder if
Mr. Ransom had made it up; then I began to hope that he had, so that
the witnessed fact should stand as proof of an insight. Without the
witnessed fact Mr. Ransom (I assume for my purpose that he invented
the tale) would be in the position of William Faulkner after his story,
A Rose for Emily, appeared. You will remember Mr. Faulkner's story.
Miss Emily, a curious spinster, conceals the dead body of her lover in
an upstairs bedroom until concealment is no longer possible. Nobody
believed this tale; it was one of Mr. Faulkner's outrageous lies; it just
couldn't have happened. Then it happened. This evidence of the decadence of the South emerged about three years later from a farmhouse

in upstate New York. A middle-aged woman had killed her lover and kept the body.

For both Mr. Ransom and Mr. Faulkner the later facts confirmed the previous insights. Yet I must confess that for another reason altogether the analogy between the scholar and the spinster teases my fancy. Both tales are tales of horror, and I submit that the greater horror, for me, is in the scholar's insincerity. The analogy, like a good one, holds on more than one level. Must we not suspect that Miss Emily had a time of it conducting her intrigue in a provincial American community and that she probably, with the lover's last breath, breathed her sigh of relief? The need of judging him as a living man had been happily removed with the removal of his breath; the contingencies of personality were happily gone; she could have him without any of the social dangers of having him. She could now proceed without interruption to the reconstruction of the history of her love. But there was always the body, and the body wrecks the analogy. Miss Emily's historical method recognized that it was the history of something it could not ignore and had to return to. But the specialist in English bibliography of the decade 1840–1850 would doubtless bury the body at once, concealing it forever; and he would never afterwards have to be reminded what he was doing the bibliography of. Or if you will give this figure yet another turn, the analogy is wrecked again, again in favor of Miss Emily. The body has got to decompose, and its existence will become shockingly known—a crisis that the historical scholars conspire among themselves to postpone indefinitely; and if the wild discourtesy of the real world reminds them of it they say, "No, you are mistaken; we buried it long ago." But have they? Can they? And that is why Miss Emily remains a somewhat endearing horror for me. It is better to pretend with Miss Emily that something dead is living than to pretend with the bibliographer that something living is dead.[2]

The bibliographer's belief that "anybody can write that" I wish to discuss later, when I get to some of the more dialectical phases of the question. Here I should like to set off against my frivolity what many literary critics have called the insincerity of the academic mind. Between the frivolity and the insincerity, between the ignorance and the irrelevant learning, the outlook for a literary criticism in our time is dark. But as a matter of fact, whatever may be said of the party of ignorance, it would be hard to maintain that anything like personal insincerity motivates the activities of the historical scholars. Every point of view entails upon its proponents, in the act of overreaching it, its own kind of insincerity. Yet the evidence for the insincerity of our bibliographer is damaging: what, if not insincerity, lies back of his professed purpose which he, when he is pressed, shamelessly repudiates? How can he spend years laying the foundations of literary criticism when he thinks that anybody can write it? If anybody can write it does it need the collaboration of many generations of scholarship to lay its foundations?

There is insincerity here no doubt; for it is plainly an instance of a professed intention that one never expects to carry out or that one vaguely expects the future to perform for us. Does this not have an ominous and familiar sound? We hear it in the world at large and on nearly every level of our experience.

We hear it in politics, and the political voice has its counterpoint in the uneasy speculation of the journalist critics about the future of literature: some ten years ago we got from England a whole series of little books called *The Future of—*; and it is seldom that we get an essay on the present state of letters or even on a single book that does not look far beyond the occasion. We are asked as citizens to live only for the future, either in the preservation of democracy or in the creation of the classless society. Mr. T. S. Eliot has discussed this question in "Literature and the Modern World," an essay which I believe has not been reprinted in any of his books; he examines the point of view of H. G. Wells and sees in it the widespread eschatology of a secular, naturalistic philosophy. As individuals today we must subordinate our spiritual life and our material satisfactions to the single purpose of gaining superior material satisfactions in the future, which will be a naturalistic Utopia of mindless hygiene and Tom Swift's gadgets. There is no doubt that the most powerful attraction offered us by the totalitarian political philosophies is the promise of irresponsible perfection in the future, to be gained at the slight cost of our present consent to extinguish our moral natures in a group mind.

The moral nature affirms itself in judgment, and we cannot or will not judge. Because the scholars as much as other people today are involved in the naturalistic temper, they also refuse to judge. The historical scholar says that we cannot judge the literature of our time because we do not know whether the future will approve of it. Is he not obviously evading his moral responsibility? I do not say he evades it as a father or as a citizen; but he does evade it in the specific field in which he ought to exercise it, since of that field he professes knowledge.

He has reasons for the Great Refusal, and the reasons are of curious interest and at the same time of critical importance. In order to express my sense of their significance I must go a long way round. I should like to begin by citing certain critical views held by Mr. Edmund Wilson, a brilliant historian of literature, who because he puts literature above research may be expected to exhibit some of the values of the historical method when it is actually applied in criticism.

Let me first make a distinction—so broad that if it is true it will be virtually a truism. Let us assume that English critics from the late Renaissance to Coleridge had a firm sense of the differences among the *genres* of literature and that they tried constantly to state those differences critically. Whether they succeeded in this task, from our point of view, is not the question; it is rather that they tried to look upon works of literature as objective existences with respect to the different forms.

Taking up this defeated critical tradition we still from time to time consider the relation of poetry to prose fiction. Our approach to this problem was adumbrated by Coleridge in a fashion that would have been unintelligible a century before his time: in Chapter XIV of *Biographia Literaria* he remarks that a work of prose fiction will often have the imaginative qualities of poetry, no essential difference between poetry and fiction being discernible. There are concealed in this view certain metaphysical assumptions, which we still use without awareness of the metaphysics. (In the study of "English" we are forbidden to "use" philosophy—which means that we are using it badly.) We say today that there is poetry in prose fiction and, wherever you have narrative, fiction in poetry. But it ought to be easy to see that the murk enveloping the question when we try to carry it further than this arises from a certain kind of fallacy of abstraction. We are thinking in terms of substance, or essence. Those who believe that poetry and prose fiction differ in some fundamental sense assume that poetry is a distinct essence; whether prose has an essence is irrelevant since it could not have the essence of poetry; and, therefore, prose fiction being a kind of prose, it is essentially different from poetry.

Now Mr. Wilson easily disposes of this argument in a famous essay called "Is Verse a Dying Technique?" (by which I understand him to mean: Is verse becoming an unpopular technique?). He boldly denies to poetry an essence distinct from the essence of prose. In denying a difference he affirms the same essence of both: he thinks in terms of essence. He shows that *Madame Bovary* contains a great deal of "poetry" and concludes that the only interesting difference between a work like Flaubert's masterpiece and the *Aeneid* is that the one is in prose, the other in verse. That is certainly a difference: it is, according to Mr. Wilson, strictly a difference of "technique"; and he assumes the likenesses in terms of a common essence. Here we get the deepest assumption of the literary historian: the subject matter alone has objective status, the specific form of the work being external and mechanical—mere technique. This essence common to all literature is human life. Both Flaubert and Virgil were concerned with it in its largest implications.

Nobody will deny this; but it is critically irrelevant to affirm it. Within the terms of this affirmation critical thought is impossible, and we succumb to the documentary routine which "correlates" this de-formed substance with its origin, which by convention is called history.

Now the writers who see in works of literature not the specific formal properties but only the amount and range of human life brought to the reader are expressionists. Back of the many varieties of expressionist theory lies the assumption of the common or the distinct essence. If I say that the essence of *Madame Bovary* is different from the essence of the *Aeneid* and Mr. Wilson says that the essences are the same, we merely shout our opinions at each other, and the louder voice prevails. The historical method will not permit us to develop a critical instrument for dealing with works of literature as existent objects; we see them as expressive of substances beyond themselves. At the historical level the work expresses its place and time, or the author's personality, but if the scholar goes further and says anything about the work, he is expressing himself. Expressionism is here a sentiment, forbidding us to think and permitting us to feel as we please. When the bored expressionist tires of the pure artistic essence he turns into the inquisitive literary historian; or he may be both at once, as indeed he often is.

The great historical scholars of our time are notoriously deficient critics, but critics they are nevertheless. I am far from believing that the bibliographer's defense of scholarship is acceptable to all the scholars, many of whom are certain that they are already doing for criticism all that is necessary. Do you want a critic? Why, we already have one—in John Livingston Lowes. Has he not given us *Convention and Revolt?* He has; but in the course of a few pages I cannot do justice to the historical scholarship that gave us the facile seesaw picture of the history of poetry, or to the poetic learning that permitted Mr. Lowes to take seriously the late Amy Lowell. The mere literary critics took Miss Lowell seriously for a while, but the literary critics were not scholars. If you will think of *Convention and Revolt* along with *The Road to Xanadu* you will see that the literary dilettante and the historical scholar can flourish, without much communication between them, in one man.

Are we not prepared here for one of the remarkable insights of the late Irving Babbitt? His *Literature and the American College*, published in 1908, is still quoted, but there is no reason to believe that its message has ever been taken seriously by the men who most need it. At that time the late J. E. Spingarn had not imported into American criticism the term expressionism. Mr. Babbitt called the dilettantes Rousseauistic impressionists; the historical scholars Baconian naturalists. Both dilettante and scholar repudiated the obligations of judgment because both alike were victims of a naturalistic philosophy. Perhaps Mr. Babbitt did not consider the possibility of their being the same man. He saw on the one hand the ignorant journalist critics, "decadent romantics," for whom intensity of feeling was the sole critical standard; and on the other hand the historical scholars, who had no critical standard at all but who amassed irrelevant information. It was—and still is—a situation in which it is virtually impossible for a young man to get a critical, literary education. If he goes to a graduate school he comes out incapacitated for criticism; if he tries to be a critic he is not unlike the ignorant impressionist who did not go to the graduate school. He cannot discuss the literary object in terms of its specific form; all that he can do is to give you its history or tell you how he feels about it. The concrete form of the play, the poem, the novel, that gave rise to the history of the feeling lies neglected on the hither side of the Styx, where Virgil explains to Dante that it is scorned alike by heaven and hell.

Mr. Babbitt saw in the aesthete and the historical scholar the same motivation. The naturalism of the scholar lies in his mechanical theory of history, a theory in which the literary object is dissolved into the determinism of forces surrounding it. The naturalism of the aesthete operates on the psychological plane; he responds to the aesthetic object in terms of sensation and if the sensation is intense the aesthetic object is good.

Mr. Babbitt scolded these erring brothers for not making a moral judgment, and it is just here that the limitations of his method appear. The moral obligation to judge does not necessarily obligate us to make a moral judgment. Mr. Babbitt's humanism contains some concealed naturalism in its insistence upon the value of the mere substance or essence of literature: the subject matter itself must be decorous in order to pass the humanist examination. The specific property of a work of literary art which differentiates it from mere historical experience he could never understand; and it is this specific property, this particular quality of the work, that puts upon us the moral obligation to form a judgment. Mr. Yvor Winters remarks that Mr. Babbitt never understood "how the moral intelligence gets into poetry." It gets in not as moral abstractions but as form, coherence of image and metaphor, control of tone and of rhythm, the union of these features. So the moral obligation to judge compels us to make not a moral but a total judgment.

The question in the end comes down to this: What as literary critics are we to judge? As literary critics we must first of all decide in what respect the literary work has a specific objectivity. If we deny its specific objectivity then not only is criticism impossible but literature also. We have got to decide what it is about the whole of a work of literature which distinguishes it from its parts—or rather the parts we can abstract from this whole and then distribute over the vast smudge of history, whence they presumably were derived. It is a question of knowing before we talk what as critics we are talking about.

From my point of view the formal qualities of a poem are the focus of the specifically critical judgment because they partake of an objectivity that the subject matter, abstracted from the form, wholly lacks. The form of "Lycidas" is Milton's specific achievement as a poet in the convention of the pastoral elegy; but this convention, which is his substance, represents in itself only a subjective selection from Milton's historical situation. Would it not be simpler to seize at once the specific quality of "Lycidas" and try to understand it than to grapple with that aspect which fades into the immense perspective of history?

It would be simpler, if not easier, to discuss the form if we had a way of discussing it; yet before we can understand a literary problem we must first confess the problem exists. We no longer admit the problem because we no longer believe in the specific quality of the work of literature, the quality that distinguishes it from a work of history or even of science. As men of letters we no longer, in fact, believe in literature; we believe rather that the knowledge offered us in even the most highly developed literary forms has something factitious and illusory about it, so that before we can begin to test its validity we must translate it into an analogy derived from the sciences. The historical method is an imitation of scientific method: we entertain as interesting and valuable that portion of the literary work to which we can apply the scientific vocabularies.

Not being a literary historian I do not know when the literary profession lost confidence in literature; I suppose it was a gradual loss; we see its beginnings in the English romantics, and we do not yet see the end. The rise of the sciences, their immense practical successes, even their moral failures, intimidated the scholars and I seem to hear them say, at first secretly and late at night when black questions cannot be gainsaid: "Milton's science is false, and the scientists say that his moral and religious ideas have no empirical validity. But if I give up Milton I give up my profession, so I had better bestir myself to study scientifically Milton's unscientific science. We must get in on the wonderful scientific triumphs of the age. Nobody believes today that the arts give us a sort of cognition at least equally valid with that of scientific method; so we will just take the arts as fields of data for more scientific investigation."

The historical method is in the long run the unhistorical method. The literary historians are not first of all historians. We seldom get from them anything like Taine on English literature; no American literary scholar has produced a work of the distinction of Carl Becker's *The Heavenly City of the Eighteenth-Century Philosophers*, a book written not in the historical method but out of the historical imagination. It is a work of literature by a mind informed with a mature point of view and seasoned with exact knowledge (by knowledge I do not mean documentation) in many fields. Could Mr. Becker have written the book had he been trained in the belief that philosophy, for example, not being "English," has no place in historical writing? Could he have written it had he been compelled to suppress all the resources of his intelligence but the single one employed in the mechanical "correlation" of literature with the undigested lump of history? Is there not an instructive moral in the distinction of Mr. Becker's prose style?

I am not attacking the study or the writing of history for use in the criticism of literature. I am attacking the historical method. I trust everybody understands what this method is. It reflects at varying distances the philosophies of monism current in the nineteenth century and still prevailing today. Because the literary scholar in his monistic naturalism cannot discern the objectivity of the forms of literature, he can only apply to literature certain abstractions which he derives, two stages removed, from the naturalistic sciences; that is to say he gets these abstractions from the historians who got them from the scientists. In the period when physics was the popular science we got historical studies of influences, conceived in terms of forces, causes, and effects; then came the biological analogies that gave us organic periods where we attended to growths and developments; and today we have a broadening of the historical method which reflects the vast extension of scientific procedure in the semi-sciences—psychology, economics, and sociology.

That this method is, in a definite sense, unhistorical it would not be hard to show. Under whatever leading analogy we employ the historical method—organism, mechanism, causality—it has the immediate effect of removing the historian himself from history, so that he cannot participate as a living imagination in a great work of literature. Even those scholars, usually men interested in the eighteenth century, who are concerned with the meaning of tradition conceive of tradition itself in terms of scientific analogies, so that there is something remote and mechanical about a tradition; and the tradition that we are interested in is almost always seen as a traditional "body" of literature, not operative today—not living, as the very word body implies.

This removal of the historian from living history has curious consequences. Because it is difficult—or too easy in some respects—to get historical documents for works of the present or recent past we refuse to study them. And we also refuse to study them because their reputations are not fixed. There is here the assumption, as I think the illusion, that the reputation of any writer is ever fixed. These two illusions—the necessity of documents for the study of literature and the fixed hierarchy of the past—are not necessarily consequences of the historical method: Milton complained of similar routines of pedantry at Cambridge. Yet perhaps more today than ever we get a systematic, semi-philosophical sanction for our refusal to study literature.

I take the somewhat naïve view that the literature of the past began somewhere a few minutes ago and that the literature of the present begins, say, with Homer. While there is no doubt that we need as much knowledge of all kinds, from all sources, as we can get if we are to see the slightest lyric in all its richness of meaning, we have nevertheless an obligation, that we perilously evade, to form a judgment of the literature of our own time. It is more than an obligation; we must do it if we would keep on living. When the scholar assumes that he is judging a work of the past from a high and disinterested position, he is actually judging it from no position at all but is only abstracting from the work those qualities that his semiscientific method will permit him to see; and this is the Great Refusal.

We must judge the past and keep it alive by being alive ourselves; and that is to say that we must judge the past not with a method or an abstract hierarchy but with the present, or with as much of the present as our poets have succeeded in elevating to the objectivity of form. For it is through the formed, objective experience of our own time that we must approach the past; and then by means of a critical mastery of our own formed experience we may test the presence and the value of form in works of the past. This critical activity is reciprocal and simultaneous. The scholar who tells us that he understands Dryden but makes nothing of Hopkins or Yeats is telling us that he does not understand Dryden.

Perhaps the same scholar acknowledges the greatness of Dryden and the even more formidable greatness of Milton and Shakespeare; and if you ask him how they became great he will reply, as I have heard him reply, that History did it and that we have got to wait until History does it, or declines to do it, to writers of our own time. Who is this mysterious person named History? We are back again with our old friend, the Great Refusal, who thrives upon the naturalistic repudiation of the moral obligation to judge. If we wait for history to judge there will be no judgment; for if we are not history then history is nobody. He is nobody when he has become the historical method.

One last feature of this illusion of the fixed hierarchy I confess I cannot understand. It is the belief that the chief function of criticism is the ranking of authors rather than their use. It is the assumption that the great writers of the past occupy a fixed position. If we alter the figure slightly, admitting that History has frozen their reputations, we must assume also that the position from which we look at them is likewise fixed; for if it were not we should see them in constantly changing relations and perspectives, and we should think their positions were changing too. If you will now see this same figure as a landscape of hills, trees, plains, you will quickly become fearful for the man who from a fixed point surveys the unchanging scene; for the man, the only man, who cannot change his position is a dead man: the only man for whom the greatness of the great poets is fixed is also dead. And so, if we may look at this Homeric simile with the eyes of Bishop Berkeley, we must conclude that the great authors are dead, too, because there is nobody to look at them. I have adapted this figure from one of the Prefaces of Henry James because it seems to me to be a good way of saying that the literature of the past can be kept alive only by seeing it as the literature of the present. Or perhaps we ought to say that the literature of the past lives in the literature of the present and nowhere else; that it is all present literature.

1. This paper was read before the English Club of Princeton University, April 10, 1940.

2. The reader will suspect that I have had in mind all along the phrase "the *corpus* of English literature," widely used by scholars and their way, no doubt, of laying literature out for burial.

Criticism, Inc.

JOHN CROWE RANSOM

Ransom's essay from The World's Body *(1938) has always been considered one of the most important landmarks in the acceptance of literary criticism as a legitimate activity of university teachers and scholars. His call to the professors to make "the erection of intelligent standards of criticism" their business was based upon a simple insight: that "the students of the future must be permitted to study literature, and not merely about literature."*

It is strange, but nobody seems to have told us what exactly is the proper business of criticism. There are many critics who might tell us, but for the most part they are amateurs. So have the critics nearly always been amateurs; including the best ones. They have not been trained to criticism so much as they have simply undertaken a job for which no specific qualifications were required. It is far too likely that what they call criticism when they produce it is not the real thing.

There are three sorts of trained performers who would appear to have some of the competence that the critic needs. The first is the artist himself. He should know good art when he sees it; but his understanding is intuitive rather than dialectical—he cannot very well explain his theory of the thing. It is true that literary artists, with their command of language, are better critics of their own art than are other artists; probably the best critics of poetry we can now have are the poets. But one can well imagine that any artist's commentary on the art-work is valuable in the degree that he sticks to its technical effects, which he knows minutely, and about which he can certainly talk if he will.

The second is the philosopher, who should know all about the function of the fine arts. But the philosopher is apt to see a lot of wood and no trees, for his theory is very general and his acquaintance with the particular works of art is not persistent and intimate, especially his acquaintance with their technical effects. Or at least I suppose so, for philosophers have not proved that they can write close criticism by writing it; and I have the feeling that even their handsome generalizations are open to suspicion as being grounded more on other generalizations, those which form their prior philosophical stock, than on acute study of particulars.

The third is the university teacher of literature, who is styled professor, and who should be the very professional we need to take charge of the critical activity. He is hardly inferior as critic to the philosopher, and perhaps not on the whole to the poet, but he is a greater disappointment because we have the right to expect more of him. Professors of literature are learned but not critical men. The professional morale of this part of the university staff is evidently low. It is as if, with conscious or unconscious cunning, they had appropriated every avenue of escape from their responsibility which was decent and official; so that it is easy for one of them without public reproach to spend a lifetime in compiling the data of literature and yet rarely or never commit himself to a literary judgment.

Nevertheless it is from the professors of literature, in this country the professors of English for the most part, that I should hope eventually for the erection of intelligent standards of criticism. It is their business.

Criticism must become more scientific, or precise and systematic, and this means that it must be developed by the collective and sustained effort of learned persons—which means that its proper seat is in the universities.

Scientific: but I do not think we need be afraid that criticism, trying to be a sort of science, will inevitably fail and give up in despair, or else fail without realizing it and enjoy some hollow and pretentious career. It will never be a very exact science, or even a nearly exact one. But neither will psychology, if that term continues to refer to psychic rather than physical phenomena; nor will sociology, as Pareto, quite contrary to his intention, appears to have furnished us with evidence for believing; nor even will economics. It does not matter whether we call them sciences or just systematic studies; the total effort of each to be effective must be consolidated and kept going. The studies which I have mentioned have immeasurably improved in understanding since they were taken over by the universities, and the same career looks possible for criticism.

Rather than occasional criticism by amateurs, I should think the whole enterprise might be seriously taken in hand by professionals. Perhaps I use a distasteful figure, but I have the idea that what we need is Criticism, Inc., or Criticism, Ltd.

The principal resistance to such an idea will come from the present incumbents of the professorial chairs. But its adoption must come from them too. The idea of course is not a private one of my own. If it should be adopted before long, the credit would probably belong to Professor

Ronald S. Crane, of the University of Chicago, more than to any other man. He is the first of the great professors to have advocated it as a major policy for departments of English. It is possible that he will have made some important academic history.

II

Professor Crane published recently a paper of great note in academic circles, on the reform of the courses in English. It appeared in *The English Journal*, under the title: "History Versus Criticism in the University Study of Literature." He argues there that historical scholarship has been overplayed heavily in English studies, in disregard of the law of diminishing returns, and that the emphasis must now be shifted to the critical.

To me this means, simply: the students of the future must be permitted to study literature, and not merely about literature. But I think this is what the good students have always wanted to do. The wonder is that they have allowed themselves so long to be denied. But they have not always been amiable about it, and the whole affair presents much comic history.

At the University of Chicago, I believe that Professor Crane, with some others, is putting the revolution into effect in his own teaching, though for the time being perhaps with a limited program, mainly the application of Aristotle's critical views. (My information is not at all exact.) The university is an opulent one, not too old to experience waves of reformational zeal, uninhibited as yet by bad traditions. Its department of English has sponsored plenty of old-line scholarship, but this is not the first time it has gone in for criticism. If the department should now systematically and intelligently build up a general school of literary criticism, I believe it would score a triumph that would be, by academic standards, spectacular. I mean that the alive and brilliant young English scholars all over the country would be saying they wanted to go there to do their work. That would place a new distinction upon the university, and it would eventually and profoundly modify the practices of many other institutions. It would be worth even more than Professor Crane's careful presentation of the theory.

This is not the first time that English professors have tilted against the historians, or "scholars," in the dull sense which that word has acquired. They did not score heavily, at those other times. Probably they were themselves not too well versed in the historical studies, so that it could be said with honest concern that they scarcely had the credentials to judge of such matters. At the same time they may have been too unproductive critically to offer a glowing alternative.

The most important recent diversion from the orthodox course of literary studies was that undertaken by the New Humanists. I regret to think that it was not the kind of diversion which I am advocating; nor the kind approved by Professor Crane, who comments briefly against it. Unquestionably the Humanists did divert, and the refreshment was grateful to anybody who felt resentful for having his literary predilections ignored under the schedule of historical learning. But in the long run the diversion proved to be nearly as unliterary as the round of studies from which it took off at a tangent. No picnic ideas were behind it.

The New Humanists were, and are, moralists; more accurately, historians and advocates of a certain moral system. Criticism is the attempt to define and enjoy the aesthetic or characteristic values of literature, but I suppose the Humanists would shudder at "aesthetic" as hard as ordinary historical scholars do. Did an official Humanist ever make any official play with the term? I do not remember it. The term "art" is slightly more ambiguous, and they have availed themselves of that; with centuries of loose usage behind it, art connotes, for those who like, high seriousness, and high seriousness connotes moral self-consciousness, and an inner check, and finally either Plato or Aristotle.

Mr. Babbitt consistently played on the terms classical and romantic. They mean any of several things each, so that unquestionably Mr. Babbitt could make war on romanticism for purely moral reasons; and his preoccupation was ethical, not aesthetic. It is perfectly legitimate for the moralist to attack romantic literature if he can make out his case; for example, on the ground that it deals with emotions rather than principles, or the ground that its author discloses himself as flabby, intemperate, escapist, unphilosophical, or simply adolescent. The moral objection is probably valid; a romantic period testifies to a large-scale failure of adaptation, and defense of that failure to adapt, to the social and political environment; unless, if the Humanists will consent, it sometimes testifies to the failure of society and state to sympathize with the needs of the individual. But this is certainly not the charge that Mr. T. S. Eliot, a literary critic, brings against romanticism. His, if I am not mistaken, is aesthetic, though he may not ever care to define it very sharply. In other words, the literary critic also has something to say about romanticism, and it might come to something like this: that romantic literature is imperfect in objectivity, or "aesthetic distance," and that out of this imperfection comes its weakness of structure; that the romantic poet does not quite realize the aesthetic attitude, and is not the pure artist. Or it might come to something else. It would be quite premature to say that when a moralist is obliged to disapprove a work the literary critic must disapprove it too.

Following the excitement produced by the Humanist diversion, there is now one due to the Leftists, or Proletarians, who are also diversionists. Their diversion is likewise moral. It is just as proper for them to ferret out class-consciousness in literature, and to make literature serve the cause of loving-comradeship, as it is for the Humanists to censure romanticism and to use the topic, and the literary exhibit, as the occasion of reviving the Aristotelian moral canon. I mean that these are procedures of the same sort. Debate could never occur between a Humanist and a Leftist on aesthetic grounds, for they are equally intent on ethical values. But the debate on ethical grounds would be very spirited, and it might create such a stir in a department conducting English studies that the conventional scholars there would find themselves slipping, and their pupils deriving from literature new and seductive excitements which would entice them away from their scheduled English exercises.

On the whole, however, the moralists, distinguished as they may be, are like those who have quarreled with the ordinary historical studies on purer or more aesthetic grounds: they have not occupied in English studies the positions of professional importance. In a department of English, as in any other going business, the proprietary interest becomes vested, and in old and reputable departments the vestees have uniformly been gentlemen who have gone through the historical mill. Their laborious Ph.D.'s and historical publications are their patents. Naturally, quite spontaneously, they would tend to perpetuate a system in which the power and the glory belonged to them. But English scholars in this country can rarely have better credentials than those which Professor Crane has earned in his extensive field, the eighteenth century. It is this which makes his disaffection significant.

It is really atrocious policy for a department to abdicate its own self-respecting identity. The department of English is charged with the understanding and the communication of literature, an art, yet it has usually forgotten to inquire into the peculiar constitution and structure of its product. English might almost as well announce that it does not regard itself as entirely autonomous, but as a branch of the department of history, with the option of declaring itself occasionally a branch of the department of ethics. It is true that the historical and the ethical studies will cluster round objects which for some reason are called artistic objects. But the thing itself the professors do not have to contemplate; and only last spring the head of English studies in a graduate school fabulously equipped made the following impromptu disclaimer to a victim who felt aggrieved at having his own studies forced in the usual direction: "This is a place for exact scholarship, and you want to do criticism.

Well, we don't allow criticism here, because that is something which anybody can do."

But one should never speak impromptu in one's professional capacity. This speech may have betrayed a fluttery private apprehension which should not have been made public: that you can never be critical and be exact at the same time, that history is firmer ground than aesthetics, and that, to tell the truth, criticism is a painful job for the sort of mind that wants to be very sure about things. Not in that temper did Aristotle labor towards a critique in at least one branch of letters; nor in that temper are strong young minds everywhere trying to sharpen their critical apparatus into precision tools, in this decade as never before.

It is not anybody who can do criticism. And for an example, the more eminent (as historical scholar) the professor of English, the less apt he is to be able to write decent criticism, unless it is about another professor's work of historical scholarship, in which case it is not literary criticism. The professor may not be without aesthetic judgments respecting an old work, especially if it is "in his period," since it must often have been judged by authorities whom he respects. Confronted with a new work, I am afraid it is very rare that he finds anything particular to say. Contemporary criticism is not at all in the hands of those who direct the English studies. Contemporary literature, which is almost obliged to receive critical study if it receives any at all, since it is hardly capable of the usual historical commentary, is barely officialized as a proper field for serious study.

Here is contemporary literature, waiting for its criticism; where are the professors of literature? They are watering their own gardens; elucidating the literary histories of their respective periods. So are their favorite pupils. The persons who save the occasion, and rescue contemporary literature from the humiliation of having to go without a criticism, are the men who had to leave the university before their time because they felt themselves being warped into mere historians; or those who finished the courses and took their punishment but were tough, and did not let it engross them and spoil them. They are home-made critics. Naturally they are not too wise, these amateurs who furnish our reviews and critical studies. But when they distinguish themselves, the universities which they attended can hardly claim more than a trifling share of the honor.

It is not so in economics, chemistry, sociology, theology, and architecture. In these branches it is taken for granted that criticism of the performance is the prerogative of the men who have had formal training in its theory and technique. The historical method is useful, and may be applied readily to any human performance whatever. But the exercise does not become an obsession with the university men working in the other branches; only the literary scholars wish to convert themselves into pure historians. This has gone far to nullify the usefulness of a departmental personnel larger, possibly, than any other, and of the lavish endowment behind it.

III

Presumably the departments of English exist in order to communicate the understanding of the literary art. That will include both criticism and also whatever may be meant by "appreciation." This latter term seems to stand for the kind of understanding that is had intuitively, without benefit of instruction, by merely being constrained to spend time in the presence of the literary product. It is true that some of the best work now being done in departments is by the men who do little more than read well aloud, enforcing a private act of appreciation upon the students. One remembers how good a service that may be, thinking perhaps of Professor Copeland of Harvard, or Dean Cross at Greeley Teachers College. And there are men who try to get at the same thing in another way, which they would claim is surer: by requiring a great deal of memory work, in order to enforce familiarity with fine poetry. These might defend their strategy by saying that at any rate the work they required was not as vain as the historical rigmarole which the scholars made their pupils recite, if the objective was really literary understanding and not external information. But it would be a misuse of terms to employ the word instruction for the offices either of the professors who read aloud or of those who require the memory work. The professors so engaged are properly curators, and the museum of which they have the care is furnished with the cherished literary masterpieces, just as another museum might be filled with paintings. They conduct their squads from one work to another, making appropriate pauses or reverent gestures, but their own obvious regard for the masterpieces is somewhat contagious, and contemplation is induced. Naturally they are grateful to the efficient staff of colleagues in the background who have framed the masterpieces, hung them in the proper schools and in the chronological order, and prepared the booklet of information about the artists and the occasions. The colleagues in their turn probably feel quite happy over this division of labor, thinking that they have done the really productive work, and that it is appropriate now if less able men should undertake a little salesmanship.

Behind appreciation, which is private, and criticism, which is public and negotiable, and represents the last stage of English studies, is historical scholarship. It is indispensable. But it is instrumental and cannot be the end itself. In this respect historical studies have the same standing as linguistic studies: language and history are aids.

On behalf of the historical studies. Without them what could we make of Chaucer, for instance? I cite the familiar locus of the "hard" scholarship, the center of any program of advanced studies in English which intends to initiate the student heroically, and once for all, into the historical discipline. Chaucer writes allegories for historians to decipher, he looks out upon institutions and customs unfamiliar to us. Behind him are many writers in various tongues from whom he borrows both forms and materials. His thought bears constant reference to classical and mediæval philosophies and sciences which have passed from our effective knowledge. An immense labor of historical adaptation is necessary before our minds are ready to make the aesthetic approach to Chaucer.

Or to any author out of our own age. The mind with which we enter into an old work is not the mind with which we make our living, or enter into a contemporary work. It is under sharp restraints, and it is quite differently furnished. Out of our actual contemporary mind we have to cancel a great deal that has come there under modern conditions but was not in the earlier mind at all. This is a technique on the negative side, a technique of suspension; difficult for practical persons, literal scientists, and aggressive moderns who take pride in the "truth" or the "progress" which enlightened man, so well represented in their own instance, has won. Then, on the positive side, we must supply the mind with the precise beliefs and ways of thought it had in that former age, with the specific content in which history instructs us; this is a technique of make-believe. The whole act of historical adaptation, through such techniques, is a marvelous feat of flexibility. Certainly it is a thing hard enough to justify university instruction. But it is not sufficient for an English program.

The achievement of modern historical scholarship in the field of English literature has been, in the aggregate, prodigious; it should be very proud. A good impression of the volume of historical learning now available for the students of English may be quickly had from inspecting a few chapters of the Cambridge History, with the bibliographies. Or, better, from inspecting one of a large number of works which have come in since the Cambridge History: the handbooks, which tell all about the authors, such as Chaucer, Shakespeare, Milton, and carry voluminous bibliographies; or the period books, which tell a good deal about whole periods of literature.

There is one sense in which it may be justly said that we can never have too much scholarship. We cannot have too much of it if the critical intelligence functions, and has the authority to direct it. There is hardly a critical problem which does not require some arduous exercises in fact-finding, but each problem is quite specific about the kind of facts it wants. Mountains of facts may have been found already, but often they have been found for no purpose at all except the purpose of piling up into a big exhibit, to offer intoxicating delights to the academic population.

To those who are æsthetically minded among students, the rewards of many a historical labor will have to be disproportionately slight. The official Chaucer course is probably over ninety-five per cent historical and linguistic, and less than five per cent aesthetic or critical. A thing of beauty is a joy forever. But it is not improved because the student has had to tie his tongue before it. It is an artistic object, with a heroic human labor behind it, and on these terms it calls for public discussion. The dialectical possibilities are limitless, and when we begin to realize them we are engaged in criticism.

IV

What is criticism? Easier to ask, What is criticism not? It is an act now notoriously arbitrary and undefined. We feel certain that the critical act is not one of those which the professors of literature habitually perform, and cause their students to perform. And it is our melancholy impression that it is not often cleanly performed in those loose compositions, by writers of perfectly indeterminate qualifications, that appear in print as reviews of books.

Professor Crane excludes from criticism works of historical scholarship and of Neo-Humanism, but more exclusions are possible than that. I should wish to exclude:

1. Personal registrations, which are declarations of the effect of the art-work upon the critic as reader. The first law to be prescribed to criticism, if we may assume such authority, is that it shall be objective, shall cite the nature of the object rather than its effects upon the subject. Therefore it is hardly criticism to assert that the proper literary work is one that we can read twice; or one that causes in us some remarkable physiological effect, such as oblivion of the outer world, the flowing of tears, visceral or laryngeal sensations, and such like; or one that induces perfect illusion, or brings us into a spiritual ecstasy; or even one that produces a catharsis of our emotions. Aristotle concerned himself with this last in making up his definition of tragedy—though he did not fail to make some acute analyses of the objective features of the work also. I have read that some modern Broadway producers of comedy require a reliable person to seat himself in a trial audience and count the laughs; their method of testing is not so subtle as Aristotle's, but both are concerned with the effects. Such concern seems to reflect the view that

art comes into being because the artist, or the employer behind him, has designs upon the public, whether high moral designs or box-office ones. It is an odious view in either case, because it denies the autonomy of the artist as one who interests himself in the artistic object in his own right, and likewise the autonomy of the work itself as existing for its own sake. (We may define a chemical as something which can effect a certain cure, but that is not its meaning to the chemist; and we may define toys, if we are weary parents, as things which keep our children quiet, but that is not what they are to engineers.). Furthermore, we must regard as uncritical the use of an extensive vocabulary which ascribes to the object properties really discovered in the subject, as: *moving, exciting, entertaining, pitiful; great,* if I am not mistaken, and *admirable,* on a slightly different ground; and, in strictness, *beautiful* itself.

2. Synopsis and paraphrase. The high-school classes and the women's clubs delight in these procedures, which are easiest of all the systematic exercises possible in the discussion of literary objects. I do not mean that the critic never uses them in his analysis of fiction and poetry, but he does not consider plot or story as identical with the real content. Plot is an abstract from content.

3. Historical studies. These have a very wide range, and include studies of the general literary background; author's biography, of course with special reference to autobiographical evidences in the work itself; bibliographical items; the citation of literary originals and analogues, and therefore what, in general, is called comparative literature. Nothing can be more stimulating to critical analysis than comparative literature. But it may be conducted only superficially, if the comparisons are perfunctory and mechanical, or if the scholar is content with merely making the parallel citations.

4. Linguistic studies. Under this head come those studies which define the meaning of unusual words and idioms, including the foreign and archaic ones, and identify the allusions. The total benefit of linguistics for criticism would be the assurance that the latter was based on perfect logical understanding of the content, or "interpretation." Acquaintance with all the languages and literatures in the world would not necessarily produce a critic, though it might save one from damaging errors.

5. Moral studies. The moral standard applied is the one appropriate to the reviewer; it may be the Christian ethic, or the Aristotelian one, or the new proletarian gospel. But the moral content is not the whole content, which should never be relinquished.

6. Any other special studies which deal with some abstract or prose content taken out of the work. Nearly all departments of knowledge may conceivably find their own materials in literature, and take them out.

Studies have been made of Chaucer's command of mediaeval sciences, of Spenser's view of the Irish question, of Shakespeare's understanding of the law, of Milton's geography, of Hardy's place-names. The critic may well inform himself of these materials as possessed by the artist, but his business as critic is to discuss the literary assimilation of them.

V

With or without such useful exercises as these, probably assuming that the intelligent reader has made them for himself, comes the critical act itself.

Mr. Austin Warren, whose writings I admire, is evidently devoted to the academic development of the critical project. Yet he must be a fair representative of what a good deal of academic opinion would be when he sees no reason why criticism should set up its own house, and try to dissociate itself from historical and other scholarly studies; why not let all sorts of studies, including the critical ones, flourish together in the same act of sustained attention, or the same scheduled "course"? But so they are supposed to do at present; and I would only ask him whether he considers that criticism prospers under this arrangement. It has always had the chance to go ahead in the hands of the professors of literature, and it has not gone ahead. A change of policy suggests itself. Strategy requires now, I should think, that criticism receive its own charter of rights and function independently. If he fears for its foundations in scholarship, the scholars will always be on hand to reprove it when it tries to function on an unsound scholarship.

I do not suppose the reviewing of books can be reformed in the sense of being turned into pure criticism. The motives of the reviewers are as much mixed as the performance, and indeed they condition the mixed performance. The reviewer has a job of presentation and interpretation as well as criticism. The most we can ask of him is that he know when the criticism begins, and that he make it as clean and definitive as his business permits. To what authority may he turn?

I know of no authority. For the present each critic must be his own authority. But I know of one large class of studies which is certainly critical, and necessary, and I can suggest another sort of study for the critic's consideration if he is really ambitious.

Studies in the technique of the art belong to criticism certainly. They cannot belong anywhere else, because the technique is not peculiar to any prose materials discoverable in the work of art, nor to anything else but the unique form of that art. A very large volume of studies is indicated by this classification. They would be technical studies of poetry, for instance, the art I am specifically discussing, if they treated its metric;

its inversions, solecisms, lapses from the prose norm of language, and from close prose logic; its tropes; its fictions, or inventions, by which it secures "aesthetic distance" and removes itself from history; or any other devices, on the general understanding that any systematic usage which does not hold good for prose is a poetic device.

A device with a purpose: the superior critic is not content with the compilation of the separate devices; they suggest to him a much more general question. The critic speculates on why poetry, through its devices, is at such pains to dissociate itself from prose at all, and what it is trying to represent that cannot be represented by prose.

I intrude here with an idea of my own, which may serve as a starting point of discussion. Poetry distinguishes itself from prose on the technical side by the devices which are, precisely, its means of escaping from prose. Something is continually being killed by prose which the poet wants to preserve. But this must be put philosophically. (Philosophy sounds hard, but it deals with natural and fundamental forms of experience.)

The critic should regard the poem as nothing short of a desperate ontological or metaphysical maneuver. The poet himself, in the agony of composition, has something like this sense of his labors. The poet perpetuates in his poem an order of existence which in actual life is constantly crumbling beneath his touch. His poem celebrates the object which is real, individual, and qualitatively infinite. He knows that his practical interests will reduce this living object to a mere utility, and that his sciences will disintegrate it for their convenience into their respective abstracts. The poet wishes to defend his object's existence against its enemies, and the critic wishes to know what he is doing, and how. The critic should find in the poem a total poetic or individual object which tends to be universalized, but is not permitted to suffer this fate. His identification of the poetic object is in terms of the universal or commonplace object to which it tends, and of the tissue, or totality of connotation, which holds it secure. How does he make out the universal object? It is the prose object, which any forthright prosy reader can discover to him by an immediate paraphrase; it is a kind of story, character, thing, scene, or moral principle. And where is the tissue that keeps it from coming out of the poetic object? That is, for the laws of the prose logic, its superfluity; and I think I would even say, its irrelevance.

A poet is said to be distinguishable in terms of his style. It is a comprehensive word, and probably means: the general character of his irrelevances, or tissues. All his technical devices contribute to it, elaborating or individualizing the universal, the core object; likewise all his material detail. For each poem even, ideally, there is distinguishable a logical object or universal, but at the same time a tissue of irrelevance from which it does not really emerge. The critic has to take the poem apart, or analyze it, for the sake of uncovering these features. With all the finesse possible, it is rude and patchy business by comparison with the living integrity of the poem. But without it there could hardly be much understanding of the value of poetry, or of the natural history behind any adult poem.

The language I have used may sound too formidable, but I seem to find that a profound criticism generally works by some such considerations. However the critic may spell them, the two terms are in his mind: the prose core to which he can violently reduce the total object, and the differentia, residue, or tissue, which keeps the object poetical or entire. The character of the poem resides for the good critic in its way of exhibiting the residuary quality. The character of the poet is defined by the kind of prose object to which his interest evidently attaches, plus his way of involving it firmly in the residuary tissue. And doubtless, incidentally, the wise critic can often read behind the poet's public character his private history as a man with a weakness for lapsing into some special form of prosy or scientific bondage.

Similar considerations hold, I think, for the critique of fiction, or of the non-literary arts. I remark this for the benefit of philosophers who believe, with propriety, that the arts are fundamentally one. But I would prefer to leave the documentation to those who are better qualified.

Is Literary Criticism Possible?[1]

ALLEN TATE

This essay, which was adapted from two conference papers delivered in 1950–51, begins with an examination of the central problems of teaching literary criticism in our universities, and finishes with ten questions that confront the reader with the philosophical dilemmas of the enterprise. In between, Tate explains why students who neglect the studies of Rhetoric and Grammar do so at their peril.

The questions that I propose to discuss in this essay will fall into two main divisions. I shall undertake to discuss, first, the teaching of literary criticism in the university. Since I am not able to *define* literary criticism, I shall be chiefly concerned with the idea of a formal relation; that is to say, supposing we knew what criticism is, what relation would it have to the humanities, of which it seems to be a constituent part? In the second division I shall try to push the discussion a little further, towards a question that has been acute in our time: Is literary criticism possible at all? The answer to this question ought logically to precede the discussion of a formal relation, for we ought to know what it is that we are trying to relate to something else. But we shall never know this; we shall only find that in teaching criticism we do not know what we are teaching, even though criticism daily talks about a vast material that we are in the habit of calling the humanities. The mere fact of this witnesses our sense of a formal relation that ought to exist between two things of the nature of which we are ignorant.

I

Literary criticism as a member of the humanities I take to be a problem of academic statesmanship inviting what we hopefully call "solutions" of both the theoretical and the practical sort. Is literary criticism properly a branch of humanistic study? That is the theoretical question, to which I shall avoid the responsibility of giving the answer. Without this answer, we cannot hope to understand the practical question: What is the place of criticism in the humanities program; on what grounds should it be there (if it should be there at all), given the kind of education that the present teachers of the humanities bring to their work?

The two questions, the theoretical and the practical, together constitute the formal question; that is to say, whatever criticism and the humanities may be, we should have to discuss their relation in some such terms as I am suggesting. But before we follow this clue we must address ourselves more candidly to the fact of our almost total ignorance.

The three grand divisions of higher education in the United States are, I believe, the Natural Sciences, the Social Sciences, and the Humanities. Of the first, I am entirely too ignorant to speak. Of the social sciences I know little, and I am not entitled to suspect that they do not really exist; I believe this in the long run because I want to believe it, the actuality of a science of human societies being repellent to me, apart from its dubious scientific credentials. Of the humanities, the division with which as poet and critic I am presumably most concerned, one must speak with melancholy as well as in ignorance. For into the humanistic bag we throw everything that cannot qualify as a science, natural or social. This discrete mixture of hot and cold, moist and dry, creates in the bag a vortex, which emits a powerful wind of ineffective heroics, somewhat as follows: We humanists bring within the scope of the humanities all the great records—sometimes we call them the remains: poetry, drama, prescientific history (Herodotus, Joinville, Bede)—of the experience of man *as* man; we are not concerned with him as vertebrate, biped, mathematician, or priest. Precisely, reply the social scientists; that is just what is wrong with you; you don't see that man is not man, that he is merely a *function*; and your records (or remains) are so full of error that we are glad to relegate them to professors of English, poets, and other dilettanti, those "former people" who live in the Past. The Past, which we can neither smell, see, taste, nor touch, was well labeled by our apostle, Mr. Carl Sandburg, as a bucket of ashes . . . No first-rate scientific mind is guilty of this vulgarity. Yet as academic statesmen, the humanists must also be practical politicians who know that they cannot stay in office unless they have an invigorating awareness of the power, and of the superior footwork, of the third-rate mind.

As for literary criticism, we here encounter a stench and murk not unlike that of a battlefield three days after the fighting is over and the armies have departed. Yet in this war nobody has suggested that criticism is one of the social sciences, except a few Marxists, who tried fifteen years ago to make it a branch of sociology. History not long ago became a social science, and saved its life by losing it; and there is no reason why sociology "oriented" toward literature should not be likewise promoted, to the relief of everybody concerned. And whatever criticism may be, we should perhaps do well to keep it with the humanities, where it can profit by the sad example of Hilaire Belloc's Jim, who failed "To keep ahold of Nurse / For fear of getting something worse."

It may not be necessary to know what criticism is; it may be quite enough to see that it is now being written, that a great deal of it was written in the past, that it is concerned with one of the chief objects of humanistic study: literature. And we therefore study it either as an "area" in itself—that is, we offer courses in its history; or as a human interest in some past age—that is, we use criticism as one way of understanding the age of Johnson or the high Renaissance. Guided by the happy theory of spontaneous understanding resulting from the collision of pure intelligence with its object—a theory injected into American education by Charles W. Eliot—we expose the student mind to "areas" of humanistic material, in the confident belief that if it is exposed to enough "areas" it will learn something. If we expose it to enough "areas" in all three grand divisions, the spontaneous intelligence will automatically become educated without thought.

The natural sciences have a high-powered rationale of their daily conquests of nature. The social sciences have a slippery analogical[2] metaphor to sustain their self-confidence. The humanities modestly offer the vision of the historical lump. This lump is tossed at the student mind, which is conceived as the miraculous combination of the *tabula rasa* and innate powers of understanding. In short, the humanities have no rationale. We suppose that it is sufficient to show that a given work—a poem, a play, a critical "document"—came before or after some other poem, play, or critical "document," or was written when something else was happening, like Alexander's invasion of India or the defeat of the Armada. When these and other correlations are perceived, the result is understanding. But the result of correlation is merely the possibility of further correlation. Our modest capacity for true understanding is frustrated. For the true rationale of humanistic study is now what it has always been, even though now it is not only in decay, but dead. I allude to the arts of rhetoric.

By rhetoric I mean the study and the use of the figurative language of experience as the discipline by means of which men govern their relations with one another in the light of truth. Rhetoric presupposes the study of two prior disciplines, grammar and logic, neither of which is much pursued today, except by specialists.

These disciplines are no longer prerequisite even to the study of philosophy. An Eastern university offers a grandiose course in Greek philosophical ideas to sophomores who will never know a syllogism from a handsaw. A graduate student who, I was told, was very brilliant in nuclear physics, decided that he wanted to take a course in *The Divine Comedy*. (Why he wanted to study Dante I do not know, but his humility was impressive.) I was assured by the academic grapevine that he understood difficult mathematical formulae, but one day in class he revealed the fact that he could neither define nor recognize a past participle. At the end of the term he confessed that nobody had ever told him that the strategies of language, or the arts of rhetoric, could be as important and exacting a discipline as the theory of equations. He had thought courses in English a little sissified; he had not been told that it might be possible, after severe application, to learn how to read. He had learned to talk without effort in infancy, in a decadent democracy, and no doubt supposed that grammar came of conditioning, and that he would get it free.

Back of this homely exemplum stands a formidable specter whose name is Cultural Decay—at a time when men are more conscious of cultures than ever before and stock their universities and museums with lumps of cultures, like inert geological specimens in a glass case. I am far from believing that a revival of the trivium, or the three primary liberal arts, would bring the dead bodies to life: revivals have a fatal incapacity to revive anything. But unless we can create and develop a hierarchy of studies that can lead not merely to further studies but to truth, one may doubt that the accelerating decline of modern culture will be checked.

Without quite knowing what literary criticism is, let us assume again that we are teaching it within the humanities division, usually in the English Department, either because it ought to be there or because nobody else wants it. For convenience we may think of the common relations between the work of the imagination and the teaching activity under four heads, which I shall put in the form of rhetorical questions:

(1) Can a given work, say *Clarissa Harlowe* or "Kubla Khan," be "taught," in such a way as to make it understood, without criticism?

(2) Can the work be taught first, and the criticism then applied as a mode of understanding?

(3) Can the criticism be presented first and held in readiness for the act of understanding, which could thus be simultaneous with the act of reading the novel or the poem?

(4) Is the purpose of teaching imaginative works to provide materials upon which the critical faculty may exercise itself in its drive toward the making of critical systems, which then perpetuate themselves without much reference to literature?

These four versions of the relation by no means exhaust its possible variations. The slippery ambiguity of the word criticism itself ought by now to be plain. But for the purposes of this localized discussion, which I am limiting for the moment to the question of how to teach, we may think of criticism as three familiar kinds of discourse about works of literature. (We must bear in mind not only our failure to know what criticism is, but another, more difficult failure resulting from it: the failure to know what literature is.) The three kinds of critical discourse are as follows: (1) acts of evaluation of literature (whatever these may be); (2) the communication of insights; and (3) the rhetorical study of the language of the imaginative work.

I am not assuming, I am merely pretending that any one of the three activities is to be found in its purity. To the extent that they may be separated, we must conclude that the two first, acts of evaluation and the communication of insights, cannot be taught, and that the third, rhetorical analysis, has not been taught effectively in this country since the rise of the historical method in literary studies.

When I first taught a college class, about eighteen years ago, I thought that anything was possible; but with every year since it has seemed a little more absurd to try to teach students to "evaluate" works of literature, and perhaps not less absurd to try to evaluate them oneself. The assumption that we are capable of just evaluation (a word that seems to have got into criticism by way of Adam Smith) is one of the subtler, if crude, abuses of democratic doctrine, as follows: all men ought to exercise independent judgment, and all men being equal, all are equally capable of it, even in literature and the arts. I have observed that when my own opinions seem most original and independent they turn out to be almost wholly conventional. An absolutely independent judgment (if such a thing were possible) would be an absolutely ignorant judgment.

Shall the instructor, then, set before the class his own "evaluations"? He will do so at the risk of disseminating a hierarchy that he may not have intended to create, and thus may be aborted, or at least stultified, the student's own reading. It is inevitable that the instructor shall say to the class that one poem is "better" than another. The student, in the degree of his intelligence, will form clear preferences or rejections that will do little harm if he understands what they are. But the teaching of literature through the assertion of preference will end up either as mere impressionism, or as the more sinister variety of impressionism that Irving Babbitt detected in the absorption of the literary work into its historical setting.

As to the communications of "insights," it would perhaps be an inquiry without benefit to anybody to ask how this elusive maid-of-all-work got into modern criticism. She is here, and perhaps we ought to be grateful, because she is obviously willing to do all the work. Insight could mean two things, separately or taken together: the perception of meanings ordinarily or hitherto undetected, and/or the synthetic awareness that brings to the text similar or contrasting qualities from other works. These awarenesses are the critical or receiving end of the Longinian "flash" proceeding from varying degrees of information and knowledge, unpredictable and largely unviable. They are doubtless a good thing for a teacher to have, but they cannot be taught to others; they can be only exhibited. If insight is like faith, a gift by the grace of God, there is not use in teaching at all—if insight-teaching is our only way of going about it. But if it is partly a gift and partly the result of labor (as Longinus thought), perhaps the teacher could find a discipline of language to expound to the class, with the hope that a latent gift of insight may be liberated.

Rhetoric is an unpopular word today, and it deserves to be, if we understand it as the "pragmatic dimension" of discourse as this has been defined by Charles W. Morris, and other semanticists and positivists. In this view rhetoric is semantically irresponsible; its use is to move people to action which is at best morally neutral; or if it is good action, this result was no necessary part of the rhetorician's purpose. The doctrine is not new; it is only a pleasantly complex and double-talking revival of Greek sophistry. But if we think of rhetoric in another tradition, that of Aristotle and of later, Christian rhetoricians, we shall be able to see it as the study of the full language of experience, not the specialized languages of method.[3] Through this full language of experience Dante and Shakespeare could arrive at truth.

This responsible use implies the previous study of the two lower, but not inferior, disciplines that I have already mentioned. One of these was once quaintly known as "grammar," the art that seems to be best learned at the elementary stage in a paradigmatic language like Latin. I think of a homely exemplum that will illustrate one of the things that have happened since the decay of grammar. I had a student at the University of Chicago who wrote a paper on T. S. Eliot's religious symbolism, in which he failed to observe that certain sequences of words in "Ash Wednesday" are without verbs: he had no understanding of the relation of the particulars to the universals in Eliot's diction. The symbols floated, in this student's mind, in a void of abstraction; the language of the poem was beyond his reach. Is the domination of historical scholarship responsible for the decline of the grammatical arts? I think that it may be; but it would not follow from its rejection that these arts or their equivalent would rise again. (One must always be prepared for the rise of nothing.) My Chicago student was laudably trying to read the text of the poem; he had nothing but a good mind and good intentions to read it with. What he had done, of course, was to abstract Eliot's symbols out of their full rhetorical context, so that they had become neither Eliot's nor anybody else's symbols. They were thus either critically useless, or potentially useful in a *pragmatic dimension* of discourse where ideas may be *power:* as the fullback is said to "bull" through the opposing line. The rhetorical disciplines, which alone seem to yield something like the full import of the work of imagination, are bypassed; and we bypass these fundamentals of understanding no less when we read our own language. All reading is translation, even in the native tongue; for translation may be described as the *tact* of mediation between universals and particulars in the complex of metaphor. As qualified translators we are inevitably rhetoricians. One scarcely sees how the student (like the Chicago student, who is also the Minnesota, the Harvard, and the Cornell student) can be expected to begin the study of rhetoric at the top, particularly if below it there is no bottom. If he begins at the top, as a "critic," he may become the victim of "insights" and "evaluations" that he has not earned, or he may parrot critical systems that his instructors have expounded or perhaps merely alluded to, in class. In any case, man being by nature, or by the nature of his language, a rhetorician, the student becomes a bad rhetorician. It is futile to expect him to be a critic when he has not yet learned how to read.

How can rhetoric, or the arts of language, be taught today? We are not likely to begin teaching something in which we do not believe: we do not believe in the uses of rhetoric because we do not believe that the full language of the human situation can be the vehicle of truth. We are not facing the problem when we circumvent it by asking the student to study the special languages of "criticism," in which we should like to believe. Can we believe in the language of humane truth without believing in the possibility of a higher unity of truth, which we must posit as *there*, even if it must remain beyond our powers of understanding? Without such a belief are we not committed to the assumption that literature has nothing to do with truth, that it is only illusion, froth on the historical current, the Platonic *gignomenon?* We languish, then, in the pragmatic vortex where ideas are disembodied into power; but power for what it is not necessary here to try to say. I turn now to literary criticism as it seems to be in itself, apart from any question of teaching it.

II

We have reached the stage of activity in individual criticism at which we begin to ask whether what we severally do has, or ought to have, a common end. What has a common end may be better reached, or at any rate more efficiently pursued, if the long ways to it are bypassed for the short ways—if happily we can agree on a common methodology, or at worst a few cooperating methodologies. The image that this enticing delusion brings to mind is that of the cheerful, patient bulldozer leveling off an uncharted landscape. The treeless plain thus made could be used as a desert—by those who can use deserts—or as an airfield from which to fly somewhere else.

The notes that follow I have put in the form of propositions, or theses, which either I or some imaginable person might be presumed to uphold at the present time. Some will be found to contradict others; but this is to be expected when we try to distinguish the aims and habits of literary critics over a period so long as a quarter of a century. The ten theses will affirm, deny, or question a belief or a practice.

I. Literary criticism is in at least one respect (perhaps more than one) like a mule: it cannot reproduce itself, though, like a mule, it is capable of trying. Its end is outside itself. If the great formal works of literature are not wholly autonomous, criticism, however theoretical it may become, is necessarily even less so. It cannot in the long run be practiced apart from what it confronts, that gives rise to it. It has no formal substance: it is always *about* something else. If it tries to be about itself, and sets up on its own, it initiates the infinite series: one criticism within another leading to another criticism progressively more formal-looking and abstract; or it is progressively more irrelevant to its external end as it attends to the periphery, the historical buzz in the rear of literature.

II. The more systematic and methodical, the "purer," criticism becomes, the less one is able to feel in it the presence of its immediate occasion. It tends more and more to *sound* like philosophical discourse. There are countless degrees, variations, and overlappings of method, but everyone knows that there are three typical directions that method may take: (1) Aesthetics, which aims at the ordering of criticism within a large synthesis of either experimental psychology or ontology; from the point of view of which it is difficult to say anything about literature that is not merely pretentious. For example: Goethe's Concrete Universal, Coleridge's Esemplastic Power, Croce's Expression. (2) Analysis of literary language, or "stylistics" (commonly supposed to be the orbit of the New Criticism). Without the correction of a total rhetoric, this *techné* must find its limit, if it is not at length to become only a habit, in the extreme "purity" of nominalism ("positivism") or of metaphysics. (3) Historical scholarship, the "purest" because the most methodical criticism of all, offers the historical reconstruction as the general possibility of literature, without accounting for the unique, miraculous superiority of *The Tempest* or of *Paradise Lost.*

III. When we find criticism appealing to phrases like "frame of reference," "intellectual discipline," or even "philosophical basis," it is not improper to suspect that the critic is asking us to accept his "criticism" on the authority of something in which he does not believe. The two first phrases contain perhaps hidden analogies to mathematics; the third, a metaphor of underpinning. This is nothing against them; all language is necessarily figurative. But used as I have indicated, the phrases have no ontological, or substantive, meaning. The critic is only avoiding the simple word truth, and begging the question. Suppose we acknowledge that the critic, as he begs this question, gives us at the same moment a new and just insight into a scene in *The Idiot* or *King Lear.* Yet the philosophical language in which he visibly expounds the insight may seem to reflect an authority that he has not visibly earned. The language of criticism had better not, then, try to be univocal. It is neither fish nor fowl, yet both, with that unpleasant taste that we get from fishing ducks.

IV. Literary criticism may become prescriptive and dogmatic when the critic achieves a coherence in the logical and rhetorical orders which exceeds the coherence of the imaginative work itself in those orders. We substitute with the critic a dialectical order for the elusive, and perhaps quite different, order of the imagination. We fall into the trap of the logicalization of parts discretely attended. This sleight of hand imposed upon the reader's good faith invites him to share the critic's own intellectual pride. Dazzled by the refractions of the critic's spectrum, the reader accepts as his own the critic's dubious superiority to the work as a whole. He is only attending serially to the separated parts in which he worships his own image. This is critical idolatry; the idols of its three great sects are the techniques of purity described in Thesis II.

V. If criticism undertakes the responsibility and the privilege of a strict theory of knowledge, the critic will need all the humility that human nature is capable of, almost the self-abnegation of the saint. Is the critic willing to test his epistemology against a selfless reading of *The Rape of the Lock, War and Peace*, or a lyric by Thomas Nashe? Or is his criticism merely the report of a quarrel between the imagined life of the work and his own "philosophy"? Has possession of the critic by a severe theory of knowledge interfered with the primary office of criticism? What is the primary office of criticism? Is it to expound and to elucidate, with as little distortion as possible, the knowledge of life contained by the novel or the poem or the play? What critic has ever done this?

VI. A work of the imagination differs from a work of the logical intellect in some radical sense that seems to lie beyond our comprehension. But this much may be said: the imaginative work admits of neither progressive correction nor substitution or rearrangement of parts; it is never obsolete, it is always up-to-date. Dryden does not "improve" Shakespeare; Shakespeare does not replace Dante, in the way that Einstein's physics seems to have "corrected" Newton's. There is no competition among poems. A good poem suggests the possibility of other poems equally good. But criticism is perpetually obsolescent and replaceable.

VII. The very terms of elucidation—the present ones, like any others—carry with them, concealed, an implicated judgment. The critic's rhetoric, laid out in his particular grammar, is the critic's mind. This enables him to see much that is there, a little that is there, nothing that is there, or something that is not there; but none of these with perfect consistency. We may ask again: to what extent is the critic obligated to dredge the bottom of his mind and to exhibit to an incredulous eye his own skeleton? We might answer the question rhetorically by saying: We are constantly trying to smoke out the critic's "position." This is criticism of criticism. Should we succeed in this game to our perfect satisfaction, we must be on guard lest our assent to or dissent from a critic's "position" mislead us unto supposing that his gift of elucidation is correspondingly impressive or no good. If absolutely just elucidation were possible, it would also be philosophically sound, even though the critic might elsewhere announce his adherence to a philosophy that we should want to question.

VIII. If the implicated judgment is made overt, is there not in it an invitation to the reader to dismiss or to accept the work before he has read it? Even though he "read" the work first? (Part of this question is dealt with in Thesis V.) Is *a priori* judgment in the long run inevitable? What unformulated assumption lurks, as in the thicket, back of T. S. Eliot's unfavorable comparison of "Ripeness is all" with "*E la sua voluntade é nostra pace*"? Is Shakespeare's summation of life naturalistic, pagan, and immature? J. V. Cunningham has shown that "Ripeness is all" is a statement within the natural law, quite as Christian as Dante's statement within the divine law. The beacon of conceptual thought as end rather than means in criticism is a standing menace to critical order because it is inevitable, human nature being what it is. One thing that human nature is, is "fallen."

IX. In certain past ages there was no distinct activity of the mind conscious of itself as literary criticism; for example, the age of Sophocles and the age of Dante. In the age of Dante the schoolmen held that poetry differed from scriptural revelation in its *historia*, or fable, at which, in poetry, the literal event could be part or even all fiction. But the other, higher meanings of poetry might well be true, in spite of the fictional plot, if the poet had the gift of anagogical, or spiritual, insight. Who was capable of knowing when the poet had achieved this insight? Is literary criticism possible without a criterion of absolute truth? Would a criterion of absolute truth make literary criticism as we know it unnecessary? Can it have a relevant criterion of truth without acknowledging an emergent order of truth in its great subject matter, literature itself?

X. Literary criticism, like the Kingdom of God on earth, is perpetually necessary and, in the very nature of its middle position between imagination and philosophy, perpetually impossible. Like man, literary criticism is nothing in itself; criticism, like man, embraces pure experience or exalts pure rationality at the price of abdication from its dual nature. It is of the nature of man and of criticism to occupy the intolerable position. Like man's, the intolerable position of criticism has its own glory. It is the only position that it is ever likely to have.

1. Part I of this essay was read at a symposium on the humanities at Vanderbilt University, October 20, 1950; Part II, at the Conference on the Philosophical Bases of Literary Criticism at Harvard University, July 23, 1951. Both parts have been amplified.

2. Analogous to the natural sciences.

3. I hope it is plain by this time that by "rhetorical analysis" and the "study of rhetoric" I do not mean the prevailing *explication of texts*. If rhetoric is the *full* language of experience, its study must be informed by a peculiar talent, not wholly reducible to method, which I have in the past called the "historical imagination," a power that has little to do with the academic routine of "historical method." For a brilliant statement of this difference, see "Art and the 'Sixth Sense'" by Philip Rahv, *Partisan Review*, March–April, 1952, pp. 225–233. The "sixth sense" is the historical imagination.

PART **2** THE NEW CRITICISM

FROM THE EARLY ESSAYS OF T. S. ELIOT AND EZRA POUND (AND OTHER innovative works such as I. A. Richards's *Principles of Literary Criticism*), and with the emergence of a number of specialized literary journals (the so-called little magazines), the New Criticism emerged in the late 1920s and early 1930s.

Many of the New Critics edited, or were mainly associated with, certain little magazines and contributed to them frequently: T. S. Eliot with Harriet Shaw Weaver's *The Egoist* (1914–19) and later with his own quarterly, the *Criterion* (1922–39); Ezra Pound with Wyndham Lewis's *Blast* (1914–15), Ford Madox Ford's *transatlantic review* (1924), Margaret Anderson's *Little Review* (1914–29), and Harriet Monroe's *Poetry* (1912); R. P. Blackmur with Lincoln Kirstein's *Hound and Horn* (1927–34); John Crowe Ransom with the *Fugitive* (1922–25) and later the *Kenyon Review* (1939). Allen Tate helped revive the *Sewanee Review* (1892) after editing the *Fugitive;* while Cleanth Brooks and Robert Penn Warren coedited the *Southern Review* (1935–42).

Nor is this an exhaustive list. Other important magazines in America include Marianne Moore's *Dial* (1925–29), the *Partisan Review* (1934–2003), and the *Hudson Review* (1947). In England, there were fewer examples; the best of them were F. R. Leavis's *Scrutiny* (1932–53) and F. W. Bateson's *Essays in Criticism* (1951). It was truly the great age of little magazines.

The history of twentieth-century literature is inextricably linked with this genre, and much of that genre's history has been forgotten. We must remember that the little magazine was an outgrowth, and the necessary vehicle, of modernism. When the modernists attempted to publish their works in the popular magazines of their day and were rebuffed, they were forced to organize their own publications in order to break into print. Only later did this give rise to the great modernist myth: a writing *avant-garde* in permanent revolt against the reading public. Their success now seems, in perfect hindsight, inexorable—but starvation was the more usual reward for those who would "épater le bourgeois." The average life of a little magazine was a year or less; exceptional ones lasted half a decade.

What the little magazines offered the serious critic was not money or fame but space. Essays in some journals could run to thirty pages, and did—

whereas most periodicals and newspapers wanted (and still want) no more than two thousand words from their critics. Within these hospitable margins, the New Critics developed the ideas and the methods that remain as relevant today as they were almost a century ago. Of course, the essays in this section cannot offer a comprehensive view of the New Criticism's animating ideas, only a representative sampling.

Suggested Further Reading

"Tradition and the Individual Talent," by T. S. Eliot (from *The Sacred Wood*, 1920)
Principles of Literary Criticism, by I. A. Richards (1924)
Seven Types of Ambiguity, by William Empson (1930)
The Well Wrought Urn, by Cleanth Brooks (1947)
"Tension in Poetry," by Allen Tate (from *Essays of Four Decades*, 1968)

FIRST PRINCIPLES

Preliminary Problems

YVOR WINTERS

This is the first chapter of Winters's book The Anatomy of Nonsense *(1943), and it admirably outlines the most basic dilemmas of the critic's task.*

First Problem

Is it possible to say that Poem A (one of Donne's *Holy Sonnets*, or one of the poems of Jonson or of Shakespeare) is better than Poem B (Collins's *Ode to Evening*) or vice versa?

If not, is it possible to say that either of these is better than Poem C (*The Cremation of Sam Magee*, or something comparable)?

If the answer is no in both cases, then any poem is as good as any other. If this is true, then all poetry is worthless; but this obviously is not true, for it is contrary to all our experience. If the answer is yes in both cases, then there follows the question of whether the answer implies merely that one poem is better than another for the speaker, or whether it means that one poem is intrinsically better than another. If the former, then we are impressionists, which is to say relativists; and are either mystics of the type of Emerson, or hedonists of the type of Stevens and Ransom. If the latter, then we assume that constant principles govern the poetic experience, and the poem (as likewise the judge) must be judged in relationship to those principles. It is important, therefore, to discover the consequences of assuming each of these positions.

If our answer to the first question is no and to the second yes, then we are asserting that we can distinguish between those poems which are of the canon and those which are not, but that within the canon all judgment is impossible. This view, if adopted, will require serious elucidation, for on the face of it, it appears inexplicable. On the other hand, one cannot deny that within the canon judgment will become more difficult, for the nearer two poems may be to the highest degrees of excellence, the harder it will be to choose between them. Two poems, in fact, might be so excellent that there would be small profit in endeavoring to say that one was better, but one could arrive at this conclusion only after a careful examination of both.

Second Problem

If we accept the view that one poem can be regarded as better than another, the question then arises whether this judgment is a matter of inexplicable intuition, or whether it is a question of intuition that can be explained, and consequently guided and improved by rational elucidation.

If we accept the view that the judgment in question is inexplicable, then we are again forced to confess ourselves impressionists and relativists, unless we can show that the intuitions of all men agree at all times, or that the intuitions of one man are invariably right and those of all others wrong whenever they differ. We obviously can demonstrate neither of these propositions.

If we start, then, with the proposition that one poem may be intrinsically superior to another, we are forced to account for differences of opinion regarding it. If two critics differ, it is possible that one is right and the other wrong, more likely that both are partly right and partly wrong, but in different respects: neither the native gifts nor the education of any man have ever been wholly adequate to many of the critical problems he will encounter, and no two men are ever the same in these respects or in any others. On the other hand, although the critic should display reasonable humility and caution, it is only fair to add that few men possess either the talent or the education to justify their being taken very seriously, even of those who are nominally professional students of these matters.

But if it is possible by rational elucidation to give a more or less clear account of what one finds in a poem and why one approves or disapproves, then communication between two critics, thought no doubt imperfect, becomes possible, and it becomes possible that they may in some measure correct each other's errors and so come more near to a true judgment of the poem.

Third Problem

If rational communication about poetry is to take place, it is necessary first to determine what we mean by a poem.

A poem is first of all a statement in words.

But it differs from all such statements of purely philosophical or theoretical nature, in that it has by intention a controlled content of feeling. In this respect, it does not differ from many works written in prose, however.

A poem differs from a work written in prose by virtue of its being composed in verse. The rhythm of verse permits the expression of more powerful feeling than is possible in prose when such feeling is needed, and it permits at all times the expression of finer shades of feeling.

A poem, then, is a statement in words in which special pains are taken with the expression of feeling. This description is merely intended to distinguish the poem from other kinds of writing; it is not offered as a complete description.

Fourth Problem

What however, are words?

They are audible sounds, or their visual symbols, invented by man to communicate his thoughts and feelings. Each word has a conceptual content, however slight; each word, exclusive, perhaps, of the particles, communicates vague associations of feeling.

The word *fire* communicates a concept; it also connotes very vaguely certain feelings, depending on the context in which we happen to place it—depending, for example, on whether we happen to think of a fire on a hearth, in a furnace, or in a forest. These feelings may be rendered more and more precise as we render the context more and more precise; as we come more and more near to completing and perfecting our poem.

Fifth Problem

But if the poem, as compared to prose, pays especial attention to feeling, are we to assume that the rational content of the poem is unimportant to its success?

The rational content cannot be eliminated from words; consequently the rational content cannot be eliminated from poetry. It is there. If it is unsatisfactory in itself, a part of the poem is unsatisfactory; the poem is thus damaged beyond argument. If we deny this, we must surely explain ourselves very fully.

If we admit this, we are faced with another problem: is it conceivable that rational content and feeling-content may both be perfect, and yet that they may be unrelated to each other, or imperfectly related? To me this is inconceivable, because the emotional content of words is generated by our experience with the conceptual content, so that a relationship is necessary.

This fact of the necessity of such relationship may fairly return us for a moment to the original question: whether imperfection of rational content damages the entire poem. If there is a necessary relationship between concept and feeling, and concept is unsatisfactory, then feeling must be damaged by way of the relationship.

Sixth Problem

If there is a relationship between concept and feeling, what is the nature of that relationship?

To answer this, let us return to the basic unit, the word. The concept represented by the word, motivates the feeling which the word communicates. It is the concept of fire which generates the feelings communicated by the word, though the sound of the word may modify these feelings very subtly, as may other accidental qualities, especially if the word be used skillfully in a given context. The accidental qualities of a word, however, such as its literary history, for example, can only modify, cannot essentially change, for these will be governed ultimately by the concept; that is, *fire* will seldom be used to signify *plum-blossom*, and so will have few opportunities to gather connotations from the concept, *plum-blossom*. The relationship, in the poem, between rational statement and feeling, is thus seen to be that of motive to emotion.

Seventh Problem

But has not this reasoning brought us back to the proposition that all poems are equally good? For if each word motivates its own feeling, because of its intrinsic nature, will not any rational statement, since it is composed of words, motivate the feeling exactly proper to it?

This is not true, for a good many reasons, of which I shall enumerate only a few of the more obvious. In making a rational statement, in purely theoretical prose, we find that our statement may be loose or exact, depending upon the relationships of the words to each other. The precision of a word depends to some extent upon its surroundings. This is true likewise with respect to the connotations of words. Two words, each of which has several usably close rational synonyms, may reinforce and clarify each other with respect to their connotations or they may not do so.

Let me illustrate with a simple example from Browning's *Serenade at the Villa:*

> So wore night; the East was gray,
>   White the broad-faced hemlock flowers.

The lines are marred by a crowding of long syllables and difficult consonants, but they have great beauty in spite of the fault. What I wish to point out, for the sake of my argument, is the relationship between the words *wore* and *gray*. The verb *wore* means literally that the night passed, but it carries with it connotations of exhaustion and attrition which belong to the condition of the protagonist; and grayness is a color which we associate with such a condition. If we change the phrase to read: "Thus night passed," we shall have the same rational meaning, and a meter quite as respectable, but no trace of the power of the line: the connotation of *wore* will be lost, and the connotation of *gray* will remain merely in a state of ineffective potentiality. The protagonist in seeing his feeling mirrored in the landscape is not guilty of motivating his feeling falsely, for we know his general motive from the poem as a whole; he is expressing a portion of the feeling motivated by the total situation through a more or less common psychological phenomenon. If the poem were such, however, that we did not know why the night *wore* instead of *passed*, we should have just cause for complaint; in fact, most of the strength of the word would probably be lost. The second line contains other fine effects, immediately with reference to the first line, ultimately with reference to the theme; I leave the reader to ana-lyze them for himself, but he will scarcely succeed without the whole poem before him.

Concepts, as represented by particular words, are affected by connota-tions due to various and curious accidents. A word may gather conno-tations from its use in folk-poetry, in formal poetry, in vulgar speech, or in technical prose: a single concept might easily be represented by four words with these distinct histories; and any one of the words might prove to be proper in a given poetic context. Words gain connotation from etymological accidents. Something of this may be seen in the English word *outrage*, in which is commonly felt, in all likelihood, something associated with *rage*, although there is no rage whatever in the original word. Similarly the word *urchin*, in modern English, seldom connotes anything related to hedgehogs, or to the familiars of the witches, by whose intervention the word arrived at its modern meaning and feeling. Yet the connotation proper to any stage in the history of such a word might be resuscitated, or a blend of connotations effected, by skillful use. Further, the connotation of a word may be modified very strongly by its function in the metrical structure. . . .

This is enough to show that exact motivation of feeling by concept is not inherent in any rational statement. Any rational statement will govern the general possibilities of feeling derivable from it, but the task of the poet is to adjust feeling to motive precisely. He has to select words containing not only the right relationships within themselves, but the right relationships to each other. The task is very difficult; and this is no doubt the reason why the great poetry of a great poet is likely to be very small in bulk.

Eighth Problem

Is it not possible, however, to escape from this relationship of motive to emotion by confining ourselves very largely to those words which denote emotion: love, envy, anger, and the like?

This is not possible, for these words, like others, represent concepts. If we should confine ourselves strictly to such a vocabulary, we should merely write didactic poetry: poetry about love in general, or about anger in general. The emotion communicated would result from our apprehension of the ideas in question. Such poetry is perfectly legitimate, but it is only one kind of poetry, and it is scarcely the kind which the Romantic theorist is endeavoring to define.

Such poetry has frequently been rendered particular by the use of allegory. The playful allegorizing of minor amoristic themes which one encounters in the Renaissance and which is possibly descended from certain neo-Platonic elements in medieval poetry may serve as illustration. Let us consider these and the subsequent lines by Thomas Lodge:

> Love in my bosom like a bee
>   Doth suck his sweet;
> Now with his wings he plays with me,
>   Now with his feet.

Love itself is a very general idea and might include many kinds of experience; the idea is limited by this allegory to the sentimental and sensual, but we still have an idea, the subdivision of the original idea, and the feeling must be appropriate to the concept. The concept is rendered concrete by the image of Cupid, whose actions, in turn, are rendered visible by comparison to the bee: it is these actions which make the poem a kind of anticipatory meditation on more or less sensual love, a meditation which by its mere tone of expression keeps the subject in its proper place as a very minor one. Sometimes the emphasis is on the mere description of the bee, sometimes on the description of Cupid, sometimes on the lover's feeling; but the feeling motivated in any passage is governed by this emphasis. The elements, once they are united in the poem, are never really separated, of course. In so far as the poet departs from his substantial theme in the direction of mere bees and flowers, he will achieve what Ransom calls irrelevance; but if there is much of this the poem will be weakened. Whether he so departs or not, the relation of motive to emotion must remain the same, within each passage. . . .

A common romantic practice is to use words denoting emotions, but to use them loosely and violently, as if the very carelessness expressed emotion. Another is to make a general statement, but seem to refer it to a particular occasion, which, however, is never indicated: the poet thus seems to avoid the didactic, yet he is not forced to understand the particular motive. Both these faults may be seen in these lines from Shelley:

> Out of the day and night
> A joy has taken flight;
>> Fresh spring, and summer, and winter hoar,
> Move my faint heart with grief, but with delight
>> No more—oh, never more.

The poet's intention is so vague; however, that he achieves nothing but stereotypes of a very crude kind.

The Romantics often tried other devices. For example, it would be possible to write a poem on fear in general, but to avoid in some measure the effect of the purely didactic by illustrating the emotion along the way with various experiences which might motivate fear. There is a danger here, though it is merely a danger, that the general idea may not dominate the poem, and that the poem may thus fall apart into a group of poems on particular experiences. There is the alternative danger, that the particular quality of the experiences may be so subordinated to the illustrative function of the experiences, that within each illustration there is merely a stereotyped and not a real relationship of motive to feeling: this occurs in Collins's *Ode to Fear*, though a few lines in the Epode come surprisingly to life. But the methods which I have just described really offer no semblance of an escape from the theory of motivation which I am defending.

Another Romantic device, if it is conscious enough to be called a device, is to offer instead of a defensible motive a false one, usually culled from landscape. This kind of writing represents a tacit admission of the principle of motivation which I am defending, but a bad application of the principle. It results in the kind of writing which I have called pseudo-reference in my volume, *Primitivism and Decadence*. One cannot believe, for example, that Wordsworth's passions were charmed away by a look at the daffodils, or that Shelley's were aroused by the sight of the leaves blown about in the autumn wind. A motive is offered, and the poet wants us to accept it, but we recognize it as inadequate. In such a poem there may be fragments of good description, which motivate a feeling more or less purely appropriate to the objects described, and these fragments may sustain our liking for the poem: this happens in Collins's *Ode to Evening*; but one will find also an account of some kind of emotion essentially irrelevant to the objects described, along with the attempt, more or less explicit, to deduce the emotion from the object.

There remains the method of the Post-Romantics, whether French Symbolists or American Experimentalists: the method of trying to extinguish the rational content of language while retaining the content of association. This method I have discussed in *Primitivism and Decadence*, and I shall discuss it again in this book.

Ninth Problem

The relationship in the poem of rational meaning to feeling we have seen to be that of motive to emotion; and we have seen that this must be a satisfactory relationship. How do we determine whether such a relationship is satisfactory? We determine it by an act of moral judgment. The question then arises whether moral judgments can be made, whether the concept of morality is or is not an illusion.

If morality can be considered real, if a theory of morality can be said to derive from reality, it is because it guides us toward the greatest happiness which the accidents of life permit: that is, toward the fullest realization of our nature, in the Aristotelian or Thomistic sense. But is there such a thing, abstractly considered, as full realization of our nature?

To avoid discussion of too great length, let us consider the opposite question: is there such a thing as obviously unfulfilled human nature? Obviously there is. We need only turn to the feeble-minded, who cannot think and so cannot perceive or feel with any clarity; or to the insane, who sometimes perceive and feel with great intensity, but whose feelings and perceptions are so improperly motivated that they are classed as illusions. At slightly higher levels, the criminal, the dissolute, the unscrupulously selfish, and various types of neurotics are likely to arouse but little disagreement as examples.

Now if we are able to recognize the fact of insanity—if in fact we are forced to recognize it—that is, the fact of the obvious maladjustment of feeling to motive, we are forced to admit the possibility of more accurate adjustment, and, by necessary sequence, of absolutely accurate adjustment, even though we admit the likelihood that most people will attain to a final adjustment but very seldom indeed. We can guide ourselves toward such an adjustment in life, as in art, by means of theory and the critical examination of special instances; but the final act of judgment is in both life and art a unique act—it is a relationship between two elements, the rational understanding and the feeling, of which only one is classificatory and of which the other has infinite possibilities of variation.

Tenth Problem

If the final act of adjustment is a unique act of judgment, can we say that it is more or less right, provided it is demonstrably within the general limits prescribed by the theory of morality which has led to it? The answer to this question is implicit in what has preceded; in fact the answer resembles exactly that reached at the end of the first problem examined. We can say that it is more or less nearly right. If extreme deviation from right judgment is obvious, then there is such a thing as right judgment. The mere fact that life may be conducted in a fairly satisfactory manner, by means of inaccurate judgment within certain limits, and that few people ever bother to refine their judgment beyond the stage which enables them to remain largely within those limits, does not mean that accurate judgment has no reality. Implicit in all that has preceded is the concept that in any moral situation, there is a right judgment as an ultimate possibility; that the human judge, or actor, will approximate it more or less nearly; that the closeness of his approximation will depend upon the accuracy of his rational understanding and of his intuition, and upon the accuracy of their interaction upon each other.

Eleventh Problem

Nothing has thus far been said about human action, yet morality is supposed to guide human action. And if art is moral, there should be a relationship between art and human action.

The moral judgment, whether good, bad, or indifferent, is commonly the prelude and instigation to action. Hastily or carefully, intelligently or otherwise, one arrives at some kind of general idea of a situation calling for action, and one's idea motivates one's feeling: the act results. The part played by will, or the lack of it, between judgment and act, the possibility that action may be frustrated by some constitutional or habitual weakness or tendency, such as cowardice or a tendency to anger, in a person of a fine speculative or poetic judgment, are subjects for a treatise on ethics or psychology; a treatise on poetry stops with the consideration of the speculative judgment, which reaches its best form and expression in poetry. In the situations of daily life, one does not, as a rule, write a poem before acting: one makes a more rapid and simple judgment. But if the poem does not individually lead to a particular act, it does not prevent action. It gives us a better way of judging representative acts than we should otherwise have. It is thus a civilizing influence: it trains our power of judgment, and should, I imagine, affect the quality of daily judgments and actions.

Twelfth Problem

What, then, is the nature of the critical process?

It will consist (1) of the statement of such historical or biographical knowledge as may be necessary in order to understand the mind and method of the writer; (2) of such analysis of his literary theories as we may need to understand and evaluate what he is doing; (3) of a rational critique of the paraphrasable content (roughly, the motive) of the poem; (4) of a rational critique of the feeling motivated—that is, of the details of style, as seen in language and technique; and (5) of the final act of judgment, a unique act, the general nature of which can be indicated, but which cannot be communicated precisely, since it consists in receiving from the poet his own final and unique judgment of his matter and in judging that judgment. It should be noted that the purpose of the first four processes is to limit as narrowly as possible the region in which the final unique act is to occur.

In the actual writing of criticism, a given task may not require all of these processes, or may not require that all be given equal emphasis; or it may be that in connection with a certain writer, whether because of the nature of the writer or because of the way in which other critics have treated him previously, one or two of these processes must be given so much emphasis that others must be neglected for lack of space. These are practical matters to be settled as the occasions arise.

The Formalist Critics

CLEANTH BROOKS

Published as the fifth part of a symposium on critical methods ("My Credo") in the Kenyon Review *in 1951, this essay is a useful summation of the New Criticism, set forth as a series of propositions.*

Here are some articles of faith I could subscribe to:

> *That literary criticism is a description and an evaluation of its object.*

> *That the primary concern of criticism is with the problem of unity—the kind of whole which the literary work forms or fails to form, and the relation of the various parts to each other in building up this whole.*

That the formal relations in a work of literature may include, but certainly exceed, those of logic.

That in a successful work, form and content cannot be separated.

That form is meaning.

That literature is ultimately metaphorical and symbolic.

That the general and the universal are not seized upon by abstraction, but got at through the concrete and the particular.

That literature is not a surrogate for religion.

That, as Allen Tate says, "specific moral problems" are the subject matter of literature, but that the purpose of literature is not to point a moral.

That the principles of criticism define the area relevant to literary criticism; they do not constitute a method for carrying out the criticism.

Such statements as these would not, however, even though greatly elaborated, serve any useful purpose here. The interested reader already knows the general nature of the critical position adumbrated—or, if he does not, he can find it set forth in writings of mine or of other critics of like sympathy. Moreover, a condensed restatement of the position here would probably beget as many misunderstandings as have past attempts to set it forth. It seems much more profitable to use the present occasion for dealing with some persistent misunderstandings and objections.

In the first place, to make the poem or the novel the central concern of criticism has appeared to mean cutting it loose from its author and from his life as a man, with his own particular hopes, fears, interests, conflicts, etc. A criticism so limited may seem bloodless and hollow. It will seem so to the typical professor of literature in the graduate school, where the study of literature is still primarily a study of the ideas and personality of the author as revealed in his letters, his diaries, and the recorded conversations of his friends. It will certainly seem so to literary gossip columnists who purvey literary chitchat. It may also seem so to the young poet or novelist, beset with his own problems of composition and with his struggles to find a subject and a style and to get a hearing for himself.

In the second place, to emphasize the work seems to involve severing it from those who actually read it, and this severance may seem drastic and therefore disastrous. After all, literature is written to be read. Wordsworth's poet was a man speaking to men. In each Sunday *Times*, Mr. J. Donald Adams points out that the hungry sheep look up and are not fed; and less strenuous moralists than Mr. Adams are bound to feel a proper revulsion against "mere aestheticism." Moreover, if we neglect the audience which reads the work, including that for which it was presumably written, the literary historian is prompt to point out that the kind of audience that Pope had did condition the kind of poetry that he wrote. The poem has its roots in history, past or present. Its place in the historical context simply cannot be ignored.

I have stated these objections as sharply as I can because I am sympathetic with the state of mind which is prone to voice them. Man's experience is indeed a seamless garment, no part of which can be separated from the rest. Yet if we urge this fact of inseparability against the drawing of distinctions, then there is no point in talking about criticism at all. I am assuming that distinctions are necessary and useful and indeed inevitable.

The formalist critic knows as well as anyone that poems and plays and novels are written by men—that they do not somehow happen—and that they are written as expressions of particular personalities and are written from all sorts of motives—for money, from a desire to express oneself, for the sake of a cause, etc. Moreover, the formalist critic knows as well as anyone that literary works are merely potential until they are read—that is, that they are recreated in the minds of actual readers, who vary enormously in their capabilities, their interests, their prejudices, their ideas. But the formalist critic is concerned primarily with the work itself. Speculation on the mental processes of the author takes the critic away from the work into biography and psychology. There is no reason, of course, why he should not turn away into biography and psychology. Such explorations are very much worth making. But they should not be confused with an account of the work. Such studies describe the process of composition, not the structure of the thing composed, and they may be performed quite as validly for the poor work as for the good one. They may be validly performed for any kind of expression—non-literary as well as literary.

On the other hand, exploration of the various readings which the work has received also takes the critic away from the work into psychology and the history of taste. The various imports of a given work may well be worth studying. I. A. Richards has put us all in his debt by demonstrating what different experiences may be derived from the same poem by an apparently homogeneous group of readers; and the scholars have pointed out, all along, how different Shakespeare appeared to an 18th Century as compared with a 19th Century audience; or how sharply divergent are the estimates of John Donne's lyrics from historical period to historical period. But such work, valuable and necessary as it may be, is to be distinguished from a criticism of the work itself. The formalist critic, because he wants to criticize the work itself, makes two assumptions: (1) he assumes that the relevant part of the author's intention is what he got actually into his work; that is, he assumes that the author's intention *as realized* is the "intention" that counts, not necessarily what he was conscious of trying to do, or what he now remembers he was then trying to do. And (2) the formalist critic assumes an ideal reader: that is, instead of focusing on the varying spectrum of possible readings, he attempts to find a central point of reference from which he can focus upon the structure of the poem or novel.

But there *is* no ideal reader, someone is prompt to point out, and he will probably add that it is sheer arrogance that allows the critic, with his own blindsides and prejudices, to put himself in the position of that ideal reader. There is no ideal reader, of course, and I suppose that the practicing critic can never be too often reminded of the gap between his reading and the "true" reading of the poem. But for the purpose of focusing upon the poem rather than upon his own reactions, it is a defensible strategy. Finally, of course, it is the strategy that all critics of whatever persuasion are forced to adopt. (The alternatives are desperate: either we say that one person's reading is as good as another's and equate those readings on a basis of absolute equality and thus deny the possibility of any standard reading. Or else we take a lowest common denominator of the various readings that have been made; that is, we frankly move from literary criticism into socio-psychology. To propose taking a consensus of the opinions of "qualified" readers is simply to split the ideal reader into a group of ideal readers.) As consequences of the distinction just referred to, the formalist critic rejects two popular tests for literary value. The first proves the value of the work from the author's "sincerity" (or the intensity of the author's feelings as he composed it). If we heard that Mr. Guest testified that he put his heart and soul into his poems, we would not be very much impressed, though I should see no reason to doubt such a statement from Mr. Guest. It would simply be critically irrelevant. Ernest Hemingway's statement in a recent issue of *Time* magazine that he counts his last novel his best is of interest for Hemingway's biography, but most readers of *Across the River and Into the Trees* would agree that it proves nothing at all about the value of the novel—that in this case the judgment is simply pathetically inept. We discount also such tests for poetry as that proposed by A. E. Housman—the bristling of his beard at the reading of a good poem. The intensity of his reaction has critical significance only in proportion as we have already learned to trust him as a reader. Even so, what it tells us is something about Housman—nothing decisive about the poem.

88 | CLEANTH BROOKS

It is unfortunate if this playing down of such responses seems to deny humanity to either writer or reader. The critic may enjoy certain works very much and may be indeed intensely moved by them. I am, and I have no embarrassment in admitting the fact; but a detailed description of my emotional state on reading certain works has little to do with indicating to an interested reader what the work is and how the parts of it are related.

Should all criticism, then, be self-effacing and analytic? I hope that the answer is implicit in what I have already written, but I shall go on to spell it out. Of course not. That will depend upon the occasion and the audience. In practice, the critic's job is rarely a purely critical one. He is much more likely to be involved in dozens of more or less related tasks, some of them trivial, some of them important. He may be trying to get a hearing for a new author, or to get the attention of the freshman sitting in the back row. He may be comparing two authors, or editing a text; writing a brief newspaper review or reading a paper before the Modern Language Association. He may even be simply talking with a friend, talking about literature for the hell of it. Parable, anecdote, epigram, metaphor—these and a hundred other devices may be thoroughly legitimate for his varying purposes. He is certainly not to be asked to suppress his personal enthusiasms or his interest in social history or in politics. Least of all is he being asked to *present* his criticisms as the close reading of a text. Tact, common sense, and uncommon sense if he has it, are all requisite if the practicing critic is to do his various jobs well.

But it will do the critic no harm to have a clear idea of what his specific job as a critic is. I can sympathize with writers who are tired of reading rather drab "critical analyses," and who recommend brighter, more amateur, and more "human" criticism. As ideals, these are excellent; as recipes for improving criticism, I have my doubts. Appropriate vulgarizations of these ideals are already flourishing, and have long flourished—in the class room presided over by the college lecturer of infectious enthusiasm, in the gossipy Book-of-the-Month Club bulletins, and in the columns of the *Saturday Review of Literature*.

I have assigned the critic a modest, though I think an important, role. With reference to the help which the critic can give to the practicing artist, the role is even more modest. As critic, he can give only negative help. Literature is not written by formula: he can have no formula to offer. Perhaps he can do little more than indicate whether in his opinion the work has succeeded or failed. Healthy criticism and healthy creation do tend to go hand in hand. Everything else being equal, the creative artist is better off for being in touch with a vigorous criticism.

But the other considerations are never equal, the case is always special, and in a given case the proper advice *could* be: quit reading criticism altogether, or read political science or history or philosophy—or join the army, or join the church.

There is certainly no doubt that the kind of specific and positive help that someone like Ezra Pound was able to give to several writers of our time is in one sense the most important kind of criticsm that there can be. I think that it is not unrelated to the kind of criticism that I have described: there is the same intense concern with the text which is being built up, the same concern with "technical problems." But many other things are involved—matters which lie outside the specific ambit of criticism altogether, among them a knowledge of the personality of the particular writer, the ability to stimulate, to make positive suggestions.

A literary work is a document and as a document can be analyzed in terms of the forces that have produced it, or it may be manipulated as a force in its own right. It mirrors the past, it may influence the future. These facts it would be futile to deny, and I know of no critic who does deny them. But the reduction of a work of literature to its causes does not constitute literary criticism; nor does an estimate of its effects. Good literature is more than effective rhetoric applied to true ideas— even if we could agree upon a philosophical yardstick for measuring the truth of ideas and even if we could find some way that transcended nose-counting for determining the effectiveness of the rhetoric.

A recent essay by Lionel Trilling bears very emphatically upon this point. (I refer to him the more readily because Trilling has registered some of his objections to the critical position that I maintain.) In the essay entitled "The Meaning of a Literary Idea," Trilling discusses the debt to Freud and Spengler of four American writers, O'Neill, Dos Passos, Wolfe, and Faulkner. Very justly, as it seems to me, he chooses Faulkner as the contemporary writer who, along with Ernest Hemingway, best illustrates the power and importance of ideas in literature. Trilling is thoroughly aware that his choice will seem shocking and perhaps perverse, "because," as he writes, "Hemingway and Faulkner have insisted on their indifference to the conscious intellectual tradition of our time and have acquired the reputation of achieving their effects by means that have the least possible connection with any sort of intellectuality or even with intelligence."

Here Trilling shows not only acute discernment but an admirable honesty in electing to deal with the hard cases—with the writers who do not clearly and easily make the case for the importance of ideas. I applaud the discernment and the honesty, but I wonder whether the whole discussion in his essay does not indicate that Trilling is really much closer to the so-called "new critics" than perhaps he is aware. For Trilling, one notices, rejects any simple one-to-one relation between the truth of the idea and the value of the literary work in which it is embodied. Moreover, he does not claim that "recognizable ideas of a force or weight are 'used' in the work," or "new ideas of a certain force and weight are 'produced' by the work." He praises rather the fact that we feel that Hemingway and Faulkner are "intensely at work upon the recalcitrant stuff of life." The last point is made the matter of real importance. Whereas Dos Passos, O'Neill, and Wolfe make us "feel that they feel that *they* have said the last word," "we seldom have the sense that [Hemingway and Faulkner] . . . have misrepresented to themselves the nature and the difficulty of the matter they work on."

Trilling has chosen to state the situation in terms of the writer's activity (Faulkner is intensely at work, etc.). But this judgment is plainly an inference from the quality of Faulkner's novels—Trilling has not simply heard Faulkner say that he has had to struggle with his work. (I take it Mr. Hemingway's declaration about the effort he put into the last novel impresses Trilling as little as it impresses the rest of us.)

Suppose, then, that we tried to state Mr. Trilling's point, not in terms of the effort of the artist, but in terms of the structure of the work itself. Should we not get something very like the terms used by formalist critics? A description in terms of "tensions," of symbolic development, of ironies and their resolution? In short, is not the formalist critic trying to describe in terms of the dynamic form of the work itself how the recalcitrancy of the material is acknowledged and dealt with?

Trilling's definition of "ideas" makes it still easier to accommodate my position to his. I have already quoted a passage in which he repudiates the notion that one has to show how recognizable ideas are "used" in the work, or new ideas are "produced" by the work. He goes on to write: "All that we need to do is account for a certain aesthetic effect as being in some important part achieved by a mental process which is not different from the process by which discursive ideas are conceived, and which is to be judged by some of the criteria by which an idea is judged." One would have to look far to find a critic "formal" enough to object to this. What some of us have been at pains to insist upon is that literature does not simply "exemplify" ideas or "produce" ideas—as Trilling acknowledges. But no one claims that the writer is an inspired idiot. He uses his mind and his reader ought to use his, in processes "not different from the process by which discursive ideas are conceived." Literature is not inimical to ideas. It thrives upon ideas, but it does not present ideas patly and neatly. It involves them with the "recalcitrant stuff of life." The literary critic's job is to deal with that involvement.

The mention of Faulkner invites a closing comment upon the critic's specific job. As I have described it, it may seem so modest that one could take its performance for granted. But consider the misreadings of Faulkner now current, some of them the work of the most brilliant critics that we have, some of them quite wrong-headed, and demonstrably so. What is true of Faulkner is only less true of many another author, including many writers of the past. Literature has many "uses"—and critics propose new uses, some of them exciting and spectacular. But all the multiform uses to which literature can be put rest finally upon our knowing what a given work "means." That knowledge is basic.

AGAINST THE FALLACIES

The Affective Fallacy

W. K. WIMSATT AND MONROE C. BEARDSLEY

In this essay, the authors describe a common critical mistake: the "confusion between the poem and its results *(what it* is *and what it* does*)," which judges a poem's worth on its psychological effect on the reader. Such affective theories ultimately lead to psychology (and to reader-response theory) rather than to objective criticism of the poem. This essay has been abridged.*

> We might as well study the properties of wine by getting drunk.
> —Eduard Hanslick, *The Beautiful in Music*

We believe ourselves to be exploring two roads which have seemed to offer convenient detours around the acknowledged and usually feared obstacles to objective criticism, both of which, however, have actually led away from criticism and from poetry. The Intentional Fallacy is a confusion between the poem and its origins, a special case of what is known to philosophers as the Genetic Fallacy. It begins by trying to derive the standard of criticism from the psychological *causes* of the poem and ends in biography and relativism. The Affective Fallacy is a confusion between the poem and its *results* (what it *is* and what it *does*), a special case of epistemological skepticism, though usually advanced as if it had far stronger claims than the over-all forms of skepticism. It begins by trying to derive the standard of criticism from the psychological effects of the poem and ends in impressionism and relativism. The outcome of either Fallacy, the Intentional or the Affective, is that the poem itself, as an object of specifically critical judgment, tends to disappear.

I

Plato's feeding and watering of the passions[1] was an early example of affective theory, and Aristotle's countertheory of catharsis was another (with modern intentionalistic analogues in theories of "relief" and "sublimation"). There was also the "transport" of the audience in the *Peri Hupsous* (matching the great soul of the poet), and this had echoes of passion or enthusiasm among eighteenth century Longinians. We have had more recently the infection theory of Tolstoy (with its intentionalistic analogue in the emotive expressionism of Veron), the *Einfühlung* or empathy of Lipps and related pleasure theories, either more or less tending to the "objectification" of Santayana: "Beauty is pleasure regarded as the quality of a thing." An affinity for these theories is seen in certain theories of the comic during the same era, the relaxation theory of Penjon, the laughter theory of Max Eastman. In their *Foundations of Aesthetics* Ogden, Richards, and Wood listed sixteen types of aesthetic theory, of which at least seven may be described as affective. Among these the theory of Synaesthesis (Beauty is what produces an equilibrium of appetencies) was the one they themselves espoused. This was developed at length by Richards in his *Principles of Literacy Criticism.*

The theories just mentioned may be considered as belonging to one branch of affective criticism, and that the main one, the emotive—unless the theory of empathy, with its transport of the self into the object, belongs rather with a parallel and equally ancient affective theory, the imaginative. This is represented by the figure of vividness so often mentioned in the rhetorics—*efficacia, enargeia,* or the *phantasiai* in Chapter XV of *Peri Hupsous.* This if we mistake not is the imagination the "Pleasures" of which are celebrated by Addison in his series of *Spectators.* It is an imagination implicit in the theories of Leibniz and Baumgarten that beauty lies in clear but confused, or sensuous, ideas; in the statement of Warton in his *Essay on Pope* that the selection of "lively pictures . . . chiefly constitutes true poetry." In our time, as the emotive form of psychologistic or affective theory has found its most impressive champion in I. A. Richards, so the imaginative form has, in Max Eastman, whose *Literary Mind* and *Enjoyment of Poetry* have much to say about vivid realizations or heightened consciousness.

The theory of intention or author psychology has been the intense conviction of poets themselves, Wordsworth, Keats, Housman, and since the romantic era, of young persons interested in poetry, the introspective amateurs and soul-cultivators. In a parallel way, affective theory has often been less a scientific view of literature than a prerogative—that of the soul adventuring among masterpieces, the contagious teacher, the poetic radiator—a magnetic rhapsode Ion, a Saintsbury, a Quiller-Couch, a William Lyon Phelps. Criticism on this theory has approximated the tone of the Buchmanite confession, the revival meeting. "To be quite frank," says Anatole France, "the critic ought to say: 'Gentle-man, I am going to speak about myself apropos of Shakespeare, apropos of Racine. . . .'" The sincerity of the critic becomes an issue, as for the intentionalist the sincerity of the poet.

A "mysterious entity called the Grand Style," says Saintsbury—something much like "the Longinian Sublime." "Whenever this per-fection of expression acquires such force that it transmutes the subject and transports the hearer or reader, then and there the Grand Style ex-ists, for so long, and in such degree, as the transmutation of the one and the transportation of the other lasts." This is the grand style, the emotive style, of nineteenth century affective criticism. A somewhat less resonant style which has been heard in our columns of Saturday and Sunday reviewing and from our literary explorers is more closely con-nected with imagism and the kind of vividness sponsored by Mr. East-man. In the *Book-of-the-Month Club News* Dorothy Canfield testifies to the power of a novel: "To read this book is like living through an expe-rience rather than just reading about it." "A poem," says Hans Zinsser,

> means nothing to me unless it can carry me away with the gentle or passionate pace of its emotion, over obstacles of reality into mead-ows and covers of illusion. . . . The sole criterion for me is whether it can sweep me with it into emotion or illusion of beauty, terror, tranquillity, or even disgust.[2]

It is but a short step to what we may call the physiological form of affec-tive criticism. Beauty, said Burke in the eighteenth century, is some-thing which "acts by relaxing the solids of the whole system." More re-cently, on the side of personal testimony, we have the oft quoted goose-flesh experience in a letter of Emily Dickinson, and the top of her head taken off. We have the bristling of the skin while Housman was shaving, the "shiver down the spine," the sensation in "the pit of the stomach." And if poetry has been discerned by these tests, truth also. "All scientists," said D. H. Lawrence to Aldous Huxley, "are liars. . . . I don't care about evidence. Evidence doesn't mean anything to me. I don't feel it *here*." And, reports Huxley, "he pressed his two hands on his solar plexus."

An even more advanced grade of affective theory, that of hallucina-tion, would seem to have played some part in the neo-classic conviction about the unities of time and place, was given a modified continuation of existence in phrases of Coleridge about a "willing suspension of dis-belief" and a "temporary half faith," and may be found today in some textbooks. The hypnotic hypothesis of E. D. Snyder might doubtless be invoked in its support. As this form of affective theory is the least theoretical in detail, has the least content, and makes the least real claim on critical intelligence, so it is in its most concrete instances not a theory but a fiction or a fact—of no critical significance. In the eighteenth century Fielding conveys a right view of the hallucinative power of drama in his comic description of Partridge seeing Garrick act the ghost scene in Hamlet. "O la! sir. . . . If I was frightened, I am not the only person. . . . You may call me coward if you will; but if that little man there upon the stage is not frightened, I never saw any man frightened in my life." Partridge is today found perhaps less often among the sophisticates at the theatre than among the myriad audience of movie and radio. It is said, and no doubt reliably, that during the war Stefan Schnabel played Nazi roles in radio dramas so convincingly that he received numerous letters of complaint, and in particular one from a lady who said that she had reported him to General MacArthur.[3]

II

A distinction can be made between those who have testified. As the systematic affective critic professes to deal not merely, if at all, with his own experiences, but with those of persons in general, his most resolute search for evidence will lead him into the dreary and antiseptic laboratory, to testing with Fechner the effects of triangles and rectangles, to inquiring what kinds of colors are suggested by a line of Keats, or to measuring the motor discharges attendant upon reading it.[4] If animals could read poetry, the affective critic might make discoveries analogous to those of W. B. Cannon about *Bodily Changes in Pain, Hunger, Fear and Rage*—the increased liberation of sugar from the liver, the secretion of adrenin from the adrenal gland. The affective critic is today actually able, if he wishes, to measure the "psychogalvanic reflex" of persons subjected to a given moving picture. But, as Herbert J. Muller in his *Science and Criticism* points out: "Students have sincerely reported an 'emotion' at the mention of the word 'mother,' although a galvanometer indicated no bodily change whatever. They have also reported no emotion at the mention of 'prostitute,' although the galvanometer gave a definite kick." Thomas Mann and a friend came out of a movie weeping copiously—but Mann narrates the incident in support of his view that movies are not Art. "Art is a *cold* sphere."[5] The gap between various levels of physiological experience and the recognition of value remains wide, in the laboratory or out.

In a similar way, general affective theory at the literary level has, by the very implications of its program, produced very little actual criticism.

The author of the ancient *Peri Hupsous* is weakest at the points where he explains that passion and sublimity are the palliatives or excuses (*alexipharmaka*) of bold metaphors, and that passions which verge on transport are the lenitives or remedies (*panakeia*) of such audacities in speech as hyperbole. The literature of catharsis has dealt with the historical and theoretical question whether Aristotle meant a medical or a lustratory metaphor, whether the genitive which follows *katharsis* is of the thing purged or of the object purified. Even the early critical practice of I. A. Richards had little to do with his theory of synaesthesis. His *Practical Criticism* depended mainly on two important constructive principles of criticism which Richards has realized and insisted upon—(1) that rhythm (the vague, if direct, expression of emotion) and poetic form in general are intimately connected with and interpreted by other and more precise parts of poetic meaning, (2) that poetic meaning is inclusive or multiple and hence sophisticated. The latter quality of poetry may perhaps be the objective correlative of the affective state synaesthesis, but in applied criticism there would seem to be not much room for synaesthesis or for the touchy little attitudes of which it is composed.

The report of some readers, on the other hand, that a poem or story induces in them vivid images, intense feelings, or heightened consciousness, is neither anything which can be refuted nor anything which it is possible for the objective critic to take into account. The purely affective report is either too physiological or it is too vague. Feelings, as Hegel has conveniently put it, "remain purely subjective affections of myself, in which the concrete matter vanishes, as though narrowed into a circle of the utmost abstraction." And the only constant or predictable thing about the vivid images which more eidetic readers experience is precisely their vividness—as may be seen by requiring a class of average pupils to draw illustrations of a short story by consulting the newest Christmas edition of a childhood classic which one knew with the illustrations of Howard Pyle N. C. Wyeth. Vividness is not the thing in the work by which the work may be identified, but the result of a cognitive structure, which *is* the thing. "The story is good," as the student so often says in his papers, "because it leaves so much to the imagination." The opaque accumulation of physical detail in some realistic novels has been an absurd reduction of plastic or graphic theory aptly dubbed by Middleton Murry "the pictorial fallacy."

Certain theorists, notably Richards, have anticipated some difficulties of affective criticism by saying that it is not intensity of emotion that characterizes poetry (murder, robbery, fornication, horse racing, war—

perhaps even chess—take care of that better), but the subtle quality of patterned emotions which play at the subdued level of disposition or attitude. We have psychological theories of aesthetic distance, detachment, or disinterestedness. A criticism on these principles has already taken important steps toward objectivity. If Eastman's theory of imaginative vividness appears today chiefly in the excited puffs of the newspaper Book Sections, the campaign of the semanticists and the balanced emotions of Richards, instead of producing their own school of affective criticism, have contributed much to recent schools of cognitive analysis, of paradox, ambiguity, irony, and symbol. It is not always true that the emotive and cognitive forms of criticism will sound far different. If the affective critic (avoiding both the physiological and the abstractly psychological form of report) ventures to state with any precision what a line of poetry *does*—as "it fills us with a mixture of melancholy and reverence for antiquity"—either the statement will be patently abnormal or false, or it will be description of what the meaning of the line *is*: "the spectacle of massive antiquity in ruins." Tennyson's "Tears, idle tears," as it deals with an emotion which the speaker at first seems not to understand, might be thought to be a specially emotive poem. "The last stanza," says Brooks in his recent analysis, "evokes an intense emotional response from the reader." But this statement is not really a part of Brooks's criticism of the poem—rather a witness of his fondness for it. "The second stanza"—Brooks might have said at an earlier point in his analysis—"gives us a momentary vivid realization of past happy experiences, then makes us sad at their loss." But he says actually: "The conjunction of the qualities of sadness and freshness is reinforced by the fact that the same basic symbol—the light on the sails of a ship hull down—has been employed to suggest both qualities." The distinction between these formulations may seem trivial, and in the first example which we furnished may be practically unimportant. Yet the difference between translatable emotive formulas and more physiological and psychologically vague ones—cognitively untranslatable—is theoretically of the greatest importance. The distinction even when it is a very faint one is at the dividing point between paths which lead to polar opposites in criticism, to classical objectivity and to the romantic reader psychology.

The critic whose formulations lean to the emotive and the critic whose formulations lean to the cognitive will in the long run produce vastly different sorts of criticism.

The more specific the account of the emotion induced by a poem, the more nearly it will be an account of the reasons for emotion, the poem itself, and the more reliable it will be as an account of what the poem is likely to induce in other—sufficiently informed—readers. It will in fact supply the kind of information which will enable readers to respond to the poem. It will talk not of tears, prickles, or other physiological symptoms, of feeling angry, joyful, hot, cold, or intense, or of vaguer states of emotional disturbance, but of shades of distinction and relation between objects of emotion. It is precisely here that the discerning literary critic has his insuperable advantage over the subject of the laboratory experiment and over the tabulator of the subject's responses. The critic is not a contributor to statistically countable reports about the poem, but a teacher or explicator of meanings. His readers, if they are alert, will not be content to take what he says as testimony, but will scrutinize it as teaching.

III

Poetry, as Matthew Arnold believed, "attaches the emotion to the idea; the idea *is* the fact." The objective critic, however, must admit that it is not easy to explain how this is done, how poetry makes ideas thick and complicated enough to attach emotions. In his essay on *Hamlet and His Problems* T. S. Eliot finds Hamlet's state of emotion unsatisfactory because it lacks an "objective correlative," a "chain of events" which are the "formula of that *particular* emotion." The emotion is "in *excess* of the facts as they appear." It is "inexpressible." Yet Hamlet's emotion must be expressible, we submit, and actually expressed too (by something) in the play; otherwise Mr. Eliot would not know it is there—in excess of the facts. That Hamlet himself or Shakespeare may be baffled by the emotion is beside the point. The second chapter of Yvor Winters's *Primitivism and Decadence* has gone much further in clarifying a distinction adumbrated by Eliot. Without embracing the extreme doctrine of Winters, that if a poem cannot be paraphrased it is a poor poem, we may yet with profit reiterate his main thesis: that there is a difference between the motive, as he calls it, or logic of an emotion, and the surface or texture of a poem constructed to describe the emotion, and that both are important to a poem. Winters has shown, we think, how there can be in effect "fine poems" about nothing. There is rational progression and there is "qualitative progression,"[6] the latter, with several subtly related modes, a characteristic of decadent poetry. Qualitative progression is the succession, the dream float, of images, not substantiated by a plot. "Moister than an oyster in its clammy cloister, I'm bluer than a wooer who has slipped in a sewer," says Morris Bishop in a recent comic poem:

Chiller than a killer in a cinema thriller,
Queerer than a leerer at his leer in a mirror,
Madder than an adder with a stone in the bladder.
If you want to know why, I cannot but reply:
    It is really no affair of yours.[7]

The term "pseudo-statement" was for Richards a patronizing term by which he indicated the attractive nullity of poems. For Winters, the kindred term "pseudo-reference" is a name for the more disguised kinds of qualitative progression and is a term of reproach. It seems to us highly significant that for another psychological critic, Max Eastman, so important a part of poetry as metaphor is in effect too pseudo statement. The vivid realization of metaphor comes from its being in some way an obstruction to practical knowledge (like a torn coat sleeve to the act of dressing). Metaphor operates by being abnormal or inept, the wrong way of saying something. Without pressing the point, we should say that an uncomfortable resemblance to this doctrine appears in Ransom's logical structure and local texture of irrelevance.

What Winters has said seems basic. To venture both a slight elaboration of this and a return to the problem of emotive semantics surveyed in our first section: it is a well known but nonetheless important truth that there are two kinds of real objects which have emotive quality, the objects which are the literal reasons for human emotion, and those which by some kind of association suggest either the reasons or the resulting emotion: the thief, the enemy, or the insult that makes us angry, and the hornet that sounds and stings somewhat like ourselves when angry; the murderer or felon, and the crow that kills small birds and animals or feeds on carrion and is black like the night when crimes are committed by men. The arrangement by which these two kinds of emotive meaning are brought together in a juncture characteristic of poetry is, roughly speaking, the simile, the metaphor, and the various less clearly defined forms of association. We offer the following crude example as a kind of skeleton figure to which we believe all the issues can be attached.

1. X feels as angry as a hornet.
2. X whose lunch has been stolen feels as angry as a hornet.

No. 1 is, we take it, the qualitative poem, the vehicle of a metaphor, an objective correlative—for nothing. No. 2 adds the tenor of the metaphor, the motive for feeling angry, and hence makes the feeling itself more specific. The total statement has a more complex and testable structure. The element of aptitude, or ineptitude, is more susceptible of discussion. "Light thickens and the crow makes wing to the rooky wood" might be a line from a poem about nothing, but initially owed much of its power, and we daresay still does, to the fact that it is spoken by a tormented murderer who, as night draws on, has sent his agents out to perform a further "deed of dreadful note."

These distinctions bear a close relation to the difference between historical statement which may be a reason for emotion because it is believed (Macbeth has killed the king) and fictitious or poetic statement, where a large component of suggestion (and hence metaphor) has usually appeared. The first of course seldom occurs pure, at least not for the public eye. The coroner or the intelligence officer may content himself with it. Not the chronicler, the bard, or the newspaper man. To these we owe more or less direct words of value and emotion (the murder, the atrocity, the wholesale butchery) and all the repertoire of suggestive meanings which here and there in history—with somewhat to start upon—a Caesar or a Macbeth—have created out of a mere case of factual reason for intense emotion a specified, figuratively fortified, and permanent object of less intense but far richer emotion. With the decline of heroes and of faith in objects as important, we have had within the last century a great flowering of poetry which has tried the utmost to do without any hero or action or fiction of these—the qualitative poetry of Winters's analysis. It is true that any hero and action when they become fictitious take the first step toward the simply qualitative, and all poetry, so far as separate from history, tends to be formula of emotion. The hero and action are taken as symbolic. A graded series from fact to quality might include: (1) the historic Macbeth, (2) Macbeth as Renaissance tragic protagonist, (3) a *Macbeth* written by Eliot, (4) a *Macbeth* written by Pound. As Winters has explained, "the prince is briefly introduced in the footnotes" of *The Waste Land*; "it is to be doubted that Mr. Pound could manage such an introduction." Yet in no one of these four stages has anything like a pure emotive poetry been produced. Even in the last stages a poetry of pure emotion is an illusion. What we have is a poetry where kings are only symbols or even a poetry of hornets and crows, rather than of human deeds. Yet a poetry about things. How these things are joined in patterns and with what names of emotion, remains always the critical question. "*The Romance of the Rose* could not, without loss," observes C. S. Lewis, "be rewritten as *The Romance of the Onion*."

Poetry is characteristically a discourse about both emotions and objects, or about the emotive quality of objects. The emotions correlative to the objects of poetry become a part of the matter dealt with—not communicated to the reader like an infection or disease, not inflicted mechanically like a bullet or knife wound, not administered like a poison, not simply expressed as by expletives or grimaces or rhythms, but presented in their objects and contemplated as a pattern of knowledge. Poetry is a way of fixing emotions or making them more permanently perceptible when objects have undergone a functional change from culture to culture, or when as simple facts of history they have lost emotive value with loss of immediacy. Though the reasons for emotion in poetry may not be so simple as Ruskin's "noble grounds for the noble emotions," yet a great deal of constancy for poetic objects of emotion—if we will look for constancy—may be traced through the drift of human history. The murder of Duncan by Macbeth, whether as history of the eleventh century or chronicle of the sixteenth, has not tended to become the subject of a Christmas carol. In Shakespeare's play it is an act difficult to duplicate in all its immediate adjuncts of treachery, deliberation, and horror of conscience. Set in its galaxy of symbols—the hoarse raven, the thickening light, and the crow making wing, the babe plucked from the breast, the dagger in the air, the ghost, the bloody hands—this ancient murder has become an object of strongly fixed emotive value. The corpse of Polyneices, a far more ancient object and partially concealed from us by the difficulties of the Greek, shows a similar pertinacity in remaining among the understandable motives of higher duty. Funeral customs have changed, but not the web of issues, religious, political, and private, woven about the corpse "unburied, unhonored, all unhallowed." Again, certain objects partly obscured in one age wax into appreciation in another, and partly through the efforts of the poet. It is not true that they suddenly arrive out of nothing. The pathos of Shylock, for example, is not a creation of our time, though a smugly modern humanitarianism, because it has slogans, may suppose that this was not felt by Shakespeare or Southampton—and may not perceive its own debt to Shakespeare. "Poets," says Shelley, "are the unacknowledged legislators of the world." And it may be granted at least that poets have been leading expositors of the laws of feeling.[8]

To the relativist historian of literature falls the uncomfortable task of establishing as discrete cultural moments the past when the poem was written and first appreciated, and the present into which the poem with its clear and nicely interrelated meanings, its completeness, balance, and tension has survived. A structure of emotive objects so complex and so reliable as to have been taken for great poetry by any past age will never, it seems safe to say, so wane with the waning of human culture as not to be recoverable at least by a willing student. And on the same grounds a confidence seems indicated for the objective discrimination of all future poetic phenomena, though the premises or materials of which such poems will be constructed cannot be prescribed or foreseen. If the exegesis of some poems depends upon the understanding of obsolete or exotic customs, the poems themselves are the most precise emotive evaluation of the customs. In the poet's finely contrived objects of emotion and in other works of art the historian finds his most reliable evidence about the emotions of antiquity—and the anthropologist, about those of contemporary primitivism. To appreciate courtly love we turn to Chrétien de Troyes and Marie de France. Certain attitudes of late fourteenth century England, toward knighthood, toward monasticism, toward the bourgeoisie, are nowhere more precisely illustrated than in the prologue to *The Canterbury Tales*. The field worker among the Zunis or the Navahos finds no informant so informative as the poet or the member of the tribe who can quote its myths.[9] In that, though cultures have changed and will change, poems remain and explain.

1. Strictly, a theory not of poetry, but of morals, as, to take a curious modern instance, Lucie Guillet's *La Poéticothérapie, Efficacités du Fluide Poétique*, Paris, 1946, is a theory not of poetry but of healing. Aristotle's catharsis is a true theory of poetry, i.e., part of a definition of poetry.

2. *As I Remember Him*, quoted by J. Donald Adams, "Speaking of Books," *New York Times Book Review*, April 20, 1947, p. 2. Mr. Adams's weekly department is a happy hunting ground for such specimens.

3. *The New Yorker*, xix (Dec. 11, 1943), 28.

4. "The final averages showed that the combined finger movements for the Byron experiments were eighteen meters longer than they were for Keats." R. C. Givler: *The Psycho-Physiological Effect of the Elements of Speech in Relation to Poetry* (Princeton, 1915), p. 62.

5. "Ueber den Film," in *Die Forderung des Tages* (Berlin, 1930), p. 387.

6. The term, as Mr. Winters indicates, is borrowed from Mr. Kenneth Burke's *Counter-Statement*.

7. *New Yorker*, xxiii (May 31, 1947), 33.

8. *Cf.* Paulhan: *The Laws of Feeling*, pp. 105, 110.

9. "The anthropologist," says Bronislaw Malinowski, "has the myth-maker at his elbow." *Myth in Primitive Psychology* (New York, 1926), 17.

The Intentional Fallacy

W. K. WIMSATT AND MONROE C. BEARDSLEY

This essay investigates whether an author's intentions need to be considered, or even understood, in studying a work of literature. The authors argue that we should judge only what exists on the page, and that looking for intentions outside *the work of literature strays beyond criticism into "sociology, biography, or other kinds of non-aesthetic history."*

> He owns with toil he wrote the following scenes;
> But, if they're naught, ne'er spare him for his pains:
> Damn him the more; have no commiseration
> For dullness on mature deliberation.
> —William Congreve, Prologue to *The Way of the World*

The claim of the author's "intention" upon the critic's judgment has been challenged in a number of recent discussions, notably in the debate entitled *The Personal Heresy*, between Professors Lewis and Tillyard. But it seems doubtful if this claim and most of its romantic corollaries are as yet subject to any widespread questioning. The present writers, in a short article entitled "Intention" for a *Dictionary*[1] of literary criticism, raised the issue but were unable to pursue its implications at any length. We argued that the design or intention of the author is neither available nor desirable as a standard for judging the success of a work of literary art, and it seems to us that this is a principle which goes deep into some differences in the history of critical attitudes. It is a principle which accepted or rejected points to the polar opposites of classical "imitation" and romantic expression. It entails many specific truths about inspiration, authenticity, biography, literary history and scholarship, and about some trends of contemporary poetry, especially its allusiveness. There is hardly a problem of literary criticism in which the critic's approach will not be qualified by his view of "intention."

"Intention," as we shall use the term, corresponds to *what he intended* in a formula which more or less explicitly has had wide acceptance. "In order to judge the poet's performance, we must know *what he intended*." Intention is design or plan in the author's mind. Intention has obvious affinities for the author's attitude toward his work, the way he felt, what made him write.

We begin our discussion with a series of propositions summarized and abstracted to a degree where they seem to us axiomatic.

1. A poem does not come into existence by accident. The words of a poem, as Professor Stoll has remarked, come out of a head, not out of a hat. Yet to insist on the designing intellect as a *cause* of a poem is not to grant the design or intention as a *standard* by which the critic is to judge the worth of the poet's performance.

2. One must ask how a critic expects to get an answer to the question about intention. How is he to find out what the poet tried to do? If the poet succeeded in doing it, then the poem itself shows what he was trying to do. And if the poet did not succeed, then the poem is not adequate evidence, and the critic must go outside the poem—for evidence of an intention that did not become effective in the poem. "Only one *caveat* must be borne in mind," says an eminent intentionalist[2] in a moment when his theory repudiates itself; "the poet's aim must be judged at the moment of the creative act, that is to say, by the art of the poem itself."

3. Judging a poem is like judging a pudding or a machine. One demands that it work. It is only because an artifact works that we infer the intention of an artificer. "A poem should not mean but be." A poem can *be* only through its *meaning*—since its medium is words—yet it *is*, simply *is*, in the sense that we have no excuse for inquiring what part is intended or meant. Poetry is a feat of style by which a complex of meaning is handled all at once. Poetry succeeds because all or most of what is said or implied is relevant; what is irrelevant has been excluded, like lumps from pudding and "bugs" from machinery. In this respect poetry differs from practical messages, which are successful if and only if we correctly infer the intention. They are more abstract than poetry.

4. The meaning of a poem may certainly be a personal one, in the sense that a poem expresses a personality or state of soul rather than a physical object like an apple. But even a short lyric poem is dramatic, the response of a speaker (no matter how abstractly conceived) to a situation (no matter how universalized). We ought to impute the thoughts and attitudes of the poem immediately to the dramatic *speaker*, and if to the author at all, only by an act of biographical inference.

5. There is a sense in which an author, by revision, may better achieve his original intention. But it is a very abstract sense. He intended to write a better work, or a better work of a certain kind, and now has done it. But it follows that his former concrete intention was not his intention. "He's the man we were in search of, that's true," says Hardy's rustic constable, "and yet he's not the man we were in search of. For the man we were in search of was not the man we wanted."

"Is not a critic," asks Professor Stoll, "a judge, who does not explore his own consciousness, but determines the author's meaning or intention, as if the poem were a will, a contract, or the constitution? The poem is not the critic's own." He has accurately diagnosed two forms of irresponsibility, one of which he prefers. Our view is yet different. The poem is not the critic's own and not the author's (it is detached from the author at birth and goes about the world beyond his power to intend about it or control it). The poem belongs to the public. It is embodied in language, the peculiar possession of the public, and it is about the human being, an object of public knowledge. What is said about the poem is subject to the same scrutiny as any statement in linguistics or in the general science of psychology.

A critic of our *Dictionary* article, Ananda K. Coomaraswamy, has argued[3] that there are two kinds of inquiry about a work of art: (1) whether the artist achieved his intentions; (2) whether the work of art "ought ever to have been undertaken at all" and so "whether it is worth preserving." Number (2), Coomaraswamy maintains, is not "criticism of any work of art *qua* work of art," but is rather moral criticism; number (1) is artistic criticism. But we maintain that (2) need not be moral criticism: that there is another way of deciding whether works of art are worth preserving and whether, in a sense, they "ought" to have been undertaken, and this is the way of objective criticism of works of art as such, the way which enables us to distinguish between a skillful murder and a skillful poem. A skillful murder is an example which Coomaraswamy uses, and in his system the difference between the murder and the poem is simply a "moral" one, not an "artistic" one, since each if carried out according to plan is "artistically" successful. We maintain that (2) is an inquiry of more worth than (1), and since (2) and not (1) is capable of distinguishing poetry from murder, the name "artistic criticism" is properly given to (2).

II

It is not so much a historical statement as a definition to say that the intentional fallacy is a romantic one. When a rhetorician of the first century A.D. writes: "Sublimity is the echo of a great soul," or when he tells us that "Homer enters into the sublime actions of his heroes" and "shares the full inspiration of the combat," we shall not be surprised to find this rhetorician considered as a distant harbinger of romanticism and greeted in the warmest terms by Saintsbury. One may wish to argue whether Longinus should be called romantic, but there can hardly be a doubt that in one important way he is.

Goethe's three questions for "constructive criticism" are "What did the author set out to do? Was his plan reasonable and sensible, and how far did he succeed in carrying it out?" If one leaves out the middle question, one has in effect the system of Croce—the culmination and crowning philosophic expression of romanticism. The beautiful is the successful intuition-expression, and the ugly is the unsuccessful; the intuition or private part of art is *the* aesthetic fact, and the medium or public part is not the subject of aesthetic at all.

> The Madonna of Cimabue is still in the Church of Santa Maria
> Novella; but does she speak to the visitor of to-day as to the Floren-
> tines of the thirteenth century?

> *Historical interpretation* labors . . . to reintegrate in us the psycho-
> logical conditions which have changed in the course of history. It
> . . . enables us to see a work of art (a physical object) as its *author
> saw it* in the moment of production.[4]

The first italics are Croce's, the second ours. The upshot of Croce's system is an ambiguous emphasis on history. With such passages as a point
of departure a critic may write a nice analysis of the meaning or "spirit"
of a play by Shakespeare or Corneille—a process that involves close historical study but remains aesthetic criticism—or he may, with equal
plausibility, produce an essay in sociology, biography, or other kinds of
nonaesthetic history.

III

> I went to the poets; tragic, dithyrambic, and all sorts. . . . I took them
> some of the most elaborate passages in their own writings, and asked
> what was the meaning of them. . . . Will you believe me? . . . there
> is hardly a person present who would not have talked better about
> their poetry than they did themselves. Then I knew that not by wis-
> dom do poets write poetry, but by a sort of genius and inspiration.

That reiterated mistrust of the poets which we hear from Socrates may
have been part of a rigorously ascetic view in which we hardly wish to
participate, yet Plato's Socrates saw a truth about the poetic mind which
the world no longer commonly sees—so much criticism, and that the
most inspirational and most affectionately remembered, has proceeded
from the poets themselves.

Certainly the poets have had something to say that the critic and professor could not say; their message has been more exciting: that poetry
should come as naturally as leaves to a tree, that poetry is the lava of the
imagination, or that it is emotion recollected in tranquillity. But it is
necessary that we realize the character and authority of such testimony.
There is only a fine shade of difference between such expressions and
a kind of earnest advice that authors often give. Thus Edward Young,
Carlyle, Walter Pater:

> I know two golden rules from *ethics*, which are no less golden in
> *Composition*, than in life. 1. Know *thyself*; 2dly, *Reverence thyself*.

This is the grand secret for finding readers and retaining them: let him who would move and convince others, be first moved and convinced himself. Horace's rule, *Si vis me flere*, is applicable in a wider sense than the literal one. To every poet, to every writer, we might say: Be true, if you would be believed.

Truth! there can be no merit, no craft at all, without that. And further, all beauty is in the long run only *fineness* of truth, or what we call expression, the finer accommodation of speech to that vision within.

And Housman's little handbook to the poetic mind yields this illustration:

> Having drunk a pint of beer at luncheon—beer is a sedative to the brain, and my afternoons are the least intellectual portion of my life—I would go out for a walk of two or three hours. As I went along, thinking of nothing in particular, only looking at things around me and following the progress of the seasons, there would flow into my mind, with sudden and unaccountable emotion, sometimes a line or two of verse, sometimes a whole stanza at once.

This is the logical terminus of the series already quoted. Here is a confession of how poems were written which would do as a definition of poetry just as well as "emotion recollected in tranquillity"—and which the young poet might equally well take to heart as a practical rule. Drink a pint of beer, relax, go walking, think on nothing in particular, look at things, surrender yourself to yourself, search for the truth in your own soul, listen to the sound of your own inside voice, discover and express the *vraie vérité*.

It is probably true that all this is excellent advice for poets. The young imagination fired by Wordsworth and Carlyle is probably closer to the verge of producing a poem than the mind of the student who has been sobered by Aristotle or Richards. The art of inspiring poets, or at least of inciting something like poetry in young persons, has probably gone further in our day than ever before. Books of creative writing such as those issued from the Lincoln School are interesting evidence of what a child can do.[5] All this, however, would appear to belong to an art separate from criticism—to a psychological discipline, a system of self-development, a yoga, which the young poet perhaps does well to notice, but which is something different from the public art of evaluating poems.

Coleridge and Arnold were better critics than most poets have been, and if the critical tendency dried up the poetry in Arnold and perhaps in Coleridge, it is not inconsistent with our argument, which is that judgment of poems is different from the art of producing them. Coleridge has given us the classic "anodyne" story, and tells what he can about the genesis of a poem which he calls a "psychological curiosity," but his definitions of poetry and of the poetic quality "imagination" are to be found elsewhere and in quite other terms.

It would be convenient if the passwords of the intentional school, "sincerity," "fidelity," "spontaneity," "authenticity," "genuineness," "originality," could be equated with terms such as "integrity," "relevance," "unity," "function," "maturity," "subtlety," "adequacy," and other more precise terms of evaluation — in short, if "expression" always meant aesthetic achievement. But this is not so.

"Aesthetic" art, says Professor Curt Ducasse, an ingenious theorist of expression, is the conscious objectification of feelings, in which an intrinsic part is the critical moment. The artist corrects the objectification when it is not adequate. But this may mean that the earlier attempt was not successful in objectifying the self, or "it may also mean that it was a successful objectification of a self which, when it confronted us clearly, we disowned and repudiated in favor of another."[6] What is the standard by which we disown or accept the self? Professor Ducasse does not say. Whatever it may be, however, this standard is an element in the definition of art which will not reduce to terms of objectification. The evaluation of the work of art remains public; the work is measured against something outside the author.

IV

There is criticism of poetry and there is author psychology, which when applied to the present or future takes the form of inspirational promotion; but author psychology can be historical too, and then we have literary biography, a legitimate and attractive study in itself, one approach, as Professor Tillyard would argue, to personality, the poem being only a parallel approach. Certainly it need not be with a derogatory purpose that one points out personal studies, as distinct from poetic studies, in the realm of literary scholarship. Yet there is danger of confusing personal and poetic studies; and there is the fault of writing the personal as if it were poetic.

There is a difference between internal and external evidence for the meaning of a poem. And the paradox is only verbal and superficial that what is (1) internal is also public: it is discovered through the semantics and syntax of a poem, through our habitual knowledge of the language, through grammars, dictionaries, and all the literature which is the source of dictionaries, in general through all that makes a language and culture; while what is (2) external is private or idiosyncratic; not a part of the work as a linguistic fact: it consists of revelations (in journals, for example, or letters or reported conversations) about how or why the poet wrote the poem—to what lady, while sitting on what lawn, or at the death of what friend or brother. There is (3) an intermediate kind of evidence about the character of the author or about private or semiprivate meanings attached to words or topics by an author or by a coterie of which he is a member. The meaning of words is the history of words, and the biography of an author, his use of a word, and the associations which the word had for *him*, are part of the word's history and meaning.[7] But the three types of evidence, especially (2) and (3), shade into one another so subtly that it is not always easy to draw a line between examples, and hence arises the difficulty for criticism. The use of biographical evidence need not involve intentionalism, because while it may be evidence of what the author intended, it may also be evidence of the meaning of his words and the dramatic character of his utterance. On the other hand, it may not be all this. And a critic who is concerned with evidence of type (1) and moderately with that of type (3) will in the long run produce a different sort of comment from that of the critic who is concerned with (2) and with (3) where it shades into (2).

The whole glittering parade of Professor Lowes's *Road to Xanadu*, for instance, runs along the border between types (2) and (3) or boldly traverses the romantic region of (2). "'Kubla Khan,'" says Professor Lowes, "is the fabric of a vision, but every image that rose up in its weaving had passed that way before. And it would seem that there is nothing haphazard or fortuitous in their return." This is not quite clear—not even when Professor Lowes explains that there were clusters of associations, like hooked atoms, which were drawn into complex relation with other clusters in the deep well of Coleridge's memory, and which then coalesced and issued forth as poems. If there was nothing "haphazard or fortuitous" in the way the images returned to the surface, that may mean (1) that Coleridge could not produce what he did not have, that he was limited in his creation by what he had read or otherwise experienced, or (2) that having received certain clusters of associations, he was bound to return them in just the way he did, and that the value of the poem may be described in terms of the experiences on which he had to draw. The latter pair of propositions (a sort of Hartleyan associationism which Coleridge himself repudiated in the *Biographia*) may not be assented to. There were certainly other combinations, other poems, worse or better, that might have been written by men who had read Bartram and Purchas and Bruce and Milton. And this will be true no matter how many times we are able to add to the brilliant complex of Coleridge's reading. In certain flourishes (such as the sentence we have quoted) and in chapter headings like "The Shaping Spirit," "The Magical Synthesis," "Imagination Creatrix," it may be that Professor Lowes pretends to say more about the actual poems than he does. There is a certain deceptive variation in these fancy chapter titles; one expects to pass on to a new stage in the argument, and one finds—more and more sources, more and more about "the streamy nature of association."[8]

"Wohin der Weg?" quotes Professor Lowes for the motto of his book. "Kein Weg! Ins Unbetretene." Precisely because the way is *unbetreten*, we should say, it leads away from the poem. Bartram's *Travels* contains a good deal of the history of certain words and of certain romantic Floridian conceptions that appear in "Kubla Khan." And a good deal of that history has passed and was then passing into the very stuff of our language. Perhaps a person who has read Bartram appreciates the poem more than one who has not. Or, by looking up the vocabulary of "Kubla Khan" in the *Oxford English Dictionary*, or by reading some of the other books there quoted, a person may know the poem better. But it would seem to pertain little to the poem to know that *Coleridge* had read Bartram. There is a gross body of life, of sensory and mental experience, which lies behind and in some sense causes every poem, but can never be and need not be known in the verbal and hence intellectual composition which is the poem. For all the objects of our manifold experience, for every unity, there is an action of the mind which cuts off roots, melts away context—or indeed we should never have objects or ideas or anything to talk about.

It is probable that there is nothing in Professor Lowes's vast book which could detract from anyone's appreciation of either *The Ancient Mariner* or "Kubla Khan." We next present a case where preoccupation with evidence of type (3) has gone so far as to distort a critic's view of a poem (yet a case not so obvious as those that abound in our critical journals).

In a well known poem by John Donne appears this quatrain:

> Moving of th' earth brings harmes and feares,
>   Men reckon what it did and meant,
> But trepidation of the spheares,
>   Though greater farre, is innocent.

A recent critic in an elaborate treatment of Donne's learning has written of this quatrain as follows:

> He touches the emotional pulse of the situation by a skillful allusion to the new and the old astronomy. . . . Of the new astronomy, the "moving of the earth" is the most radical principle; of the old, the "trepidation of the spheres" is the motion of the greatest complexity.

. . . The poet must exhort his love to quietness and calm upon his departure; and for this purpose the figure based upon the latter motion (trepidation), long absorbed into the traditional astronomy, fittingly suggests the tension of the moment without arousing the "harmes and feares" implicit in the figure of the moving earth.[9]

The argument is plausible and rests on a well substantiated thesis that Donne was deeply interested in the new astronomy and its repercussions in the theological realm. In various works Donne shows his familiarity with Kepler's *De Stella Nova*, with Galileo's *Siderius Nuncius*, with William Gilbert's *De Magnete*, and with Clavius's commentary on the *De Sphaera* of Sacrobosco. He refers to the new science in his Sermon at Paul's Cross and in a letter to Sir Henry Goodyer. In *The First Anniversary* he says the "new philosophy calls all in doubt." In the *Elegy on Prince Henry* he says that the "least moving of the center" makes "the world to shake."

It is difficult to answer argument like this, and impossible to answer it with evidence of like nature. There is no reason why Donne might not have written a stanza in which the two kinds of celestial motion stood for two sorts of emotion at parting. And if we become full of astronomical ideas and see Donne only against the background of the new science, we may believe that he did. But the text itself remains to be dealt with, the analyzable vehicle of a complicated metaphor. And one may observe: (1) that the movement of the earth according to the Copernican theory is a celestial motion, smooth and regular, and while it might cause religious or philosophic fears, it could not be associated with the crudity and earthiness of the kind of commotion which the speaker in the poem wishes to discourage; (2) that there is another moving of the earth, an earthquake, which has just these qualities and is to be associated with the tear-floods and sigh-tempests of the second stanza of the poem; (3) that "trepidation" is an appropriate opposite of earthquake, because each is a shaking or vibratory motion; and "trepidation of the spheres" is "greater far" than an earthquake, but not much greater (if two such motions can be compared as to greatness) than the annual motion of the earth; (4) that reckoning what it "did and meant" shows that the event has passed, like an earthquake, not like the incessant celestial movement of the earth. Perhaps a knowledge of Donne's interest in the new science may add another shade of meaning, an overtone to the stanza in question, though to say even this runs against the words. To make the geocentric and heliocentric antithesis the core of the metaphor is to disregard the English language, to prefer private evidence to public, external to internal.

V

If the distinction between kinds of evidence has implications for the historical critic, it has them no less for the contemporary poet and his critic. Or, since every rule for a poet is but another side of a judgment by a critic, and since the past is the realm of the scholar and critic, and the future and present that of the poet and the critical leaders of taste, we may say that the problems arising in literary scholarship from the intentional fallacy are matched by others which arise in the world of progressive experiment.

The question of "allusiveness," for example, as acutely posed by the poetry of Eliot, is certainly one where a false judgment is likely to involve the intentional fallacy. The frequency and depth of literary allusion in the poetry of Eliot and others has driven so many in pursuit of full meanings to the *Golden Bough* and the Elizabethan drama that it has become a kind of commonplace to suppose that we do not know what a poet means unless we have traced him in his reading—a supposition redolent with intentional implications. The stand taken by F. O. Matthiessen is a sound one and partially forestalls the difficulty.

> If one reads these lines with an attentive ear and is sensitive to their sudden shifts in movement, the contrast between the actual Thames and the idealized vision of it during an age before it flowed through a megalopolis is sharply conveyed by that movement itself, whether or not one recognizes the refrain to be from Spenser.

Eliot's allusions work when we know them—and to a great extent even when we do not know them, through their suggestive power.

But sometimes we find allusions supported by notes, and it is a nice question whether the notes function more as guides to send us where we may be educated, or more as indications in themselves about the character of the allusions. "Nearly everything of importance . . . that is apposite to an appreciation of 'The Waste Land,'" writes Matthiessen of Miss Weston's book; "has been incorporated into the structure of the poem itself, or into Eliot's Notes." And with such an admission it may begin to appear that it would not much matter if Eliot invented his sources (as Sir Walter Scott invented chapter epigraphs from "old plays" and "anonymous" authors, or as Coleridge wrote marginal glosses for *The Ancient Mariner*). Allusions to Dante, Webster, Marvell, or Baudelaire doubtless gain something because these writers existed, but it is doubtful whether the same can be said for an allusion to an obscure Elizabethan:

> The sound of horns and motors, which shall bring
> Sweeney to Mrs. Porter in the spring.

"Cf. Day, *Parliament of Bees*": says Eliot,

> When of a sudden, listening, you shall hear,
> A noise of horns and hunting, which shall bring
> Actaeon to Diana in the spring,
> Where all shall see her naked skin.

The irony is completed by the quotation itself; had Eliot, as is quite conceivable, composed these lines to furnish his own background, there would be no loss of validity. The conviction may grow as one reads Eliot's next note: "I do not know the origin of the ballad from which these lines are taken: it was reported to me from Sydney, Australia." The important word in this note—on Mrs. Porter and her daughter who washed their feet in soda water—is "ballad." And if one should feel from the lines themselves their "ballad" quality, there would be little need for the note. Ultimately, the inquiry must focus on the integrity of such notes as parts of the poem, for where they constitute special information about the meaning of phrases in the poem, they ought to be subject to the same scrutiny as any of the other words in which it is written. Matthiessen believes the notes were the price Eliot "had to pay in order to avoid what he would have considered muffling the energy of his poem by extended connecting links in the text itself." But it may be questioned whether the notes and the need for them are not equally muffling. F. W. Bateson has plausibly argued that Tennyson's "The Sailor Boy" would be better if half the stanzas were omitted, and the best versions of ballads like "Sir Patrick Spens" owe their power to the very audacity with which the minstrel has taken for granted the story upon which he comments. What then if a poet finds he cannot take so much for granted in a more recondite context and rather than write informatively, supplies notes? It can be said in favor of this plan that at least the notes do not pretend to be dramatic, as they would if written in verse. On the other hand, the notes may look like unassimilated material lying loose beside the poem, necessary for the meaning of the verbal symbol, but not integrated, so that the symbol stands incomplete.

We mean to suggest by the above analysis that whereas notes tend to seem to justify themselves as external indexes to the author's *intention*, yet they ought to be judged like any other parts of a composition (verbal arrangement special to a particular context), and when so judged their reality as parts of the poem, or their imaginative integration with the rest of the poem, may come into question. Matthiessen, for instance, sees that Eliot's titles for poems and his epigraphs are informative apparatus, like the notes. But while he is worried by some of the notes and thinks that Eliot "appears to be mocking himself for writing the note at the same time that he wants to convey something by it," Matthiessen believes that the "device" of epigraphs "is not at all open to the objection of not being sufficiently structural." "The *intention*," he says, "is to enable the poet to secure a condensed expression in the poem itself." "In each case the epigraph is *designed* to form an integral part of the effect of the poem." And Eliot himself, in his notes, has justified his poetic practice in terms of intention.

> The Hanged Man, a member of the traditional pack, fits my purpose in two ways: because he is associated in my mind with the Hanged God of Frazer, and because I associate him with the hooded figure in the passage of the disciples to Emmaus in Part V. . . . The man with Three Staves (an authentic member of the Tarot pack) I associate, quite arbitrarily, with the Fisher King himself.

And perhaps he is to be taken more seriously here, when off guard in a note, than when in his Norton Lectures he comments on the difficulty of saying what a poem means and adds playfully that he thinks of prefixing to a second edition of *Ash Wednesday* some lines from *Don Juan*:

> I don't pretend that I quite understand
> My own meaning when I would be *very* fine;
> But the fact is that I have nothing planned
> Unless it were to be a moment merry.

If Eliot and other contemporary poets have any characteristic fault, it may be in *planning* too much.

Allusiveness in poetry is one of several critical issues by which we have illustrated the more abstract issue of intentionalism, but it may be for today the most important illustration. As a poetic practice allusiveness would appear to be in some recent poems an extreme corollary of the romantic intentionalist assumption, and as a critical issue it challenges and brings to light in a special way the basic premise of intentionalism. The following instance from the poetry of Eliot may serve to epitomize the practical implications of what we have been saying. In Eliot's "Love Song of J. Alfred Prufrock," toward the end, occurs the line: "I have heard the mermaids singing, each to each," and this bears a certain resemblance to a line in a Song by John Donne, "Teach me

to heare Mermaides singing," so that for the reader acquainted to a certain degree with Donne's poetry, the critical question arises: Is Eliot's
line an allusion to Donne's? Is Prufrock thinking about Donne? Is Eliot
thinking about Donne? We suggest that there are two radically different
ways of looking for an answer to this question. There is (1) the way of
poetic analysis and exegesis, which inquires whether it makes any sense
if Eliot-Prufrock *is* thinking about Donne. In an earlier part of the
poem, when Prufrock asks, "Would it have been worth while, . . . To
have squeezed the universe into a ball," his words take half their sadness
and irony from certain energetic and passionate lines of Marvell's "To
His Coy Mistress." But the exegetical inquirer may wonder whether
mermaids considered as "strange sights" (to hear them is in Donne's
poem analogous to getting with child a mandrake root) have much to
do with Prufrock's mermaids, which seem to be symbols of romance
and dynamism, and which incidentally have literary authentication, if
they need it, in a line of a sonnet by Gérard de Nerval. This method of
inquiry may lead to the conclusion that the given resemblance between
Eliot and Donne is without significance and is better not thought of, or
the method may have the disadvantage of providing no certain conclusion. Nevertheless, we submit that this is the true and objective way of
criticism, as contrasted to what the very uncertainty of exegesis might
tempt a second kind of critic to undertake: (2) the way of biographical
or genetic inquiry, in which, taking advantage of the fact that Eliot is
still alive, and in the spirit of a man who would settle a bet, the critic
writes to Eliot and asks what he meant, or if he had Donne in mind. We
shall not here weigh the probabilities—whether Eliot would answer
that he meant nothing at all, had nothing at all in mind—a sufficiently
good answer to such a question—or in an unguarded moment might
furnish a clear and, within its limit, irrefutable answer. Our point is that
such an answer to such an inquiry would have nothing to do with the
poem "Prufrock"; it would not be a critical inquiry. Critical inquiries,
unlike bets, are not settled in this way. Critical inquiries are not settled
by consulting the oracle.

1. *Dictionary of World Literature*, Joseph T. Shipley, ed. (New York, 1942), 326–29.

2. J. E. Spingarn, "The New Criticism," in *Criticism in America* (New York, 1924), 24–25.

3. Anada K. Coomaraswamy, "Intention," in *American Bookman*, I (1944), 41–48.

4. It is true that Croce himself in his Ariosto, *Shakespeare and Corneille* (London, 1920), chap.
VII, "The Practical Personality and the Poetical Personality," and in his *Defence of Poetry* (Oxford,
1933), 24, and elsewhere, early and late, has delivered telling attacks on emotive geneticism, but the
main drive of the *Aesthetic* is surely toward a kind of cognitive intentionalism.

5. See Hughes Mearns, *Creative Youth* (Garden City, 1925), esp. 10, 27–29. The technique of
inspiring poems has apparently been outdone more recently by the study of inspiration in successful
poets and other artists. See, for instance, Rosamond E. M. Harding, *An Anatomy of Inspiration*
(Cambridge, 1940); Julius Portnoy, *A Psychology of Art Creation* (Philadelphia, 1942); Rudolf Arnheim

and others, *Poets at Work* (New York, 1947); Phyllis Bartlett, *Poems in Process* (New York, 1951); Brewster Ghiselin (ed.), *The Creative Process: A Symposium* (Berkeley and Los Angeles, 1952).

6. Curt Ducasse, *The Philosophy of Art* (New York, 1929), 116.

7. And the history of words *after* a poem is written may contribute meanings which if relevant to the original pattern should not be ruled out by a scruple about intention.

8. Chaps. VIII, "The Pattern," and XVI, "The Known and Familiar Landscape," will be found of most help to the student of the poem.

9. Charles M. Coffin, *John Donne and the New Philosophy* (New York, 1927), 97–98.

Pure and Impure Poetry

ROBERT PENN WARREN

Originally delivered as a lecture at Princeton University in 1942, and subsequently published in the Kenyon Review, *this essay remains the best examination of the concept of "pure" poetry—a much debated and important critical term in the symbolist and modernist vocabulary.*

Critics are rarely faithful to their labels and their special strategies. Usually the critic will confess that no one strategy—the psychological, the moralistic, the formalistic, the historical—or combination of strategies, will quite work the defeat of the poem. For the poem is like the monstrous Orillo in Boiardo's *Orlando Innamorato.* When the sword lops off any member of the monster, that member is immediately rejoined to the body, and the monster is as formidable as ever. But the poem is even more formidable than the monster, for Orillo's adversary finally gained a victory by an astonishing feat of dexterity: he slashed off both the monster's arms and quick as a wink seized them and flung them into the river. The critic who vaingloriously trusts his method to account for the poem, to exhaust the poem, is trying to emulate this dexterity: he thinks that he, too, can win by throwing the lopped-off arms into the river. But he is doomed to failure. Neither fire nor water will suffice to prevent the rejoining of the mutilated members to the monstrous torso. There is only one way to conquer the monster: you must eat it, bones, blood, skin, pelt, and gristle. And even then the monster is not dead, for it lives in you, is assimilated into you, and you are different, and somewhat monstrous yourself, for having eaten it.

So the monster will always win, and the critic knows this. He does not want to win. He knows that he must always play stooge to the monster. All he wants to do is to give the monster a chance to exhibit again its miraculous power.

With this fable, I shall begin by observing that poetry wants to be pure. And it always succeeds in this ambition. In so far as we have poetry at all, it is always pure poetry; that is, it is not non-poetry. The poetry of Shakespeare, the poetry of Pope, the poetry of Herrick, is pure, in so far as it is poetry at all. We call the poetry "higher" or "lower," we say "more powerful" or "less powerful" about it, and we are, no doubt, quite right in doing so. The souls that form the great rose of Paradise are seated in banks and tiers of ascending blessedness, but they are all saved, they are all perfectly happy; they are all "pure," for they have all been purged of mortal taint. This is not to say, however, that if we get poetry from one source, such a single source, say Shakespeare, should suffice us in as much as we can always appeal to it, or that, since all poetry is equally pure, we engage in a superfluous labor in trying to explore or create new sources of poetry. No, for we can remember that every soul in the great rose is precious in the eyes of God. No soul is the substitute for another.

Poetry wants to be pure, but poems do not. At least, most of them do not want to be too pure. The poems want to give us poetry, which is pure, and the elements of a poem, in so far as it is a good poem, will work together toward that end, but many of the elements, taken in themselves, may actually seem to contradict that end, or be neutral toward the achieving of that end. Are we then to conclude that, because neutral or recalcitrant elements appear in poems, even in poems called great, these elements are simply an index to human frailty, that in a perfect world there would be no dross in poems which would, then, be perfectly pure? No, it does not seem to be merely the fault of our world, for the poems include, deliberately, more of the so-called dross than would appear necessary. They are not even as pure as they might be in this imperfect world. They mar themselves with cacophonies, jagged rhythms, ugly words and ugly thoughts, colloquialisms, clichés, sterile technical terms, head work and argument, self-contradictions, clevernesses, irony, realism—all things which call us back to the world of prose and imperfection.

Sometimes a poet will reflect on this state of affairs, and grieve. He will decide that he, at least, will try to make one poem as pure as possible. So he writes:

> Now sleeps the crimson petal, now the white;
> Nor waves the cypress in the palace walk;
> Nor winks the gold fin in the porphyry font:
> The firefly wakens: waken thou with me.

We know the famous garden. We know how all nature conspires here to express the purity of the moment: how the milk-white peacock glimmers like a ghost, and how like a ghost the unnamed "she" glimmers on to her tryst; how earth lies "all Danaé to the stars," as the beloved's heart lies open to the lover; and how, in the end, the lily folds up her sweetness, "and slips into the bosom of the lake," as the lovers are lost in the sweet dissolution of love.

And we know another poet and another garden. Or perhaps it is the same garden, after all:

> I arise from dreams of thee
> In the first sweet sleep of night,
> When the winds are breathing low
> And the stars are shining bright.
> I arise from dreams of thee,
> And a spirit in my feet
> Hath led me—who knows how?
> To thy chamber window, Sweet!

We remember how, again, all nature conspires, how the wandering airs "faint," how the Champak's odors "pine," how the nightingale's complaint "dies upon her heart," as the lover will die upon the beloved's heart. Nature here strains out of nature, it wants to be called by another name, it wants to spiritualize itself by calling itself another name. How does the lover get to the chamber window? He refuses to say how, in his semi-somnambulistic daze, he got there. He blames, he says, "a spirit in my feet," and hastens to disavow any knowledge of how that spirit operates. In any case, he arrives at the chamber window. Subsequent events and the lover's reaction toward them are somewhat hazy. We only know that the lover, who faints and fails at the opening of the last stanza, and who asks to be lifted from the grass by a more enterprising beloved, is in a condition of delectable passivity, in which distinctions blur out in the "purity" of the moment.

Let us turn to another garden: the place, Verona; the time, a summer night, with full moon. The lover speaks:

> But soft! what light through yonder window breaks?
> It is the east. . . .

But we know the rest, and know that this garden, in which nature for the moment conspires again with the lover, is the most famous of them all, for the scene is justly admired for its purity of effect, for giving us the very essence of young, untarnished love. Nature conspires beneficently here, but we may chance to remember that beyond the garden wall strolls Mercutio, who can celebrate Queen Mab, but who is always aware that nature has other names as well as the names the pure poets and pure lovers put upon her. And we remember that Mercutio outside the wall, has just said:

> . . . 'twould anger him
> To raise a spirit in his mistress's circle
> Of some strange nature, letting it there stand
> Till she had laid it and conjured it down.

Mercutio has made a joke, a bawdy joke. That is bad enough, but worse, he has made his joke witty and, worst of all, intellectually complicated in its form. Realism, wit, intellectual complication—these are the enemies of the garden purity.

But the poet has not only let us see Mercutio outside the garden wall. Within the garden itself, when the lover invokes nature, when he spiritualizes and innocently trusts her, and says,

> Lady, by yonder blessed moon I swear,

the lady herself replies,

> O, swear not by the moon, the inconstant moon,
> That monthly changes in her circled orb.

The lady distrusts "pure" poems, nature spiritualized into forgetfulness. She has, as it were, a rigorous taste in metaphor, too; she brings a logical criticism to bear on the metaphor which is too easy; the metaphor must prove itself to her, must be willing to subject itself to scrutiny beyond the moment's enthusiasm. She injects the impurity of an intellectual style into the lover's pure poem.

And we must not forget the voice of the nurse, who calls from within, a voice which, we discover, is the voice of expediency, of half-measures, of the view that circumstances alter cases—the voice of prose and imperfection.

It is time to ask ourselves if the celebrated poetry of this scene, which as poetry is pure, exists despite the impurities of the total composition, if the effect would be more purely poetic were the nurse and Mercutio absent and the lady a more sympathetic critic of pure poems. I do not think so. This effect might even be more vulnerable poetically if the impurities were purged away. Mercutio, the lady, and the nurse are critics of the lover, who believes in pure poems, but perhaps they are necessary. Perhaps the lover can only be accepted in their context. The poet seems to say: "I know the worst that can be said on this subject, and I am giving fair warning. Read at your own risk." So the poetry arises from a recalcitrant and contradictory context; and finally involves that context.

Let us return to one of the other gardens, in which there is no Mercutio or nurse, and in which the lady is more sympathetic. Let us mar its purity by installing Mercutio in the shrubbery, from which the poet was so careful to banish him. You can hear his comment when the lover says:

> And a spirit in my feet
> Hath led me—who knows how?
> To thy chamber window, Sweet!

And we can guess what the wicked tongue would have to say in response to the last stanza.

It may be that the poet should have made his peace early with Mercutio, and have appealed to his better nature. For Mercutio seems to be glad to cooperate with a poet. But he must be invited; otherwise, he is apt to show a streak of merry vindictiveness about the finished product. Poems are vulnerable enough at best. Bright reason mocks them like sun from a wintry sky. They are easily left naked to laughter when leaves fall in the garden and the cold winds come. Therefore, they need all the friends they can get, and Mercutio, who is an ally of reason and who himself is given to mocking laughter, is a good friend for a poem to have.

On what terms does a poet make his peace with Mercutio? There are about as many sets of terms as there are good poets. I know that I have loaded the answer with the word *good* here, that I have implied a scale of excellence based, in part at least, on degree of complication. I shall return to this question. For the moment, however, let us examine a poem whose apparent innocence and simple lyric cry should earn it a place in any anthology of "pure poetry."

> Western wind, when wilt thou blow
> That the small rain down can rain?
> Christ, that my love were in my arms
> And I in my bed again!

The lover, grieving for the absent beloved, cries out for relief. Several kinds of relief are involved in the appeal to the wind. First there is the relief that would be had from the sympathetic manifestation of nature. The lover, in his perturbation of spirit, invokes the perturbations of nature. He exclaims,

> Western wind, when wilt thou blow

and Lear exclaims,

> Blow, winds, and crack your cheeks! rage! blow!

Second, there is the relief that would be had by the fulfillment of grief—the frost of grief, the drouth of grief broken, the full anguish expressed, then the violence allayed in the peace of tears. Third, there is the relief that would be had in the excitement and fulfillment of love itself. There seems to be a contrast between the first two types of relief and the third type; speaking loosely, we may say that the first two types are romantic and general, the third type realistic and specific. So much for the first two lines.

In the last two lines, the lover cries out for the specific solace of his case: reunion with his beloved. But there is a difference between the two lines. The first is general, and romantic. The phrase "in my arms" does not seem to mean exactly what it says. True, it has a literal meaning, if we can look close at the words, but it is hard to look close because of the romantic aura—the spiritualized mist about them.[1] But with the last line the perfectly literal meaning suddenly comes into sharp focus. The mist is rifted and we can look straight at the words, which, we discover with a slight shock of surprise, do mean exactly what they say. The last line is realistic and specific. It is not even content to say,

> And I in bed again!

It is, rather, more scrupulously specific, and says,

> And I in *my* bed again![2]

All of this does not go to say that the realistic elements here are to be taken as cancelling, or negating, the romantic elements. There is no ironical leer. The poem is not a celebration of carnality. It is a faithful lover who speaks. He is faithful to the absent beloved, and he is also faithful to the full experience of love. That is, he does not abstract one aspect of the experience and call it the whole experience. He does not strain nature out of nature; he does not over-spiritualize nature. This nameless poet would never have said, in the happier days of his love, that he had been led to his Sweet's chamber window by "a spirit in my feet"; and he certainly would not have added the coy disavowal, "who knows how?" But because the nameless poet refused to over-spiritualize nature, we can accept the spirituality of the poem.

Another poem gives us another problem.

> Ah, what avails the sceptered race,
>   Ah, what the form divine!
> What every virtue, every grace!
>   Rose Aylmer, all were thine.

Rose Aylmer, whom those wakeful eyes
      May weep, but never see,
A night of memories and of sighs
      I consecrate to thee.

This is another poem about lost love: a "soft" subject. Now to one kind of poet the soft subject presents a sore temptation. Because it is soft in its natural state, he is inclined to feel that to get at its poetic essence he must make it softer still, that he must insist on its softness, that he must render it as "pure" as possible. At first glance, it may seem that Landor is trying to do just that. What he says seems to be emphatic, unqualified, and open. Not every power, grace, and virtue could avail to preserve his love. That statement insists on the pathetic contrast. And in the next stanza, wakefulness and tearfulness are mentioned quite unashamedly, along with memories and sighs. It is all blurted out, as pure as possible.

But only in the paraphrase is it "blurted." The actual quality of the first stanza is hard, not soft. It is a chiseled stanza, in which formality is insisted upon. We may observe the balance of the first and second lines; the balance of the first half with the second half of the third line, which recapitulates the structure of the first two lines; the balance of the two parts of the last line, though here the balance is merely a rhythmical and not a sense balance as in the preceding instances; the binders of discreet alliteration, repetition, and assonance. The stanza is built up, as it were, of units which are firmly defined and sharply separated, phrase by phrase, line by line. We have the formal control of the soft subject, ritual and not surrender.

But in the second stanza the rigor of this formality is somewhat abated, as the more general, speculative emphasis (why cannot pomp, virtue, and grace avail?) gives way to the personal emphasis, as though the repetition of the beloved's name had, momentarily, released the flood of feeling. The first line of the second stanza spills over into the second; the "wakeful eyes" as subject find their verb in the next line, "weep," and the *wake-weep* alliteration, along with the rest after *weep*, points up the disintegration of the line, just as it emphasizes the situation. Then with the phrase "but never see" falling away from the long thrust of the rhetorical structure to the pause after *weep*, the poem seems to go completely soft, the frame is broken. But, even as the poet insists on "memories and sighs" in the last two lines he restores the balance. Notice the understatement of "A night." It says: "I know that life is a fairly complicated affair, and that I am committed to it and to its complications. I intend to stand by my commitment, as a man of integrity, that is, to live despite the grief. Since life is complicated, I cannot, if I am to live, spare too much time for indulging grief. I can give *a* night, but not all nights." The lover, like the hero of Frost's poem "Stopping by Woods on a Winter Evening," tears himself from the temptation of staring into the treacherous, delicious blackness, for he, too, has "promises to keep." Or he resembles the Homeric heroes who, after the perilous passage is made, after their energy has saved their lives, and after they have beached their craft and eaten their meal, can then set aside an hour before sleep to mourn the comrades lost by the way—the heroes who, as Aldous Huxley says, understand realistically a whole truth as contrasted with a half-truth.

Is this a denial of the depth and sincerity of the grief? The soft reader, who wants the poem pure, may be inclined to say so. But let us look at the last line to see what it gives us in answer to this question. The answer seems to lie in the word *consecrate*. The meter thrusts this word at us; we observe that two of the three metrical accents in the line fall on syllables of this word forcing it beyond its prose emphasis. The word is important and the importance is justified, for the word tells us that the single night is not merely a lapse into weakness, a trivial event to be forgotten when the weakness is overcome. It is, rather, an event of the most extreme and focal importance, an event formally dedicated, "set apart for sacred uses," an event by which other events are to be measured. So the word *consecrate* formalizes, philosophizes, ritualizes the grief; it specifies what style in the first stanza has implied.

But here is another poem of grief, grief at the death of a child:

> There was such speed in her little body,
> And such lightness in her footfall,
> It is no wonder that her brown study
> Astonishes us all.
>
> Her wars were bruited in our high window.
> We looked among orchard trees and beyond
> Where she took arms against her shadow,
> Or harried unto the pond
>
> The lazy geese, like a snow cloud
> Dripping their snow on the green grass,
> Tricking and stopping, sleepy and proud,
> Who cried in goose, Alas,
>
> For the tireless heart within the little
> Lady with rod that made them rise
> From their noon apple dreams, and scuttle
> Goose-fashion under the skies!

But now go the bells, and we are ready;
In one house we are sternly stopped
To say we are vexed at her brown study,
Lying so primly propped.

Another soft subject, softer, if anything, than the subject of "Rose Aylmer," and it presents the same problem. But the problem is solved in a different way.

The first stanza is based on two time-honored clichés: first, "Heaven, won't that child ever be still, she is driving me distracted"; and second, "She was such an active, healthy-looking child, would you've ever thought she would just up and die?" In fact, the whole poem develops these clichés, and exploits, in a backhand fashion, the ironies implicit in their inter-relation. And in this connection, we may note that the fact of the clichés, rather than more original or profound observations, at the root of the poem is important; there is in the poem the contrast between the staleness of the clichés and the shock of the reality. Further, we may note that the second cliché is an answer, savagely ironical in itself, to the first: the child you wished would be still *is* still, despite all that activity which your adult occupations deplored.

But such a savage irony is not the game here. It is too desperate, too naked, in a word, too pure. And ultimately, it is, in a sense, a meaningless irony if left in its pure state, because it depends on a mechanical, accidental contrast in nature, void of moral content. The poem is concerned with modifications and modulations of this brute, basic irony, modulations and modifications contingent upon an attitude taken toward it by a responsible human being, the speaker of the poem. The savagery is masked, or ameliorated.

In this connection, we may observe, first, the phrase "brown study." It is not the "frosted flower," the "marmoreal immobility," or any one of a thousand such phrases which would aim for the pure effect. It is merely the brown study which astonishes—a phrase which denies, as it were, the finality of the situation, underplays the pathos, and merely reminds one of those moments of childish pensiveness into which the grown-up cannot penetrate. And the phrase itself is a cliché—the common now echoed in the uncommon.

Next, we may observe that stanzas two, three, and four simply document, with a busy yet wavering rhythm (one sentence runs through the three stanzas) the tireless naughtiness which was once the cause of rebuke, the naughtiness which disturbed the mature going-on in the room with the "high window." But the naughtiness has been transmuted, by events just transpired, into a kind of fanciful story-book dream-world, in which geese are whiter than nature, and the grass greener, in which geese speak in goose language, saying "Alas," and have apple dreams. It is a drowsy, delicious world, in which the geese are bigger than life, and more important. It is an unreal (now unreal because lost), stylized world. Notice how the phrase "the little lady with rod" works: the detached, grown-up primness of "little lady"; the formal, stiff effect gained by the omission of the article before *rod*; the slightly unnatural use of the word *rod* itself, which sets some distance between us and the scene (perhaps with the hint of the fairy story, a magic wand, or a magic rod—not a common, every-day stick). But the stanzas tie back into the premises of the poem in other ways. The little girl, in her naughtiness, warred against her shadow. Is it crowding matters too hard to surmise that the shadow here achieves a sort of covert symbolic significance? The little girl lost her war against her "shadow," which was always with her. Certainly the phrase "tireless heart" has some rich connotations. And the geese which say "Alas!" conspire with the family to deplore the excessive activity of the child. (They do not conspire to express the present grief, only the past vexation—an inversion of the method of the pastoral elegy, or of the method of the first two garden poems.)

The business of the three stanzas, then, may be said to be two-fold. First, they make us believe more fully in the child and therefore in the fact of the grief itself. They "prove" the grief, and they show the deliciousness of the lost world which will never look the same from the high window. Second, and contrarywise, they "transcend" the grief, or at least give a hint of a means for transcending the immediate anguish: the lost world is, in one sense, redeemed out of time, it enters the pages of the picture book where geese speak, where the untrue is true, where the fleeting is fixed. What was had cannot, after all, be lost. (By way of comparison—a comparison which, because extreme, may be helpful—I cite the transcendence in *La Recherche du Temps Perdu*.) The three stanzas, then, to state it in another way, have validated the first stanza and have prepared for the last.

The three stanzas have made it possible for us to say, when the bell tolls, "we are ready." Some kind of terms, perhaps not the best terms possible but some kind, have been made with the savage underlying irony. But the terms arrived at do not prevent the occasion from being a "stern" one. The transcendence is not absolute, and in the end is possible only because of an exercise of will and self-control. Because we control ourselves, we can say "vexed" and not some big word. And the word itself picks up the first of the domestic clichés on which the poem is based—the outburst of impatience at the naughty child who, by dying, has performed her most serious piece of naughtiness. But now the word comes to us charged with the burden of the poem, and further, as re-echoed here by the phrase "brown study," charged by the sentence in which it occurs: we are gathered formally, ritualistically, sternly together to say the word *vexed*.[3] *Vexed* becomes the ritualistic, the summarizing word.

I have used the words *pure* and *impure* often in the foregoing pages, and I confess that I have used them rather loosely. But perhaps it has been evident that I have meant something like this: the pure poem tries to be pure by excluding, more or less rigidly, certain elements which might qualify or contradict its original impulse. In other words the pure poems want to be, and desperately, all of a piece. It has also been evident, no doubt, that the kinds of impurity which are admitted or excluded by the various little anthology pieces which have been analyzed, are different in the different poems. This is only to be expected, for there is not one doctrine of "pure poetry"—not one definition of what constitutes impurity in poems—but many. And not all of the doctrines are recent. When, for example, one cites Poe as the father of *the* doctrine of pure poetry, one is in error; Poe simply fathered *a* particular doctrine of pure poetry. One can find other doctrines of purity long antedating Poe. When Sir Philip Sidney, for example, legislated against tragic-comedy, he was repeating a current doctrine of purity. When Ben Jonson told William Drummond that Donne, for not keeping of accent, deserved hanging, he was defending another kind of purity, and when Dryden spoke to save the ear of the fair sex from metaphysical perplexities in amorous poems, he was defending another kind of purity, just as he was defending another when he defined the nature of the heroic drama. The 18th century had a doctrine of pure poetry, which may be summed up under the word *sublimity*, but which involved two corollary doctrines, one concerning diction and the other concerning imagery. But at the same time that this century, by means of these corollary doctrines, was tidying up and purifying, as Mr. Monk and Mr. Henn have indicated, the doctrine derived from Longinus, it was admitting into the drama certain impurities which the theorists of the heroic drama would not have admitted.[4]

But when we think of the modern doctrine of pure poetry, we usually think of Poe, as critic and poet, perhaps of Shelley, of the Symbolists, of the Abbé Brémond, perhaps of Pater, and certainly of George Moore and the Imagists. We know Poe's position: the long poem is "a flat contradiction in terms," because intense excitement, which is essential in poetry, cannot be long maintained; the moral sense and the intellect function more satisfactorily in prose than in poetry, and, in fact, "Truth" and the "Passions," which are for Poe associated with intellect and the moral sense, may actually be inimical to poetry; vagueness, suggestiveness, are central virtues, for poetry has for "its object an *indefinite* instead of a *definite* pleasure"; poetry is not supposed to undergo close inspection, only a cursory glance, for it, "above all things, is a beautiful painting whose tints, to minute inspection, are confusion worse confounded, but start out boldly to the cursory glance of the connoisseur"; poetry aspires toward music, since it is concerned with "indefinite sensations, to which music is an *essential*, since the comprehension of sweet sound is our most indefinite conception"; melancholy is the most poetical effect and enters into all the higher manifestations of beauty. We know, too, the Abbé Brémond's mystical interpretation, and the preface to George Moore's anthology, and the Imagist manifesto.

But these views are not identical. Shelley, for instance, delights in the imprecision praised and practiced by Poe, but he has an enormous appetite for "Truth" and the "Passions," which are, except for purposes of contrast, excluded by Poe. The Imagist manifesto, while excluding ideas, endorses precision rather than vagueness in rendering the image, and admits diction and objects which would have seemed impure to Poe and to many poets of the 19th century, and does not take much stock in the importance of verbal music: George Moore emphasizes the objective aspect of his pure poetry, which he describes as "something which the poet creates outside his own personality," and this is opposed to the subjective emphasis in Poe and Shelley; but he shares with both an emphasis on verbal music; and with the former a distaste for ideas.

But more recently, the notion of poetic purity has emerged in other contexts, contexts which sometimes obscure the connection of the new theories with the older theories. For instance Max Eastman has a theory. "Pure poetry," he says in *The Literary Mind*, "is the pure effort to heighten consciousness." Mr. Eastman, we discover elsewhere in his book, would ban idea from poetry, but his motive is different from, say, the motive of Poe, and the difference is important: Poe would kick out the ideas because the ideas hurt the poetry, and Mr. Eastman would kick out the ideas because the poetry hurts the ideas. Only the scientist, he tells us, is entitled to have ideas on any subject, and the rest of the citizenry must wait to be told what attitude to take toward the ideas which they are not permitted to have except at second-hand. Literary truth, he says, is truth which is "uncertain or comparatively unimportant." But he assigns the poet a function—to heighten consciousness. But in the light of this context we would have to rewrite his original definition: pure poetry is the pure effort to heighten consciousness, but the consciousness which is heightened must not have any connection with ideas, must involve no attitude toward any ideas.

Furthermore, to assist the poet in fulfilling the assigned function, Mr. Eastman gives him a somewhat sketchy doctrine of "pure" poetic diction. For instance, the word *bloated* is not admissible into a poem because it is, as he testifies, "sacred to the memory of dead fish," and the word *tangy* is; though he knows not exactly how, "intrinsically poetic." The notion of a vocabulary which is intrinsically poetic seems, with Mr. Eastman, to mean a vocabulary which indicates agreeable or beautiful objects. So we might rewrite the original definition to read: pure poetry is the pure effort to heighten consciousness, but the consciousness which is heightened must be a consciousness exclusively of agreeable or beautiful objects—certainly not a consciousness of any ideas.

In a recent book, *The Idiom of Poetry*, Frederick Pottle has discussed the question of pure poetry. He distinguishes another type of pure poetry in addition to the types already mentioned. He calls it the "Elliptical," and would include in it symbolist and metaphysical poetry (old and new) and some work by poets such as Collins, Blake, and Browning. He observes—without any pejorative implication, for he is a critical relativist and scarcely permits himself the luxury of evaluative judgments—that the contemporary product differs from older examples of the elliptical type in that "the modern poet goes much farther in employing private experiences or ideas than would formerly have been thought legitimate." To the common reader, he says, "the prime characteristic of this kind of poetry is not the nature of its imagery but its obscurity: its urgent sugges- tion that you add something to the poem without telling you what that something is." This omitted "something" he interprets as the prose "frame," to use his word, the statement of the occasion, the logical or narrative transitions, the generalized application derived from the poem, etc. In other words, this type of pure poetry contends that "the effect would be more powerful if we could somehow manage to feel the im- ages fully and accurately without having the effect diluted by any words put in to give us a 'meaning'—that is, if we could expel all the talk *about* the imaginative realization and have the pure realization itself."[5]

For the moment I shall pass the question of the accuracy of Mr. Pot- tle's description of the impulse of Elliptical Poetry and present the ques- tion which ultimately concerns him. How pure does poetry need to be in practice? That is the question which Mr. Pottle asks. He answers by say- ing that a great degree of impurity *may* be admitted, and cites our famous didactic poems, *The Faerie Queene, The Essay on Man, The Vanity of Human Wishes, The Excursion.* That is the only answer which the rela- tivist, and nominalist, can give. Then he turns to what he calls the hard- est question in the theory of poetry: what kind of prosaism is acceptable and what is not? His answer, which he advances very modestly, is this:

... the element of prose is innocent and even salutary when it appears as—take your choice of three metaphors—a background on which the images are projected, or a frame in which they are shown, or a thread on which they are strung. In short, when it serves a *structural* purpose. Prose in a poem seems offensive to me when ... the prosaisms are sharp, obvious, individual, and ranked coordinately with the images.

At first glance this looks plausible, and the critic has used the sanctified word *structural*. But at second glance we may begin to wonder what the sanctified word means to the critic. It means something rather mechanical—background, frame, thread. The structure is a showcase, say a jeweler's showcase, in which the little jewels of poetry are exhibited, the images. The showcase shouldn't be ornamental itself ("sharp, obvious, individual," Mr. Pottle says), for it would then distract us from the jewels; it should be chastely designed, and the jewels should repose on black velvet and not on flowered chintz. But Mr. Pottle doesn't ask what the relation among the bright jewels should be. Apparently, not only does the showcase bear no relation to the jewels, but the jewels bear no relation to each other. Each one is a shining little focus of heightened consciousness, or pure realization, existing for itself alone. Or perhaps he should desire that they be arranged in some mechanical pattern, such a pattern, perhaps, as would make it easier for the eye to travel from one little jewel to the next when the time comes to move on. Structure becomes here simply a device of salesmanship, a well arranged showcase.

It is all mechanical. And this means that Mr. Pottle, after all, is himself an exponent of pure poetry. He locates the poetry simply in the images, the nodes of "pure realization." This means that what he calls the "element of prose" include definition of situation, movement of narrative, logical transition, factual description, generalization, ideas. Such things, for him, do not participate in the poetic effect of the poem; in fact, they work against the poetic effect, and so, though necessary as a frame, should be kept from being "sharp, obvious, individual."[6]

I have referred to *The Idiom of Poetry*, first, because it is such an admirable and provocative book, sane, lucid, generous-spirited, and second, because, to my mind, it illustrates the insidiousness with which a doctrine of pure poetry can penetrate into the theory of a critic who is suspicious of such a doctrine. Furthermore, I have felt that Mr. Pottle's analysis might help me to define the common denominator of the various doctrines of pure poetry.

That common denominator seems to be the belief that poetry is an essence that is to be located at some particular place in a poem, or in some particular element. The exponent of pure poetry persuades himself that he has determined the particular something in which the poetry inheres, and then proceeds to decree that poems shall be composed, as nearly as possible, of that element and of nothing else. If we add up the things excluded by various critics and practitioners, we get a list about like this:

1. ideas, truths, generalizations, "meaning"
2. precise, complicated, "intellectual" images
3. unbeautiful, disagreeable, or neutral materials
4. situation, narrative, logical transition
5. realistic details, exact descriptions, realism in general
6. shifts in tone or mood
7. irony
8. metrical variation, dramatic adaptations of rhythm, cacophony, etc.
9. meter itself
10. subjective and personal elements

No one theory of pure poetry excludes all of these items, and, as a matter of fact, the items listed are not on the same level of importance. Nor do the items always bear the same interpretation. For example, if one item seems to be central to discussions of pure poetry, it is the first: "ideas," it is said, "are not involved in the poetic effect, and may even the inimical to it." But this view can be interpreted in a variety of ways. If it is interpreted as simply meaning that the paraphrase of a poem is not equivalent to the poem, that the poetic gist is not to be defined as the statement embodied in the poem with the sugar-coating as bait, then the view can be held by opponents as well as exponents of any theory of pure poetry. We might scale down from this interpretation to the other extreme interpretation that the poem should merely give the sharp image in isolation. But there are many complicated and confused variations possible between the two extremes. There is, for example, the interpretation that "ideas," though they are not involved in the poetic effect, must appear in poems to provide, as Mr. Pottle's prosaisms do, a kind of frame, or thread, for the poetry—a spine to support the poetic flesh or a Christmas tree on which the baubles of poetry are hung.[7] T. S. Eliot has said something of this sort:

The chief use of the "meaning" of a poem, in the ordinary sense, may be (for here again I am speaking of some kinds of poetry and not all) to satisfy one habit of the reader, to keep his mind diverted and quiet, while the poem does its work upon him: much as the imaginary burglar is always provided with a bit of nice meat for the house-dog.

Here, it would seem, Mr. Eliot has simply inverted the old sugar-coated pill theory: the idea becomes the sugar-coating and the "poetry" becomes the medicine. This seems to say that the idea in a poem does not participate in the poetic effect, and seems to commit Mr. Eliot to a theory of pure poetry. But to do justice to the quotation, we should first observe that the parenthesis indicates that the writer is referring to some sort of provisional and superficial distinction and not to a fundamental one, and second observe that the passage is out of its context. In the context, Mr. Eliot goes on to say that some poets "become impatient of this 'meaning' [explicit statement of ideas in logical order] which seems superfluous, and perceive possibilities of intensity through its elimination." This may mean either of two things. It may mean that ideas do not participate in the poetic effect, or it may mean, though they do participate in the poetic effect, they need not appear in the poem in an explicit and argued form. And this second reading would scarcely be a doctrine of pure poetry at all, for it would involve poetic casuistry and not poetic principle.

We might, however, illustrate the second interpretation by glancing at Marvell's "Horatian Ode" on Cromwell. Marvell does not give us narrative; he does not give us an account of the issues behind the Civil War; he does not state the two competing ideas which are dramatized in the poem, the idea of "sanction" and the idea of "efficiency." But the effect of the poem does involve these two factors; the special reserved, scarcely resolved, irony, which is realized in the historical situation, is an irony derived from unstated materials and ideas. It is, to use Mr. Pottle's term again, a pure poem in so far as it is elliptical in method, but it is anything but a pure poem if by purity we mean the exclusion of idea from participation in the poetic effect. And Mr. Eliot's own practice implies that he believes that ideas do participate in the poetic effect. Otherwise, why did he put the clues to his ideas in the notes at the end of *The Waste Land* after so carefully excluding any explicit statement of them from the body of the poem? If he is regarding those ideas as mere bait—the "bit of nice meat for the house-dog"—he has put the ideas in a peculiar place, in the back of the book—like giving the dog the meat on the way out of the house with the swag or giving the mouse the cheese after he is in the trap. All this would lead one to the speculation that Marvell and Mr. Eliot have purged away statement of ideas from their poems, not because they wanted the ideas to participate less in the poetry, but because they wanted them to participate more fully, intensely, and immediately. This impulse, then, would account for the characteristic type of image, types in which precision, complication, and complicated intellectual relation to the theme are exploited; in other words, they are trying—whatever may be their final success—to carry the movement of mind to the center of the process. On these grounds they are the exact opposite of poets who, presumably on grounds of purity, exclude the movement of mind from the center of the poetic process—from the internal structure of the poem—but pay their respect to it as a kind of footnote, or gloss, or application coming at the end. Marvell and Eliot, by their cutting away of frame, are trying to emphasize the participation of ideas in the poetic process. Then Elliptical Poetry is not, as Mr. Pottle says it is, a pure poetry at all if we regard intention; the elliptical poet is elliptical for purposes of inclusion, not exclusion.

But waiving the question of Elliptical Poetry, no one of the other theories does—or could—exclude all the items on the list above. And that fact may instruct us. If all of these items were excluded, we might not have any poem at all. For instance, we know how some critics have pointed out that even in the strictest imagist poetry idea creeps in—when the image leaves its natural habitat and enters a poem it begins to "mean" something. The attempt to read ideas out of the poetic party violates the unity of our being and the unity of our experience. "For this reason," as Santayana puts it, "philosophy, when a poet is not mindless, enters inevitably into his poetry, since it has entered into his life; or rather, the detail of things and the detail of ideas pass equally into his verse, when both alike lie in the path that has led him to his ideal. To object to theory in poetry would be like objecting to words there; for words, too, are symbols without the sensuous character of the things they stand for; and yet it is only by the net of new connections which words throw over things, in recalling them, that poetry arises at all. Poetry is an attenuation, a rehandling, an echo of crude experience; it is itself a theoretic vision of things at arm's length." Does this not lead us to the conclusion that poetry does not inhere in any particular element but depends upon the set of relationships, the structure, which we call the poem?

Then the question arises: what elements cannot be used in such a structure? I should answer that nothing that is available in human experience is to be legislated out of poetry. This does not mean that anything can be used in *any* poem, or that some materials or elements may not prove more recalcitrant than others, or that it might not be easy to have too much of some things. But it does mean that, granted certain contexts, any sort of material, a chemical formula for instance, might appear functionally in a poem. It also may mean that, other things being equal, the greatness of a poet depends upon the extent of the area of experience that he can master poetically.

Can we make any generalizations about the nature of the poetic structure? First, it involves resistances, at various levels. There is the tension between the rhythm of the poem and the rhythm of speech (a tension which is very low at the extreme of free verse and at the extreme of verse such as that of *Ulalume*, which verges toward a walloping doggerel); between the formality of the rhythm and the informality of the language; between the particular and the general, the concrete and the abstract; between the elements of even the simplest metaphor; between the beautiful and the ugly; between ideas (as in Marvell's poem); between the elements involved in irony (as in *Bells for John Whiteside's Daughter* or *Rose Aylmer*); between prosaisms and poeticisms (as in *Western Wind*). This list is not intended to be exhaustive; it is intended to be merely suggestive. But it may be taken to imply that the poet is like the jiujitsu expert; he wins by utilizing the resistance of his opponent—the materials of the poem. In other words, a poem, to be good, must earn itself. It is a motion toward a point of rest, but if it is not a resisted motion, it is motion of no consequence. For example, a poem which depends upon stock materials and stock responses is simply a toboggan slide, or a fall through space. And the good poem must, in some way, involve the resistances; it must carry something of the context of its own creation; it must come to terms with Mercutio. This is another way of saying that a good poem involves the participation of the reader; it must, as Coleridge puts it, make the reader into "an active creative being." Perhaps we can see this most readily in the case of tragedy: the determination of good and evil is not a "given" in tragedy, it is something to be earned in the process, and even the tragic villain must be "loved." We must kill him, as Brutus killed Caesar, not as butchers but as sacrificers. And all of this adds up to the fact that the structure is a dramatic structure, a movement through action toward rest, through complication toward simplicity of effect.

In the foregoing discussion, I have deliberately omitted reference to another type of pure poetry, a type which, in the context of the present war, may well become dominant. Perhaps the most sensible description of this type can be found in an essay by Herbert Muller:

> If it is not the primary business of the poet to be eloquent about these matters [faith and ideals], it still does not follow that he has more dignity or wisdom than those who are, or that he should have more sophistication. At any rate the fact is that almost all poets of the past did freely make large, simple statements, and not in their prosy or lax moments.

Mr. Muller then goes on to illustrate by quoting three famous large, simple statements:

> In la sua voluntade e nostra pace

and

> We are such stuff
> As dreams are made on; and our little lives
> Are rounded with a sleep.

and

> The mind is its own place, and in itself
> Can make a heaven of hell, a hell of heaven.

Mr. Muller is here attacking the critical emphasis on ironic tension in poetry. His attack really involves two lines of argument. First, the poet is not wiser than the statesman, philosopher, or saint, people who are eloquent about faith and ideals and who say what they mean, without benefit of irony. This Platonic (or pseudo-Platonic) line of argument is, I think, off the point in the present context. Second, the poets of the past have made large, simple affirmations, have said what they meant. This line of argument is very much on the point.

Poets *have* tried very hard, for thousands of years, to say what they mean. But they have not only tried to say what they mean, they have tried to prove what they mean. The saint proves his vision by stepping cheerfully into the fires. The poet, somewhat less spectacularly, proves his vision by submitting it to the fires of irony—to the drama of his structure—in the hope that the fires will refine it. In other words, the poet wishes to indicate that his vision has been earned, that it can survive reference to the complexities and contradictions of experience. And irony is one such device of reference.

In this connection let us look at the first of Mr. Muller's exhibits. The famous line occurs in Canto III of the *Paradiso*. It is spoken by Piccarda Donati, in answer to Dante's question as to why she does not desire to rise higher than her present sphere, the sphere of the moon. But it expresses, in unequivocal terms, a central theme of the *Commedia*, as of Christian experience. On the one hand, it may be a pious truism, fit for sampler work, and on the other hand, it may be a burning conviction, tested and earned. Dante, in his poem, sets out to show how it has been earned and tested. One set of ironic tensions, for instance, which centers about this theme concerns the opposition between the notion of human justice and the notion of divine justice. The story of Paolo and Francesca is so warm, appealing, and pathetic in its human terms and their punishment so savage and unrelenting, so incommensurable, it seems, with the fault, that Dante, torn by the conflict, falls down as a dead body falls. Or Farinata, the enemy of Dante's house, is presented by the poet in terms of his human grandeur, which now, in Hell, is transmuted into a superhuman grandeur,

> com' avesse l'inferno in gran dispitto.

Ulysses remains a hero, a hero who should draw special applause from Dante, who defined the temporal end of man as the conquest of knowledge. But Ulysses is damned, as the great Brutus is damned, who hangs from the jaws of the fiend in the lowest pit of traitors. So divine justice is set over against human pathos, human dignity, human grandeur, human intellect, human justice. And we recall how Virgil, more than once, reminds Dante that he must not apply human standards to the sights he sees. It is this long conflict, which appears in many forms, this ironic tension, which finally gives body to the simple eloquence of the line in question; the statement is meaningful, not for what it says, but for what has gone before. It is earned. It has been earned by the entire poem.

I do not want to misrepresent Mr. Muller. He does follow his quotations by the sentence: "If they are properly qualified in the work as a whole, they may still be taken straight, they *are* [he italicizes the word] taken so in recollection as in their immediate impact." But can this line be taken so in recollection, and was it taken so in its "immediate impact"? And if one does take it so, is he not violating, very definitely, the poet's meaning, for the poet means the *poem*, he doesn't mean the line.

It would be interesting to try to develop the contexts of the other passages which Mr. Muller quotes. But in any case, he was simply trying, in his essay, to guard against what he considered to be, rightly or wrongly, a too narrow description of poetry; he was not trying to legislate all poetry into the type of simple eloquence, the unqualified statement of "faith and ideas." But we have already witnessed certain, probably preliminary, attempts to legislate literature into becoming a simple, unqualified, "pure" statement of faith and ideal. We have seen the writers of the 1920s called the "irresponsibles." We have seen writers such a Proust, Eliot, Dreiser, and Faulkner, called writers of the "death drive." Why are these writers condemned? Because they have tried, within the limits of their gifts, to remain faithful to the complexities of the problems with which they were dealing, because they refused to take the easy statement as solution, because they tried to define the context in which, and the terms by which, faith and ideals could be earned. But this method will scarcely satisfy the mind which is hot for certainties; to that mind it will seem merely an index to lukewarmness, indecision,

disunity, treason. The new theory of purity would purge out all complexities and all ironies and all self-criticism. And this theory will forget
that the hand-me-down faith, the hand-me-down ideals, no matter what
the professed content, is in the end not only meaningless but vicious. It
is vicious because, as parody, it is the enemy of all faith.

1. It may be objected here that I am reading the phrase "in my arms" as a twentieth century reader. I
confess the fact. Certainly, several centuries have passed since the composition of the little poem, and
those centuries have thickened the romantic mist about the words, but it is scarcely to be believed that
the sixteenth century was the clear, literal Eden dawn of poetry when words walked without the fig leaf.

2. In connection with the word *my* in this line, we may also feel that it helps to set over the comfort and satisfaction there specified against the bad weather of the first two lines. We may also glance at
the word *small* in the second line. It is the scrupulous word, the word that, realistically, makes us believe
in the rain. But, too, it is broader in its function. The storm which the lover invokes will not rend the
firmament, it will not end the world; it will simply bring down the "small" rain, a credible rain.

3. It might be profitable, in contrast with this poem, to analyze *After the Burial*, by James Russell
Lowell, a poem which is identical in situation. But in Lowell's poem the savagery of the irony is
unqualified. In fact, the whole poem insists, quite literally, that qualification is impossible: the
scheme of the poem is to set up the brute fact of death against possible consolations. It insists on
"tears," the "thin-worn locket," the "anguish of deathless hair," "the smallness of the child's grave,"
the "little shoe in the corner." It is a poem which, we might say, does not progress, but ends where it
begins, resting in the savage irony from which it stems; or we might say that it is a poem without any
"insides" for the hero of the poem is not attempting to do anything about the problem which confronts
him—it is a poem without issue, without conflict, a poem of unconditional surrender. In other words,
it tries to be a pure poem, pure grief, absolutely inconsolable. It is a strident poem, and strident in its
rhythms. The fact that we know this poem to be an expression of a bereavement historically real
makes it an embarrassing poem, as well. It is a naked poem.

4. Samuel Holt Monk: *The Sublime: a Study of Critical Theories in XVIII-Century England*, and
T. R. Henn: *Longinus and English Criticism*.

5. F. W. Bateson, in *English Poetry and the English Language*, discusses the impulse in contemporary poetry. Tennyson, he points out in connection with *The Sailor Boy*, dilutes his poetry
by telling a story as well as writing a poem, and "a shorter poem would have spoilt his story." The
claims of prose conquer the claims of poetry. Of the Victorians in general: "The dramatic and
narrative framework of their poems, by circumventing the disconcerting plunges into *medias res*
which are the essence of poetry, brings it down to a level of prose. The reader knows where he is; it
serves the purpose of introduction and note." Such introduction and notes in the body of the poem
itself are exactly what Mr. Pottle says is missing in Elliptical Poetry. Mr. Bateson agrees with Poe in
accepting intensity as the criterion of the poetic effect, and in accepting the corollary that a poem
should be short. But he, contradicting Poe, seems to admire precise and complicated incidental effects.

6. Several other difficulties concerning Mr. Pottle's statement may suggest themselves. First, since
he seems to infer that the poetic essence resides in the image, what view would he take of meter and
rhythm? His statement, strictly construed, would mean that these factors do not participate in the
poetic effect, but are simply part of the frame. Second, what view of dramatic poetry is implied? It
seems again that a strict interpretation would mean that the story and the images bear no essential
relation to each other, that the story is simply part of the frame. That is, the story, characters, rhythms,
and ideas, are on one level and the images, in which the poetry inheres, are on another. But Miss
Spurgeon, Mr. Knight, and other critics have given us some reason for holding that the images do
bear some relation to the business of the other items. In fact, all of the items, as M. Maritain has
said, "feelings, ideas, representations, are for the artist merely materials and means, still symbols."
That is, they are all elements in a single expressive structure.

7. Such an interpretation seems to find a parallel in E. M. Forster's treatment of plot in fiction.
Plot in his theory becomes a mere spine and does not really participate, except in a narrow, formal
sense, in the fictional effect. By his inversion of the Aristotelian principle, the plot becomes merely a
necessary evil.

THE OBJECTIVE CORRELATIVE

Hamlet and His Problems

T. S. ELIOT

In this essay from The Sacred Wood (1920), *Eliot introduced the "objective correlative" as a critical term, as well as one of his most provocative critical judgments: that Shakespeare's* Hamlet *is an artistic failure.*

Few critics have even admitted that *Hamlet* the play is the primary problem, and Hamlet the character only secondary. And Hamlet the character has had an especial temptation for that most dangerous type of critic: the critic with a mind which is naturally of the creative order, but which through some weakness in creative power exercises itself in criticism instead. These minds often find in Hamlet a vicarious existence for their own artistic realization. Such a mind had Goethe, who made of Hamlet a Werther; and such had Coleridge, who made of Hamlet a Coleridge; and probably neither of these men in writing about Hamlet remembered that his first business was to study a work of art. The kind of criticism that Goethe and Coleridge produced, in writing of Hamlet, is the most misleading kind possible. For they both possessed unquestionable critical insight, and both make their critical aberrations the more plausible by the substitution — of their own Hamlet for Shakespeare's — which their creative gift effects. We should be thankful that Walter Pater did not fix his attention on this play.

Two recent writers, Mr. J. M. Robertson and Professor Stoll of the University of Minnesota, have issued small books which can be praised for moving in the other direction. Mr. Stoll performs a service in recalling to our attention the labors of the critics of the seventeenth and eighteenth centuries,[1] observing that

> they knew less about psychology than more recent Hamlet critics, but they were nearer in spirit to Shakespeare's art; and as they insisted on the importance of the effect of the whole rather than on the importance of the leading character, they were nearer, in their old-fashioned way, to the secret of dramatic art in general.

Qua work of art, the work of art cannot be interpreted; there is nothing to interpret; we can only criticize it according to standards, in comparison to other works of art; and for "interpretation" the chief task is the presentation of relevant historical facts which the reader is not assumed to know. Mr. Robertson points out, very pertinently, how critics have failed in their "interpretation" of *Hamlet* by ignoring what ought to be very obvious; that *Hamlet* is a stratification, that it represents the efforts of a series of men, each making what he could out of the work of his predecessors. The *Hamlet* of Shakespeare will appear to us very differently if, instead of treating the whole action of the play as due to Shakespeare's design, we perceive his *Hamlet* to be superposed upon much cruder material which persists even in the final form.

We know that there was an older play by Thomas Kyd, that extraordinary dramatic (if not poetic) genius who was in all probability the author of two plays so dissimilar as *The Spanish Tragedy* and *Arden of Feversham*; and what this play was like we can guess from three clues: from *The Spanish Tragedy* itself, from the tale of Belleforest upon which Kyd's *Hamlet* must have been based, and from a version acted in Germany in Shakespeare's lifetime which bears strong evidence of having been adapted from the earlier, not from the later, play. From these three sources it is clear that in the earlier play the motive was a revenge-motive simply; that the action or delay is caused, as in *The Spanish Tragedy*, solely by the difficulty of assassinating a monarch surrounded by guards; and that the "madness" of Hamlet was feigned in order to escape suspicion, and successfully. In the final play of Shakespeare, on the other hand, there is a motive which is more important than that of revenge, and which explicitly "blunts" the latter; the delay in revenge is unexplained on grounds of necessity or expediency; and the effect of the "madness" is not to lull but to arouse the king's suspicion. The alteration is not complete enough, however, to be convincing. Furthermore, there are verbal parallels so close to *The Spanish Tragedy* as to leave no doubt that in places Shakespeare was merely revising the text of Kyd. And finally there are unexplained scenes—the Polonius-Laertes and the Polonius-Reynaldo scenes—for which there is little excuse; these scenes are not in the verse style of Kyd, and not beyond doubt in the style of Shakespeare. These Mr. Robertson believes to be scenes in the original play of Kyd reworked by a third hand, perhaps Chapman, before Shakespeare touched the play. And he concludes, with very strong show of reason, that the original play of Kyd was, like certain other revenge plays, in two parts of five acts each. The upshot of Mr. Robertson's examination is, we believe, irrefragable: that Shakespeare's *Hamlet*, so far as it is Shakespeare's, is a play dealing with the effect of a mother's guilt upon her son, and that Shakespeare was unable to impose this motive successfully upon the "intractable" material of the old play.

Of the intractability there can be no doubt. So far from being Shakespeare's masterpiece, the play is most certainly an artistic failure. In several ways the play is puzzling, and disquieting as is none of the others. Of all the plays it is the longest and is possibly the one on which Shakespeare spent most pains; and yet he has left in it superfluous and inconsistent scenes which even hasty revision should have noticed. The versification is variable. Lines like

> Look, the morn, in russet mantle clad,
> Walks o'er the dew of yon high eastern hill,

are of the Shakespeare of *Romeo and Juliet*. The lines in Act v. sc. ii,

> Sir, in my heart there was a kind of fighting
> That would not let me sleep . . .
> Up from my cabin,
> My sea-gown scarf'd about me, in the dark
> Grop'd I to find out them: had my desire;
> Finger'd their packet;

are of his quite mature. Both workmanship and thought are in an unstable condition. We are surely justified in attributing the play, with that other profoundly interesting play of "intractable" material and astonishing versification, *Measure for Measure*, to a period of crisis, after which follow the tragic successes which culminate in *Coriolanus*. *Coriolanus* may be not as "interesting" as *Hamlet*, but it is, with *Antony and Cleopatra*, Shakespeare's most assured artistic success. And probably more people have thought *Hamlet* a work of art because they found it interesting, than have found it interesting because it is a work of art. It is the "Mona Lisa" of literature.

The grounds of *Hamlet*'s failure are not immediately obvious. Mr. Robertson is undoubtedly correct in concluding that the essential emotion of the play is the feeling of a son towards a guilty mother:

> [Hamlet's] tone is that of one who has suffered tortures on the score of his mother's degradation. . . . The guilt of a mother is an almost intolerable motive for drama, but it had to be maintained and emphasized to supply a psychological solution, or rather a hint of one.

This, however, is by no means the whole story. It is not merely the "guilt of a mother" that cannot be handled as Shakespeare handled the suspicion of Othello, the infatuation of Antony, or the pride of Coriolanus. The subject might conceivably have expanded into a tragedy like these, intelligible, self-complete, in the sunlight. *Hamlet*, like the sonnets, is full of some stuff that the writer could not drag to light, contemplate, or manipulate into art. And when we search for this feeling, we find it, as in the sonnets, very difficult to localize. You cannot point to it in the speeches; indeed, if you examine the two famous soliloquies you see the versification of Shakespeare, but a content which might be claimed by another, perhaps by the author of the *Revenge of Bussy d'Ambois*, Act v. sc. i. We find Shakespeare's *Hamlet* not in the action, not in any quotations that we might select, so much as in an unmistakable tone which is unmistakably not in the earlier play.

The only way of expressing emotion in the form of art is by finding an "objective correlative"; in other words, a set of objects, a situation, a chain of events which shall be the formula of that *particular* emotion; such that when the external facts, which must terminate in sensory experience, are given, the emotion is immediately evoked. If you examine any of Shakespeare's more successful tragedies, you will find this exact equivalence; you will find that the state of mind of Lady Macbeth walking in her sleep has been communicated to you by a skilful accumulation of imagined sensory impressions; the words of Macbeth on hearing of his wife's death strike us as if, given the sequence of events, these words were automatically released by the last event in the series. The artistic "inevitability" lies in this complete adequacy of the external to the emotion; and this is precisely what is deficient in *Hamlet*. Hamlet (the man) is dominated by an emotion which is inexpressible, because it is in excess of the facts as they appear. And the supposed identity of Hamlet with his author is genuine to this point: that Hamlet's bafflement at the absence of objective equivalent to his feelings is a prolongation of the bafflement of his creator in the face of his artistic problem. Hamlet is up against the difficulty that his disgust is occasioned by his mother, but that his mother is not an adequate equivalent for it; his disgust envelops and exceeds her. It is thus a feeling which he cannot understand; he cannot objectify it, and it therefore remains to poison life and obstruct action. None of the possible actions can satisfy it; and nothing that Shakespeare can do with the plot can express Hamlet for him. And it must be noticed that the very nature of the *données* of the problem precludes objective equivalence. To have heightened the criminality of Gertrude would have been to provide the formula for a totally different emotion in Hamlet; it is just because her character is so negative and insignificant that she arouses in Hamlet the feeling which she is incapable of representing.

The "madness" of Hamlet lay to Shakespeare's hand; in the earlier play a simple ruse, and to the end, we may presume, understood as a ruse by the audience. For Shakespeare it is less than madness and more than feigned. The levity of Hamlet, his repetition of phrase, his puns, are not part of a deliberate plan of dissimulation, but a form of emotional relief. In the character Hamlet it is the buffoonery of an emotion which can find no outlet in action; in the dramatist it is the buffoonery of an emotion which he cannot express in art. The intense feeling, ecstatic or terrible, without an object or exceeding its object, is something which every person of sensibility has known; it is doubtless a study to pathologists. It often occurs in adolescence: the ordinary person puts these feelings to sleep, or trims down his feeling to fit the business world; the artist keeps it alive by his ability to intensify the world to his emotions. The Hamlet of Laforgue is an adolescent; the Hamlet of Shakespeare is not, he has not that explanation and excuse. We must simply admit that here Shakespeare tackled a problem which proved too much for him. Why he attempted it at all is an insoluble puzzle; under compulsion of what experience he attempted to express the inexpressibly horrible, we cannot ever know. We need a great many facts in his biography; and we should like to know whether, and when, and after or at the same time as what personal experience, he read Montaigne, II. xii., *Apologie de Raimond Sebond*. We should have, finally, to know something which is by hypothesis unknowable, for we assume it to be an experience which, in the manner indicated, exceeded the facts. We should have to understand things which Shakespeare did not understand himself.

1. I have never, by the way, seen a cogent refutation of Thomas Rymer's objections to *Othello*.

The Metaphysical Poets

T. S. ELIOT

Originally published in the Times Literary Supplement *in 1921, and therefore not included in* The Sacred Wood, *this essay elevated Donne to his central place in the modernist canon; it also introduced the idea of the "dissociation of sensibility" to explain why the methods of the metaphysical poets should be preferred to their Romantic successors. Eliot here, in hailing Donne and his ilk, justified and promoted the difficult poetry of modernism to his generation.*

By collecting these poems[1] from the work of a generation more often named than read, and more often read than profitably studied, Professor Grierson has rendered a service of some importance. Certainly the reader will meet with many poems already preserved in other anthologies, at the same time that he discovers poems such as those of Aurelian Townshend or Lord Herbert of Cherbury here included. But the function of such an anthology as this is neither that of Professor Saintsbury's admirable edition of Caroline poets nor that of the *Oxford Book of English Verse*. Mr. Grierson's book is in itself a piece of criticism and a provocation of criticism; and we think that he was right in including so many poems of Donne, elsewhere (though not in many editions) accessible, as documents in the case of "metaphysical poetry." The phrase has long done duty as a term of abuse or as the label of a quaint and pleasant taste. The question is to what extent the so-called metaphysicals formed a school (in our own time we should say a "movement"), and how far this so-called school or movement is a digression from the main current.

Not only is it extremely difficult to define metaphysical poetry, but difficult to decide what poets practice it and in which of their verses. The poetry of Donne (to whom Marvell and Bishop King are sometimes nearer than any of the other authors) is late Elizabethan, its feeling often very close to that of Chapman. The "courtly" poetry is derivative from Jonson, who borrowed liberally from the Latin; it expires in the next century with the sentiment and witticism of Prior. There is finally the devotional verse of Herbert, Vaughan, and Crashaw (echoed long after by Christina Rossetti and Francis Thompson); Crashaw, sometimes more profound and less sectarian than the others, has a quality which returns through the Elizabethan period to the early Italians. It is difficult to find any precise use of metaphor, simile, or other conceit, which is common to all the poets and at the same time important enough as an element of style to isolate these poets as a group. Donne, and often Cowley, employ a device which is sometimes considered characteristically "metaphysical"; the elaboration (contrasted with the condensation) of a figure of speech to the farthest stage to which ingenuity can carry it. Thus Cowley develops the commonplace comparison of the world to a chess-board through long stanzas (*To Destiny*), and Donne, with more grace, in A *Valediction*, the comparison of two lovers to a pair of compasses. But elsewhere we find, instead of the mere explication of the content of a comparison, a development by rapid association of thought which requires considerable agility on the part of the reader.

> On a round ball
> A workeman that hath copies by, can lay
> An Europe, Afrique, and an Asia,
> And quickly make that, which was nothing, *All*,
> > So doth each teare,
> > Which thee doth weare,
> A globe, yea, world by that impression grow,
> Till thy tears mixt with mine doe overflow

> This world, by waters sent from thee, my heaven dissolved so.

Here we find at least two connections which are not implicit in the first figure, but are forced upon it by the poet: from the geographer's globe to the tear, and the tear to the deluge. On the other hand, some of Donne's most successful and characteristic effects are secured by brief words and sudden contrasts:

> A bracelet of bright hair about the bone,

where the most powerful effect is produced by the sudden contrast of associations of "bright hair" and of "bone." This telescoping of images and multiplied associations is characteristic of the phrase of some of the dramatists of the period which Donne knew; not to mention Shakespeare, it is frequent in Middleton, Webster, and Tourneur, and is one of the sources of the vitality of their language.

Johnson, who employed the term "metaphysical poets," apparently having Donne, Cleveland, and Cowley chiefly in mind, remarks of them that "the most heterogeneous ideas are yoked by violence together." The force of this impeachment lies in the failure of the conjunction, the fact that often the ideas are yoked but not united; and if we are to judge of styles of poetry by their abuse, enough examples may be found in Cleveland to justify Johnson's condemnation. But a degree of heterogeneity of material compelled into unity by the operation of the poet's mind is omnipresent in poetry. We need not select for illustration such a line as:

Notre âme est un trois-mâts cherchant son Icarie;

we may find it in some of the best lines of Johnson himself *(The Vanity of Human Wishes)*:

His fate was destined to a barren strand,
A petty fortress, and a dubious hand;
He left a name at which the world grew pale,
To point a moral, or adorn a tale—

where the effect is due to a contrast of ideas, different in degree but the same in principle, as that which Johnson mildly reprehended. And in one of the finest poems of the age (a poem which could not have been written in any other age), the *Exequy* of Bishop King, the extended comparison is used with perfect success: the idea and the simile become one, in the passage in which the Bishop illustrates his impatience to see his dead wife, under the figure of a journey:

Stay for me there; I will not faile
To meet thee in that hollow Vale.
And think not much of my delay;
I am already on the way,
And follow thee with all the speed
Desire can make, or sorrows breed.
Each minute is a short degree,
And ev'ry houre a step towards thee.
At night when I betake to rest,
Next morn I rise nearer my West
Of life, almost by eight houres sail,
Than when sleep breath'd his drowsy gale. . .
But heark! My Pulse, like a soft Drum

> Beats my approach, tells Thee I come;
> And slow howere my marches be,
> I shall at last sit down by Thee.

(In the last few lines there is that effect of terror which is several times attained by one of Bishop King's admirers, Edgar Poe.) Again, we may justly take these quatrains from Lord Herbert's Ode, stanzas which would, we think, be immediately pronounced to be of the metaphysical school:

> So when from hence we shall be gone,
>   And be no more, nor you, nor I,
>   As one another's mystery,
> Each shall be both, yet both but one.
>
> This said, in her up-lifted face,
>   Her eyes, which did that beauty crown,
>   Were like two starrs, that having faln down,
> Look up again to find their place:
>
> While such a moveless silent peace
>   Did seize on their becalmed sense,
>   One would have thought some influence
> Their ravished spirits did possess.

There is nothing in these lines (with the possible exception of the stars, a simile not at once grasped, but lovely and justified) which fits Johnson's general observations on the metaphysical poets in his essay on Cowley. A good deal resides in the richness of association which is at the same time borrowed from and given to the word "becalmed"; but the meaning is clear, the language simple and elegant. It is to be observed that the language of these poets is as a rule simple and pure; in the verse of George Herbert this simplicity is carried as far as it can go—a simplicity emulated without success by numerous modern poets. The *structure* of the sentences, on the other hand, is sometimes far from simple, but this is not a vice; it is a fidelity to thought and feeling. The effect, at its best, is far less artificial than that of an ode by Gray. And as this fidelity induces variety of thought and feeling, so it induces variety of music. We doubt whether, in the eighteenth century, could be found two poems in nominally the same meter, so dissimilar as Marvell's *Coy Mistress* and Crashaw's *Saint Teresa*; the one producing an effect of great speed by the use of short syllables, and the other an ecclesiastical solemnity by the use of long ones:

> Love, thou art absolute sole lord
> Of life and death.

If so shrewd and sensitive (though so limited) a critic as Johnson failed to define metaphysical poetry by its faults, it is worth while to inquire whether we may not have more success by adopting the opposite method: by assuming that the poets of the seventeenth century (up to the Revolution) were the direct and normal development of the precedent age; and, without prejudicing their case by the adjective "metaphysical," consider whether their virtue was not something permanently valuable, which subsequently disappeared, but ought not to have disappeared. Johnson has hit, perhaps by accident, on one of their peculiarities, when he observes that "their attempts were always analytic"; he would not agree that, after the dissociation, they put the material together again in a new unity.

It is certain that the dramatic verse of the later Elizabethan and early Jacobean poets expresses a degree of development of sensibility which is not found in any of the prose, good as it often is. If we except Marlowe, a man of prodigious intelligence, these dramatists were directly or indirectly (it is at least a tenable theory) affected by Montaigne. Even if we except also Jonson and Chapman, these two were notably erudite, and were notably men who incorporated their erudition into their sensibility: their mode of feeling was directly and freshly altered by their reading and thought. In Chapman especially there is a direct sensuous apprehension of thought, or a re-creation of thought into feeling, which is exactly what we find in Donne:

> . . . in this one thing, all the discipline
> Of manners and of manhood is contained;
> A man to join himself with th' Universe
> In his main sway, and make in all things fit
> One with that All, and go on, round as it;
> Not plucking from the whole his wretched part,
> And into straits, or into nought revert,
> Wishing the complete Universe might be
> Subject to such a rag of it as he;
> But to consider great Necessity.

We compare this with some modern passage:

> No, when the fight begins within himself,
> A man's worth something. God stoops o'er his head,

> Satan looks up between his feet—both tug—
> He's left, himself, i' the middle; the soul wakes
> And grows. Prolong that battle through his life!

It is perhaps somewhat less fair, though very tempting (as both poets are concerned with the perpetuation of love by offspring), to compare with the stanzas already quoted from Lord Herbert's Ode the following from Tennyson:

> One walked between his wife and child,
> With measured footfall firm and mild,
> And now and then he gravely smiled.
>
> The prudent partner of his blood
> Leaned on him, faithful, gentle, good,
> Wearing the rose of womanhood.
>
> And in their double love secure,
> The little maiden walked demure,
> Pacing with downward eyelids pure.
>
> These three made unity so sweet,
> My frozen heart began to beat,
> Remembering its ancient beat.

The difference is not a simple difference of degree between poets. It is something which had happened to the mind of England between the time of Donne or Lord Herbert of Cherbury and the time of Tennyson and Browning; it is the difference between the intellectual poet and the reflective poet. Tennyson and Browning are poets, and they think; but they do not feel their thought as immediately as the odor of a rose. A thought to Donne was an experience; it modified his sensibility. When a poet's mind is perfectly equipped for its work, it is constantly amalgamating disparate experience; the ordinary man's experience is chaotic, irregular, fragmentary. The latter falls in love, or reads Spinoza, and these two experiences have nothing to do with each other, or with the noise of the typewriter or the smell of cooking; in the mind of the poet these experiences are always forming new wholes.

We may express the difference by the following theory: The poets of the seventeenth century, the successors of the dramatists of the sixteenth, possessed a mechanism of sensibility which could devour any kind of experience. They are simple, artificial, difficult, or fantastic, as their predecessors were; no less nor more than Dante, Guido Cavalcanti, Guinizelli, or Cino. In the seventeenth century a dissociation of sensibility set in, from which we have never recovered; and this dissociation, as is natural, was aggravated by the influence of the two most powerful poets of the century, Milton and Dryden. Each of these men performed certain poetic functions so magnificently well that the magnitude of the effect concealed the absence of others. The language went on and in some respects improved; the best verse of Collins, Gray, Johnson, and even Goldsmith satisfies some of our fastidious demands better than that of Donne or Marvell or King. But while the language became more refined, the feeling became more crude. The feeling, the sensibility, expressed in the *Country Churchyard* (to say nothing of Tennyson and Browning) is cruder than that in the *Coy Mistress*.

The second effect of the influence of Milton and Dryden followed from the first, and was therefore slow in manifestation. The sentimental age began early in the eighteenth century, and continued. The poets revolted against the ratiocinative, the descriptive; they thought and felt by fits, unbalanced; they reflected. In one or two passages of Shelley's *Triumph of Life*, in the second *Hyperion*, there are traces of a struggle toward unification of sensibility. But Keats and Shelley died, and Tennyson and Browning ruminated.

After this brief exposition of a theory—too brief, perhaps, to carry conviction—we may ask, what would have been the fate of the "metaphysical" had the current of poetry descended in a direct line from them, as it descended in a direct line to them? They would not, certainly, be classified as metaphysical. The possible interests of a poet are unlimited; the more intelligent he is the better; the more intelligent he is the more likely that he will have interests: our only condition is that he turn them into poetry, and not merely meditate on them poetically. A philosophical theory which has entered into poetry is established, for its truth or falsity in one sense ceases to matter, and its truth in another sense is proved. The poets in question have, like other poets, various faults. But they were, at best, engaged in the task of trying to find the verbal equivalent for states of mind and feeling. And this means both that they are more mature, and that they wear better, than later poets of certainly not less literary ability.

It is not a permanent necessity that poets should be interested in philosophy, or in any other subject. We can only say that it appears likely that poets in our civilization, as it exists at present, must be *difficult*. Our civilization comprehends great variety and complexity, and this variety and complexity, playing upon a refined sensibility, must produce various and complex results. The poet must become more and more comprehensive, more allusive, more indirect, in order to force, to dislocate if necessary, language into his meaning. (A brilliant and extreme statement of this view, with which it is not requisite to associate oneself, is that of M. Jean Epstein, *La Poésie d'aujourd'hui.*) Hence we get something which looks very much like the conceit—we get, in fact, a method curiously similar to that of the "metaphysical poets," similar also in its use of obscure words and of simple phrasing.

> O géraniums diaphanes, guerroyeurs sortilèges,
> Sacrilèges monomanes!
> Emballages, dévergondages, douches! O pressoirs
> Des vendanges des grands soirs!
> Layettes aux abois,
> Thyrses au fond des bois!
> Transfusions, représailles,
> Relevailles, compresses et l'éternal potion.
> Angélus! n'en pouvoir plus
> De débâcles nuptiales! de débâcles nuptiales!

The same poet could write also simply:

> Elle est bien loin, elle pleure,
> Le grand vent se lamente aussi . . .

Jules Laforgue, and Tristan Corbière in many of his poems, are nearer to the "school of Donne" than any modern English poet. But poets more classical than they have the same essential quality of transmuting ideas into sensations, of transforming an observation into a state of mind.

> Pour l'enfant, amoureux de cartes et d'estampes,
> L'univers égal à son vaste appétit.
> Ah, que le monde est grand à la clarté des lampes!
> Aux yeux du souvenir que le monde est petit!

In French literature the great master of the seventeenth century—Racine—and the great master of the nineteenth—Baudelaire—are in some ways more like each other than they are like any one else. The greatest two masters of diction are also the greatest two psychologists, the most curious explorers of the soul. It is interesting to speculate whether it is not a misfortune that two of the greatest masters of diction in our language, Milton and Dryden, triumph with a dazzling disregard of the soul. If we continued to produce Miltons and Drydens it might not so much matter, but as things are it is a pity that English poetry has remained so incomplete. Those who object to the "artificiality" of Milton or Dryden sometimes tell us to "look into our hearts and write." But that is not looking deep enough; Racine or Donne looked into a good deal more than the heart. One must look into the cerebral cortex, the nervous system, and the digestive tracts.

May we not conclude, then, that Donne, Crashaw, Vaughan, Herbert and Lord Herbert, Marvell, King, Cowley at his best, are in the direct current of English poetry, and that their faults should be reprimanded by this standard rather than coddled by antiquarian affection? They have been enough praised in terms which are implicit limitations because they are "metaphysical" or "witty," "quaint" or "obscure," though at their best they have not these attributes more than other serious poets. On the other hand, we must not reject the criticism of Johnson (a dangerous person to disagree with) without having mastered it, without having assimilated the Johnsonian canons of taste. In reading the celebrated passage in his essay on Cowley we must remember that by wit he clearly means something more serious than we usually mean today; in his criticism of their versification we must remember in what a narrow discipline he was trained, but also how well trained; we must remember that Johnson tortures chiefly the chief offenders, Cowley and Cleveland. It would be a fruitful work, and one requiring a substantial book, to break up the classification of Johnson (for there has been none since) and exhibit these poets in all their difference of kind and of degree, from the massive music of Donne to the faint, pleasing tinkle of Aurelian Townshend—whose *Dialogue Between a Pilgrim and Time* is one of the few regrettable omissions from the excellent anthology of Professor Grierson.

1. *Metaphysical Lyrics and Poems of the Seventeeth Century: Donne to Butler*. Selected and edited, with an Essay, by Herbert J. C. Grierson (Oxford: Clarendon Press. London; Milford).

The Isolation of Modern Poetry

DELMORE SCHWARTZ

In this essay, originally published in the Kenyon Review *in 1941, Schwartz argues that, as modern poets have become isolated individuals without a function in industrial societies, their poetry has become more obscure and narrowly focused on their own lives. Schwartz also explains why modern poetry is always lyric poetry, while narrative and dramatic verse have almost disappeared.*

The characteristic of modern poetry which is most discussed is of course its difficulty, its famous obscurity. Certain discussions, usually by contemporary poets, have done much to illuminate the new methods and forms of contemporary poetry. Certain other discussions have illustrated an essential weakness inherent in all readers, the fact that the love of one kind of writing must often interfere with the understanding of another kind. Wordsworth was undoubtedly thinking of this weakness when he wrote, in his justly well-known preface, that

> It is supposed that by the act of writing in verse an Author makes a formal engagement that he will gratify certain known habits of association; that he not only apprises the reader that certain classes of ideas and expression will be found in his book, but that others will be carefully excluded.

This seems to me to be a perfect statement of the first barrier which intervenes between the reader and any kind of writing with which he is not familiar. But it is far from being sufficient as a defense of modern poetry. Wordsworth was engaged in defending his poetry against the habitual expectations of the reader accustomed to Dryden, Pope, and Johnson. It is necessary now to defend the modern poet against the reader accustomed to Wordsworth. The specific difference between such a poet as Wordsworth and the typical modern poet requires a specific explanation.

There is another defense of the modern poet which seems utterly insufficient to me. It is said that the modern poet must be complex because modern life is complicated. This is the view of Mr. T. S. Eliot, among others. "It appears likely," he says, "that poets in our civilization, as it exists at present, must be *difficult*. Our civilization comprehends great variety and complexity, and this variety and complexity, playing upon a refined sensibility, must produce various and complex results." Mr. Eliot's explanation seems to me not so much wrong as superficial. I need hardly say that Mr. Eliot is seldom superficial in any regard; here, however, I think he is identifying the surface of our civilization with the surface of our poetry. But the complexity of modern life, the disorder of the traffic on a business street or the variety of reference in the daily newspaper is far from being the same thing as the difficulties of syntax, tone, diction, metaphor, and allusion which face the reader in the modern poem. If one is the product of the other, the causal sequence involves a number of factors on different levels, and to imply, as I think Mr. Eliot does, that there is a simple causal relationship between the disorder of modern life and the difficulty of modern poetry is merely to engender misunderstanding by oversimplification.

Now obscurity is merely one of the peculiar aspects of modern poetry. There are others which are just as important. Nothing could be more peculiar than the fact that modern poetry is lyric poetry. Almost without exception there is a failure or an absence of narrative or dramatic writing in verse. With the possible exception of Hardy and Robinson, it is impossible to think of any modern poet who will be remembered for his writing in any form other than that of the lyric.

It is obvious by contrast that the major portion of the poetry of the past, of poetry until we reach the latter half of the 19th century, is narrative and dramatic as well as lyrical in its most important moments; and it is equally evident that all of that poetry is never obscure in the modern sense.

I need not mention further characteristics of modern poetry which co-exist with its obscurity and its limitation to the lyric form. The two characteristics seem to me to be closely related to each other and to spring from the essential condition of the modern poet. The way in which this condition, if that is the adequate word for what I mean, the way in which this essential circumstance affects the modern poet is a rather involved matter, but had better be stated bluntly and crudely at this point. The modern poet has been very much affected by the condition and the circumstance that he has been separated from the whole life of society. This separation has taken numerous forms and has increased continually. It is a separation which occurs with an uneven development in all the matters with which the modern poet must concern himself. Different poets have been differently affected, and their efforts to cope with this separation have been various. But there is a common denominator which points to a common cause.

The beginning of the process of separation, if one can rightly discern a beginning in such things, is the gradual destruction of the world-picture which, despite many changes, had for a long time been taken for granted by the poet. Amid much change, development, and modification, the Bible had provided a view of the universe which circumscribed the area in which anyone ventured to think, or use his imagination. It would of course be a serious mistake to suppose that this view of the universe had not been disturbed in numerous ways long before the modern poet arrived upon the scene. But it is doubtful if the poet before the time of Blake felt a conflict between two pictures of the world, the picture provided by the Bible and the one provided by the physical sciences.

In Blake's rage against Newton and Voltaire, in his interest, as a poet, in the doctrine of Swedenborg, and in his attempt to construct his own view of the universe, we come upon the first full example of this difficulty of the poet. There is a break between intellect and sensibility; the intellect finds unreasonable what the sensibility and the imagination cannot help but accept because of centuries of imagining and feeling in terms of definite images of the world. Milton's use of a Ptolemaic cosmology, though he knew that the Copernican one was mathematically superior, is an example from a still earlier period; it shows with exactitude the extent to which the poet depended upon the traditional world-picture of Western culture. After Blake, the Romantic poets are further instances; not only were they intensely interested in new conceptions of the world, new philosophies; but in turning to Nature as they did, they displayed their painful sense that the poet no longer belonged to the society into which he was born, and for which, presumably, he was writing his verse.

But these authors are not modern poets. And it was not until the middle of the 19th century that the progress of the physical sciences brought forth a body of knowledge which was in serious and open conflict with the picture of the world which had been in use for so long a time. This conflict had been going on, of course, for centuries, but it was not until we come to an occasion like the publication of the Darwinian theory that the conflict becomes so radical and so obvious that no poet of ambition can seriously avoid it. I am not referring to any conflict between religious doctrine and scientific knowledge, for this conflict, if it actually exists, is hardly the direct concern of the poet at any time. It is a question of the conflict between the sensibility of the poet, the very images which he viewed as the world, and the evolving and blank and empty universe of 19th century science.

The development of modern culture from Darwin and Huxley to Freud, Marx, and the author of *The Golden Bough*, has merely extended, hastened, and intensified this process of removing the picture of the world which the poet took for granted as the arena of his imagination, and putting in its place another world-picture which he could not use. This is illustrated broadly in the career of such a poet as Yeats. Hearing as a young man that man was descended from the ape, Yeats occupied himself for many years with theosophy, black magic, and the least respectable forms of psychical research, all in the effort to gain a view of the universe and of man which would restore dignity and importance to both man and the universe. We may invent an illustration at this point and suppose that when Yeats or any other modern poet of similar interests heard of how many million light years the known regions of the universe comprise, he felt a fundamental incongruity between his own sense of the importance of human lives and their physical smallness in the universe. This is merely a difficulty in *imagining*—one has an image of a very small being in an endless world; but that's just the point, the difficulty with images. The philosopher and the theologian know that size is not a particularly important aspect of any thing; but the poet must see, and what he has had to see was this incongruity between the importance man attributes to himself and his smallness against the background of the physical world of 19th century science.

Now this is only one aspect of the poet's isolation; it is the aspect in which the sensibility of the poet has been separated from the theoretical knowledge of his time. The isolation of the modern poet has, however, taken an even more difficult form, that of being separated by poetry from the rest of society. Here one must guard against a simple view of what this separation has amounted to in any particular context. It is not a simple matter of the poet lacking an audience, for that is an effect, rather than a cause, of the character of modern poetry. And it is not, on the other hand, the simple matter of the poet being isolated from the usual habits and customs and amusements of his time and place; for if this were the trouble, then the poet could perhaps be justly accused of retiring to his celebrated ivory tower; and it would then be quite reasonable to advise the poet as some have done: to tell him that he ought to get "experience," see the world, join a political party, make sure that he participates in the habitual activities of his society.

The fundamental isolation of the modern poet began not with the poet and his way of life; but rather with the whole way of life of modern society. It was not so much the poet as it was poetry, culture, sensibility, imagination, that were isolated. On the one hand, there was no room in the increasing industrialization of society for such a monster as the cultivated man; a man's taste for literature had at best nothing to do with most of the activities which constituted daily life in an industrial society. On the other hand, culture, since it could not find a place in modern life, has fed upon itself increasingly and has created its own autonomous satisfactions, removing itself further all the time from any essential part in the organic life of society.

Stated thus, this account may seem abstract and even implausible. It would be best before going further to mention certain striking evidences of what has taken place. There is, for instance, the classic American joke about how bored father is at the opera or the concert; the poet too has been an essentially comic figure, from time to time. But this homely instance may seem merely the product of vulgarity and lack of taste. A related tendency which has been much observed by foreigners is the belief in America that women were supposed to be interested in literature, culture, and "such things," while men had no time for such trivial delights because they were busy with what is called *business*. But this instance may seem local in that it is American and inconclusive since it has to do with the poet's audience rather than with the poet himself. There is then a third example, one which seems almost dramatic to me, the phenomenon of American authors of superior gifts going to Europe and staying there. Henry James is the most convincing case; one can scarcely doubt that he lived in Europe because there the divorce between culture and the rest of life, although it had begun, had by no means reached the point which was unavoidable in America. George Santayana, Ezra Pound, and T. S. Eliot are cases which come later in time; we do not know exactly why these men went to Europe; the significant fact is that they did not come back to America. I do not merely wish to suggest a critical view of the rôle of culture in American life, for the same process was occurring in Europe, though at a slower rate and with local modifications. The important point is the intuitive recognition on the part of both the artist and the rest of the population that culture and sensibility—and thus the works by means of which they sustained their existence—did not belong, did not fit into the essential workings of society.

At this point, it might be objected that culture has never played a very important part in the life of any society; it has only engaged the attention and devotion of the elect, who are always few in number. This view seems utterly false to me, and for the sake of showing briefly how false it has been historically, I quote one of the greatest living classical scholars on the part that dramatic tragedy played in the life of Periclean Athens. Werner Jaeger writes that

> After the state organized the dramatic performances held at the festival of Dionysus, tragedy more and more evoked the interest and participation of the entire people. . . . Its power over them was so vast that they held it responsible for the spirit of the whole state . . . it is no exaggeration to say that the tragic festival was the climax of the city's life. (*Paideia*, p. 245–246.)

No contrast could be more extreme than this one between the function of the Greek dramatist and that of the modern poet in their respective societies.

One significant effect of this divorce has been the poet's avowal of the doctrine of Art for Art's Sake, a doctrine which is meaningful only when viewed in the context in which it is always announced, that is, to repeat, a society which had no use and no need for Art, other than as a superfluous amusement or decoration. And another significant and related effect is the sentiment of the poet, and at times his convinced belief, that he has no connection with or allegiances to anything else. Nowhere is this belief stated with more clarity than in the following prose poem by Baudelaire, who in so many ways is either the first or the typical modern poet:

The Stranger

"Whom do you love most of all, enigmatic man, tell me? Your father, your mother, your brother, or your sister?"

"I have neither father, mother, brother, nor sister."

"Do you love your friends then?"

"You have just used a word whose meaning remains unknown to me to this very day."

"Do you love your country, then?"

"I ignore the latitude in which it is situated."

"Then do you love Beauty?"

"I love her with my whole will; she is a goddess and immortal."

"Do you love gold?"

"I hate it as you hate God."

"Well then: extraordinary stranger, what *do* you love?"

"I love the clouds . . . the clouds which pass . . . far away . . . far away . . . the marvelous clouds!"

It would be possible to take this stranger who is the modern poet with less seriousness, if he were merely affecting a pose, attempting to dramatize himself or be clever. The shocking passages in modern poetry have sometimes been understood in this way as Bohemianism, and the conventional picture or caricature of the poet has been derived from this Bohemianism, considered as a surface. But the sentiments which Baudelaire attributes to his stranger are the deepest feelings of the modern poet. He does feel that he is a stranger, an alien, an outsider; he finds himself without a father or mother, or he is separated from them by the opposition between his values as an artist and their values as respectable members of modern society. This opposition cannot be avoided because not a government subsidy, nor yearly prizes, nor a national academy can disguise the fact that there is no genuine place for the poet in modern life. He has no country, no community, insofar as he is a poet, and his greatest enemy is money, since poetry does not yield him a livelihood. It is natural then that he should emphasize his allegiance, his devotion to Beauty, that is to say, to the practice of Art and the works of art which already exist. And thus it is that Baudelaire's stranger announces that what he loves most of all is to look at the clouds, that is, to exercise his own sensibility. The modern poet has had nothing to do, no serious activity other than the cultivation of his own sensibility. There is a very famous passage in Walter Pater advising just this course.

From this standpoint, the two aspects of modern poetry which I marked at the start can be seen as natural and almost inevitable developments. In cultivating his own sensibility, the modern poet participated in a life which was removed from the lives of other men, who, insofar as they could be considered important characters, were engaged in cultivating money or building an industrial society. This it became increasingly impossible for the poet to write about the lives of other men; for not only was he removed from their lives, but, above all, the culture and the sensibility which made him a poet could not be employed when the proposed subject was the lives of human beings in whom culture and sensibility had no organic function. There have been unsuccessful efforts on the part of able poets to write about bankers and about railroad trains, and in such examples the poet has been confronted by what seems on the surface a technical problem, the extraordinary difficulty of employing poetic diction, meter, language, and metaphor in the contexts of modern life. It is not that contemporary people do not speak or think poetically; human beings at any time in general do not speak or think in ways which are immediately poetic, and if they did there would be no need for poetry. The trouble has been that the idiom of poetic style and the normal thought and speech of the community have been moving in opposite directions and have had little or no relationship to each other. The normal state of affairs occurs when poetry is continually digesting the prose of its time, and folk art and speech are providing sustenance for major literary efforts.

Since the only life available to the poet as a man of culture has been the cultivation of his own sensibility, that is the only subject available to him, if we may assume that a poet can only write about subjects of which he has an absorbing experience in every sense.[1] Thus we find that in much modern poetry, the poet is writing about other poetry, just as in modern painting the art works and styles of the past have so often become the painter's subject. For writing about other poetry and in general about works of art is the most direct way of grasping one's sensibility as a subject. But more than that, since one can only write about one's sensibility, one can only write lyric poetry. Dramatic and narrative poetry require a grasp of the lives of other men, and it is precisely these lives, to repeat, that are outside the orbit of poetic style and poetic sensibility. An analogous thing has, of necessity, happened in the history of the novel; the development of the autobiographical novel has resulted in part from the inability of the novelist to write about any one but himself or other people in relation to himself.

From this isolation of poetic sensibility the obscurity of modern poetry also arises. The poet is engaged in following the minutest movements, tones, and distinctions of his own being as a poetic man. Because this private life of his sensibility is the chief subject available to him, it becomes increasingly necessary to have recourse to new and special uses of language. The more the poet has cultivated his own sensibility, the more unique and special has his subject, and thus his method, become. The common language of daily life, its syntax, habitual sequences, and processes of association, are precisely the opposite of what he needs, if he is to make poetry from what absorbs him as a poet, his own sensibility.

Sometimes, indeed, the poet has taken this conflict between sensibility and modern life as his subject. The early fiction of Thomas Mann concerns itself repeatedly with the opposition between the artist and the bourgeoisie, and in such a story as "Tonio Kröger" we see the problem most explicitly; the artist feels at home nowhere and he suffers from an intense longing to be normal and bourgeois himself. Again, there is the famous device of modern poetry which was invented by Laforgue and used most successfully by T. S. Eliot, the ironic contrast between a past in which culture was an important part of life and the present in which the cultural monument sits next to vulgarity and insensitivity. This has been misunderstood very often as a yearning to go back to a past idyllically conceived. It is nothing of the kind; it is the poet's conscious experience of the isolation of culture from the rest of society.

I would like to cite one more instance of this condition. Four years ago one of the very best modern poets lectured and read his own poetry at Harvard. As a normal citizen, this man is an executive of an important corporation. It may reasonably be presumed that most of his writing is done on holidays and vacations. At the conclusion of his reading of his own poetry, this poet and business man remarked to one of the instructors who had welcomed him: "I wonder what the boys at the office would think of this."

But I have spoken throughout as if this isolation was in every sense a misfortune. It is certainly a misfortune so far as the life of the whole community is concerned; this is evident in the character of popular taste, in the kind of fiction, play, and movie which is successful, as compared with the popular authors of the 19th century, who were very often the best authors also. But on the other hand, it seems to me that the period of modern poetry, the age which begins with Baudelaire, is undoubtedly one in which the art of poetry has gained not only in the number of fine poets, but in technical resources of all kinds. If the enforced isolation of the poet has made dramatic and narrative poetry almost impossible, it has, on the other hand, increased the uses and powers of languages in the most amazing and the most valuable directions.

I have also spoken as if this isolation of the poet had already reached its conclusion. Whether it has or not, and whether it would be entirely desirable that it should, may be left as unanswered and perhaps unanswerable questions. It is true, at any rate, that during the past ten years a new school of poets has attempted to free itself from the isolation of poetry by taking society itself as the dominant subject.[2] The attempt has been a brilliant and exciting one in many ways; the measure of its success is not yet clear, particularly since it has been inspired by the present crisis of society; and its relative popularity may also be limited to contemporary and transient interests. But the very nature of the effort testifies in its own way to the isolation which haunts modern poetry, and from which these poets have been trying to escape.

1. The connection between the way in which an author lives and his writing is of course a complicated one. But how close the connection is and how effective can be seen if we ask ourselves: would Eliot have written *The Waste Land* as we know it, if he had lived in London? Would Pound have written the later *Cantos*, if he had not lived on the Italian Riviera? Would either have written, using culture as they have, if they were not expatriate Americans? Certainly Joyce might not have written *Finnegans Wake* if he had not taught in a Berlitz school and Perse could not have written *Anabase* if he had not been sent to Asia as a diplomat, and Yeats might not have written his later poetry, if he had lived on Lady Gregory's estate.

2. These are the poets who, significantly enough, have invented the recurrent figures of "the island," as a symbol of isolation. From the point of view of this essay, the leading themes of the Agrarian-Regionalist poets, such as Tate and Ransom, would represent another, very different effort to get back to the center of the community and away from the poet's isolation.

CLOSE READING

Texts from Housman

RANDALL JARRELL

Originally published in the Kenyon Review *in 1939, this essay embodies the central New Critical method: "close reading." An almost word-by-word examination of a few poems by A. E. Housman allows Jarrell to draw some startling conclusions about the author and his beliefs.*

The logic poetry has or pretends to have generally resembles induction more than deduction. Of four possible procedures (dealing entirely with particulars, dealing entirely with generalizations, inferring the relatively general from the relatively particular, and deducing the particular from the more general), the third is very much the most common, and the first and second are limits which "pure" and didactic poetry timidly approach. The fourth is seldom seen. In this essay I am interested in that variety of the third procedure in which the generalizations are implicit. When such generalizations are simple ones, very plainly implied by the particulars of the poem, there will be little tendency to confuse this variety of the third procedure with the first procedure; when they are neither simple nor very plainly implied, the poem will be thought of as "pure" (frequently, "nature") poetry. This is all the more likely to occur since most "pure" poetry is merely that in which the impurity, like the illegitimate child of the story, is "such a little one" that we feel it ought to be disregarded. Of these poems of implicit generalization there is a wide range, extending from the simplest, in which the generalizations are made obvious enough to vex the average reader (some of the "Satires of Circumstance," for instance), to the most complicated, in which they entirely escape his observation ("To the Moon"). The two poems of Housman's which I am about to analyze are more nearly of the type of "To the Moon."

II

Crossing alone the nighted ferry
With the one coin for fee,

Whom, on the wharf of Lethe waiting,
Count you to find? Not me.

The brisk fond lackey to fetch and carry,
The true, sick-hearted slave,
Expect him not in the just city
And free land of the grave.

The first stanza is oddly constructed; it manages to carry over several more or less unexpressed statements, while the statement it makes on the surface, grammatically, is arranged so as to make the reader disregard it completely. Literally, the stanza says: *Whom do you expect to find waiting for you? Not me.* But the denying and elliptical *not me* is not an answer to the surface question; that question is almost rhetorical, and obviously gets a *me*; the *not me* denies *And I'll satisfy your expectations and be there?*—the implied corollary of the surface question; and the flippant and brutal finality of the *not me* implies that the expectations are foolish. (A belief that can be contradicted so carelessly and completely—by a person in a position to know—is a foolish one.) The stanza says: *You do expect to find me and ought not to* and *You're actually such a fool as to count on my being there?* and *So I'll be there, eh? Not me.*

Some paraphrases of the two stanzas will show how extraordinarily much they do mean; they illustrate the quality of poetry that is almost its most characteristic, compression. These paraphrases are not very imaginative—the reader can find justification for any statement in the actual words of the poem. (Though not in any part considered in isolation. The part as part has a misleading look of independence and reality, just as does the word as word; but it has only that relationship to the larger contexts of the poem that the words which compose it have to it, and its significance is similarly controlled and extended by those larger units of which it is a part. A poem is a sort of onion of contexts, and you can no more locate any of the important meanings exclusively in a part than you can locate a relation in one of its terms. The significance of a part may be greatly modified or even in extreme cases completely reversed by later and larger parts and by the whole. This will be illustrated in the following discussion: most of the important meanings attached to the first stanza do not exist when the stanza is considered in isolation.) And the paraphrases are not hypertrophied, they do not even begin to be exhaustive.

Stanza I: Do you expect me to wait patiently for you there, just as I have done on earth? expect that, in hell, after death, things will go on for you just as they do here on earth? that there, after crossing and drinking

Lethe and oblivion, I'll still be thinking of human you, still be waiting faithfully there on the wharf for you to arrive, with you still my only interest, with me still your absolutely devoted slave—just as we are here? Do you really? Do you actually suppose that you yourself, then, will be able to expect it? Even when dead, all alone, on that grim ferry, in the middle of the dark forgetful river, all that's left of your human life one coin, you'll be stupid or inflexible or faithful enough to *count* on (you're sure, are you, so sure that not even a doubt enters your mind?) finding me waiting there? How are we to understand an inflexibility that seems almost incredible? Is it because you're pathetically deluded about love's constancy, my great lasting love for you? (This version makes the *you* sympathetic; but it is unlikely, an unstressed possibility, and the others do not.) Or is it that you're so sure of my complete enslavement that you know death itself can't change it? Or are you so peculiarly stupid that you can't even conceive of any essential change away from your past life and knowledge, even after the death that has destroyed them both? Or is it the general inescapable stupidity of mankind, who can conceive of death only in human and vital terms? (Housman's not giving the reasons, when the reasons must be thought about if the poem is to be understood, forces the reader to make them for himself, and to see that there is a wide range that must be considered. This is one of the most important principles of compression in poetry; these implied foundations or justifications for a statement might be called *bases*.) Are you actually such a fool as to believe that? So I'll be there? Not me. You're wrong. These things are really different.

One of the most important elements in the poem is the tone of the *not me*. Its casualness, finality, and matter-of-fact bluntness give it almost the effect of slang. It is the crudest of denials. There is in it a laconic brutality, an imperturbable and almost complacent vigor; it has certainly a sort of contempt. Contempt for what? Contempt at himself for his faithlessness? contempt at himself for his obsessing weakness—for not being faithless now instead of them? Or contempt at her, for being bad enough to keep things as they are, for being stupid enough to imagine that they will be so always? The tone is both threatening and disgusted. It shivers between all these qualities like a just-thrown knife. And to what particular denial does this tone attach? how specific, how general a one? These are changes a reader can easily ring for himself; but I hope he will realize their importance. Variations of this formula of alternative possibilities make up one of the most valuable resources of the poet.

The second stanza is most thoroughly ambiguous; there are two entirely different levels of meaning for the whole, and most of the parts exhibit a comparable stratification. I give a word-for-word analysis:

Do not expect me to be after death what I was alive and human: the *fond* (1. *foolish*; 2. *loving*—you get the same two meanings in the synonym *doting*) *brisk* (the normal meanings are favorable: *full of life, keenly alive or alert, energetic*; but here the context forces it over into *officious, undignified, solicitous, leaping at your every word*—there is a pathetic ignoble sense to it here) *lackey* (the most contemptuous and degrading form of the word *servant*: a servile follower, a toady) *to fetch and carry* (you thought so poorly of me that you let me perform nothing but silly menial physical tasks; thus, our love was nothing but the degrading relationship of obsequious servant and contemptuous master), *the true* (1. *constant, loyal, devoted, faithful*; 2. *properly so-called, ideally or typically such*—the perfectly slavish slave) *sick-hearted* (1. cowardly, disheartened in a weak discouraged ignoble way, as a Spartan would have said of helots, "These sick-hearted slaves"; 2. sick at heart at the whole mess, his own helpless subjection. There was a man in one of the sagas who had a bad boil on his foot; when he was asked why he didn't limp and favor it, he replied: "One walks straight while the leg is whole." If the reader imagines this man as a slave he will see sharply the more elevated sense of the phrase *sick-hearted slave*) *slave* (1. the conventional hardly meant sense in which we use it of lovers, as an almost completely dead metaphor; this sense has very little force here; or 2. the literal *slave*: the relation of slave to master is not pleasant, not honorable, is between lovers indecent and horrible, but immensely comprehensive—their love is made even more compulsive and even less favorable). But here I leave the word-by-word analysis for more general comment. I think I hardly need remark on the shock in this treatment, which forces over the conventional unfelt terms into their literal degrading senses; and this shock is amplified by the paradoxical fall through *just city* and *free land* into *the grave*. (Also, the effect of the *lackey / carry* and versification of the first line of the stanza should be noted.)

Let me give first the favorable literal surface sense of *the just city and free land of the grave*, its sense on the level at which you take Housman's Greek underworld convention seriously. The house of Hades is the *just city* for a number of reasons: in it are the three just judges; in it are all the exemplary convicts, from Ixion to the Danaïdes, simply dripping with justice; here justice is meted equally to the anonymous and rankless dead; there is no corruption here. It is the *free land* because here the king and the slave are equal (though even on the level of death as the Greek underworld, the horrid irony has begun to intrude—Achilles knew, and Housman knows, that it is better to be the slave of a poor farmer than king among the hosts of the dead); because here we are free at last from life; and so on and so on.

But at the deeper level, the *just* fastened to *city*, the *city* fastened to *grave*, have an irony that is thorough. How are we to apply *just* to a place where corruption and nothingness are forced on good and bad, innocent and guilty alike? (From Housman's point of view it might be called mercy, but never justice.) And the *city* is as bad; the cemetery looks like a city of the graves, of the stone rectangular houses—but a city without occupations, citizens, without life: a shell, a blank check that can never be filled out. And can we call a land *free* whose inhabitants cannot move a finger, are compelled as completely as stones? And can we call the little cave, the patch of darkness and pressing earth, the *land* of the grave?

And why are we told to expect him not, the slave, the lackey, in the just city and free land of the grave? Because he is changed now, a citizen of the Greek underworld, engrossed in its games and occupations, the new interests that he has acquired? Oh no, the change is complete, not from the old interests to new ones, but from any interests to none; do not expect him because he has ceased to exist, he is really, finally different now. It is foolish to expect *anything* of the world after death. But we can expect nothingness; and that is better than this world, the poem is supposed to make us feel; there, even though we are overwhelmed impartially and completely, we shall be free of the evil of this world—a world whose best thing, love, is nothing but injustice and stupidity and slavery. This is why the poet resorts to the ambiguity that permits him to employ the adjectives *just* and *free:* they seem to apply truly on the surface level, and ironically at the other; but in a way they, and certainly the air of reward and luck and approbation that goes with them, apply truly at the second level as well. This is the accusation and condemnation of life that we read so often in Housman: that the grave seems better, we are glad to be in it.

We ought not to forget that this poem is a love poem by the living "me" of the poem to its equally living "you": *when we are dead, things will be different—and I'm glad of it.* It is, considerably sublimated, the formula familiar to such connections: *I wish I were dead;* and it has more than a suspicion of the child's *when I'm dead, then they'll be sorry.* It is an accusation that embodies a very strong statement of the underlying antagonism, the real ambivalence of most such relationships. The condemnation applied to the world for being bad is extended to the *you* for not being better. And these plaints are always pleas; so the poem has an additional force. Certainly this particular-seeming little poem turns out to be general enough: it carries implicit in it attitudes (aggregates of related generalizations) toward love, life, and death.

III

It nods and curtseys and recovers
    When the wind blows above,
The nettle on the graves of lovers
    That hanged themselves for love.

The nettle nods, the wind blows over,
    The man, he does not move,
The lover of the grave, the lover
    That hanged himself for love.

This innocent-looking little nature poem is actually, I think, a general quasi-philosophical piece meant to infect the reader with Housman's own belief about the cause of any action. (I am afraid it is a judgment the reader is likely neither to resist nor recognize.) The nettle and the wind are Housman's specific and usual symbols. Housman's poetry itself is a sort of homemade nettle wine ("Out of a stem that scored the hand / I wrung it in a weary land"); the nettle has one poem entirely to itself, XXXII in *More Poems*. No matter what you sow, only the nettle grows; no matter what happens, it flourishes and remains—"the numberless, the lonely, the thronger of the land." It peoples cities, it waves above the courts of kings; "and touch it and it stings." Stating what symbols "mean" is a job the poet has properly avoided; but, roughly, the nettle stands for the hurting and inescapable conditions of life, the prosperous (but sympathetically presented and almost admiringly accepted) evil of the universe—"great Necessity," if you are not altogether charmed by it. What the wind is Housman states himself (in "On Wenlock Edge the wood's in trouble"; but it is given the same value in several other poems, notably "The weeping Pleiads wester"): the "tree of man" is never quiet because the wind, "the gale of life," blows through it always.

What I said just before the analysis of the first stanza of "Crossing alone the nighted ferry" is true here too; many of one's remarks about the first stanza of this poem will be plausible or intelligible only in the light of one's consideration of the whole poem. In the first line, *It nods and curtseys and recovers*, there is a shock which grows out of the contrast between this demure performance and its performer, the Housman nettle. The nettle is merely repeating above the grave, compelled by the wind, what the man in the grave did once, when the wind blew through him. So living is (we must take it as being) just a repetition of little meaningless nodding actions, actions that haven't even the virtue of being our own—since the wind forces them out of us; life as the wind makes man as the tree or nettle helpless and determined. This illustrates the general principle that in poetry you make judgments by your own pre-liminary choice of symbols, and force the reader who accepts the symbols to accept the judgments implicit in them. A symbol, like Bowne's "concept," is a nest of judgments; the reader may accept the symbols, and then be cautious about accepting judgments or generalizations, but the damage is done.

The images in the poem are quite general: "the nettle on the graves of lovers that hanged themselves for love" is not any one nettle, not really any particular at all, but a moderately extensive class. (If Housman were writing a pure poem, a nature poem, he would go about it differently; here the generality is insisted on—any lover, any nettle will do well enough: if you prove something for *any* you prove it for *all*, and Housman is arranging all this as a plausible *any*.) There is of course irony, at several levels, in a nettle's dancing obliviously (*nod* and *curtsey* and *recover* add up to *dance*) on the grave of the dead lover. All flesh is grass; but worse here, because the grass which is the symbol for transitoriness outlasts us. (The reader may say, remembering *The stinging nettle only will still be found to stand:* "But the nettle is a symbol of lasting things to Housman, not of transitory ones." Actually it manages for both here, for the first when considered as a common symbol, for the second when considered as Housman's particular one. But this ambiguity in symbols is frequent; without it they would be much less useful. Take a similar case, *grass*: this year's grass springs up and withers, and is shorter than man; but *grass*, all grass, lasts forever. With people we have different words for the two aspects, *men* and *man*. The whole business of thinking of the transitory grass as just the same more lasting than man—in one form or another, one of the stock poetic subjects—is a beautiful fallacy that goes like this: *Grass*—the year-after-year process—is more lasting than *men*; substituting *man* for *men* and this year's blade for the endless grass, you end by getting a proposition that everybody from Job on down or up has felt, at one time or another, thoroughly satisfactory.) Why a nettle to dance on the grave? Because in English poetry flowers grow on the graves of these lovers who have died for love, to show remembrance; Housman puts the nettle there, for forgetfulness. In the other poems the flower "meant" their love—here the nettle means it. All the nettle's actions emphasize its indifference and removedness. The roses in the ballads were intimately related to the lovers, and entwined themselves above the graves—the nature that surrounded the lovers was thoroughly interested in their game, almost as human as they; the nettle above this grave is alone, inhuman and casual, the representative of a nature indifferent to man.

The fifth and sixth lines of the poem are there mainly to establish this shocking paradox: here is a sessile thing, a plant, that curtseys and nods, while the man, the most thoroughly animate of all beings, cannot even move. Looked at in the usual way this is gloomy and mortifying, and that is the surface force it has here; but looked at in another way, Housman's way, there is a sort of triumph in it: the most absolute that man can know. That is what it is for Housman. Once man was tossed about helplessly and incessantly by the wind that blew through him—now the toughest of all plants is more sensitive, more easily moved than he. In other words, death is better than life, nothing is better than anything. Nor is this a silly adolescent pessimism peculiar to Housman, as so many critics assure you. It is better to be dead than alive, best of all never to have been born—said a poet approvingly advertised as seeing life steadily and seeing it whole; and if I began an anthology of such quotations there it would take me a long time to finish. The attitude is obviously inadequate and just as obviously important.

The triumph here leads beautifully into the poem's final statement: the triumph at being in the grave, one with the grave, prepares us for the fact that it was the grave, not any living thing, that the lover loved, and hanged himself for love of. The statement has some plausibility: hanging yourself for love of someone is entirely silly, so far as any possession or any furthering of your love is concerned, but if you are in love with death, killing yourself is the logical and obvious and only way to consummate your love. For the lover to have killed himself for love of a living thing would have been senseless; but his love for her was only ostensible, concealing—from himself too—the "common wish for death," his real passion for the grave.

But if this holds for this one case; if in committing this most sincere and passionate, most living of all acts (that is, killing yourself for love; nothing else shows so complete a contempt for death and consequences, so absolute a value placed on another living creature), the lover was deceiving himself about his motives, and did it, not for love of anything living, but because of his real love for death; then everybody must do everything for the same reason. (This is a judgment too exaggerated for anyone to expect to get away with, the reader may think; but judgments of life tend to this form—"Vanity, vanity, all is vanity.") For the lover is the perfectly simplified, extreme case. This is what is called a crucial experiment. (It is one of Mill's regular types of induction.) The logic runs: If you can prove that in committing this act—an act about the motives of which the actor is so little likely to be deceived, an act so little likely to have the love of death as its motive—the actor was deceived, and had the love of death as his motive, then you can prove it for any other act the motive of which is more likely to be the love of death, and about the motives of which it is more likely that the actor might be deceived.

But for the conclusion to be true the initial premise must be true, the lover's one motive must have been the wish for death; and Housman has of course not put in even a word of argument for the truth of that premise, he has merely stated it, with the most engaging audacity and dogmatism—has stated it innocently, as a fact obvious as any other of these little natural facts about the wind and the nettle and the cemetery. He has produced it not as a judgment but as a datum, and the sympathetic reader has accepted it as such. He is really treating it as a percept, and percepts have no need for proof, they are neither true nor false, they are just there. If he had tried to prove the truth of the premise he would have convinced only those who already believed in the truth of the conclusion, and those people (i.e., himself) didn't need to be convinced. With the poem as it is, the reader is convinced; or if he objects, the poet can object disingenuously in return, "But you've made the absurd error of taking hypothetical reasoning as categorical. My form is: *If* A, *then* B; I'm not interested in *proving* A. Though, of course, if you decide to remove the *if*, and assert A, then B is asserted also; and A is awfully plausible, isn't it?— just part of the data of the poem; you could hardly reject it, could you?"

Two of the generalizations carried over by this poem—that our actions are motivated by the wish for death, that our ostensible reasons for acts are merely rationalizations, veneers of apparent motive overlying the real levels of motivation—are, in a less sweeping form, psychological or psychoanalytical commonplaces today. But I am not going to hold up Housman's poem as a masterly anticipation of our own discoveries; so far as I can see, Housman was not only uninterested but incapable in such things, and pulled these truths out of his pie, not because of wit, but because of the perverse and ingenious obstinacy that pulled just such gloomy judgments out of any pie at all. Here the shock and unlikeliness of what he said were what recommended it to him; and the discovery that these have been mitigated would merely have added to his gloom.

Some Post-Symbolist Structures

HUGH KENNER

In this essay, originally published in 1972, Kenner traces how the structures and syntax of poetry in English were altered by poets coming to terms with the French symbolists of the nineteenth century.

Part of the discovery of Language that was going on in the early nineteenth century was the discovery of Anglo-Saxon, which fascinated the young Lewis Carroll by being not-quite-English. People were exclaiming over the "epic" qualities of *The Battle of Brunanburh* as though it were a fragment of the *Iliad*, and citing, in that Romantic-vernacular heyday, bits from which you could extract a kind of sense without knowing except in the most general way what any of the words might denote. Lewis Carroll's imitation of this effect is better known than any of the Anglo-Saxon models he had in mind—

> And, as in uffish thought he stood,
>   The Jabberwock, with eyes of flame,
> Came whiffling through the tulgey wood,
>   And burbled as it came!

"Somehow it seems to fill my head with ideas," said Alice, "—only I don't exactly know what they are!" This gets cited in books on linguistics nowadays, with careful demonstrations of how much we can actually know without knowing the words.

The Romantic enthusiasts had discovered how thoroughly reader and writer can rely on the structural pattern of English. "Structure," so understood, corresponds to a higher level of generalization than "grammar" and "syntax." It is thanks to our understanding of structural patterns that we can enjoy a feeling of inwardness with such an utterance as "All mimsy were the borogoves," connecting the verb-form "were" with the -*s* termination on "borogoves," divining (how?) an inverted construction, assigning adverbial rather than adjectival force to "all," and concluding, faster than thought, that the borogoves, whatever they may be, are in a state of total mimsiness of which we can form no idea.

To state in detail and in order of application the exceedingly intricate rules by which we make structural sense of any utterance that may confront us has been the work of a generation of linguists, the most recent of whom are suggesting that the job is barely begun. Though this work has nearly all been done in the twentieth century its field of operation was discovered in the nineteenth, and largely by poets confronting the baffling fact, much later formulated by Eliot, that poetry can communicate before it is understood. Elizabeth Sewell in her pioneering work *The Field of Nonsense* has pointed to the analogy between the work of Mallarmé in France and the work of the English nonsense-writers Lear and Carroll. Nonsense-verse builds intelligible structures without intelligible words; thus Lear discovered you could create Coleridgean or Tennysonian effects with a minimum of reliance on words that are in the dictionary—

. . . over the stark Grumboolian plain.

And Tennyson, as though returning the compliment, dedicated to Edward Lear a poem whose first five lines features three adjectives and two nouns of which hardly anyone is likely to know the exact significance:

> Illyrian woodlands, echoing falls
> Of water, sheets of summer glass,
> The long divine Peneïan pass,
> The vast Akrokeraunian walls,
>
> Tomohrit, Athos, all things fair . . .

This is very likely the only appearance anywhere of the word *Akrokeraunian*; one understands that these are very splendid and ancient walls without examining that word's credentials. Tennyson seems to have remembered *infames scopulos Acroceraunia* from Horace (1.iii.20) and inserted his pseudo-kappas to point up the derivation from Greek words meaning high-thundering. We are no doubt to imagine the sheer sides of mountains from which thunderbolts are hurled, and Acroceraunia, for that matter, is the Latin name of a rocky promontory in Epirus. Yet, prompted as we are to think of walls, not of mountains, we feel curiously little need of such information. Akrokeraunian walls rise, it may be, from a Grumboolian plain, in a landscape made wholly of linguistic structures, and once this possibility was under control poetry could never be the same. By 1853, the date of Tennyson's poem, acute eyes might have sighted on the furthest horizon, slouching toward Dublin to be born, the rough beast *Finnegans Wake*.

If we look at Tennyson's line more carefully we discover that the structural and the rhetorical principles can be separated. Our sense of linguistic structures can establish with perfect exactness the relationship between words; thus anyone reasonably familiar with English knows at once that *Akrokeraunian* is an adjective: that it denotes some quality of those walls. We are drawing on a different order of knowledge when we divine from its formidable length and sound that the quality it denotes has to do with exotic impressiveness, and we are really doing more than the poem asks us to do when we poke into its etymology, assign it a meaning, and find that its meaning turns the meaning of *walls* into a metaphor for cliffs. From the structural point of view, *Akrokeraunian* is a six-syllable phenomenon that comes between *vast* and *walls* and has the same kind of syntactic function that *vast* has. It is clear that Tennyson could have drafted the line with a blank in it, to be filled up later by six appropriate syllables, and seeing the line in his work-sheet with that blank in it we should know at once that the missing six syllables would constitute one or more adjectives. In fact a prose draft of the whole poem is quite conceivable, a floor-plan of its syntax, with blanks where all the interesting words were to be installed. The plan would be of no interest whatever; it would run,

> [A lot of things] you describe so well I felt I was there; and as I read I felt I was in the golden age; and for me [a lot of exotic images] seemed realities.

This is the substance of Tennyson's compliment to Lear; we can probably agree that it is as banal as that of a thank-you note, and that the handsomeness of the compliment will depend on his success with the parts in square brackets. Such a draft, in fact, is so trivial we may feel fairly sure Tennyson never wrote one, but rather devised his clots of gorgeous words and then cobbled together the connective matter in the middle. This is no more than most of us would expect. We have been taught to ask scornfully what poetry may have to do with prose drafts, and are unsurprised when paraphrase, which is like an attempt to recover a prose original, yields little of interest.

But not always. At Westminster School, late in the sixteenth century, the young Ben Jonson acquired from his famous master William Camden a precept he never forgot, that before writing verse he should work out his sense in prose, and knowing this we may often be astonished at how little alteration the prose draft seems to have undergone in the course of being transmuted. When he makes the stone speak to passersby over the grave of the lady named Elizabeth, what it has to say defies paraphrase because it is already identical in structure and diction with any paraphrase we might venture to make:

> Would'st thou heare, what man can say
> In a little? Reader, stay.
> Under-neath this stone doth lye
> As much beautie, as could dye:
> Which in life did harbour give
> To more vertue, than doth live.
> If, at all, shee had a fault,
> Leave it buryed in this vault.
> One name was Elizabeth,
> Th'other let it sleepe with death:
> Fitter, where it dyed, to tell,
> Than that it liv'd at all. Farewell.

The stone has three statements to make about Elizabeth, three cere-monious sentences, the middle one short. Before entering on these statements it asks if we want to hear them, and bids us pause if so. At the end it bids us, in one word, Farewell. That is all; and in working out the structure of those three central sentences Jonson worked out his poem also. This defeats the Romantic distinctions between prose and verse; it becomes verse only in becoming decorously neat, and in being neat and quiet it imitates the qualities of the neat quiet lady whose virtue is reti-cence now as it was when she lived.

> Would'st thou heare, what man can say
> In a little?

means both, observe the virtues of this poem, small as this stone, and still more, be instructed in the qualities of this lady, whose life was a state-ment here completed by death, a statement the poem rephrases.

We can scarcely think about the poem except syntactically, nor is it easy to imagine Jonson thinking his way into it, while it was unwritten, by any but a syntactic route. Neither are the words bright jewels to jus-tify the structures, nor are the structures, as they were for Tennyson, an unobtrusive mounting for the words. We may find it profitable to adduce another pre-Romantic poem for which no one would claim decorous neatness, yet for which, as much as for Jonson, the structures that hold the words in relation are exactly as indispensable as the words they hold. That great baroque structure the opening sentence of *Paradise Lost* is grown from a kernel sentence Milton seems to have imitated from the beginning of the *Iliad. Mēnin aeide thea,* Homer commences, "Wrath sing, goddess . . . ," and Homer goes on to explain what he means by the wrath of Achilles and the mischief it did. "Disobedience sing, Muse," commences Milton, placing the key words in the same order as Homer's but appending his explanations directly to the words they amplify. Having specified "Man's first disobedience" he elaborates on it at once, summa-rizing the whole drama of loss and redemption in a circular structure which begins with "the fruit of that forbidden tree" and ends ("one greater man" having negated the disobedient man) with "regain that blissful seat," thirty-eight words occupying in the sentence the place of one word in Homer. Then comes, just where it comes in Homer, the imperative "sing"; then, as in Homer, the vocative, "Heavenly Muse," which he proceeds to elaborate just as he had elaborated the word "disobedience," by way of establishing to what Muse a Christian poet may address himself. The verb stands unadorned in the middle, "sing"; the words before it and after it, "disobedience" and "Muse," receive par-allel amplification.

Whether from the custom of diagramming sentences in classrooms or from the writings of Noam Chomsky, we are all familiar with the notion of a long sentence elaborated from a kernel sentence, and with the principle that there is no other way to arrive at syntactic English. We may be less familiar with the fact that the kernel sentence, after it has generated the elaborate sentence, may or may not prove to be of any rhetorical salience. For Milton the kernel sentence is clearly salient. As he elaborates, he releases the latent energies of his predicate and his subject, showing us all that may be implicit, since Adam, in *disobedience*, all that may be implicit, since the Holy Spirit revealed himself, in *Muse*: two words which, he allows us to feel, are expanding across his page their own inherent orderly energies. The kernel sentence does not simply permit all this, it contains all this, and if, as we read on in *Paradise Lost*, we chance to forget those majestic elaborations, it will remain true that the Muse singing of disobedience comprises the poem's business.

But this is not an invariable practice; in particular, it is not Symbolist practice. In the minor Tennyson poem we have looked at, the kernel sentence, far from mapping the poem's business, reduces to nothing but "I felt . . . and I felt . . . ," the merest excuse for the rest of the poem to assemble its sonorities and exoticisms. And we may say that Tennyson was working toward a new poetic which he never succeeded in formulating, and that it got formulated instead in France. About ten years after Tennyson's homage to Lear, we find the very young Stéphane Mallarmé composing in ten Alexandrine couplets a poem called "Soupir," a single long sinuous sentence whose subject and verb are not huddled inconspicuously away, but so disposed as to command a maximum of evocative detail. Its kernel sentence appears to be "Mon âme monte vers l'Azur," my soul mounts toward the azure, the azure of the infinite pale sky being already for Mallarmé, it would seem, an ultimate and a word of great power. Arthur Symons's translation is faithful to the features we are interested in:

SIGH

My soul, calm sister, towards thy brow, whereon scarce grieves
An autumn strewn already with its russet leaves,
And towards the wandering sky of thine angelic eyes,
Mounts, as in melancholy gardens may arise
Some faithful fountain sighing whitely towards the blue!
—Towards the blue pale and pure that sad October knew,
When, in those depths, it mirrored languors infinite,
And agonizing leaves upon the waters white,

Windily drifting, traced a furrow cold and dun,
Where, in one long last ray, lingered the yellow sun.

This is a subtle piece of syntactic engineering. Symons remarks that "a delicate emotion, a figure vaguely defined, a landscape magically evoked, blend in a single effect." So they do; they are present like overlayered transparencies, not sorted out as the first sentence of *Paradise Lost* sorts things out. But Mallarmé does not huddle these elements together and allow us to associate them; he makes use of the remarkable sentence he is constructing, a sentence the progress of which uncoils like a plot. "My soul," he commences, both beginning the poem and giving the sentence its subject; then "towards," so that we know we are to expect a verb of motion, and for three lines the poem relies on that expectation to assimilate details we would not have expected:

My soul, calm sister, towards thy brow, whereon scarce grieves
An autumn strewn already with its russet leaves,
And towards the wandering sky of thine angelic eyes,
Mounts . . .

Already we have the woman and the landscape, and the qualities felt in the woman have given rise to the landscape. We also have, it would seem, a sentence completed. And yet two-thirds of the poem is still to be produced, and produced not by tacking more things on but by generating a new syntactic necessity. He does this economically, in plain sight, with such assurance we hardly see it done, and are apt to wonder where the rest of the poem came from. Yet if we watch closely it is easy to see what he does: he effects a mutation in the kernel sentence.

We have said that the kernel sentence seems to be, "My soul mounts towards the azure." This is not strictly true. The kernel sentence is complete in the opening lines, before the azure has been mentioned. It is, "My soul mounts toward your brow and toward the sky of your eyes." That mention of "sky" prepares for the mutation; the mutation itself occurs immediately after the verb. For the line that begins with the poem's main verb goes on,

Mounts, as in melancholy gardens may arise
Some faithful fountain sighing whitely towards the blue!

—all very orderly, an adverbial clause telling how the soul mounts and comparing its aspiration to a fountain's. The fountain mounts toward the sky but never gets there: its energy goes into striving. But instead of leaving us with this trim analogy, Mallarmé commences a new line by reduplicating the phrase with which the last line ended: "—Towards the blue pale and pure that sad October knew . . . ," and since we cannot help connecting the energy of *towards* with *mounts*, we connect, without noticing, the subject of *mounts* and that aspiration toward blueness. And there is the soul, mounting toward the azure sky, the kernel sentence mutated by a fountain's intervention. This works because each of its key elements, *My soul, mounts, towards the blue*, occupies a rhetorical strong point where a line commences, while the previous constructions in "towards" have expended themselves in less prominent niches. And with the soul mounting toward the azure and the fountain playing, he can allow the rest of the poem to concern itself with the still water in the fountain's basin:

> —Towards the blue pale and pure that sad October knew,
> When, in those depths, it mirrored languors infinite,
> And agonizing leaves upon the waters white,
> Windily drifting, traced a furrow cold and dun,
> Where, in one long last ray, lingered the yellow sun.

Since *it* may refer to the blue or to October, there is some blurring of the relative pronoun, less evident in Symons's translation than in the French, where it governs not one verb but two. It appears to be a calculated blurring; Mallarmé shows every sign of interest in the sentence he is putting together, and of awareness that such linguistic chemistries as he aspires to need shaped vessels to contain them. His syntactic arrangements, unlike Tennyson's, are like the interconnected glass vessels on a laboratory bench, of virtually sculptural interest in themselves, yet functional and everywhere transparent, to let us watch the colors change within them. Yet they are unlike Milton's too, not to mention Jonson's, in being strangely devoid of independent interest. Confronted by "My soul mounts toward your brow and toward the sky of your eyes," we may legitimately ask what it may mean. Unlike Tennyson's kernel sentence, it contains words vital to the poem's chemistry as well as to its syntactic legitimacy. Yet it is already sufficiently a piece of opportunism to be saying, in itself, nothing very forceful: nothing of the order of "Disobedience sing, Muse."

We have seen that Mallarmé's formal kernel sentence is supplanted by a mutant version composed of words that open lines. Many of his poems exploit that order of nearly geometrical coherence. He will make of the first and the last words of a poem a thematic phrase which the intervening words fill in like a chord. His most famous sonnet begins "Le vierge . . ." and ends " . . . Cygne": "the virgin swan." His *Toast Funèbre* to the memory of Gautier is enclosed within the words "O . . . nuit": "O night." His memorial sonnet to Edgar Allan Poe not only announces in its first line that eternity will change Poe's mere self into what he was meant to be, but has for its first word "tel" and its last "futur." The Poe sonnet moreover is made of Poe-words, dark Gothicisms, sortilege and hydra and a black flood and a tomb and blasphemy; it does not fail to capitalize *Poète* in its second line to anticipate the *Poe* of its twelfth; it manages to resonate with basement metaphysics like *Eureka* itself; and amid its controlled semi-penetrabilities three isolated strong lines like bars of steel assert the aphoristic weight of the French Alexandrine. These may be the most important facts about the sonnet, and all of them except the presence of the three strong lines may be gathered by a scanning eye that does not actually *read* it. So far are we on the way toward *la poésie concrète*, and Mallarmé as we know from his last work was to carry that possibility still further, and dispose clusters of words in pure spatial contingency on a page otherwise white.

Such instances may help us describe Mallarmé's syntactic structures: they are ways, among other ways, of governing the exact relationship of the poem's elements, and all his ways, including his syntactic ones, have something of the geometer's economy about them. This is in part because the French language contains more syntactic orthodoxies than does the English. When the French writer does something so simple as place the adjective before the noun instead of after, he can anticipate a seismic dislocation in the sensibility of the French reader.

English usage being less rigid, the poet who attempts comparable effects in English must go to greater extremes. In 1896, after some years of hearing from Symons and others about what was going on in France, W. B. Yeats attempted some syntactic legerdemain of his own: a twenty-four-line poem that consists of one sentence, and like so many poems of Mallarmé's proceeds by systematic digression from its formal structure. Indeed the importance of the kernel sentence is vanishingly small. It is simply "I press my heart . . . and I hear. . . ." And so little are we likely to ask what it means, that we are even unlikely to notice it, amid Yeats's exploitation of the pliancy of English subordinate structures.

HE REMEMBERS FORGOTTEN BEAUTY

> When my arms wrap you round I press
> My heart upon the loveliness
> That has long faded from the world;

The jeweled crowns that kings have hurled
In shadowy pools, when armies fled;
The love-tales wrought with silken thread
By dreaming ladies upon cloth
That has made fat the murderous moth;
The roses that of old time were
Woven by ladies in their hair,
The dew-cold lilies ladies bore
Through many a sacred corridor
Where such grey clouds of incense rose
That only God's eyes did not close:
For that pale breast and lingering hand
Come from a more dream-heavy land,
A more dream-heavy hour than this;
And when you sigh from kiss to kiss
I hear white Beauty sighing, too,
For hours when all must fade like dew,
But flame on flame, and deep on deep,
Throne over throne, where in half sleep,
Their swords upon their iron knees,
Brood her high lonely mysteries.

Are we prepared to say without hesitation where those flames come from, and those swords and those thrones? Their ring is Miltonic (pre-Raphaelite Miltonic), but we are far from Milton, whose effort in his long sentences is to keep clear whereabouts we are from moment to moment as the sentence works itself out. Yeats's effort is nearly the opposite, as we can tell from the way he revised this ending. The version he published in 1896 heard white Beauty sighing, too

For hours when all must fade like dew
Till there be naught but throne on throne
Of seraphs, brooding each alone,
A sword upon his iron knees,
On her most lonely mysteries.

This is clear enough, at least in structure: Beauty sighs for those hours when everything will fade except the seraphs who brood on Beauty's mysteries. "Till there be naught but . . . ," runs the governing structure: we cannot mistake it. But he seems to have disliked a structure we could not mistake, and three years later the ending was revised to run as it now does in the definitive edition:

> I hear white Beauty sighing, too,
> For hours when all must fade like dew
> But flame on flame, and deep on deep,
> Throne over throne where in half sleep,
> Their swords upon their iron knees,
> Brood her high lonely mysteries.

This not only substitutes "high lonely mysteries" for "seraphs," it makes everything turn on an "all but" construction which we are almost certain not to notice. The phrase "when all must fade like dew" has such a ring of completeness that only by nearly scholastic effort, and with a printed text to pore over, can we force the "But" that opens the next line to give up its air of magisterial disjunction and link itself with "all."

Yeats is willing to dissolve one strong effect into another, leaving us with no clear idea how they are supposed to be related, though structural relations are specified in the text if we choose to undertake the work of recovering them. Thus we can determine that eleven successive lines develop from four nouns (*crowns, tales, roses, lilies*) that are all in apposition to the noun *loveliness*; that three lines about the pale breast and the lingering hand return us to a person we had quite forgotten, the *you* of the poem's opening; and that a new kernel sentence in parallel with the first one, *when you sigh I hear* . . . , paralleling *when my arms wrap you round I press* . . . , presides over the second lobe of the poem. Yet the way these kernel sentences preside is curiously oblique. Each serves to introduce an abstract noun, the first one *loveliness* and the second one *Beauty*, which nouns are the real seeds from which the enchanted thickets grow. And these nouns are not the objects of the main verbs in the kernel sentences, but abstractions produced within subordinate clauses which those verbs have produced. The effect is to move our attention as far as may be from the thrust of subject-verb-object. The structure is formal, elaborate, symmetrical, and syntactically faultless; and yet only by a very great effort of attention is the reader likely to discover what it is.

Tennyson's structures, which are equally unassertive, turn out when we disengage them to be informal, asymmetrical, and unimportant. They enable him, while he deploys his sumptuousness of diction, to fulfill the schoolmarm's requirement that the sentence shall parse, and they tend to comprise its least effectual words. The Yeatsian structure, though elaboration encumbers and conceals it, has been an object of the poet's careful attention, and though it may never chance to attract our notice its presence does matter, and not merely to the schoolmarm in us. Its presence underwrites the feel of ceremony and formality Yeats's poems of the 1890s characteristically yield. Those were the years when Yeats was being a Symbolist, meeting people familiar with what was going on in Paris, listening during the year he roomed with Symons while Symons talked out the still-unwritten *Symbolist Movement in Literature,* or expounded the translations he was then making, which Yeats called "the most accomplished metrical translations of our time," adding that the ones from Mallarmé "may have given elaborate form to my verses of those years, to the latter poems of *The Wind Among the Reeds,* to *The Shadowy Waters.*" In 1937, looking again at Mallarmé in a translation, Roger Fry's this time, he called that way of working "the road I and others of my time went for certain furlongs. It is not the way I go now, but one of the legitimate roads."

Yeats did not abandon the intricate long sentence; each stanza of *Byzantium* is one sentence, each stanza of *Coole Park, 1929,* each stanza of *Ancestral Houses,* each but three of the twelve stanzas of *In Memory of Major Robert Gregory.* What he abandoned was the Mallarméan way of proceeding by digressions from the sentence's main business. By transposing this particular method into English, and discovering its possibilities and limitations, he may have saved other poets time. Other poets, certainly, whose later work is quite unlike Yeats's later work because they did not adopt Yeats's final attitude to syntax, display in their early as well as their later work a debt to Symbolist syntax which is less than obvious if only because Yeats had already explored the obvious.

Thus instead of progress by digressions we encounter progress by ellipses. In Mallarmé's "Soupir," we may remember, Arthur Symons discovered a delicate emotion, a figure vaguely divined, a landscape magically evoked, three things that would seem not to be related but are blended into a single effect. The trick of the blending was to make the elements digress from a kernel sentence which holds them firmly in relation to one another and allows the reader's mind to overlay them. But if they can be held firmly by some other means, the kernel sentence may simply be omitted.

One way of holding them, giving each element in the poem its identity and still persuading the mind that they relate, is by metrical definition, as in Ezra Pound's 1912 poem "The Return," in which a strong metrical figure —

> Gods of the winged shoe!
>
> With them the silver hounds,
>
> sniffing the trace of air

— dominates the part characterized by verbs in the past tense, enforcing the contrast between the emphatic way the gods once *were,* and

> the tentative
> Movements, and the slow feet,
> The trouble in the pace and the uncertain
> Wavering

that expresses their unstable way of returning *now*. The poem encompasses a long historical span, from Sappho's time, say, to H.D.'s, but no kernel sentence makes a statement to that effect. The sentences of which the poem is made are very simple: "See, they return"; "These were the souls of blood"; while no syntax specifies the coherence of the poem as a whole. We may feel that a statement of some length has been made but that important syntactic members of this statement have dropped out. And yet nothing has dropped out; we have, thanks to the rhythmic definition, every necessary element, held in place in the poem's continuum so exactly that alterations of tense will specify everything.

Or we encounter progress by incantation, as in Eliot's "Marina." Some parts of "Marina" can be treated as sentences and some parts cannot; nor can "Marina" as a whole be treated as though it were a long statement, even a statement of which parts are missing. Its organization is not syntactic at all. One probably wants to call it "musical," based on associations and recurrences, among them the Shakespearean associations aroused by the title. It is as far as Eliot ever went in that particular direction, but the direction is implicit in most of his work, and confirmed as well by work of Valéry's: the poem faced toward a domain of waking dream, so certain of its diction that we concede it a coherence it need not find means of specifying. It has no paraphrasable structure at all, and yet seems to affirm its elusive substance as authoritatively as Mozart.

Eliot admired Tennyson when Tennyson was out of fashion, and now that Eliot too is out of fashion it is pertinent to recall his great indebtedness to Symons's *Symbolist Movement in Literature*. Everyone remembers how he discovered Laforgue in that book; we tend to forget how quickly he dropped Laforgue, and also tend not to notice how tenaciously he developed hints from Mallarmé, of whom he and Valéry are the principal heirs. I think Donald Davie has been alone in insisting that Eliot's sensibility is post-Symbolist. Yet surely he imitated the unseen eyebeam that falls in *Burnt Norton* on flowers that seem looked at, from "le regard diaphane" which in *Toast Funèbre* rests on unfading because verbal flowers; surely the intent insistence on a silence into which "words, after speech, reach" (for "that which is only living / Can only die") reflects Mallarmé's best-known preoccupation. *Burnt Norton*, by intention a counter-poem to *The Waste Land*, is also a sustained homage to Mallarmé, the austere codifier of its difficult art. The art is in touch with

Tennyson's as well, and with Edward Lear's. The inventory of its structures remains to be made, so long, ironically, despite all Eliot's warnings, was criticism preoccupied with his "ideas." What Mallarmé wrote darkly of Poe, that the dipsomaniac who went by that name would be transformed by the operations of Eternity not into some myth but precisely into himself, we may see exemplified, more convincingly than in Poe's case, when Eliot is sufficiently forgotten to be rediscovered. His work may then seem a compendium of examples for such a survey of post-Symbolist structures as this paper has hinted at.

PART 3

TECHNIQUES AND TRUTHS

THE NEW CRITICS NEVER TIRED OF TWO WORDS: *FORM* AND *TECHNIQUE*. In fact, these terms defined the battleground where the historical scholars lost their way, and were ultimately defeated. Allen Tate, in annihilating the methods of the old regime, maintained that "[t]he question in the end comes down to this: What as literary critics are we to judge? As literary critics we must first of all decide in what respect the literary work has a specific objectivity. If we deny its specific objectivity then not only is criticism impossible but literature also." He then reasoned: "From my point of view the formal qualities of a poem are the focus of the specifically critical judgment because they partake of an objectivity that the subject matter, abstracted from the form, wholly lacks." This was the philosophical justification for the New Critical practice of treating each literary work as an organic whole in which *form* and *subject* were integral (rather than treating *form* as merely the vehicle for the author's social and historical interests, an approach that Tate derided as "the historical method").

This did not mean that modern poets should be required to use only the forms and techniques inherited from older generations. In fact, they were constantly encouraged by most of the New Critics to be original in their meters. John Crowe Ransom explained the necessity of such experimentation by the modernists: "They do not find sufficient profit in that traditional poetic labor which consists in the determinate metering of a determinate discourse. I have argued that some ontological triumph, something impossible for pure discourse, may be secured in this way. They are acquainted with the technique, and find it too easy. The well-metered discourse is impaired for them because it is transparently artful; they want a more direct and less formal knowledge."

Whether such experimentation was, indeed, *necessary* to modern poetry remains an interesting debate. Ezra Pound, the twentieth century's great innovator of verse technique, found the motto of modernism engraved on the bathtub of a Chinese emperor: "Make it new." This obsession with originality (which Randall Jarrell described so well in his essay "The End of the Line") was almost inescapable in its day—though nearly a century later, the notion that a perpetual revolution of poetic technique is really necessary, or even possible, is questionable. Certainly, the neoclassical wing of the New Criticism—ruled by Yvor Winters and his disciples—found these trends excessive and even grotesque, with some reason. (Winters's book *Primitivism and Decadence* is essentially a disapproving examination of modernist poetry techniques.)

This debate (inaugurated with Pound's early essays on imagism and crystallized in a much later line of his poetry that "to break the pentameter . . . was the first heave" of modernism) has never ended. The major premise of so much recent American poetry is simply "To be modern is to be experimental." That is a vulgar simplification of certain tendencies. Confronted with the modernist distaste for the rules of classical prosody, subsequent generations have mistakenly dispensed with prosody altogether. The *vers libre* movement has led to truly free verse, which (as T. S. Eliot wrote in 1917) is merely chaos.

Included in this section is the key document of the *vers libre* movement that Ezra Pound launched in 1913, along with Eliot's prescient essay concerning its practice. John Crowe Ransom and Randall Jarrell provide two views of the modernist poets' unique (Ransom would say *ontologically distinct*) approach to their craft, while J. V. Cunningham's essay dares his fellow versifiers to view traditional meters and forms as the final outpost of the *avant-garde*. Finally, Yvor Winters provides the reader with a brief overview of the main critical theories of literature, before proposing his own absolutism regarding poetry as a moral discipline.

Suggested Further Reading

"The Influence of Meter on Poetic Convention," by Yvor Winters (from *Primitivism and Decadence*, 1937)

"The Audible Reading of Poetry," by Yvor Winters (from *The Function of Literature*, 1943)

Literary Essays of Ezra Pound, edited by T. S. Eliot (1954)

"The Music of Poetry," by T. S. Eliot (from *On Poetry and Poets*, 1957)

"The Concept of Meter: An Exercise in Abstraction," by W. K. Wimsatt (from *Hateful Contraries*, 1965)

BREAKING THE PENTAMETER

A Retrospect

EZRA POUND

From Pound's first essay collection, Pavannes and Divisions *(1918),
this piece set forth the rules and direction of the imagist poets, and
thus is central to understanding the practice (and malpractice) of
free verse in English in our own day.*

There has been so much scribbling about a new fashion in poetry,
that I may perhaps be pardoned this brief recapitulation and retrospect.

In the spring or early summer of 1912, "H. D.," Richard Aldington and
myself decided that we were agreed upon the three principles following:

1. Direct treatment of the "thing" whether subjective or objective.

2. To use absolutely no word that does not contribute to the presentation.

3. As regarding rhythm: to compose in the sequence of the musical
phrase, not in sequence of a metronome.

Upon many points of taste and of predilection we differed, but agreeing
upon these three positions we thought we had as much right to a group
name, at least as much right, as a number of French "schools" proclaimed
by Mr. Flint in the August number of Harold Monro's magazine for 1911.

This school has since been "joined" or "followed" by numerous people
who, whatever their merits, do not show any signs of agreeing with
the second specification. Indeed *vers libre* has become as prolix and as
verbose as any of the flaccid varieties that preceded it. It has brought
faults of its own. The actual language and phrasing is often as bad as
that of our elders without even the excuse that the words are shoveled
in to fill a metric pattern or to complete the noise of a rhyme-sound.
Whether or no the phrases followed by the followers are musical must
be left to the reader's decision. At times I can find a marked meter in
"vers libres," as stale and hackneyed as any pseudo-Swinburnian, at times
the writers seem to follow no musical structure whatever. But it is, on
the whole, good that the field should be ploughed. Perhaps a few good
poems have come from a new method, and if so it is justified.

Criticism is not a circumscription or a set of prohibitions. It provides
fixed points of departure. It may startle a dull reader into alertness. That

little of it which is good is mostly in stray phrases; or if it be an older artist helping a younger it is in great measure but rules of thumb, cautions gained by experience.

I set together a few phrases on practical working about the time the first remarks on imagisme were published. The first use of the word "Imagiste" was in my note to T. E. Hulme's five poems, printed at the end of my "Ripostes" in the autumn of 1912. I reprint my cautions from *Poetry* for March, 1913.

A Few Don'ts

An "Image" is that which presents an intellectual and emotional complex in an instant of time. I use the term "complex" rather in the technical sense employed by the newer psychologists, such as Hart, though we might not agree absolutely in our application.

It is the presentation of such a "complex" instantaneously which gives that sense of sudden liberation; that sense of freedom from time limits and space limits; that sense of sudden growth, which we experience in the presence of the greatest works of art.

It is better to present one Image in a lifetime than to produce voluminous works.

All this, however, some may consider open to debate. The immediate necessity is to tabulate A LIST OF DON'TS for those beginning to write verses. I can not put all of them into Mosaic negative.

To begin with, consider the three propositions (demanding direct treatment, economy of words, and the sequence of the musical phrase), not as dogma—never consider anything as dogma—but as the result of long contemplation, which, even if it is some one else's contemplation, may be worth consideration.

Pay no attention to the criticism of men who have never themselves written a notable work. Consider the discrepancies between the actual writing of the Greek poets and dramatists, and the theories of the Graeco-Roman grammarians, concocted to explain their meters.

Language

Use no superfluous word, no adjective which does not reveal something.

Don't use such an expression as "dim lands of *peace*." It dulls the image. It mixes an abstraction with the concrete. It comes from the writer's not realizing that the natural object is always the *adequate* symbol.

Go in fear of abstractions. Do not retell in mediocre verse what has already been done in good prose. Don't think any intelligent person is going to be deceived when you try to shirk all the difficulties of the unspeakably difficult art of good prose by chopping your composition into line lengths.

What the expert is tired of today the public will be tired of tomorrow.

Don't imagine that the art of poetry is any simpler than the art of music, or that you can please the expert before you have spent at least as much effort on the art of verse as the average piano teacher spends on the art of music.

Be influenced by as many great artists as you can, but have the decency either to acknowledge the debt outright, or to try to conceal it.

Don't allow "influence" to mean merely that you mop up the particular decorative vocabulary of some one or two poets whom you happen to admire. A Turkish war correspondent was recently caught red-handed babbling in his dispatches of "dove-grey" hills, or else it was "pearl-pale," I can not remember.

Use either no ornament or good ornament.

Rhythm and Rhyme

Let the candidate fill his mind with the finest cadences he can discover, preferably in a foreign language,[1] so that the meaning of the words may be less likely to divert his attention from the movement; e.g. Saxon charms, Hebridean Folk Songs, the verse of Dante, and the lyrics of Shakespeare — if he can dissociate the vocabulary from the cadence. Let him dissect the lyrics of Goethe coldly into their component sound values, syllables long and short, stressed and unstressed, into vowels and consonants.

It is not necessary that a poem should rely on its music, but if it does rely on its music that music must be such as will delight the expert.

Let the neophyte know assonance and alliteration, rhyme immediate and delayed, simple and polyphonic, as a musician would expect to know harmony and counterpoint and all the minutiae of his craft. No time is too great to give to these matters or to any one of them, even if the artist seldom have need of them.

Don't imagine that a thing will "go" in verse just because it's too dull to go in prose.

Don't be "viewy"—leave that to the writers of pretty little philosophic essays. Don't be descriptive; remember that the painter can describe a landscape much better than you can, and that he has to know a deal more about it.

When Shakespeare talks of the "Dawn in russet mantle clad" he presents something which the painter does not present. There is in this line of his nothing that one can call description; he presents.

Consider the way of the scientists rather than the way of an advertising agent for a new soap.

The scientist does not expect to be acclaimed as a great scientist until he has *discovered* something. He begins by learning what has been discovered already. He goes from that point onward. He does not bank on being a charming fellow personally. He does not expect his friends to applaud the results of his freshman class work. Freshmen in poetry are unfortunately not confined to a definite and recognizable class room. They are "all over the shop." Is it any wonder "the public is indifferent to poetry"?

Don't chop your stuff into separate *iambs*. Don't make each line stop dead at the end, and then begin every next line with a heave. Let the beginning of the next line catch the rise of the rhythm wave, unless you want a definite longish pause.

In short, behave as a musician, a good musician, when dealing with that phase of your art which has exact parallels in music. The same laws govern, and you are bound by no others.

Naturally, your rhythmic structure should not destroy the shape of your words, or their natural sound, or their meaning. It is improbable that, at the start, you will be able to get a rhythm-structure strong enough to affect them very much, though you may fall a victim to all sorts of false stopping due to line ends and cæsurae.

The Musician can rely on pitch and the volume of the orchestra. You can not. The term harmony is misapplied in poetry; it refers to simultaneous sounds of different pitch. There is, however, in the best verse a sort of residue of sound which remains in the ear of the hearer and acts more or less as an organ-base.

A rhyme must have in it some slight element of surprise if it is to give pleasure; it need not be bizarre or curious, but it must be well used if used at all.

Vide further Vildrac and Duhamel's notes on rhyme in *"Technique Poétique."*

That part of your poetry which strikes upon the imaginative *eye* of the reader will lose nothing by translation into a foreign tongue; that which appeals to the ear can reach only those who take it in the original.

Consider the definiteness of Dante's presentation, as compared with Milton's rhetoric. Read as much of Wordsworth as does not seem too unutterably dull.[2]

If you want the gist of the matter go to Sappho, Catullus, Villon, Heine when he is in the vein, Gautier when he is not too frigid; or, if you have not the tongues, seek out the leisurely Chaucer. Good prose will do you no harm, and there is good discipline to be had by trying to write it.

Translation is likewise good training, if you find that you original matter "wobbles" when you try to rewrite it. The meaning of the poem to be translated can not "wobble."

If you are using a symmetrical form, don't put in what you want to say and then fill up the remaining vacuums with slush.

Don't mess up the perception of one sense by trying to define it in terms of another. This is usually only the result of being too lazy to find the exact word. To this clause there are possibly exceptions.

The first three simple prescriptions will throw out nine-tenths of all the bad poetry now accepted as standard and classic; and will prevent you from many a crime of production.

" . . . *Mais d'abord il faut être un poète,*" as MM. Duhamel and Vildrac have said at the end of their little book, "*Notes sur la Technique Poétique.*"

• • •

Since March 1913, Ford Madox Hueffer has pointed out that Wordsworth was so intent on the ordinary or plain word that he never thought of hunting for *le mot juste.*

John Butler Yeats has handled or man-handled Wordsworth and the Victorians, and his criticism, contained in letters to his son, is now printed and available.

I do not like writing *about* art, my first, at least I think it was my first essay on the subject, was a protest against it.

Prolegomena[3]

Time was when the poet lay in a green field with his head against a tree and played his diversion on a ha'penny whistle, and Caesar's predecessors conquered the earth, and the predecessors of golden Crassus embezzled, and fashions had their say, and let him alone. And presumably he was fairly content in this circumstance, for I have small doubt that the occasional passerby, being attracted by curiosity to know why any one should lie under a tree and blow diversion on a ha'penny whistle, came and conversed with him, and that among these passers-by there was on occasion a person of charm or a young lady who had not read *Man and Superman*; and looking back upon this naïve state of affairs we call it the age of gold.

Metastasio, and he should know if any one, assures us that this age endures—even though the modern poet is expected to holloa his verses down a speaking tube to the editors of cheap magazines—S. S. McClure, or some one of that sort—even though hordes of authors meet in dreariness and drink healths to the "Copyright Bill"; even though these things be, the age of gold pertains. Imperceivably, if you like, but pertains. You meet unkempt Amyclas in a Soho restaurant and chant together of dead and forgotten things—it is a manner of speech among poets to chant of dead, half-forgotten things, there seems no special harm in it; it has always been done—and it's rather better to be a clerk in the Post Office than to look after a lot of stinking, verminous sheep—and at another hour of the day one substitutes the drawing-room for the restaurant and tea is probably more palatable than mead and mare's milk, and little cakes than honey. And in this fashion one survives the resignation of Mr. Balfour, and the iniquities of the American customs-house, *e quel bufera infernal*, the periodical press. And then in the middle of it, there being apparently no other person at once capable and available one is stopped and asked to explain oneself.

I begin on the chord thus querulous, for I would much rather lie on what is left of Catullus's parlor floor and speculate the azure beneath it and the hills off to Salo and Riva with their forgotten gods moving unhindered amongst them, than discuss any processes and theories of art whatsoever. I would rather play tennis. I shall not argue.

Credo

Rhythm. —I believe in an "absolute rhythm," a rhythm, that is, in poetry which corresponds exactly to the emotion or shade of emotion to be expressed. A man's rhythm must be interpretative, it will be, therefore, in the end, his own, uncounterfeiting, uncounterfeitable.

Symbols. —I believe that the proper and perfect symbol is the natural object, that if a man use "symbols" he must so use them that their symbolic function does not obtrude; so that *a* sense, and the poetic quality of the passage, is not lost to those who do not understand the symbol as such, to whom, for instance, a hawk is a hawk.

Technique. —I believe in technique as the test of a man's sincerity; in law when it is ascertainable; in the trampling down of every convention that impedes or obscures the determination of the law, or the precise rendering of the impulse.

Form. —I think there is a "fluid" as well as a "solid" content, that some poems may have form as a tree has form, some as water poured into a vase. That most symmetrical forms have certain uses. That a vast number of subjects cannot be precisely, and therefore not properly rendered in symmetrical forms.

"Thinking that alone worthy wherein the whole art is employed."[4] I think the artist should master all known forms and systems of metric, and I have with some persistence set about doing this, searching particularly into those periods wherein the systems came to birth or attained their maturity. It has been complained, with some justice, that I dump my note-books on the public. I think that only after a long struggle will poetry attain such a degree of development, or, if you will, modernity, that it will vitally concern people who are accustomed, in prose, to Henry James and Anatole France, in music to Debussy. I am constantly contending that it took two centuries of Provence and one of Tuscany to develop the media of Dante's masterwork, that it took the latinists of the Renaissance, and the Pleiade, and his own age of painted speech to prepare Shakespeare his tools. It is tremendously important that great poetry be written, it makes no jot of difference who writes it. The experimental demonstrations of one man may save the time of many—hence my furore over Arnaut Daniel—if a man's experiments try out one new rime, or dispense conclusively with one iota of currently accepted nonsense, he is merely playing fair with his colleagues when he chalks up his result.

No man ever writes very much poetry that "matters." In bulk, that is, no one produces much that is final, and when a man is not doing this highest thing, this saying the thing once for all and perfectly; when he is not matching Ποχιλόθρον, άθάνατ Αφρόδιτα, or "Hist—said Kate the Queen," he had much better be making the sorts of experiment which may be of use to him in his later work, or to his successors.

"The lyf so short, the craft so long to lerne." It is a foolish thing for a man to begin his work on a too narrow foundation, it is a disgraceful thing for a man's work not to show steady growth and increasing fineness from first to last.

As for "adaptations"; one finds that all the old masters of painting recommend to their pupils that they begin by copying masterwork, and proceed to their own composition.

As for "Every man his own poet," the more every man knows about poetry the better. I believe in every one writing poetry who wants to; most do. I believe in every man knowing enough of music to play "God bless our home" on the harmonium, but I do not believe in every man giving concerts and printing his sin.

The mastery of any art is the work of a lifetime. I should not discriminate between the "amateur"' and the "professional." Or rather I should discriminate quite often in favor of the amateur, but I should discriminate between the amateur and the expert. It is certain that the present chaos will endure until the Art of poetry has been preached down the amateur gullet, until there is such a general understanding of the fact that poetry is an art and not a pastime; such a knowledge of technique; of technique of surface and technique of content, that the amateurs will cease to try to drown out the masters.

If a certain thing was said once for all in Atlantis or Arcadia, in 450 Before Christ or in 1290 after, it is not for us moderns to go saying it over, or to go obscuring the memory of the dead by saying the same thing with less skill and less conviction.

My pawing over the ancients and semi-ancients has been one strug-gle to find out what has been done, once for all, better than it can ever be done again, and to find out what remains for us to do, and plenty does remain, for if we still feel the same emotions as those which launched the thousand ships, it is quite certain that we come on these feelings dif-ferently, through different nuances, by different intellectual gradations. Each age has its own abounding gifts yet only some ages transmute them into matter of duration. No good poetry is ever written in a man-ner twenty years old, for to write in such a manner shows conclusively that the writer thinks from books, convention and *cliché*, and not from life, yet a man feeling the divorce of life and his art may naturally try to resurrect a forgotten mode if he finds in that mode some leaven, or if he think he sees in it some element lacking in contemporary art which might unite that art again to its sustenance, life.

In the art of Daniel and Cavalcanti, I have seen that precision which I miss in the Victorians, that explicit rendering, be it of external nature, or of emotion. Their testimony is of the eyewitness, their symptoms are first hand.

As for the nineteenth century, with all respect to its achievements, I think we shall look back upon it as a rather blurry, messy sort of a period, a rather sentimentalistic, mannerish sort of a period. I say this without any self-righteousness, with no self-satisfaction.

As for there being a "movement" or my being of it, the conception of poetry as a "pure art" in the sense in which I use the term, revived with Swinburne. From the puritanical revolt to Swinburne, poetry had been merely the vehicle—yes, definitely, Arthur Symons's scruples and feelings about the word not withholding—the ox-cart and post-chaise for trans-mitting thoughts poetic or otherwise. And perhaps the "great Victorians," though it is doubtful, and assuredly the "nineties" continued the devel-opment of the art, confining their improvements, however, chiefly to sound and to refinements of manner.

Mr. Yeats has once and for all stripped English poetry of its per-damnable rhetoric. He has boiled away all that is not poetic—and a good deal that is. He has become a classic in his own lifetime and *nel mezzo del cammin*. He has made our poetic idiom a thing pliable, a speech without inversions.

Robert Bridges, Maurice Hewlett, and Frederic Manning are[5] in their different ways seriously concerned with overhauling the metric, in testing the language and its adaptability to certain modes. Ford Hueffer is making some sort of experiments in modernity. The Provost of Oriel continues his translation of the *Divina Commedia*.

As to Twentieth century poetry, and the poetry which I expect to see written during the next decade or so, it will, I think, move against poppy-cock, it will be harder and saner, it will be what Mr. Hewlett calls "nearer the bone." It will be as much like granite as it can be, its force will lie in its truth, its interpretative power (of course, poetic force does always rest there); I mean it will not try to seem forcible by rhetorical din, and luxurious riot. We will have fewer painted adjectives impeding the shock and stroke of it. At least for myself, I want it so, austere, direct, free from emotional slither.

• • •

What is there now, in 1917, to be added?

Re Vers Libre

I think the desire for vers libre is due to the sense of quantity reasserting itself after years of starvation. But I doubt if we can take over, for English, the rules of quantity laid down for Greek and Latin, mostly by Latin grammarians.

I think one should write vers libre only when one "must," that is to say, only when the "thing" builds up a rhythm more beautiful than that of set meters, or more real, more a part of the emotion of the "thing," more germane, intimate, interpretative than the measure of regular accentual verse; a rhythm which discontents one with set iambic or set anapaestic.

Eliot has said the thing very well when he said, "No *vers* is *libre* for the man who wants to do a good job."

As a matter of detail, there is vers libre with accent heavily marked as a drum-beat (as par example my "Dance Figure"), and on the other hand I think I have gone as far as can profitably be gone in the other direction (and perhaps too far). I mean I do not think one can use to any advantage rhythms much more tenuous and imperceptible than some I have used. I think progress lies rather in an attempt to approximate classical quantitative meters (NOT to copy them) than in a carelessness regarding such things.[6]

• • •

I agree with John Yeats on the relation of beauty to certitude. I prefer satire, which is due to emotion, to any sham of emotion.

I have had to write, or at least I have written a good deal about art, sculpture, painting, and poetry. I have seen what seemed to me the best of contemporary work reviled and obstructed. Can any one write prose of permanent or durable interest when he is merely saying for one year what nearly every one will say at the end of three or four years? I have been battistrada for a sculptor, a painter, a novelist, several poets. I wrote also of certain French writers in *The New Age* in nineteen twelve or eleven.

I would much rather that people would look at Brzeska's sculpture and Lewis's drawings, and that they would read Joyce, Jules Romains, Eliot, than that they should read what I have said of these men, or that I should be asked to republish argumentative essays and reviews.

All that the critic can do for the reader or audience or spectator is to focus his gaze or audition. Rightly or wrongly I think my blasts and essays have done their work, and that more people are now likely to go to the sources than are likely to read this book.

Jammes's "Existences" in "*La Triomphe de la Vie*" is available. So are his early poems. I think we need a convenient anthology rather than descriptive criticism. Carl Sandburg wrote me from Chicago, "It's hell when poets can't afford to buy each other's books." Half the people who care, only borrow. In America so few people know each other that the difficulty lies more than half in distribution. Perhaps one should make an anthology: Romains's "Un Etre en Marche' and 'Prières," Vildrac's "Visite." Retrospectively the fine wrought work of Laforgue, the flashes of Rimbaud, the hard-bit lines of Tristan Corbière, Tailhade's sketches in "Poèmes Aristophanesques," the "Litanies" of De Gourmont.

• • •

It is difficult at all times to write of the fine arts, it is almost impossible unless one can accompany one's prose with many reproductions. Still I would seize this chance or any chance to reaffirm my belief in Wyndham Lewis's genius, both in his drawings and his writings. And I would name an out of the way prose book, the "*Scenes and Portraits*" of Frederic Manning, as well as James Joyce's short stories and novel, "Dubliners" and the now well known "Portrait of the Artist" as well as Lewis's "Tarr," if, that is, I may treat my strange reader as if he were a new friend come into the room, intent on ransacking my bookshelf.

Only Emotion Endures

"Only emotion endures." Surely it is better for me to name over the few beautiful poems that still ring in my head than for me to search my flat for back numbers of periodicals and rearrange all that I have said about friendly and hostile writers.

The first twelve lines of Padraic Colum's "Drover"; his "O Woman shapely as a swan, on your account I shall not die"; Joyce's "I hear an army"; the lines of Yeats that ring in my head and in the heads of all young men of my time who care for poetry: Braseal and the Fisher-man, "The fire that stirs about her when she stirs"; the later lines of "The Scholars," the faces of the Magi; William Carlos Williams's "Postlude," Aldington's version of "Atthis," and "H. D.'"s "waves like pine tops'," and her verse in "Des Imagistes" the first anthology; Hueffer's "How red your lips are'" in his translation from Von der Vogelweide, his "Three Ten," the general effect of his "On Heaven"; his sense of the prose values or prose qualities in poetry; his ability to write poems that half-chant and are spoiled by a musician's additions; beyond these a poem by Alice Corbin, "One City Only," and another ending "But slid-ing water over a stone." These things have worn smooth in my head and I am not through with them, nor with Aldington's "In Via Sestina" nor his other poems in "Des Imagistes," though people have told me their flaws. It may be that their content is too much embedded in me for me to look back at the words.

I am almost a different person when I come to take up the argument for Eliot's poems.

1. This is for rhythm, his vocabulary must of course be found in his native tongue.
2. Vide infra.
3. *Poetry and Drama* (then the *Poetry Review*, edited by Harold Monro), Feb. 1912.
4. Dante, *De Volgari Eloquio.*
5. (Dec. 1911).
6. Let me date this statement 20 Aug. 1917.

Reflections on *Vers Libre*

T. S. ELIOT

One of Eliot's first published pieces of prose was this shrewd exami-nation of the fallacies and challenges of the then-emerging vers libre *movement. Most of the deformations of contemporary poetic versification in America are anticipated and explained in this re-markable essay.*

Ceux qui possèdent *leur* vers libre y tiennent:
on n'abandonne que *le* vers libre.

— Duhamel et Vildrac

A lady, renowned in her small circle for the accuracy of her stop-press information of literature, complains to me of a growing pococurantism.

"Since the Russians came in I can read nothing else. I have finished Dostoevski, and I do not know what to do." I suggested that the great Russian was an admirer of Dickens, and that she also might find that author readable. "But Dickens is a sentimentalist; Dostoevski is a realist." I reflected on the amours of Sonia and Rashkolnikov, but forbore to press the point, and I proposed *It Is Never Too Late to Mend*. "But one cannot read the Victorians at all!" While I was extracting the virtues of the proposition that Dostoevski is a Christian, while Charles Reade is merely pious, she added that she could not longer read any verse but *vers libre*.

It is assumed that *vers libre* exists. It is assumed that *vers libre* is a school; that it consists of certain theories; that its group or groups of theorists will either revolutionize or demoralize poetry if their attack upon the iambic pentameter meets with any success. *Vers libre* does not exist, and it is time that this preposterous fiction followed the *élan vital* and the eighty thousand Russians into oblivion.

When a theory of art passes it is usually found that a groat's worth of art has been bought with a million of advertisement. The theory which sold the wares may be quite false, or it may be confused and incapable of elucidation, or it may never have existed. A mythical revolution will have taken place and produced a few works of art which perhaps would be even better if still less of the revolutionary theories clung to them. In modern society such revolutions are almost inevitable. An artist, happens upon a method, perhaps quite unreflectingly, which is new in the sense that it is essentially different from that of the second-rate people about him, and different in everything but essentials from that of any of his great predecessors. The novelty meets with neglect; neglect provokes attack; and attack demands a theory. In an ideal state of society one might imagine the good New growing naturally out of the good Old, without the need for polemic and theory; this would be a society with a living tradition. In a sluggish society, as actual societies are, tradition is ever lapsing into superstition, and the violent stimulus of novelty is required. This is bad for the artist and his school, who may become circumscribed by their theory and narrowed by their polemic; but the artist can always console himself for his errors in his old age by considering that if he had not fought nothing would have been accomplished.

Vers libre has not even the excuse of a polemic; it is a battle-cry of freedom, and there is no freedom in art. And as the so-called *vers libre* which is good is anything but "free," it can better be defended under some other label. Particular types of *vers libre* may be supported on the choice of content, or on the method of handling the content. I am aware that many writers of *vers libre* have introduced such innova-tions, and that the novelty of their choice and manipulation of material is confused—if not in their own minds, in the minds of many of their readers—with the novelty of the form. But I am not here concerned with imagism, which is a theory about the use of material; I am only concerned with the theory of the verse-form in which imagism is cast. If *vers libre* is a genuine verse-form it will have a positive definition. And I can define it only in negatives: (1) absence of pattern, (2) absence of rhyme, (3) absence of meter.

The third of these qualities is easily disposed of. What sort of a line that would be which would not scan at all I cannot say. Even in the popular American magazines, whose verse columns are now largely given over to *vers libre*, the lines are usually explicable in terms of prosody. Any line can be divided into feet and accents. The simpler meters are a repetition of one combination, perhaps a long and a short, or a short and a long syllable, five times repeated. There is, however, no reason why, within the single line, there should be any repetition; why there should not be lines (as there are) divisible only into feet of different types. How can the grammatical exercise of scansion make a line of this sort more intelligible? Only by isolating elements which occur in other lines, and the sole purpose of doing this is the production of a similar effect elsewhere. But repetition of effect is a question of pattern.

Scansion tells us very little. It is probable that there is not much to be gained by an elaborate system of prosody, but the erudite complexi-ties of Swinburnian meter. With Swinburne, once the trick is perceived and the scholarship appreciated, the effect is somewhat diminished. When the unexpectedness, due to the unfamiliarity of the meters to English ears, wears off and is understood, one ceases to look for what one does not find in Swinburne; the inexplicable line with the music which can never be recaptured in other words. Swinburne mastered his technique, which is a great deal, but he did not master it to the extent of being able to take liberties with it, which is everything. If anything promising for English poetry is hidden in the meters of Swinburne, it probably lies far beyond the point to which Swinburne has developed them. But the most interesting verse which has yet been written in our language has been done either by taking a very simple form, like the iambic pentameter, and constantly withdrawing from it, or taking no form at all, and constantly approximating to a very simple one. It is this contrast between fixity and flux, this unperceived evasion of monotony, which is the very life of verse.

I have in mind two passages of contemporary verse which would be called *vers libre*. Both of them I quote because of their beauty:

> Once, in finesse of fiddles found I ecstasy,
> In the flash of gold heels on the hard pavement.
> Now see I
> That warmth's the very stuff of poesy.
> Oh, God, make small
> The old star-eaten blanket of the sky,
> That I may fold it round me and in comfort lie.

This is a complete poem. The other is part of a much longer poem:

> There shut up in his castle, Tairiran's,
> She who had nor ears nor tongue save in her hands,
> Gone—ah, gone—untouched, unreachable—
> She who could never live save through one person,
> She who could never speak save to one person,
> And all the rest of her a shifting change,
> A broken bundle of mirrors . . .—

It is obvious that the charm of these lines could not be, without the constant suggestion and the skilful evasion of iambic pentameter.

At the beginning of the seventeenth century, and especially in the verse of John Webster, who was in some ways a more cunning technician than Shakespeare, one finds the same constant evasion and recognition of regularity. Webster is much freer than Shakespeare, and that his fault is not negligence is evidenced by the fact that it is often at moments of the highest intensity that his verse acquires this freedom. That there is also carelessness I do not deny, but the irregularity of carelessness can be at once detected from the irregularity of deliberation. (In *The White Devil* Brachiano dying, and Cornelia mad, deliberately rupture the bonds of pentameter.)

> I recover, like a spent taper, for a flash
> and instantly go out.

• • •

> Cover her face; mine eyes dazzle; she died young.

• • •

> You have cause to love me, I did enter you in my heart
> Before you would vouchsafe to call for the keys.

• • •

> This is a vain poetry: but I pray you tell me
> If there were proposed me, wisdom, riches, and beauty,
> In three several young men, which should I choose?

These are not lines of carelessness. The irregularity is further enhanced by the use of short lines and the breaking up of lines in dialogue, which alters the quantities. And there are many lines in the drama of this time which are spoilt by regular accentuation.

> I loved this woman in spite of my heart. (*The Changeling*)

> I would have these herbs grow up in his grave. (*The White Devil*)

> Whether the spirit of greatness or of woman . . . (*The Duchess of Malfi*)

The general charge of decadence cannot be preferred. Tourneur and Shirley, who I think will be conceded to have touched nearly the bottom of the decline of tragedy, are much more regular than Webster or Middleton. Tourneur will polish off a fair line of iambics even at the cost of amputating a preposition from its substantive, and in the *Atheist's Tragedy* he has a final "of" in two lines out of five together.

We may therefore formulate as follows: the ghost of some simple meter should lurk behind the arras in even the "freest" verse; to advance menacingly as we doze, and withdraw as we rouse. Or, freedom is only true freedom when it appears against the background of an artificial limitation.

Not to have perceived the simple truth that *some* artificial limitation is necessary except in moments of the first intensity is, I believe, a capital error of even so distinguished a talent as that of Mr. E. L. Masters. The *Spoon River Anthology* is not material of the first intensity; it is reflective, not immediate; its author is a moralist, rather than an observer. His material is so near to the material of Crabbe that one wonders why he should have used a different form. Crabbe is, on the whole, the more intense of the two; he is keen, direct, and unsparing. His material is prosaic, not in the sense that it would have been better done in prose, but in the sense of requiring a simple and rather rigid verse-form and this Crabbe has given it. Mr. Masters requires a more rigid verse-form than either of the two contemporary poets quoted above, and his epitaphs suffer from the lack of it.

So much for meter. There is no escape from meter; there is only mastery. But while there obviously is escape from rhyme, the *vers librists* are by no means the first out of the cave.

The boughs of the trees
Are twisted
By many bafflings;
Twisted are
The small-leafed boughs.
But the shadow of them
Is not the shadow of the mast head
Nor of the torn sails.

* * *

When the white dawn first
Through the rough fir-planks
Of my hut, by the chestnuts,
Up at the valley-head,
Came breaking, Goddess,
I sprang up, I threw round me
My dappled fawn-skin . . .

Except for the more human touch in the second of these extracts a hasty observer would hardly realize that the first is by a contemporary, and the second by Matthew Arnold.

I do not minimize the services of modern poets in exploiting the possibilities of rhymeless verse. They prove the strength of a Movement, the utility of a Theory. What neither Blake nor Arnold could do alone is being done in our time. "Blank verse" is the only accepted rhymeless verse in English — the inevitable iambic pentameter. The English ear is (or was) more sensitive to the music of the verse and less dependent upon the recurrence of identical sounds in this meter than in any other. There is no campaign against rhyme. But it is possible that excessive devotion to rhyme has thickened the modern ear. The rejection of rhyme is not a leap at facility; on the contrary, it imposes a much severer strain upon the language. When the comforting echo of rhyme is removed, success or failure in the choice of words, in the sentence structure, in the order, is at once more apparent. Rhyme removed, the poet is at once held up to the standards of prose. Rhyme removed, much ethereal music leaps up from the word, music which has hitherto chirped unnoticed in the expanse of prose. Any rhyme forbidden, many Shagpats were unwigged.

And this liberation from rhyme might be as well a liberation *of* rhyme. Freed from its exacting task of supporting lame verse, it could be applied with greater effect where it is most needed. There are often passages in an unrhymed poem where rhyme is wanted for some special effect, for a sudden tightening-up, for a cumulative insistence, or for an abrupt change of mood. But formal rhymed verse will certainly not lose its place. We only need the coming of a Satirist—no man of genius is rarer—to prove that the heroic couplet has lost none of its edge since Dryden and Pope laid it down. As for the sonnet I am not so sure. But the decay of intricate formal patterns has nothing to do with the advent of *vers libre*. It had set in long before. Only in a closely-knit and homogeneous society, where many men are at work on the same problems, such a society as those which produced the Greek chorus, the Elizabethan lyric, and the Troubadour canzone, will the development of such forms ever be carried to perfection. And as for *vers libre*, we conclude that it is not defined by absence of pattern or absence of rhyme, for other verse is without these; that it is not defined by non-existence of meter, since even the *worst* verse can be scanned; and we conclude that the division between Conservative Verse and *vers libre* does not exist, for there is only good verse, bad verse, and chaos.

Poets Without Laurels

JOHN CROWE RANSOM

In this essay from The World's Body *(1938),* Ransom brilliantly explains how modern poets used new techniques in order to examine
new realities of experience. In the concluding chapter of his book
The New Criticism (1941), *he defended the modern poets this way:
"The fundamental consideration is that the moderns are well instructed in the practice of the traditionalists. But this is what has
happened: they find the old practice trite, and ontologically inadequate for them. Yet they lack any consistent conception of what a
new practice might be [. . .] and therefore they work by taking liberties with the old practice, and irregularize and de-systematize it,
without denying it."*

The poets I refer to in the title are the "moderns": those whom a
small company of adept readers enjoys, perhaps enormously, but the
general public detests; those in whose hands poetry as a living art has
lost its public support.

Consequently I do not refer to such poets as Edna St. Vincent Millay
and Robert Frost, who are evidently influenced by modernism without
caring to "go modern" in the sense of joining the revolution; which is
very much as if they had stopped at a mild or parlor variety of socialism,
when all about them the brave, or at least the doctrinaire, were march-
ing under the red banner. Probably they are wise in their time; they
have laurels deservedly and wear them gracefully. But they do not define
the issue which I wish to discuss. And still less do I refer to poets like E. A.
Robinson, Sturge Moore, and John Masefield, who are even less modern; though I have no intention of questioning their laurels either. I refer
to poets with no laurels.

I do not wish to seem to hold the public responsible for their condition,
as if it had suddenly become phlegmatic, cruel, and philistine. The poets
have certainly for their part conducted themselves peculiarly. They could
not have estranged the public more completely if they had tried; and
smart fellows as they are, they know very well what they have been doing,
and what they are still stubborn in doing, and what the consequences are.

For they have failed more and more flagrantly, more and more deliberately, to identify themselves with the public interests, as if expressly to renounce the kind affections which poets had courted for centuries. Accordingly, they do not only encounter public indifference, they sometimes encounter active hostility. A Pulitzer committeeman, I hear, says about some modernist poet whose book is up for judgment: "He will never get the award except over my dead body." The violence of the remark seems to exceed the occasion, but it is not exceptional.

Poets used to be bards and patriots, priests and prophets, keepers of the public conscience, and, naturally, men of public importance. Society crowned them with wreaths of laurel, according to the tradition which comes to us from the Greeks and is perpetuated by official custom in England—and in Oklahoma. Generally the favor must have been gratefully received. But modern poets are of another breed. It is as if all at once they had lost their prudence as well as their piety, and formed a compact to unclasp the chaplet from their brows, inflicting upon themselves the humility of delaureation, and retiring from public responsibility and honors. It is this phenomenon which has thrown critical theory into confusion.

Sir Philip Sidney made the orthodox defense of poetry on the ground of the poet's service to patriotism and virtue:

> He doth not only show the way, but giveth so sweet a
> prospect into the way, as will entice any man to enter into it.

And what was the technique of enticement?

> With a tale forsooth he cometh unto you, with a tale which
> holdeth children from play, and old men from the chimney
> corner.

The poets, therefore, told entrancing tales, which had morals. But the fact was, also, that the poets were not always content to win to virtue by indirection, or enticement, but were prepared to preach with almost no disguise, and to become sententious and repetitious, and the literature which they created is crowded with precise maxims for the moralists. There it stands on the shelves now. Sometimes the so-called poet has been only a moralist with a poetic manner. And all the poets famous in our tradition, or very nearly all, have been poets of a powerful moral cast.

So I shall try a preliminary definition of the poet's, traditional function on behalf of society: he proposed to make virtue delicious. He compounded a moral effect with an aesthetic effect. The total effect was not a pure one, but it was rich, and relished highly. The name of the moral effect was goodness; the name of the aesthetic effect was beauty. Perhaps these did not have to coexist, but the planners of society saw to it that they should; they called upon the artists to reinforce morality with charm. The artists obliged.

When they had done so, the public did not think of attempting to distinguish in its experience as reader the glow which was aesthetic from the glow which was moral. Most persons probably could not have done this; many persons cannot do it today. There is yet no general recognition of the possibility that an aesthetic effect may exist by itself, independent of morality or any other useful set of ideas. But the modern poet is intensely concerned with this possibility, and he has disclaimed social responsibility in order to secure this pure aesthetic effect. He cares nothing, professionally, about morals, or God, or native land. He has performed a work of dissociation and purified his art.

There are distinct styles of "modernity," but I think their net results, psychologically, are about the same. I have in mind what might be called the "pure" style and what might be called the "obscure" style.

A good "pure" poem is Wallace Stevens's "Sea Surface Full of Clouds"—famous perhaps, but certainly not well known. I shall have to deal with it summarily. Time and place, "In that November off Tehuantepec." The poem has five uniform stanzas, presenting as many surface effects beheld at breakfast time "after the slopping of the sea by night grew still." The first surface made one think of rosy chocolate and gilt umbrellas; the second, of chophouse chocolate and sham umbrellas; the third, of porcelain chocolate and pied umbrellas; the fourth, of musky chocolate and frail umbrellas; the fifth, of Chinese chocolate and large umbrellas. Nothing could be more discriminating than these details, which induct us respectively into the five fields of observation. The poem has a calculated complexity, and its technical competence is so high that to study it, if you do that sort of thing, is to be happy. That it has not been studied by a multitude of persons is due to a simple consideration which strikes us at once: the poem has no moral, political, religious, or sociological values. It is not about "res publica," the public thing. The subject matter is trifling.

Poetry of this sort, as it was practiced by some French poets of the nineteenth century, and as it is practiced by many British and American poets now, has been called pure poetry, and the name is accurate. It is nothing but poetry; it is poetry for poetry's sake, and you cannot get a moral out of it. But it was to be expected that it would never win the public at large. The impulse which led readers to the old poetry was at least as much moral as it was aesthetic, while the new poetry cannot count on any customers except those specializing in strict aesthetic effects. But the modern poets intend to rate only as poets, and would probably think it meretricious to solicit patronage by making moral overtures.

As an example of "obscure" poetry, though not the most extreme one, I cite Allen Tate's "Death of Little Boys." Here are some of its verses:

> Then you will touch at the bedside, torn in two,
> Gold curls now deftly intricate with gray
> As the windowpane extends a fear to you
> From one peeled aster drenched with the wind all day. . . .
>
> Till all the guests, come in to look, turn down
> Their palms; and delirium assails the cliff
> Of Norway where you ponder, and your little town
> Reels like a sailor drunk in his rotten skiff.

There is evidently a wide difference between Stevens and Tate, as poets. Tate has an important subject, and his poem is a human document, with a contagious fury about it: Stevens, pursuing purity, does not care to risk such a subject. But Tate, as if conscious that he is close to moralizing and sententiousness, builds up deliberately, I imagine, an effect of obscurity; for example, he does not care to explain the private meaning of his windowpane and his Norwegian cliff; or else, by some feat, he permits these bright features to belong to his total image without permitting them to reveal any precise meaning, either for himself or for his reader. Stevens, however, is objective from beginning to end; he completes all his meanings, knowing these will have little or no moral importance.

Pure or obscure, the modern poet manages not to slip into the old-fashioned moral-beautiful compound. If pure, he will not consider a subject which lends itself to moralization; that is, a subject of practical interest. It is his chief problem to find then a subject which has any interest at all. If, however, he prefers the other road, he may take the subject nearest his own humanity, a subject perhaps of terrifying import; but in treating it will stop short of all moral or theoretical conclusions, and confuse his detail to the point where it leaves no positive implications.

To be more technical: it is as if the pure poet presented a subject and declined to make any predication about it or even to start predication; and as if the obscure poet presented a subject in order to play with a great deal of important predication without ever completing any.

Personally, I prefer the rich obscure poetry to the thin pure poetry. The deaths of little boys are more exciting than the sea surfaces. It may be that the public preference, however, is otherwise. The public is inclined simply to ignore the pure poetry, because it lacks practical usefulness; but, to hate the obscure poetry, because it looks important enough to attend to, and yet never yields up any specific fruit. Society, through its spokesmen the dozens of social-minded critics, who talk the necessity of "communication," is now raging with indignation, or it may be with scorn, against the obscure poetry which this particular generation of poets has deposited. Nevertheless, both types of poetry, obscure as well as pure, aim at poetic autonomy; that is, speaking roughly, at purity.

Modern poetry in this respect is like modern painting. European painting used to be nearly as social a thing as poetry. It illustrated the sacred themes prescribed by the priests, whether popularly (Raphael) or esoterically and symbolically (Michelangelo); did the portraits of kings and cardinals, and the scenes of battles and great occasions; worked up allegorical and sentimental subjects. But more or less suddenly it asserted its independence. So we find Impressionists, doing the most innocent tricks with landscapes and mere objects; and we find Cézanne, painting so many times and so lovingly his foolish little bowl of fruits. The procedure was a strange one for the moral laity, who could detect nothing of importance there; and indeed nothing of public importance was there, only matters of technical interest to painters, and to persons who found painting sufficient. Later, and today, we find painters taking up the most heroic human material again in the most promising manner, yet arriving at no explicit meaning and, on the whole, simply playing with its powerful symbols. (Not all painters, of course.)

Apostate, illaureate, and doomed to outlawry the modern poets may be. I have the feeling that modernism is an unfortunate road for them to have taken. But it was an inevitable one. It is not hard to defend them from imputations against their honor and their logic. It is probably a question of whether we really know them, and understand their unusual purpose, and the powerful inhibitions they impose upon themselves.

But let us approach the matter from a slightly different angle. Poets have had to become modern because the age is modern. Its modernism envelops them like a sea, or an air. Nothing in their thought can escape it.

Modern poetry is pure poetry. The motive behind it cannot be substantially different from the motive behind the other modern activities, which is certainly the driving force of all our modernism. What is its name? "Purism" would be exact, except that it does not have the zealous and contriving sound we want. "Platonism" would do, provided there were time to come to an agreement about the essential meaning of Plato's act. I think the name "Puritanism" will describe this motive, if I may extend a little a term whose application in history has been mostly religious and moral.

Our period differs outwardly from other periods because it first differs inwardly. Its spiritual temper is puritanical; that is, it craves to perfect the parts of experience separately or in their purity, and is a series of isolated perfections. These have often been brilliant. But perhaps the modern program, on the whole, is not the one under which men maintain their best health and spirits. A little fear to that effect is beginning to cloud the consciousness of the brilliant moderns.

And here I conclude my defense of the modern poet. He is a good workman, and his purpose is really quite orthodox in its modernism. But it is no better.

The development of modern civilization has been a grand progression in which Puritanism has invaded first one field and then another.

The first field perhaps was religion. The religious impulse used to join to itself and dominate and hold together nearly all the fields of human experience; politics, science, art, and even industry, and by all means moral conduct. But Puritanism came in the form of the Protestant Reformation and separated religion from all its partners. Perhaps the most important of these separations was that which lopped off from religion the aesthetic properties which simple-hearted devotees and loving artists had given it. The aesthetic properties constituted the myth, which to the temperamental Protestants became superstition, and the ceremonial, which became idolatry. Under the progressive zeal of the Reformation the being of God has become rarefied in the degree that it has been purified, until we find difficulty in grasping it, and there are people who tell me, just as there are people who tell the reader, that religion as a living force here in the Western world is spent. Theology is purer or more abstract than ever before, but it would seem to belong exclusively to theologians, and it cannot by itself assemble together all those who once delighted in the moral precepts, the music and the pomp, the social communion, and the concrete Godhead, of the synthetic institution which was called religion.

Next, or perhaps at the same time, Puritanism applied itself to morality. Broad as the reach of morality may be, it is distinct enough as an experience to be capable of purification. We may say that its destiny was to become what we know as sociology, a body of positivistic science. It had to be emancipated from its religious overlords, whose authority, after all, was not a moral one. Then it had to be emancipated from the dictates of taste, or aesthetic, and this latter emancipation was the harder, and perhaps the more needless. The Greeks, though they were incipient Puritans, scarcely attempted it. They had a compound phrase meaning "beautiful-good," which even their philosophers used habitually as the name of something elemental and indissoluble. Suspicion was aroused in Greeks by a goodness which could not produce beauty, just as to a man like Spenser the idea of virtue was incomplete until it flowered into poetic form, and just as to the sympathetic French artist our new American liberty was not quite won until identifiable with an able-bodied demi-goddess lifting a torch. The splitting up of the moral-beautiful compound for the sake of the pure moral article is visibly at work in the New Testament, and in the bourgeois cult of plainness in seventeenth-century England, and in the finicky private life of a Puritan moralist like Kant, and today in moral or sociological treatises (and authors) which neither exhibit nor discuss charm. Now, it is true that we moralize with "maximum efficiency" when we do it technically, or abstractly, but when that comes to be the rule we no longer approach a moral discussion with anything but a moral interest. To be moral is no longer to be "decent," and it looks as if moral appeal had become something less wide and less instant than it was.

Then Puritanism worked upon politics. I am not prepared to go deeply into this, but it is evident that purification consisted in taking the state away from the church, from the monarch, from the feudal aristocracy, from any other concrete attachments, in order that it might propel itself by the force of pure statecraft. Progress in this direction meant constitutionalism, parliamentarianism, republicanism. A modern state like ours is transparent in the perfection of its logic. But that does not make it the more realistic. It is obliged to count upon a universal and continuous will on the part of the citizens to accept an abstract formula of political action. But such a will may not be there. The population, not being composed exclusively of politicians, is inclined to delegate statecraft to those who profess it. The old mixed states had a greater variety of loyalties to appeal to.

Puritanism is an ideal which not all persons are strong enough to realize, but only those with great power of concentration. Its best chance of success lies in individual projects. Accordingly, Puritanism fairly came into its own in the vast multitude of private enterprises which go together to make modern science. Galileo and Kepler found science captive to religious dogma. America, the paradise of Puritanism, was not yet in being, but England was; and there presently, while other Puritanisms were going on, Lord Bacon was able to anticipate the complete emancipation of science by virtue of its adoption of the pure experimental method. Now, there have been other incubi besides religion resting upon science at one time or another; and chiefly the tendency of poetry to haunt its deliberations. Poetry is a figurative way of expression, science is a technical or abstract way; but since science employs language, the figurative associations are hard to keep out. In earlier days poetry kept close to science, and it did not seem so strange if Lucretius wanted to set forth the body of accepted science in verse. But poetry now cannot attend science into its technical labyrinth. The result is greater success for scientists, but not necessarily their greater happiness as men; and the general understanding on our part that we will follow science if we are scientists, but otherwise will leave it to the scientists.

It was but one step that Puritanism had to go from there into the world of business, where the material sciences are systematically applied. The rise of the modern business world is a development attendant upon the freedom which it has enjoyed; upon business for business's sake, or pure business, or "laissez faire," with such unconditioned principles as efficiency, technological improvement, and maximum productivity. If I wished to attack the record of business, I should by now have been long anticipated. It is common opinion that business as a self-contained profession has created business men who are defective in their humanity; that the conduct of business his made us callous to personal relations and to social justice; and that many of the occupations which business has devised are, in the absence of aesthetic standards, servile.

All these exclusions and specializations, and many more, have been making modern life what it is. It is significant that every specialization on the list has had to resist the insidious charms of aesthetic experience before its own perfection could arise. (Evidently the aesthetic interest is remarkably catholic among our faculties in its affinities; ready to attach itself easily to almost any sort of moment; a ubiquitous element in experience, it might be thought, which it would be unhealthy to cast out.) But the energy of so deep an impulse as Puritanism had to flow through all the channels, and to come to its last outlet in a pure art, a pure poetry. Those who have not observed the necessity may choose to hold its predestined agents the poets in contempt, or in amazement. The poets are in the spirit of their time. On the one hand, they have been pushed out of their old attachments, whereby they used to make themselves useful to public causes, by the specialists who did not want the respective causes to be branded with amateurism. On the other hand, they are moved by a universal tendency into their own appropriate kind of specialization, which can be, as they have been at pains to show, as formidable as any other.

Considerations of this kind, I feel sure, have been more or less precisely within the intuition of all modern poets, and have motivated their performance. Technically, they are quite capable of writing the old compound poetry, but they cannot bring themselves to do it; or rather, when they have composed it in unguarded moments, as modern poets still sometimes do, they are under the necessity of destroying it immediately. There is no baffling degree of virtuosity in the old lines,

Roll on, thou deep and dark blue Ocean, roll!
Ten thousand fleets sweep over thee in vain:
Man marks the earth with ruin, his control
Stops with the shore.

The modern poet can accomplish just as elegant a rumination as this; but thinks it would commit him to an anachronism, for this is the style of an older period. In that period, though it was a comparatively late one, and though this poet thought he was in advance of it, the prophets of society were still numbering and tuning their valuable reflections before they saw fit to release them; and morality, philosophy, religion, science, and art could still meet comfortably in one joint expression, though perhaps not with the same distinction they might have gained if they had had their pure and several expressions. A passage of Byron's if sprung upon an unsuspecting modern would be felt immediately as "dating"; it would be felt as something that did very well for those dark ages before the modern mind achieved its own disintegration and perfected its faculties serially.

Even as readers, we must testify readily to the force of this time-principle. We sometimes pore over an old piece of poetry for so long that we fall under its spell and forget that its spirit is not our spirit. But we began to read it in a peculiar manner; by saying to ourselves, This is early Greek epic, This is seventeenth-century English drama. By means of one of the ripest and subtlest powers in us, that is, the historical sense, we made an adaptation of our minds to its mind, and were able to suspend those centuries which had intervened. Those centuries had made our minds much more knowing and at the same time, it is to be feared, much less suggestible. Yet it is not exactly with our own minds that we are reading the old poetry; otherwise we could not read it. For when we come back to our own world there begins to function in us a different style of consciousness altogether. And if we had begun to read a poetry of this old sort by saying, This was written last night by the poet around the corner, we could not have put up with it. If we throw away impatiently a contemporaneous poetry which displays archaisms of diction, what will we do with that which displays archaisms of temper? It looks spurious; for we require our art, and the living artists require it too, to be as contemporaneous as our banking or our locomotion.

What, then, is the matter with a pure poetry? The question is really more theoretical than practical. A school, an age, is involved by such a question, not merely some small poem or poet. And there is nothing the matter with this particular branch of purity which is not the matter with our other modern activities. All are affected by Puritanism, just as the vegetation is affected, generally and indifferently, by the climate.

It is impossible to answer the question categorically because the items are intangible. But we find ourselves reasoning about it as well as we can, which is as follows.

You may dissociate the elements of experience and exploit them separately. But then at the best you go on a schedule of small experiences, taking them in turn, and trusting that when the rotation is complete you will have missed nothing. And at the worst you will become so absorbed in some one small experience that you will forget to go on and complete the schedule; in that case you will have missed something. The theory that excellence lies in the perfection of the single functions, and that society should demand that its members be hard specialists, assumes that there is no particular harm in missing something. But I do not see why. A maniac with a fixed idea is a variety of specialist, and an absorbing specialty is a small mania.

As for poetry, it seems to me a pity that its beauty should have to be cloistered and conventual, if it is "pure," or teasing and evasive, if it is "obscure." The union of beauty with goodness and truth has been common enough to be regarded as natural. It is the dissociation which is unnatural and painful.

But when we talk about simple and compound experiences, we are evidently employing a chemical mode of speech to represent something we cannot quite make out. Units of consciousness are hard to handle scientifically; it takes more science than we have. Max Eastman thinks the future of literary criticism is bound up with the future of psychology, and very likely it is; but it is difficult to share his sanguine expectations of that science. It cannot become as effective a science as chemistry.

Nevertheless, I shall make a tentative argument from the analogy of chemistry. Lemonade is only a mechanical mixture, not very interesting to chemists. Aside from the water, a drop of lemonade contains lemon and sugar in no standard proportions. If it tastes too sour, add sugar, and if it tastes too sweet, add lemon. (And do not forget to stir the mixture.) No matter what the final proportions, you can still detect in the lemonade the sweet taste and the sour; though this is too abstract a matter to bother about if the lemonade is satisfactory, for in that case you simply drink it.

Table salt, however, is a true chemical compound; a molecule of it is $NaCl$. Understanding this, you do not claim to know the taste either of sodium or of chlorine when you say you are acquainted with the taste of salt. Whatever the Na was and however it tasted by itself, it gave up that identity when it compounded with Cl; and *vice versa*.

$NaCl$ is found in the state of nature, where it is much commoner than either of its constituents. But suppose the chemists decided to have nothing to do with $NaCl$ because of its compoundness, and undertook to extract from it the pure Na and Cl to serve on the table. Suppose they made war on all the natural compounds, broke them down into the hundred or so atomic elements, and asked us to live on these alone. The beneficiaries would regard this service as well-meaning but mistaken.

But we provide the necessities for our minds and affections with more harshness than we dare use on our stomachs and bodies—so inferior in precision is our knowledge of minds to our knowledge of bodies. Poets are now under the influence of a perfectly arbitrary theory which I have called Puritanism. They pursue A, an aesthetic element thought always to have the same taste and to be the one thing desirable for poets. They will not permit the presence near it of M, the moral element, because that will produce the lemonade MA, and they do not approve of lemonade. In lemonade the A gets itself weakened and neutralized by the M.

But it is possible that MA is not a drop of lemonade after all, but a true molecule, into which the separate M and the separate A have disappeared and out of which an entirely new taste is born. The effects which we attribute to a poet like Virgil, or Milton, are on the following order: pious, philosophical, imaginative, sonorous, and the like. But perhaps the effect which we actually receive from the poetry is not that of an aggregate or series or mechanical mixture of distinct properties but only the single effect of a compound. In that event the properties will exist separate only in our minds, by a later act of qualitative analysis, and they will not really be in the poetry in their own identities.

Is the old-fashioned full poetry a mechanical mixture like lemonade or a chemical compound like table salt? That is probably the most important question which the modern critics have opened up to speculation. There are many corollary questions along with it, like these: When does the display of doctrine in poetry incur the charge of didacticism? And must the poet also bear arms—that is, like the economist and the social reformer, view his performance in the light of a utility rather than an end?

Now some poetry, so-called, is not even lemonade, for the ingredients have not been mixed, much less compounded. Lumps of morality and image lie side by side, and are tasted in succession. T. S. Eliot thinks that this has been the character of a great deal of English poetry since the age of Dryden. Such poetry occupies some of the best room in the library, and takes up some of the best time of the earnest student of literature. It is decidedly one of the causes of that revulsion of feeling on the part of the modern poet which drives him away from the poetic tradition.

When our critical theory is complete, perhaps we shall be able to distinguish various combinations of elements passing for poetry; thus, poetry by assemblage, poetry by mixture, and poetry by composition. The last of these sounds the best.

I suggest that critics and philosophers fix their most loving attention upon certain natural compounds in human experience. But I say so diffidently, and not too hopefully. It will take a long time to change the philosophical set which has come over the practice of the poets. The intellectual climate in which they live will have to be altered first.

The End of the Line

RANDALL JARRELL

Originally published in the Nation *in 1942, Jarrell's essay explained the essential connection between the romantic and modernist schools of poetry. "The end of the line" was his phrase for the death of modernism, and for an era when all poetic styles seemed to be practiced simultaneously: "Today, for the poet, there is an embarrassment of choices: young poets can choose — do choose — to write anything from surrealism to imitations of Robert Bridges; the only thing they have no choice about is making their own choice."*

What has impressed everyone about modernist poetry is its *differentness.* The familiar and rather touching "I like poetry — but not modern poetry" is only another way of noticing what almost all criticism has emphasized: that modernist poetry is a revolutionary departure from the romantic poetry of the preceding century. Less far-reaching changes would have seemed a revolutionary disaster to "conventional" poets, critics, and readers, who were satisfied with romantic poetry; a revolutionary improvement to more "advanced" poets and critics, who disliked romanticism with the fervor of converts. *Romantic* once again, after almost two centuries, became a term of simple derogation; correspondingly, there grew up a rather blank cult of the "classical," and poets like Eliot hinted that poets like Pound might be the new classicism for which all had been waiting.

All this seems to me partially true, essentially false. The change from romantic poetry was evolutionary, not revolutionary: the modernists were a universe away from the great-grandfathers they admired; they *were* their fathers, only more so. I want to sketch this evolution. But if the reader understands me to be using *romantic* as an unfavorably weighted term, most of what I say will be distorted. Some of the tendencies of romanticism are bad; some of the better tendencies, exaggerated enough, are bad; but a great deal of the best poetry I know is romantic. Of course, one can say almost that about any of the larger movements into which critics divide English poetry; and one might say even better things about the "classical tradition" in English poetry, if there were one. (It is not strange that any real movement, compared to this wax monster, comes off nowhere; but it is strange that anyone should take the comparison for a real one.) If I pay more attention to unfortunate or exaggerated romantic tendencies, it is because these are the most characteristic: the "good" tendencies of movements are far more alike than the "bad" ones, and a proof that two movements are essentially similar needs to show that they share each other's vices.

Modernist poetry—the poetry of Pound, Eliot, Crane, Tate, Stevens, Cummings, MacLeish, et cetera—appears to be and is generally considered to be a violent break with romanticism; it is actually, I believe, an extension of romanticism, an end product in which most of the tendencies of romanticism have been carried to their limits. Romanticism—whether considered as the product of a whole culture or, in isolation, as a purely literary phenomenon—is necessarily a process of extension, a vector; it presupposes a constant experimentalism, the indefinite attainment of "originality," generation after generation, primarily by the novel extrapolation of previously exploited processes. (Neoclassicism, in theory at least, is a static system.) All these romantic tendencies are exploited to their limits; and the movement which carries out this final exploitation, apparently so different from earlier stages of the same process, is what we call modernism. Then, at last, romanticism is confronted with an impasse, a critical point, a genuinely novel situation that it can meet successfully only by contriving genuinely novel means—that is, means which are not romantic; the romantic means have already been exhausted. Until these new means are found, romanticism operates by repeating its last modernist successes or by reverting to its earlier stages; but its normal development has ended, and—the momentum that gave it most of its attraction gone—it becomes a relatively eclectic system, much closer to neoclassicism than it has hitherto been. (A few of these last romanticists resort to odd varieties of neoclassicism.) If this account seems unlikely to the reader, let me remind him that a similar course of development is extremely plain in modern music.

A good many factors combine to conceal the essentially romantic character of modernist poetry. (1) A great quantitative change looks like a qualitative one: for instance, the attenuation or breaking up of form characteristic of romanticism will not be recognized or tolerated by the average romantic when it reaches its limit in modernist poetry. (2) The violent contrast between the modernist limits of romantic tendencies and the earlier stages of these tendencies, practiced belatedly and eclectically by "conventional" poets, is an importance source of confusion. (3) Most of the best modern criticism of poetry is extremely anti-romantic — a poet's criticism is frequently not a reflection of but a compensation for his own poetry; and this change in theory has helped to hide the lack of any essential change in practice. (4) Modernist poems, while possessing some romantic tendencies in hyper-trophied forms, often lack others so spectacularly that the reader disregards those they still possess; and these remaining tendencies may be too common for him to be conscious of them as specifically romantic. (Most of the romantic qualities that poetry has specialized in since 1800 seem to the average reader "normal" or "poetic," what poetry inescapably is.) (5) Romanticism holds in solution contradictory tendencies which, isolated and exaggerated in modernism, look startlingly opposed both to each other and to the earlier stages of romanticism. (6) Both modernist and conventional critics have been unable to see the fundamental similarities between modernist and romantic poetry because they were unwilling to see anything but differences: these were to the former a final recommendation, and to the latter a final condemnation.

• • •

We can understand modernist poetry better by noticing where and how it began. The English poetry that we call *fin de siècle* — the most important tendency of its time — was a limit of one easily recognizable extension of romanticism. These "decadent" poets were strongly influenced by Baudelaire, Verlaine, and similar French poets. Rimbaud, Laforgue, and Corbière — who had already written "modern" poetry — had no influence on them. Why? Because a section of French poetry was developing a third of a century ahead of English poetry: Rimbaud wrote typically modernist poetry in the 1870's; in the nineties a surrealist play, Jarry's *Ubu Roi*, scared the young Yeats into crying: "After us the Savage God!" France, without England's industrial advantages and enormous colonial profits, had had little of the Victorian prosperity which slowed up the economic and political rate of change in England — had still less of that complacent mercantile Christianity the French dismissed as "English hypocrisy." And — if we stick to a part of the culture, literature — the rate of change could be greater in France because romanticism was more of a surface phenomenon there. English poetry was not *ready* to be influenced by French modernism for many years. Meanwhile, there were two movements particularly suited to criticism. Accompanying the triumph of prose naturalism there was a prosy, realistic, rather limited reaction against "decadent" poetry (it included Robinson, Frost,

Masters, Masefield, some of the Georgians, etc.). The other movement,
imagism, carried three or four romantic tendencies to their limits with
the perfection of a mathematical demonstration.

French modernist poetry first influenced poetry in English through
Americans who, lacking a determining or confining tradition of their
own, were particularly accessible and susceptible: Pound and Eliot (like
Picasso, Stravinsky, and Joyce) were in some sense expatriates in both
space and time. They imported modernism into English rather more
deliberately and openly than Wordsworth and Coleridge had imported
romanticism; but all Pound's early advice to poets could be summed up
in a sentence half of which is pure Wordsworth: Write like prose, like
speech—and *read French poetry!* The work of this most influential of
modern poets, Ezra Pound, is a recapitulation of the development of our
poetry from late romanticism to modernism. His early work is a sort of
anthology of romantic sources: Browning, early Yeats, the *fin de siècle*
poets, Villon and the troubadours (in translations of imitations that
remind one of Swinburne's and Rossetti's), Heine. *His* variety of imagism is partly a return to the fresh beginnings of romantic practices,
from their diluted and perfunctory ends; partly an extension to their limits of some of the most characteristic obsessions of romanticism—for instance, its passion for "pure" poetry, for putting everything in terms of
sensation and emotion, with logic and generalizations excluded; and
partly an adaptation of the exotic procedures of Chinese poetry, those
silks that swathe a homely heart. When Pound first wrote poems that
are modernist in every sense of the word, their general "feel" is reminis-
cent of what one might call a lowest common denominator of Corbière,
Laforgue, and Rimbaud; but Heine had by no means disappeared;
and the original Cantos I and II, gone now, were still full of Browning. But if Eliot was willing to base his form on Browning's (the dramatic monologue is primarily a departure from the norm of ordinary
poetry; but in modernist poetry this departure *itself becomes the norm*),
he had no interest in Browning's content and manner; in even his earliest poems one is seeing romanticism through Laforgue, and one can
reconstruct this romanticism, in the pure form in which it had once
existed, only from Eliot's remarks about his early feelings for Rossetti
and Swinburne . . . All during this time the Irish expatriate Joyce was
making his way from late-romantic lyrics (in verse, though there is
much that is similar in his early prose) to the modernist poetry (in prose)
that crops up here and there in *Ulysses,* and that is everywhere in
Finnegans Wake.

But it would take fifty or a hundred pages to write about this development in terms of specific poets. One can indicate the resemblances

of romanticism and modernism more briefly, by making a list of some of the general characteristics of modernist poetry:

(1) A pronounced experimentalism: "originality" is everyone's aim, and novel techniques are as much prized as new scientific discoveries. Eliot states it with surprising naïveté: "It is exactly as wasteful for a poet to do what has been done already as for a biologist to rediscover Mendel's discoveries." (2) External formlessness, internal disorganization: these are justified either as the disorganization necessary to express a disorganized age or as new and more complex forms of organization. Language is deliberately disorganized, meter becomes irregular or disappears; the rhythmical flow of verse is broken up into a jerky half-prose *collage* or *montage*. (3) Heightened emotional intensity; violence of every sort. (4) Obscurity, inaccessibility: logic, both for structure and for texture, is neglected; without this for a ground the masses of the illogical or alogical lose much of their effectiveness. The poet's peculiar erudition and allusiveness (compare the Alexandrian poet Lycophron) consciously restrict his audience to a small, highly specialized group; the poet is a specialist like everyone else. He intimidates or overawes the public by an attitude one may paraphrase as: "The poet's cultivation and sensibility are of a different order from those of his readers; even if he tried to talk down to them—and why should he try?—he would talk about things they have never heard of, in ways they will never understand." But he did not despair of their understanding a slap in the face. (5) A lack of restraint or proportion: all tendencies are forced to their limits, even contradictory tendencies—and not merely in the same movement but, frequently, in the same poet or the same poem. Some modernist poetry puts an unparalleled emphasis on texture, connotation, violently "interesting" language (attained partly by an extension of romantic principles, partly by a more violent rhetoric based on sixteenth- and seventeenth-century practices); but there has never before been such prosaic poetry—conversational-colloquial verse without even a pretense at meter. (6) A great emphasis on details—on parts, not wholes. Poetry is essentially lyric: the rare narrative or expository poem is a half-fortuitous collocation of lyric details. Poetry exploits particulars and avoids and condemns generalizations. (7) A typically romantic preoccupation with sensation, perceptual nuances. (8) A preoccupation with the unconscious, dreams, the stream of consciousness, the irrational: this *surréaliste* emphasis might better have been called *sousréaliste*. (9) Irony of every type: Byronic, Laforguian, dryly metaphysical, or helplessly sentimental. Poetry rejects a great deal, accepts a little, and is embarrassed by that little. (10) *Fauve* or neo-primitive elements. (11) Modernist poets, though they may write about the ordinary life of the time, are removed from it, have highly specialized relations

with it. The poet's naturalism is employed as indictment, as justification for his own isolation; prosaic and sordid details become important as what writers like Wallace Stevens and William Carlos Williams somewhat primitively think of as the *anti-poetic*. Contemporary life is condemned, patronized, or treated as a disgraceful aberration or special case, compared to the past; the poet hangs out the window of the Ivory Tower making severe but obscure remarks about what is happening below—he accepts the universe with several (thin) volumes of reservations. What was happening below was bad enough; the poet could characterize it, truthfully enough, with comparative forms of all those adjectives that Goethe and Arnold had applied to their ages. But its disasters, at least, were of unprecedented grandeur; it was, after all, "the very world, which is the world / Of all of us,—the place where, in the end, / We find our happiness or not at all"; and the poet's rejection or patronizing acceptance of it on his own terms—and, sometimes, what terms they were!—hurt his poetry more than he would have believed. (12) Individualism, isolation, alienation. The poet is not only different from society, he is as different as possible from other poets; all this differentness is exploited to the limit—is used as subject matter, even. Each poet develops an elaborate, "personalized," bureaucratized machinery of effect; *refine your singularities* is everybody's maxim. (13) These poets, typically, dislike and condemn science, industrialism, humanitarianism, "progress," the main tendencies of Western development; they want to trade the present for a somewhat idealized past, to turn from a scientific, commercial, and political world view to one that is literary, theological, and personal.

This complex of qualities is essentially romantic, and the poetry that exhibits it is the culminating point of romanticism.

It is the end of the line. Poets can go back and repeat the ride; they can settle in attractive, atavistic colonies along the railroad; they can repudiate the whole system, à la Yvor Winters, for some neoclassical donkey caravan of their own. But Modernism As We Knew It—the most successful and influential body of poetry of this century—is dead. Compare a 1940 issue of *Poetry* with a 1930 issue. Who could have believed that modernism would collapse so fast? Only someone who realized that modernism is a limit which it is impossible to exceed. How can poems be written that are more violent, more disorganized, more obscure, more—supply your own adjective—than those that have already been written? But if modernism could go no further, it was equally difficult for it to stay where it was: how could a movement completely dynamic in character, as "progressive" as the science and industrialism it accompanied, manage to become static or retrogressive without going to pieces? Among modernist poets, from 1910 to 1925, there was the same feeling of confident excitement, of an individual but irregularly cooperative experimentalism, of revolutionary discoveries just around the corner, that one regularly sees at certain stages in the development of a science; they had ahead of them the same Manifest Destiny that poets have behind them today. Today, for the poet, there is an embarrassment of choices: young poets can choose—do choose—to write anything from surrealism to imitations of Robert Bridges; the only thing they have no choice about is making their own choice. The Muse, forsaking her sterner laws, says to everyone: "Do what you will." Originality can no longer be recognized by, and condemned or applauded for, its obvious experimentalism; the age offers to the poet a fairly heartless eclecticism or a fairly solitary individuality. He can avoid being swept along by the current—there is no current; he can congratulate himself on this, and see behind him, glittering in the distance of time, all those bright streams sweeping people on to the wildest of excesses, the unlikeliest of triumphs.

For a long time society and poetry have been developing in the same direction, have been carrying certain tendencies to their limits: how could anyone fail to realize that the excesses of modernist poetry are the necessary concomitants of the excesses of late-capitalist society? (An example too pure and too absurd even for allegory is Robinson Jeffers, who must prefer a hawk to a man, a stone to a hawk, because of an individualism so exaggerated that it contemptuously rejects affections, obligations, relations of any kind whatsoever, and sets up as a nostalgically awaited goal the war of all against all. Old Rocky Face, perched on his sea crag, is the last of *laissez faire*; Free Economic Man at the end of his rope.) How much the modernist poets disliked their society, and how much they resembled it! How often they contradicted its letter and duplicated its spirit! They rushed, side by side with their society, to the limits of all tendencies. When, at the beginning of the thirties, these limits were reached, what became of these individualists? They turned toward anything collective: toward Catholicism, communism, distributism, social credit, agrarianism; they wrote neoclassical criticism or verse; they wrote political (Marxist or fellow traveler) criticism or verse; they stopped writing; and when they read the verse of someone like E. E. Cummings, as it pushed on into the heart of that last undiscovered continent, *e. e. cummings*, they thought of this moral impossibility, this living fossil, with a sort of awed and incredulous revulsion.

I have no space to write of later developments. Auden was so influential because his poetry was the only novel and successful reaction away from modernism; and a few years later Dylan Thomas was so influential—

in England—because his poetry was the only novel and successful reaction away from Auden. But his semi-surrealist experimentalism could be as good as it was, and as influential as it was, only in a country whose poets had never carried modernism to the limits of its possibilities. No one can understand these English developments if he forgets that, while we were having the modernism of Pound, Stevens, Williams, Moore, Eliot, Tate, Crane, Cummings, and all the rest, England was having the modernism of the Sitwells.

I am afraid that my hypothesis about romanticism and modernism, without the mass of evidence that can make a theory plausible, or the tangle of extensions and incidental insights that can make it charming, may seem improbable or unpleasant to some of my readers. It is intended to be partial: I have not written about the hard or dry or "classical" tendencies of some modern verse—what Empson and Marianne Moore have in common, for instance; and I have not listed the differences between modernism and romanticism that everybody has seen and stated. But I hope that nobody will dislike my article because he thinks is an attack on romanticism or modernism. This has been description, not indictment. Burke said that you can't indict a whole people, and I hope I am not such a fool as to indict a century and a half of a world. Besides, so far as its poetry is concerned, it was wonderful. Wordsworth and Blake and Heine, Baudelaire and Corbière, Hardy and Yeats and Rilke—the names crowd in; and there are dozens more. That some of these poets were, sometimes, as strange as they were wonderful; that some of their successors were, alas, rather stranger: all this is as true as it is obvious. But the "classical" prejudice which hints that these poets were somehow deceived and misguided as (say) Dryden and Valéry were not seems every year more grotesque. One repeats to oneself, *Whom God deceives is well deceived,* and concludes that if these poets were not classical, so much the worse for classicism.

The Problem of Form

J. V. CUNNINGHAM

In only a few pages, and with implacable logic, Cunningham here attacks the philosophy of the vers libre *movement, and thus much of our contemporary poetic practice. The indispensability of meter has never been argued for more succinctly.*

I shall stipulate that there is a problem of form in the poetry of our day, but I shall treat *form*, for the moment, as an undefined term, and I shall not until later specify the nature of some of the problems. I am, at the outset, interested in pointing to certain generalities, and to certain broad, simpleminded, pervasive attitudes and dualisms, of which the problem in poetry is to a large extent only a localization. These will give in outline the larger context of the problem.

To begin with, it is apparent that in our society we have too many choices. When we ask the young what they are going to do when they grow up, we should not be surprised or amused that the answers are whimsical and bewildered. The young poet today has a large and not too discriminated anthology of forms to realize: only illiterate ignorance or having made the pilgrimage to Gambier or to Los Altos will reduce the scope of options to manageable size—and even then there will be a hankering for further options. On the other hand, the young poet 250 years ago had it easy in this respect. He wrote octosyllabic or decasyllabic couplets, and the rhetoric and areas of experience of each were fairly delimited. For recreation he wrote a song in quatrains, and once or twice in a lifetime a Pindaric ode.

We come now to those attitudes and dualisms that make the problem of particular forms peculiarly our problem. We are a democratic society and give a positive value to informality, though some of the ladies still like to dress up. We will have nothing to do with the formal language and figured rhetoric of the *Arcadia*, for that is the language and rhetoric of a hierarchical and authoritarian society in which ceremony and formality were demanded by and accorded to the governing class. Instead, we praise, especially in poetry, what we call the accents of real speech—that is, of uncalculated and casual utterance, and sometimes even of vulgar impropriety. Now, if this attitude is a concomitant of the Democratic Revolution, the value we give to antiformality, to the deliberate violation of form and decorum, is a concomitant of its sibling, the Romantic Revolution. The measured, or formal, the contrived, the artificial are, we feel, insincere; they are perversions of the central value of our life, genuineness of feeling. "At least I was honest," we say with moral benediction as we leave wife and child for the sentimental empyrean.

If informality and antiformality are positive values, then the problem of form is how to get rid of it. But to get rid of it we must keep it; we must have something to get rid of. To do this we need a method, and we have found it in our dualisms of science and art, of intellectual and emotional, of regularity and irregularity, of norm and variation. We have been convinced, without inquiry or indeed adequate knowledge, that the regularities of ancient scientific law, of Newton's laws of motion, are regularities of matter, not of spirit, and hence are inimical to human significance. And so we embrace the broad, pervasive, simpleminded, and scarcely scrutinized proposition that regularity is meaningless and irregularity is meaningful—to the subversion of Form. For one needs only so much regularity as will validate irregularity. But Form is regularity.

So we come to definition. The customary distinctions of form and matter, or form and content, are in the discussion of writing at least only usable on the most rudimentary level. For it is apparent to any poet who sets out to write a sonnet that the form of the sonnet is the content, and its content the form. This is not a profundity, but the end of the discussion. I shall define form, then, without a contrasting term. It is that which remains the same when everything else is changed. This is not at all, I may say, a Platonic position. It is rather a mathematical and, as it should be, linguistic notion: $a^2 - b^2 = (a + b)(a - b)$ through all the potentialities of a and b. The form of the simple declarative sentence in English is in each of its realizations.

It follows, then, that form is discoverable by the act of substitution. It is what has alternative realizations. And the generality or particularity of a form lies in the range or restriction of alternatives. It follows, also, that the form precedes its realization, even in the first instance, and that unique form, or organic form in the sense of unique form, is a contradiction in terms. For it is the essence of form to be repetitive, and the repetitive is form. It follows, further, that there may be in a given utterance simultaneously a number of forms, so that the common literary question, What is the form of this work? can only be answered by a tacit disregard of all the forms other than the one we are momently concerned with.

It is time for illustration. Donne has a little epigram on Hero and Leander:

> Both robbed of air, we both lie in one ground,
> Both whom one fire had burnt, one water drowned.

What are the forms of this poem? First, both lines are decasyllabic in normal iambic pattern. Second, they rhyme. Third, it is phrased in units of four and six syllables in chiasmic order. Fourth, there are three "both's" and three "one's" in overlapping order. Fifth, the whole story of the lovers is apprehended, summarized, and enclosed in the simple scheme or form of the four elements. Finally, it is recognizably an epigram. Now Sir Philip Sidney, a few years earlier, in one of the *Arcadia* poems has the following lines:

> Man oft is plagued with air, is burnt with fire,
> In water drowned, in earth his burial is.

The lines are decasyllabic in normal iambic pattern. The adjacent lines do not rhyme, for the form of the poem is terza rima, an alternative form. It is phrased in units of six and four in chiasmic order. The first line repeats "with," the second "in." Man, not Hero and Leander, is apprehended in the scheme of the four elements, and in both cases the order of the elements is not formally predetermined. Finally, it is not an epigram, but part of an eclogue.

I have illustrated in these examples and in this analysis something of the variety of what may be distinguished as form: literary kind, conceptual distinctions, and all the rhetorical figures of like ending, equal members, chiasmus, and the various modes of verbal repetition. That some of the forms of Sidney's lines are repeated in Donne's, with the substitution of Hero and Leander for man, shows they have alternate realizations, and that so many operate simultaneously shows, not that a literary work has form, but that it is a convergence of forms, and forms of disparate orders. It is the coincidence of forms that locks in the poem.

Indeed, it is the inherent coincidence of forms in poetry, in metrical writing, that gives it its place and its power—a claim for poetry perhaps more accurate and certainly more modest than is customary. For this is the poet's *Poetics*: prose is written in sentences; poetry in sentences and lines. It is encoded not only in grammar, but also simultaneously in meter, for meter is the principle or set of principles, whatever they may be, that determines the line. And as we perceive of each sentence that it is grammatical or not, so the repetitive perception that this line is metrical or that it is not, that it exemplifies the rules or that it does not, is the metrical experience. It is the ground bass of all poetry.

And here in naked reduction is the problem of form in the poetry of our day. It is before all a problem of meter. We have lost the repetitive harmony of the old tradition, and we have not established a new. We have written to vary or violate the old line, for regularity we feel is meaningless and irregularity meaningful. But a generation of poets, acting on the principles and practice of significant variation, have at last nothing to vary from. The last variation is regularity.

POETRY AS A MORAL DISCIPLINE

Foreword to *Primitivism and Decadence*

YVOR WINTERS

In this foreword to Primitivism and Decadence: A Study of American Experimental Poetry *(1937),* Winters describes (and destroys)
*the three main theories of literature—the didactic, the hedonistic,
and the romantic—before defining his own moralistic theory. Winters, in his absolutism, admits of no compromise, and he is frequently
unanswerable: "Our universities, in which relativistic doctrines are
widely taught, can justify their existence only in terms of a doctrine
of absolute truth."*

There have been various ideas regarding the nature and function of
literature during the twenty-five hundred years or so that literature has
been seriously discussed. One might think, off-hand, that the possibilities were limitless; but they are actually limited and even narrowly
limited—the ideas are all classifiable under a fairly small number of
headings. I shall not attempt an historical survey but shall merely attempt a brief classificatory survey. The theories in question can all be
classified, I believe, under three headings: the didactic, the hedonistic,
and the romantic. I am not in sympathy with any of these, but with a
fourth, which for lack of a better term I call the moralistic. This concept
of literature has not been adequately defined in the past so far as my
limited knowledge extends, but I believe that it has been loosely implicit
in the inexact theorizing which has led to the most durable judgments
in the history of criticism.

The didactic theory of literature is simple; it is this: that literature offers us useful precepts and explicit moral instruction. If the theory is
sound, then literature is useful; but the question arises as to whether there
may not be other fields of study, such as religion or ethics, which may
accomplish the same end more efficiently. The question is usually met
by the Horatian formula, which combines the didactic with the hedonistic, telling us that the function of literature is to provide instruction
(or profit) in conjunction with pleasure, to make instruction palatable.
Of this I shall say more later. There arises another question in connection with the didactic theory: can one say, as someone—I believe it was

Kenneth Burke—has remarked, that *Hamlet* was written to prove that procrastination is the thief of time, or to prove something comparably simple? Or is there more than that to *Hamlet*? And if there is more, is it worth anything? It seems obvious to me that there is more and that it is worth a great deal, that the paraphrasable content of the work is never equal to the work, and that our theory of literature must account not only for the paraphrasable content but for the work itself. The didactic theory of literature fails to do this.

The hedonist sees pleasure as the end of life, and literature either as a heightener of pleasure or as the purveyor of a particular and more or less esoteric variety of pleasure. The term *pleasure* is applied indiscriminately to widely varying experiences: we say, for example, that we derive pleasure from a glass of good whisky and that we derive pleasure from reading *Hamlet*. The word is thus misleading, for it designates two experiences here which have little relationship to each other. There is a great range in the kinds of pleasure advocated in various hedonistic philosophies, but in general one might remark this defect which is common to nearly all, perhaps to all, such systems: pleasure is treated as an end in itself, not as a by-product of something else. If we recognize that certain feelings which are loosely classifiable as forms of pleasure result from our recognition of various kinds of truth and from the proper functioning of our natures in the process of this recognition, we then have a principle which may enable us to distinguish these pleasures from pleasures less important or less desirable, such as the pleasures or satisfactions which we derive from the gratification of physical appetites or from the excitement of stimulants, and a principle which may even enable us to evaluate relatively to each other the higher pleasures themselves. But pleasure then becomes incidental and not primary, and our system can no longer be classified as properly hedonistic. Furthermore, there is this distinction at least between hedonistic ethics and hedonistic aesthetics: hedonistic ethics, as in the philosophy of Epicurus, may take on a somewhat passive or negativistic character; that is pleasure may come to be more or less nearly identified simply with the avoidance of pain. But one cannot praise a poem or a picture merely by saying that it gives no pain: the experience of the poem or of the picture must be strongly positive. Hedonistic theories of literature tend in the main, and this is especially true in the past two hundred years, to take one of two forms.

The first might be connected with the name of Walter Pater. According to this view there is a close relation between hedonistic ethics and hedonistic aesthetics. Pleasure is the aim of life. Pleasure consists in intensity of experience; that is in the cultivation of the feelings for their own sake, as a good in themselves. And literature, or at any rate the arts in general, can provide a finer technique of such cultivation than can any other mode of activity. We meet here the first difficulty which I mentioned in connection with hedonistic doctrines; namely, that unless we have illicit relations with some non-hedonistic ethical theory, we have no way of distinguishing among the many and diverse excitements that are commonly described as pleasurable. And we shall discover, as a matter of human nature which is recorded in the history of literature and the other arts, that this search for intensity of experience leads inevitably to an endless pursuit either of increasing degrees of violence of emotion or of increasingly elusive and more nearly meaningless nuances, and ultimately to disillusionment with art and with life. It is possible, of course, that art and life are really worthless, but on the other hand it is possible that they are valuable. And until we have made sure that our hedonistic theory offers a true description of human experience, that no better description is possible, we should be unwise to commit ourselves to it, for the ultimate consequences appear both certain and unfortunate.

The second form of hedonistic theory tends to dissociate the artistic experience sharply from all other experience. T. S. Eliot, for example, tells us that the human experience about which the poem appears to be written has been transmuted in the aesthetic process into something new which is different in kind from all other experience. The poem is not then, as it superficially appears, a statement about a human experience, but is a thing in itself. The beginnings of this notion are to be found in Poe and are developed further by the French Symbolists, notably by Mallarmé. The aim of the poem so conceived is again pleasure, pleasure conceived as intensity of emotion; but the emotion is of an absolutely special sort. Some such notion of the artistic experience is the essential concept of Santayana's aesthetics; in fact, it is essential to almost any treatment of "aesthetics" as a branch of philosophy, and one will find it everywhere in the work of the academic aestheticians of the past half-century. The nature of the "aesthetic" experience as conceived in these terms has never been clearly defined; we commonly meet here a kind of pseudo-mysticism. The chief advantage of this kind of hedonism over the Paterian variety is that one can adhere to it without adhering to a doctrine of ethical hedonism, for art and life are absolutely severed from each other. Eliot, for example, considers himself a Christian. The chief disadvantage is that it renders intelligible discussion of art impossible, and it relegates art to the position of an esoteric indulgence, possibly though not certainly harmless, but hardly of sufficient importance to merit a high position among other human activities. Art, however, has always been accorded a high position, and a true theory of art should be able to account for this fact.

Certain theorists who have been aware that art is more than moral precept on the one hand and more than a search for cultivated excitement on the other have tried to account for its complexity by combining the didactic and the hedonistic theories: this gives us the Horatian formula, that art combines profit with pleasure. When this formula occurs, as it often does, in the writing of a great poet or of some other person who takes his poetry seriously, it apparently represents a somewhat rough and ready recognition of the fact that poetry has intellectual content and something more; that its power is real and cannot be accounted for too easily. But if one regard the doctrine itself, and regard it as pure theory, it is unsatisfactory; or at any rate it relegates art to an unsatisfactory position. For the didactic element in art so conceived will be no more efficient as didacticism than we have seen it to be before: that is, the serious moralist may quite reasonably argue that he prefers to get his teaching in a more direct and compact form; and the pleasure is still in the unhappy predicament in which we found it in the purely hedonistic theory.

The Romantic theory of literature takes account more seriously than the theories which I have thus far mentioned of the power which literature seems to exert over human nature, and to that extent offers a more realistic view of literature. I am concerned with literature which may be loosely described as artistic: that is, with literature which communicates not only thought but also emotion. I do not like the expression *imaginative literature*, for in its colloquial acceptation the phrase excludes too much: it excludes the persuasive and hortatory, for example, the sermon and the political tract; and *imagination* as a term of sophisticated criticism has been used so variously and so elusively, especially during the past hundred and fifty years, that I am not quite sure what it means. But the power of artistic literature is real: if we consider such writers as Plato, Augustine, Dante, Shakespeare, Rousseau, Voltaire, Emerson, and Hitler, to go no further, we must be aware that such literature has been directly and indirectly one of the greatest forces in human history. The Gospels gave a new direction to half the world; *Mein Kampf* very nearly reversed that direction. The influence of Rimbaud and of Mallarmé is quite as real but has operated more slowly and with less of obvious violence. It behooves us to discover the nature of artistic literature, what it does, how it does it, and how one may evaluate it. It is one of the facts of life, and quite as important a fact as atomic fission. In our universities at present, for example, one or another of the hedonistic views of literature will be found to dominate, although often colored by Romantic ideas, with the result that the professors of literature, who for the most part are genteel but mediocre men, can make but a poor defense of their profession, and the professors of science, who are frequently men of great intelligence but of limited interests and education, feel a politely disguised contempt for it; and thus the study of one of the most pervasive and powerful influences on human life is traduced and neglected.

The Romantics, however, although they offer a relatively realistic view of the power of literature, offer a fallacious and dangerous view of the nature both of literature and of man. The Romantic theory assumes that literature is mainly or even purely an emotional experience, that man is naturally good, that man's impulses are trustworthy, that the rational faculty is unreliable to the point of being dangerous or possibly evil. The Romantic theory of human nature teaches that if man will rely upon his impulses, he will achieve the good life. When this notion is combined, as it frequently is, with a pantheistic philosophy or religion, it commonly teaches that through surrender to impulse man will not only achieve the good life but will achieve also a kind of mystical union with the Divinity: this, for example, is the doctrine of Emerson. Literature thus becomes a form of what is known popularly as self-expression. It is not the business of man to understand and improve himself, for such an effort is superfluous: he is good as he is, if he will only let himself alone, or, as we might say, let himself go. The poem is valuable because it enables us to share the experience of a man who has let himself go, who has expressed his feelings, without hindrance, as he has found them at a given moment. The ultimate ideal at which such a theory aims is automatism. There is nothing in the theory to provide a check on such automatism; if the individual man is restrained by some streak of personal but unformulated common sense, by some framework of habit derived from a contrary doctrine, such as Christian doctrine, or by something in his biological inheritance, that is merely his good fortune — the Romantic doctrine itself will not restrain him. The Romantic doctrine itself will urge him toward automatism. And the study of history seems to show that if any doctrine is widely accepted for a long period of time, it tends more and more strongly to exact conformity from human nature, to alter human nature. The Romantic theory of literature and of human nature has been the dominant theory in western civilization for about two and a half centuries. Its influence is obviously disastrous in literature and is already dangerous in other departments of human life.

There are certain other general notions of human nature and of values which are related to the notions which I have been discussing, but which are not exactly correlative with them. I shall refer to them rather baldly as determinism, relativism, and absolutism.

Determinism is that theory of the universe which holds that the whole is a single organism, pursuing a single and undeviating course which has been predestined by God or determined by its own nature. It sees the human being simply as a part of this organism, with no independent force of his own. One must distinguish sharply between a deterministic theory and a theory which recognizes the real existence of influences outside of the individual, whether those influences be historical, biological, or other. One may even take a pessimistic view of such influences without being a determinist. If one admits that man may understand in some measure the conditions of his existence, that as a result of such understanding he may choose a mode of action, that as a result of such choice he may persevere in the mode of action chosen, and that as a result of his perseverance he may in some measure alter the conditions of his existence, then one is not a determinist. Few people who profess deterministic doctrines are willing to envisage clearly their implications, however. As a result, one will find all three of the views of poetry which I have mentioned held by determinists.

It is natural that deterministic and Romantic theories should coincide, for Romanticism teaches the infinite desirability of automatism, and determinism teaches the inevitability of automatism. Determinism is Romanticism in a disillusioned mood; Henry Adams is little more than the obverse side of Emerson, the dark side of the moon. And since hedonism is, like determinism, an anti-intellectualistic philosophy and is somewhat vague in all its tenets, it is not surprising that determinists should sometimes appear as hedonists: since they cannot control in any measure the courses of their lives, the determinists sometimes find solace in seeking pleasure along the way, without stopping to consider that such a search is a willful activity involving at least limited consideration and choice. It is curious that the didactic view of literature should so often be adopted by determinists, however, for the determinist really has no right to the didactic method. Yet the most vigorous, one might say the most religious, of the various species of determinist, such for example as the Calvinists of the past and the Marxists of the present, are commonly the most didactic of men, both in their literature and in their behavior.

The absolutist believes in the existence of absolute truths and values. Unless he is very foolish, he does not believe that he personally has free access to these absolutes and that his own judgments are final; but he does believe that such absolutes exist and that it is the duty of every man and of every society to endeavor as far as may be to approximate them. The relativist, on the other hand, believes that there are no absolute truths, that the judgment of every man is right for himself. I am aware that many persons believe that they have arrived at some kind of compromise between these two positions, but actually no compromise is possible. Any such attempt at compromise, if closely examined, will exhibit an ultimate allegiance to one position or the other or else will exhibit simple confusion. It is popular at present to profess relativism and yet in important matters to act as if we were absolutists. Our ideas of justice, which we endeavor to define by law and for which wars are often fought, can be defended only by invoking moral absolutism. Our universities, in which relativistic doctrines are widely taught, can justify their existence only in terms of a doctrine of absolute truth. The professor of English Literature, who believes that taste is relative yet who endeavors to convince his students that *Hamlet* is more worthy of their attention than some currently popular novel, is in a serious predicament, a predicament which is moral, intellectual, and in the narrowest sense professional, though he commonly has not the wit to realize the fact.

The Romantic is almost inescapably a relativist, for if all men follow their impulses there will be a wide disparity of judgments and of actions and the fact enforces recognition. The Emersonian formula is the perfect one: that is right for me which is after my constitution; that is right for you which is after yours; the common divinity will guide each of us in the way which is best for him. The hedonist is usually a relativist and should logically be one, but there is often an illicit and veiled recognition of absolutism in his attempts to classify the various pleasures as more or less valuable, not for himself alone but in general. The defender of the didactic view of literature has been traditionally an absolutist, but he is not invariably so: didacticism is a method, and when one sees literature only as didacticism one sees it as a method, and the method may be used, as Emerson used it, to disseminate relativistic doctrine.

The theory of literature which I defend in these essays is absolutist. I believe that the work of literature, in so far as it is valuable, approximates a real apprehension and communication of a particular kind of objective truth. The form of literature with which I am for the most part concerned is the poem; but since the poem exhausts more fully than any other literary form the inherent possibilities of language, what I say about poetry can be extended to include other literary forms with relatively unimportant qualifications, and in point of fact I devote considerable space to other literary forms. The poem is a statement in words about a human experience. Words are primarily conceptual, but through use and because human experience is not purely conceptual, they have acquired connotations of feeling. The poet makes his statement in such a way as to employ both concept and connotation as efficiently as possible. The poem is good in so far as it makes a defensible rational statement about a given human experience (the experience need not be real but must be in some sense possible) and at the same time communicates the emotion which ought to be motivated by that rational understanding of that experience. This notion of poetry, whatever its defects, will account both for the power of poetry and of artistic literature in general over its readers and for the seriousness with which the great poets have taken their art. Milton, for example, did not write *Paradise Lost* to give pleasure to Professor So-and-So, nor did he write it to give free rein to his emotions; he wrote it in order to justify the ways of God to men, and the justification involved not merely a statement of theory but a conformity of the emotional nature of men with the theory.

Poetry, and in a less definite fashion all artistic literature, involves not only the two aspects of language which I have just mentioned, but also the rhythmic and the formal. Rhythm, for reasons which I do not wholly understand, has the power of communicating emotion; and as a part of the poem it has the power of qualifying the total emotion. What we speak of loosely as the "form" of a poem is probably, at least for the most part, two-fold: we have on the one hand the rational structure of the poem, the orderly arrangement and progression of thought; and we have on the other a kind of rhythm broader and less easily measurable than the rhythm of the line—the poem exists in time, the mind proceeds through it in time, and if the poet is a good one he takes advantage of this fact and makes the progression rhythmical. These aspects of the poem will be efficient in so far as the poet subordinates them to the total aim of the poem.

One criticism which has been made of me repeatedly is this: that I wish to discard every poem to which I make objections. This is not true. Probably no poem is perfect in the eye of God. So far as I am concerned, a good many poems approach so nearly to perfection that I find them satisfactory. But there are many poems which seem to me obviously imperfect and even very seriously imperfect, which I have no wish to discard. Some of these I have analyzed both in respect to their virtues and to their defects; others, because of the nature of my discussion, mainly with reference to their defects; but I have dealt with few works which do not seem to me to have discernible virtues, for to do otherwise would seem to me a waste of time. If we were all to emulate Hart Crane, the result would be disastrous to literature and to civilization; it is necessary to understand the limitations of Hart Crane, which are of the utmost seriousness; but when we understand those limitations, we are in a position to profit by his virtues with impunity, and his virtues are sometimes very great. If we are not aware of his limitations but are sufficiently sensitive to guess in some fashion at his virtues, he may easily take possession of us wholly. This difficulty indicates the function of criticism.

Certain poetry of the sixteenth and seventeenth centuries approximates most closely the qualities which seem to me the best. It seems to me, as it has seemed to many others, that there has been a general deterioration of the quality of poetry since the opening of the eighteenth century. Like many others, I have endeavored to account for this deterioration. It would surprise no one if I stated that Collins's *Ode to Evening* was an imperfect and secondary poem if judged in comparison with all English poetry; but it arouses antagonism when I give reasons, partly because there is a general dislike for reasons, and partly because my reasons are not complimentary to the orthodoxies of our time. I regret the antagonism, but since I believe my reasons to be sound and the matter in general serious, I must maintain my position and take the consequences. These essays, then, endeavor not only to defend a theory of poetry and to judge certain writers with reference to that theory, but to outline as far as this kind of writing permits certain historical tendencies and the reasons for them. I do this in the hope that my efforts may in some small measure contribute to the alteration of these tendencies; our literary culture (to mention nothing more) appears to me to be breaking up, and the rescue of it appears to me a matter of greater moment than the private feelings of some minor poet or scholar.

I should perhaps call attention to one other matter in connection with my aims. It seems to me impossible to judge the value of any idea in a vacuum. That is, the hedonistic view of literature may conceivably appear sound, or the relativistic view of literature and morals may appear sound, if the idea is circumscribed by a few words. But either idea implies a fairly complete description of a large range of human experience, and if the description does not agree with the facts as we are forced to recognize them, then something is wrong. I am acquainted, for example, with the arguments which prove that the wall is not there, but if I try to step through the wall, I find that the wall is there notwithstanding the arguments. During the past century or so, the number of poets who have endeavored to conform their practice to the ideas which seem to me unsound has been rather large, and we can judge the ideas more or less dearly in the light of these experiments. . . .

Finally, I am aware that my absolutism implies a theistic position, unfortunate as this admission may be. If experience appears to indicate that absolute truths exist, that we are able to work toward an approximate apprehension of them, but that they are antecedent to our apprehension and that our apprehension is seldom and perhaps never perfect, then there is only one place in which those truths may be located, and I see no way to escape this conclusion. I merely wish to point out that my critical and moral notions are derived from the observation of literature and of life, and that my theism is derived from my critical and moral notions. I did not proceed from the opposite direction.

Editor's Note: The first paragraph, omitted here, reads as follows: "The essays now reprinted in this volume are the work of more than fifteen years. Although this collection, like any collection of essays, suffers from its miscellaneous character, there is a single theory of literature developed throughout and a single theory of the history of literature since the Renaissance. These theories are developed mainly with reference to American literature. It may be of some service to the reader if I recapitulate briefly."

The final paragraph, also omitted, reads as follows: "All of the concepts outlined briefly and incompletely in this foreword, with the exception of that mentioned in the last paragraph, will be found more fully explained at various points in the present volume. These remarks are not offered as a complete statement, but are offered merely as a guide and an introduction."

The Morality of Poetry

YVOR WINTERS

This is the first chapter of Winters's book Primitivism and Decadence *(1937), and it is the best introduction to his absolutism regarding moral and aesthetic judgment. Winters insisted that every metrical variation, "no matter how slight, is exactly perceptible and as a result can be given exact meaning as an act of moral perception."*

Before attempting to elucidate or to criticize a poetry so difficult and evasive as that of the best moderns, it would appear wise to summarize as clearly as possible those qualities for which one looks in a poem. We may say that a poem in the first place should offer us new perceptions, not only of the exterior universe, but of human experience as well; it should add, in other words, to what we have already seen. This is the elementary function for the reader. The corresponding function for the poet is a sharpening and training of his sensibilities; the very exigencies of the medium as he employs it in the act of perception should force him to the discovery of values which he never would have found without the convening of all the conditions of that particular act, conditions one or more of which will be the necessity of solving some particular difficulty such as the location of a rhyme or the perfection of a cadence without disturbance to the remainder of the poem. The poet who suffers from such difficulties instead of profiting by them is only in a rather rough sense a poet at all.

If, however, the difficulties of versification are a stimulant merely to the *poet*, the reader may argue that he finds them a hindrance to himself and that he prefers some writer of prose who appears to offer him as much with less trouble to all concerned. The answer to such a reader is that the appearance of equal richness in the writer of prose is necessarily deceptive.

For language is a kind of abstraction, even at its most concrete; such a word as "cat," for instance, is generic and not particular. Such a word becomes particular only in so far as it gets into some kind of experiential complex, which qualifies it and limits it, which gives it, in short, a local habitation as well as a name. Such a complex is the poetic line or other unit, which, in turn, should be a functioning part of the larger complex, or poem. This is, I imagine, what Mallarmé should have had in mind when he demanded that the poetic line be a new word, not found in any dictionary, and partaking of the nature of incantation (that is, having the power to materialize, or perhaps it would be more accurate to say, *being*, a new experience).[1]

The poem, to be perfect, should likewise be a new word in the same sense, a word of which the line, as we have defined it, is merely a syllable. Such a word is, of course, composed of much more than the sum of its words (as one normally uses the term) and its syntax. It is composed of an almost fluid complex, if the adjective and the noun are not too nearly contradictory, of relationships between words (in the normal sense of the term), a relationship involving rational content, cadences, rhymes, juxtapositions, literary and other connotations, inversions, and so on, almost indefinitely. These relationships, it should be obvious, extend the poet's vocabulary incalculably. They partake of the fluidity and unpredictability of experience and so provide a means of treating experience with precision and freedom. If the poet does not wish, as, actually, he seldom does, to reproduce a given experience with approximate exactitude, he can employ the experience as a basis for a new experience that will be just as real, in the sense of being particular, and perhaps more valuable.

Now verse is more valuable than prose in this process for the simple reasons that its rhythms are faster and more highly organized than are those of prose, and so lend themselves to a greater complexity and compression of relationship, and that the intensity of this convention renders possible a greater intensity of other desirable conventions, such as poetic language and devices of rhetoric. The writer of prose must substitute bulk for this kind of intensity; he must define his experience ordinarily by giving all of its past history, the narrative logic leading up to it, whereas the experiential relations given in a good lyric poem, though particular in themselves, are applicable without alteration to a good many past histories. In this sense, the lyric is general as well as particular; in fact, this quality of transferable or generalized experience might be regarded as the defining quality of lyrical poetry.

What I have just said should make plain the difficulty of comprehending a poem exactly and fully; its total intention may be very different from its paraphrasable, or purely logical content. If one take, for example, Mr. Allen Tate's sonnet, *The Subway*, and translate it into good scholarly prose, using nothing but the rational content of the poem as a reference, one will find the author saying that as a result of his ideas and of his metropolitan environment, he is going mad. Now as a matter of fact, the poem says nothing of the sort:

> Dark accurate plunger down the successive knell
> Of arch on arch, where ogives burst a red
> Reverberance of hail upon the dead
> Thunder, like an exploding crucible!
> Harshly articulate, musical steel shell
> Of angry worship, hurled religiously
> Upon your business of humility
> Into the iron forestries of hell!
>
> Till broken in the shift of quieter
> Dense altitudes tangential of your steel,
> I am become geometries—and glut
> Expansions like a blind astronomer
> Dazed, while the worldless heavens bulge and reel
> In the cold revery of an idiot.

The sonnet indicates that the author has faced and defined the possibility of the madness that I have mentioned (a possibility from the consideration of which others as well as himself may have found it impossible to escape) and has arrived at a moral attitude toward it, an attitude which is at once defined and communicated by the poem. This attitude is defined only by the entire poem, not by the logical content alone; it is a matter not only of logical content, but of feeling as well. The feeling is particular and unparaphrasable, but one may indicate the nature of it briefly by saying that it is a feeling of dignity and of self-control in the face of a situation of major difficulty, a difficulty which the poet fully apprehends. This feeling is inseparable from what we call poetic form, or unity, for the creation of a form is nothing more nor less than the act of evaluating and shaping (that is, controlling) a given experience. It should be obvious that any attempt to reduce the rational content of such a poem would tend to confuse or even to eliminate the feeling: the poem consists in the relationship between the two.

To reënforce my point, I shall take the liberty of quoting another poem, this one by Mr. Howard Baker, in which something comparable occurs. The title is *Pont Neuf*:

Henry the Fourth rides in bronze,
His shoulders curved and pensive, thrust
Enormously into electric
Blazonments of a Christmas trust.

Children pass him aghast and pleased,
Reflective of the flickerings
Of jerky bears and clowns. Alone,
Astute to all the bickerings

Of age and death rides Henry the Grand.
A lean tug shudders in the Seine;
And Notre Dame is black, a relic
Of the blood of other men.

Peace to the other men! And peace
To the mind that has no century,
And sees the savage pull the statue down,
And down the bear and clown.

The spiritual control in a poem, then, is simply a manifestation of
the spiritual control within the poet, and, as I have already indicated, it
may have been an important means by which the poet arrived at a realization of spiritual control. This conception must not be confused with the
conception of the poem as a safety valve, by which feeling is diverted
from action, by which the writer escapes from an attitude by pouring it
into his work and leaving it behind him. The conception which I am trying to define is a conception of poetry as a technique of contemplation,
of comprehension, a technique which does not eliminate the need of philosophy or of religion, but which, rather, completes and enriches them.

One feels, whether rightly or wrongly, a correlation between the control evinced within a poem and the control within the poet behind it.
The laxity of the one ordinarily appears to involve laxity in the other. The
rather limp versification of Mr. Eliot and of Mr. MacLeish is inseparable from the spiritual limpness that one feels behind the poems, as the
fragmentary, ejaculatory, and over-excited quality of a great many of the
poems of Hart Crane is inseparable from the intellectual confusion upon
which these particular poems seem to rest (for examples, *The Dance,
Cape Hatteras,* and *Atlantis*). Crane possessed great energy, but his faculties functioned clearly only within a limited range of experience (*Repose of Rivers, Voyages II, Faustus and Helen II*). Outside of that range
he was either numb (*My Grandmother's Love-letters* and *Harbor Dawn*)

or unsure of himself and hence uncertain in his detail (as in *The River*, a very powerful poem in spite of its poor construction and its quantities of bad writing) or both (see *Indiana*, probably one of the worst poems in modern literature). Many of the poems of Mr. Eliot and of Mr. MacLeish could be reduced by paraphrase to about the same thing as my paraphrase of Mr. Tate's sonnet; the difference between them and Mr. Tate in this connection is that, as the form of nearly all of their poems is much looser to start with, the process of paraphrasing would constitute a much slighter act of betrayal. And we must not forget that this quality, form, is not something outside the poet, something "æsthetic," and superimposed upon his moral content; it is essentially a part, in fact it may be the decisive part, of the moral content, even though the poet may be arriving at the final perfection of the condition he is communicating while he communicates it and in a large measure as a result of the act and technique of communication. For the communication is first of all with himself: it is, as I have said, the last refinement of contemplation.

I should pause here to remark that many writers have sought to seize the fluidity of experience by breaking down the limits of form, but that in so doing, they defeat their own ends. For, as I have shown, writing, as it approaches the looseness of prose and departs from the strictness of verse, tends to lose the capacity for fluid or highly complex relationships between words; language, in short, reapproaches its original stiffness and generality; and one is forced to recognize the truth of what appears a paradox, that the greatest fluidity of statement is possible where the greatest clarity of form prevails. It is hard to see how the existence of such a work as Mr. Joyce's latest creation[2] can be anything but precarious, in spite of its multitudes of incidental felicities; for it departs from the primary condition of prose — coherent and cumulative logic or narrative — without, since it is, finally, prose, achieving the formal precision of verse. These remarks should not be construed, however, as an argument against free verse, though, with proper qualifications, they could be brought to bear in such an argument. The free verse that is really verse — the best, that is, of W. C. Williams, H. D., Miss Moore, Wallace Stevens, and Ezra Pound — is, in its peculiar fashion, the antithesis of free, and the evaluation of this verse is a difficult problem in itself.

Thus we see that the poet, in striving toward an ideal of poetic form at which he has arrived through the study of other poets, is actually striving to perfect a moral attitude toward that range of experience of which he is aware. Such moral attitudes are contagious from poet to poet, and, within the life of a single poet, from poem to poem. The presence of Hardy and Arnold, let us say, in so far as their successful works offer us models and their failures warnings or unfulfilled suggestions, should make it easier to write good poetry; they should not only aid us, by providing standards of sound feeling, to test the soundness of our own poems, but, since their range of experience is very wide, they should aid us, as we are able to enter and share their experience, to grow into regions that we had not previously mastered or perhaps even discovered. The discipline of imitation is thus valuable if it leads to understanding and assimilation. Too often a minor poet or other reader will recognize in such a master the validity of only that part of the master's experience which corresponds to his own limited range, and will rule out the poetry to which he is consequently numb as sentimental or otherwise imperfect. Inflexibility of critical opinion in such matters is not particularly conducive to growth.

Random experiment may have a related value: one may hit on a form (perhaps the rough idea or draft of a form) which induces some new state or states of mind. I regard as fallacious the notion that form is determined by a precedent attitude or a precedent subject matter, at least invariably: the form (that is, the general idea of a certain type of form) *may* precede, and the attitude, in any case, is never definite till the form is achieved.[3] It does not follow that any attitude resulting from random experiment is intrinsically desirable; undesirable attitudes, like desirable, are contagious and may spread widely; it is here that criticism becomes necessary. A failure, however, to achieve something valuable may offer a valuable suggestion to someone else. The poet who has succeeded once or twice in mastering difficult and central emotions and in recording his mastery for future reference should find it easier to succeed again.

I am not endeavoring in the two foregoing paragraphs to establish poetry as a substitute for philosophy or for religion. Religion is highly desirable if it is really available to the individual; the study of philosophy is always available and is of incalculable value as a preliminary and as a check to activities as a poet and as a critic (that is, as an intelligent reader). I am, then, merely attempting to define a few of the things which poetry does.

It would perhaps be wise to add another caution: I suffer from no illusion that any man who can write a good poem has a naturally sweet moral temper or that the man who has written three good poems is a candidate for canonization. Literary history is packed with sickening biographies. But it is worth noting that the poetry of such a man, say, as Rochester (who in this is typical of his age) displays a mastery of an extremely narrow range of experience, and that his moral brutality falls almost wholly in those regions (nearly every region save that of worldly manners, if we except some few poems, notably *Upon Nothing*, *Absent from Thee*, and, possibly, *A Song of a Young Lady to Her Ancient Lover*, in which last there is a curious blending of the erotic with deep moral feeling) with which his poetry fails to deal or with which it deals badly.

This statement requires elucidation. Rochester frequently writes of his debauchery, and sometimes writes well of it, but in the best poems on the subject, in such poems as *The Maim'd Debauchee* and *Upon Drinking in a Bowl*, he writes, as do his contemporaries in the comedy, as a witty and satirical gentleman: the wit inspired by the material is mastered, and other aspects of the material are ignored. In the worst poems on more or less similar material (for examples, the numerous lampoons upon Charles II and upon Nell Gwyn) we have a grossness of feeling comparable to that of his worst actions. All of this, however, detracts not in the least from the quality of Rochester's best poetry, which is remarkably fine; Rochester seldom extends the standards which he recognizes into fields to which they are inapplicable, and hence he is seldom guilty of false evaluation. In reading him, one is aware that he is a sound and beautiful poet, and that there are greater poets. That is all of which one has a right to be aware.[4]

If a poem, in so far as it is good, represents the comprehension on a moral plane of a given experience, it is only fair to add that some experiences offer very slight difficulties and some very great, and that the poem will be the most valuable, which, granted it achieves formal perfection, represents the most difficult victory. In the great tragic poets, such as Racine or Shakespeare, one feels that a victory has been won over life itself, so much is implicated in the subject matter; that feeling is the source of their power over us, whereas a slighter poet will absorb very little of our experience and leave the rest untouched.

This requisite seems to be ignored in a large measure by a good many contemporary poets of more or less mystical tendencies, who avoid the difficult task of mastering the more complex forms of experience by setting up a theoretic escape from them and by then accepting that escape with a good deal of lyrical enthusiasm. Such an escape is offered us, I fear, by Hart Crane, in one of the most extraordinary sections of his volume, *The Bridge*,[5] in the poem called *The Dance*, and such escapes are often employed by Mr. Yeats. In the religious poets of the past, one encounters this vice very seldom; the older religions are fully aware that the heart, to borrow the terms of a poem by Janet Lewis, is untranslatable, whatever may be true of the soul, and that one can escape from the claims of the world only by understanding those claims and by thus accustoming oneself to the thought of eventually putting them by. This necessity is explicitly the subject of one of Sidney's greatest sonnets, *Leave me, O Love, which reachest but to dust*, and of the greatest poem by George Herbert, *Church Monuments*; one can find it elsewhere. The attitude is humane, and does not belittle nor evade the magnitude of the task; it is essentially a tragic attitude.

For this reason, the religious fervor of Gerard Hopkins, of John Donne, or of George Herbert should weaken but little the force of most of their poems for the non-believer, just as the deterministic doctrines, whatever their nature and extent, to be found in Hardy, should not weaken for us those poems which do not deal too pugnaciously with the doctrines, and for the same reason. Though a belief in any form of determinism should, if the belief is pushed to its logical ends, eliminate the belief in, and consequently the functioning of, whatever it is that we call the will, yet there is no trace of any kind of disintegration in Hardy's poetic style, in his sense of form, which we have seen to be, so far as writing is concerned, identical with the will or the ability to control and shape one's experience. The tragic necessity of putting by the claims of the world without the abandonment of self-control, without loss of the ability to go on living, for the present, intelligently and well, is just as definitely the subject of Hardy's poetry as of Herbert's. We have in both poets a common moral territory which is far greater than are the theological regions which they do not share; for, on the one hand, the fundamental concepts of morality are common to intelligent men regardless of theological orientation, except in so far as morality may be simply denied or ignored, and, on the other hand, the Absolute is in its nature inscrutable and offers little material for speculation, except in so far as it is a stimulus to moral speculation. It would be difficult, I think, to find a devotional poem of which most of the implications were not moral and universal. So with Hardy: his determinism was mythic and animistic and tended to dramatize the human struggle, whereas a genuinely rational and coherent determinism would have eliminated the human struggle. He was thrown back upon traditional literacy and folk wisdom in working out moral situations, and for these situations his mythology provided a new setting, sometimes magnificent, sometimes melodramatic, but, thanks to its rational incompleteness, not really destructive of a working morality. Like many another man who has been unable to think clearly, he was saved by the inability to think coherently: had he been coherent, he would probably have been about as interesting as Godwin; as it is, his professed beliefs and his working beliefs have only a little in common, and the former damage his work only in a fragmentary way, as when satires of circumstance are dragged into a novel or isolated in a poem to prove a point (and they can prove nothing, of course) and usually to the detriment of coherent feeling and understanding.

Crane's attitude, on the other hand, often suggests a kind of theoretic rejection of all human endeavor in favor of some vaguely apprehended but ecstatically asserted existence of a superior sort. As the exact nature of the superior experience is uncertain, it forms a rather uncertain and infertile source of material for exact poetry; one can write poetry about it only by utilizing in some way more or less metaphorical the realm of experience from which one is trying to escape; but as one *is* endeavoring to escape from this realm, not to master it and understand it, one's feelings about it are certain to be confused, and one's imagery drawn from it is bound to be largely formulary and devoid of meaning. That is, in so far as one endeavors to deal with the Absolute, not as a means of ordering one's moral perception but as the subject itself of perception, one will tend to say nothing, despite the multiplication of words. In *The Dance* there seems to be an effort to apply to each of two mutually exclusive fields the terms of the other. This is a vice of which Rochester was not guilty.

Crane's best work, such as *Repose of Rivers* and *Voyages II*, is not confused, but one feels that the experience is curiously limited and uncomplicated: it is between the author, isolated from most human complications, and Eternity. Crane becomes in such poems a universal symbol of the human mind in a particular situation, a fact which is the source of his power, but of the human mind in very nearly the simplest form of that situation, a fact which is the source of his limitation.

Objective proof of this assertion cannot be found in the poems, any more than proof of the opposite quality can be found in Hardy; it is in each poet a matter of feeling invading the poetry mainly by way of the non-paraphrasable content: one feels the fragility of Crane's finest work, just as one feels the richness of Hardy's. Hardy is able to utilize, for example, great ranges of literary, historical, and other connotations in words and cadences; one feels behind each word the history of the word and the generations of men who embodied that history; Hardy gets somehow at the wealth of the race. It should be observed again how the moral discipline is involved in the literary discipline, how it becomes, at times, almost a matter of living philology. From the greater part of this wealth Crane appears to be isolated and content to remain isolated. His isolation, like Hardy's immersion, was in part social and unavoidable, but a clearer mind and a more fixed intention might have overcome much of the handicap.

I should like to forestall one possible objection to the theory of poetry which I am trying to elucidate. Poetry, as a moral discipline, should not be regarded as one more means of escape. That is, moral responsibility should not be transferred from action to paper in the face of a particular situation. Poetry, if pursued either by the poet or by the reader, in the manner which I have suggested, should offer a means of enriching one's awareness of human experience and of so rendering greater the possibility of intelligence in the course of future action; and it should offer likewise a means of inducing certain more or less constant habits of feeling, which should render greater the possibility of one's acting, in a future situation, in accordance with the findings of one's improved intelligence. It should, in other words, increase the intelligence and strengthen the moral temper; these effects should naturally be carried over into action, if, through constant discipline, they are made permanent acquisitions. If the poetic discipline is to have steadiness and direction, it requires an antecedent discipline of ethical thinking and of at least some ethical feeling, which may be in whole or in part the gift of religion or of a social tradition, or which may be largely the result of individual acquisition by way of study. The poetic discipline includes the antecedent discipline and more: it is the richest and most perfect technique of contemplation.

This view of poetry in its general outline is not original, but is a restatement of ideas that have been current in English criticism since the time of Sidney, that have appeared again in most of the famous apologists for poetry since Sidney, especially in Arnold and in Newman. In summarizing these ideas, I have merely endeavored to illuminate a few of the more obscure relationships and to dispose of them in such a way as to prepare the reader for various analyses of poetic method which I intend, in other essays, to undertake. Poetic morality and poetic feeling are inseparable; feeling and technique, or structure, are inseparable. Technique has laws which govern poetic (and perhaps more general) morality more widely than is commonly recognized. It is my intention to examine them.

1. Stéphane Mallarmé: *Avant-Dire* du *Traité du Verbe*, par René Ghil. Giraud, 18 Rue Drouot, Paris. 1886. Actually, Mallarmé seems to have had more in mind, though he should have had no more, in my opinion. The margin of difference is the margin in which post-romantic theory has flourished and from which post-romantic poetry has sprung. I quote the entire curious passage:

> "Un désir indéniable à l'époque est de séparer comme en vue d'attributions différentes, le double état de la parole, brut ou immédiate ici, à là essentiel.
>
> "Narrer, enseigner, même décrire, cela va et encore qu'a chacun suffirait peut-être, pour échanger toute pensée humaine, de prendre ou de mettre dans la main d'autrui en silence une pièce de monnaie, l'emploi élémentaire du discours dessert l'universel reportage dont, la Littérature exceptée, participe tout, entre les genres d'écrits contemporains.
>
> "A quoi bon la merveille de transposer un fait de nature en sa presque disparition vibratoire selon le jeu de la parole cependant, si ce n'est pour qu'on émane, sans la gêne d'un proche ou concret rappel, la notion pure?
>
> "Je dis: une fleur! et, hors de l'oubli où ma voix relègue aucun contour, en tant que quelque chose d'autre que les calices sus, musicalement se lève, idée rieuse ou altière, l'absente de tons bouquets.
>
> "Au contraire d'une fonction de numéraire facile et représentatif, comme le traite d'abord la foule, le parler qui est, après tout, rêve et chant, retrouve chez le poète, par nécessité constitutive d'un art consacré aux fictions, sa virtualité.

"Le vers qui de plusieurs vocables refait un mot total, neuf, étranger à la langue et comme incantatoire, achève cet isolement de la parole: niant, d'un trait souverain, le hasard demeuré aux termes malgré l'artifice de leur retrempe alternée en le sens et la sonorité, et vous cause cette surprise de n'avoir ouï jamais tel fragment ordinaire d'élocution, en même temps que la réminiscence de l'objet nommé baigne dans une clairvoyante atmosphère."

This is in some respects an admirable summary, and is certainly important historically. The entire tendency of the passage is to encourage the elimination of the rational from poetry. One should observe the sequence: "narrer, enseigner, *même* décrire," as if description were more nearly poetic than the other activities. The word *essentiel*, at the end of the first paragraph, is the crux of the whole passage. The critic says that words have an obvious (that is, a rational) meaning, and a fringe of feeling, which he chooses to call essential: if only one kind of content is essential, we are naturally inclined to try to eliminate the other, and we have in this confusion, which reappears spontaneously, and without any discernible indebtedness to Mallarmé, in each successive generation of post-romantic poets, the real basis for post-romantic obscurantism. The sound idea that a poem is more than its rational content is thus perverted and distorted.

2. Entitled at this writing (1935) *Work in Progress.* (Ultimately published as *Finnegans Wake.*)

3. As a single example, consider the manner in which the Petrarchan experimenters in England, most of them feeble poets and the best of them given to empty and inflated reasoning, worked out the technique of reasoning elaborately in graceful lyrical verse and bequeathed that technique to the 17th century: the form preceded the matter.

4. *The Collected Poems of John Wilmot, Earl of Rochester*, edited by John Hayward. The Nonesuch Press, 16 Great James St., London, W.C. 1926.

5. *The Bridge*, by Hart Crane, Horace Liveright: N. Y.: 1930.

PART 4 — APPRAISING POETS AND PERIODS

THE REVOLUTION THAT THE NEW CRITICS CREATED IN THE TEACHING OF literary criticism—which was codified in Robert Penn Warren and Cleanth Brooks's textbook anthology *Understanding Poetry,* and widely adopted in the American universities after 1938—carried with it a revolution in taste as well. The canon of American literature was quickly established, while the canon of British literature was altered and amended, sometimes radically. For example, the romantic school of poets was displaced from its privileged perch (few New Critics had anything good to say about Shelley, Byron, or Wordsworth) while the school of the metaphysical poets—also known as the school of Donne—was raised to its prominent position. T. S. Eliot reignited interest in the more obscure Elizabethan dramatists; he also published W. H. Auden. Ezra Pound elevated the reputation of Landor while encouraging Basil Bunting and Louis Zukofsky. Randall Jarrell almost single-handedly focused critical attention on Walt Whitman and Robert Frost when they were both relatively neglected. So the New Critics did not merely raise the dead; they enthroned the living. According to Delmore Schwartz, they were responsible for sparking a literary revival in American literature that had

> resurrected [Henry] James, and given the novels of Faulkner and Fitzgerald the attention of which they were deprived by the concerns of criticism during the depression; and classic American literature has established itself clearly and fully. We have only to think of Melville, Emily Dickinson, and Mark Twain to see there has been a real advance: the gulf between the present and the past which existed in virtually every other period has been greatly diminished, and this has come about chiefly because so many critics are teachers.

The New Critics were the first generation to discuss living authors in college classrooms. Consequently, poets and writers who would ordinarily have remained neglected were read, anthologized, and employed by universities as teachers. One has only to consider the career of Hart Crane—whose difficult verse and self-destructive personality made him his era's *poète maudit*—to know that the sympathetic attention he received from such critics as Allen Tate and Yvor Winters probably saved him from utter obscurity. (This is not a trivial matter. Not only do poets perish while waiting for their audience to arrive, but their works disappear as well. The great French poet Tristan Corbière owes his reputation entirely to a relative who pressed his book into the hands of Paul Verlaine. Some of Arthur Rimbaud's greatest poems have never been recovered; very few of his books escaped the printer's warehouse. *One* copy of Isidore Ducasse's *Poésies* survived in the Bibliothèque Nationale for André Breton and Louis Aragon to discover.)

The end of the New Criticism should probably be dated by the last book of the last New Critic (W. K. Wimsatt's *Day of the Leopards,* 1976) or by the rise of the next critical movement to dominate the American universities, the aptly named deconstruction movement. This changing of the generations was heralded by a coarsening of style. Where the New Critics had courted the educated public with their elegant prose, the deconstructionists wrote only for their fellow professors in an almost impenetrable language. In the last forty years, literary scholarship aped this embarrassing trend with a surfeit of pseudoscientific jargon and a strangling of common sense. Under various names (structuralism, post-structuralism, deconstruction) the rise of so-called Literary Theory effectively divorced criticism from its audience outside the universities. Of this pseudosophisticated style, Randall Jarrell complained that "if the two bears that ate the forty-two little children who said to Elisha, 'Go up, thou baldhead'—if they, after getting their Ph.D.'s from the University of Göttingen, had retired to Atta Troll's Castle and written a book called A *Prolegomena to Every Future Criticism of Finnegans Wake,* they might have written so."

Suggested Further Reading

Revaluation: Tradition and Development in English Poetry, by F. R. Leavis (1936)
Maule's Curse: Seven Studies in the History of American Obscurantism, by Yvor
    Winters (1938)
Selected Essays, by T. S. Eliot (2nd ed.; 1950)
Poetry and the Age, by Randall Jarrell (1953)
Form & Value in Modern Poetry, by R. P. Blackmur (1957)

T. S. Eliot: Thinker and Artist

CLEANTH BROOKS

Originally published in the Sewanee Review, *this essay argues for the central place of T. S. Eliot in twentieth-century literature because of the essential unity of his artistic work. Whether one accepts or rejects Eliot's Christian sensibility is immaterial, Brooks asserts, because Eliot's poems do not sermonize but dramatize the spiritual crisis of our age. "In a time of grave disorder, Eliot has moved toward a restoration of order."*

Eliot's career is no loose bundle of unrelated activities but possesses an essential unity. Indeed, once discovered, this unity of purpose becomes increasingly evident. Few literary men in our history have so consistently related all their activities to a coherent set of principles. And the consistency of his various writings reflects the quality of the man. In a time of disorder, Eliot moved toward a restoration of order—toward the restoration of order that poetry alone, perhaps, can give.

Thus, Eliot's fundamental reassessment of the twentieth-century literary and cultural situation was *not* expressed in his poetry alone. The poetry arose out of a mental and spiritual activity that necessarily showed itself in literary and social criticism, not only in his brilliant essays on the Elizabethan dramatists, for example, but also in a work like *Notes towards the Definition of Culture*.

When one discusses literature, few things are so deadly as the recital of abstract statements and wide generalizations. Moreover, it seems impertinent to treat a poet in this fashion, especially a poet who succeeded so brilliantly in giving his ideas concrete embodiment and who devoted so much of his discursive prose to this very split in the modern mind, this dissociation of sensibility, in which Eliot saw not only the distemper of literature but a symptom of a more general disease. Let me try to illustrate the essential unity of Eliot's work from a single topic, his treatment of the urban scene. In an essay written near the end of his life he has told us how he discovered that the urban scene was proper material for poetry, and specifically the special material for his own poetry. The passage I mean to quote begins with some observations on literary influences and what a poet can learn from earlier poets.

Then, among influences, there are the poets from whom one has learned some one thing, perhaps of capital importance to oneself, though not necessarily the greatest contribution these poets have made. I think that from Baudelaire I learned first, a precedent for the poetical possibilities, never developed by any poet writing in my own language, the more sordid aspects of the modern metropolis, of the possibility of fusion between the sordidly realistic and the phantasmagoric, the possibility of the juxtaposition of the matter-of-fact and the fantastic. From him, as from Laforgue, I learned that the sort of material that I had, the sort of experience that an adolescent had had, in an industrial city in America, could be the material for poetry; and that the source of new poetry might be found in what had been regarded hitherto as the impossible, the sterile, the intractably unpoetic. That, in fact, the business of the poet was to make poetry out of the unexplored resources of the unpoetical; that the poet, in fact, was committed by his profession to turn the unpoetical into poetry. A great poet can give a younger poet everything that he has to give him in a very few lines. It may be that I am indebted in Baudelaire chiefly for half a dozen lines out of the whole of *Fleurs du Mal*; and that his significance for me is summed up in the lines:

> Fourmillante cité, cité pleine de rêves,
> Où le spectre en plein jour raccroche le passant!

I knew what *that* meant, because I had lived it before I knew that I wanted to turn it into verse on my own account.

I want to consider further both Eliot's notion that the poet, by his very profession, is committed "to turn the unpoetical into poetry", and his idea that poetry is a fusion of opposites—in this instance, a fusion of "the sordidly realistic and the phantasmagoric," of "the matter-of-fact and the fantastic."

Poetry is evidently not to be thought of as a bouquet of "poetic" objects. The implication is that the materials the poet uses are not in themselves poetic. To be agreeable or pleasant or charming is not the same thing as being poetic. Poetic value is a quality of a different order. It is not a *property* of objects but a relationship among them, a relationship discovered and established by the poet. Moreover, the relationship may be one of tension in which the materials pull against each other and resist any easy reconciliation. In this instance it is the realistic and the phantasmagoric that may seem intractable, or the matter-of-fact and the fantastic.

All of this Eliot had said before, and, because he had said it before, in this rather late essay he could afford to touch upon it lightly. But when he first enunciated this view of tension in poetry, it very much needed saying—or at least needed re-saying. And his statement of this conception, together with the poems that embodied it, inspired the literary revolution that is sometimes given Eliot's name.

It is useful to refer to another passage in which Eliot discusses the poet's use of what the Victorians sometimes regarded as hopelessly unpromising materials for poetry. The Victorian in this instance is Matthew Arnold commenting upon the ugliness of the world of Robert Burns. After quoting Arnold's rather prim observation to the effect that "no one can deny that it is of advantage to a poet to deal with a beautiful world," Eliot suddenly rounds on the nineteenth-century critic and quite flatly denies his basic assumption. The essential advantage for a poet, Eliot remarks, is *not* that of having a beautiful world with which to deal, but rather "to be able to see beneath both beauty and ugliness; to see the boredom, and the horror, and the glory." "The vision of the horror and the glory," he rather acidly concludes, "was denied to Arnold, but he knew something of the boredom."

This is excellent polemics: the hard backhand drive that rifles across the court and just dusts the opponent's back line. Yet the reader may wonder at the energy with which Eliot rejects Arnold. He may wonder too at what may seem an almost gratuitous reference to "boredom," not, surely, an obvious member of a cluster that would include "horror" and "glory." But references to boredom often come into Eliot's account of urban life, and we have in this passage mention of concerns central to his poetry.

They are indeed central to his experience of the modern metropolis where so many people find themselves caught in a world of monotonous repetition, an aimless circling without end or purpose. Eliot's early poetry is full of it:

> The morning comes to consciousness
> Of faint stale smells of beer
> From the sawdust-trampled street
> With all its muddy feet that press
> To early coffee-stands.
>
> With the other masquerades
> That time resumes,

One thinks of all the hands
That are raising dingy shades
In a thousand furnished rooms.

· · ·

They are rattling breakfast plates in basement kitchens,
And along the trampled edges of the street
I am aware of the damp souls of housemaids
Sprouting despondently at area gates.

· · ·

At the violet hour, the evening hour that strives
Homeward, and brings the sailor home from sea,
The typist home at teatime, clears her breakfast, lights
Her stove, and lays out food in tins.

· · ·

Let us go, through certain half-deserted streets,
The muttering retreats
Of restless nights in one-night cheap hotels
And sawdust restaurants with oyster-shells:
Streets that follow like a tedious argument
Of Insidious intent. . . .

The wanderer moving through the deserted city streets long past mid-
night walks through a genuine nightmare in which

the floors of memory
And all its clear relations,
Its divisions and precisions

are dissolved, a fantastic world in which every street lamp that one passes

Beats like a fatalistic drum. . .

Yet when the wanderer turns to his own door, he steps out of one horror
into a worse horror:

The lamp said,
'Four o'clock,

Here is the number on the door.
Memory!
You have the key,
The little lamp spreads a ring on the stair.
Mount.
The bed is open; the tooth-brush hangs on the wall,
Put your shoes at the door, sleep, prepare for life.'

The last twist of the knife.

The wound in which this knife is twisted is modern man's loss of meaning and purpose. When life to which one expects to rise after sleep—a daylight world of clear plans and purposes—turns out to be simply a kind of automatism, as absurd as the bizarre world of the nightmare streets, the knife in the wound is given a final agonizing twist.

It may be useful to remind the reader, especially the reader who finds that Eliot's Anglo-Catholicism sticks in his craw and prevents his swallowing the poetry, that in passages of the sort that I have been quoting, we are not getting sermonizing but drama, not generalizations about facts but responses to situations, not statements about what ought to be but renditions of what is.

Eliot once remarked that prose has to do with ideals; poetry, with reality. The statement has proved puzzling to many a reader who has been brought up on just the opposite set of notions, but Eliot's observation seems to me profoundly true. Discursive prose is the medium for carrying on arguments, drawing conclusions, offering solutions. Poetry is the medium *par excellence* for rendering a total situation—for letting us know what it feels like to take a particular action or hold a particular belief or simply to look at something with imaginative sympathy.

Here are some presentations of reality—an urban vignette, a winter evening in the city:

The winter evening settles down
With smell of steaks in passageways.
Six o'clock.
The burnt-out ends of smoky days.
And now a gusty shower wraps
The grimy scraps
Of withered leaves about your feet
And newspapers from vacant lots;
The showers beat
On broken blinds and chimney-pots,

And at the corner of the street
A lonely cab-horse steams and stamps.

And then the lighting of the lamps.

The Song of the third Thames-daughter:

'Trams and dusty trees.
Highbury bore me. Richmond and Kew
Undid me. By Richmond I raised my knees
Supine on the floor of a narrow canoe.'

'My feet are at Moorgate, and my heart
Under my feet. After the event
He wept. He promised "a new start."
I made no comment. What should I resent?'

'On Margate Sands.
I can connect
Nothing with nothing.
The broken fingernails of dirty hands.
My people humble people who expect
Nothing.'
                    la la

Even the raffish Sweeney's recital of his philosophy—a view of life
held, incidentally, by many of Sweeney's betters—is a bit of reality too;
for it is a dramatic projection of a man, not an abstract formulation. Its
very rhythms testify to a personality and an attitude.

Birth, and copulation, and death.
That's all the facts when you come to brass tacks:
Birth, and copulation, and death.
I've been born, and once is enough.

Readers have responded powerfully to such passages, even readers
who hold very different conceptions of what the world ought to be. What
is primarily at stake in all these passages is not the reader's approval or
rejection of a statement, but his response to authentic reality. The only
compulsion to respond is that exerted by the authority of the imagination. Perhaps the poet can never do more than exert such authority; but
in any case he cannot afford to do less.

This matter of the reader's response has another and more special aspect. Eliot suggests that many of those who live in the modern world have been drugged and numbed by it. One task of the poet is to penetrate their torpor, to awaken them to full consciousness of their condition, to let them see where they are. The theme recurs throughout Eliot's poetry from the earliest poems to the latest.

The people who inhabit *The Waste Land* cling to their partial oblivion. They say:

> Winter kept us warm, covering
> Earth in forgetful snow, feeding
> A little life with dried tubers.

Or like the old women of Canterbury, they may say:

> We do not wish anything to happen.
> Seven years we have lived quietly,
> Succeeded in avoiding notice,
> Living and partly living.

The trivial daily actions, they point out, at least marked

> a limit to our suffering.
> Every horror had its definition,
> Every sorrow had a kind of end. . . .

What they dread now is the "disturbance" of the seasons, the decisive break in the numbing routine that will wake them out of their half-life.

But the partially numbed creatures may be, and usually are, people of the contemporary world. They may, for example, be like the characters in *The Family Reunion* who do not want anything to rumple their rather carefully arranged lives—who want things to be "normal"—and who cannot see that—to use their nephew's words—the event that they call normal "is merely the unreal and the unimportant."

They may be like certain well-bred inhabitants of Boston, Massachusetts:

> . . . evening quickens faintly in the street
> Wakening the appetite of life in some
> And to others bringing the *Boston Evening Transcript.* . . .

Or they may be the bored drawing-room characters in "The Love Song of J. Alfred Prufrock" whom Prufrock would like to confront with the truth about themselves. He would like to say to them:

'I am Lazarus, come from the dead,
Come back to tell you all, I shall tell you all'. . . .

But he well knows that these overcivilized and desiccated people would
not be impressed by the Lazarus of the New Testament, much less by a
self-conscious man "with a bald spot in the middle of [his] hair," a man
aware of the fact that he wears a "necktie rich and modest, but asserted
by a simple pin." In any case, these people would not understand the
talk of a man who had experienced real death or real life.

The themes that run through so much of Eliot's poetry—life that is
only a half-life because it cannot come to terms with death, the liberation
into true living that comes from the acceptance of death, the ecstatic moment that partakes of both life and death:

> . . . I could not
> Speak, and my eyes failed, I was neither
> Living nor dead, and I knew nothing,
> Looking into the heart of light, the silence.

These and the other themes that recur in Eliot's poetry bear the closest
relation to his concern with the boredom and the horror and the glory
that he finds in our contemporary metropolitan life. They also bear the
closest relationship to the sense of unreality that pervades a world that
has lost the rhythm of the seasons, has lost any sense of community, and,
most of all, has lost a sense of purpose. Such a world *is* unreal: the sordid and the matter-of-fact to not erase the phantasmagoric but accentu-
ate it. The spectre does indeed in broad daylight reach out to grasp the
passerby. London, "under the brown fog of a winter noon" as well as
"under the brown fog of a winter dawn," is seen as an "Unreal City," and
the crowds flowing across London Bridge might be in Dante's Hell:

> I had not thought death had undone so many.
> Sighs, short and infrequent, were exhaled,
> And each man fixed his eyes before his feet.

The echo of *The Divine Comedy* is not merely a flourish or an attempt
to touch up the modern scene by giving it literary overtones. What con-
nects the modern scene with Dante's "Inferno" is the poet's insight into
the nature of hell. The man who sees the crowds flowing over London
Bridge as damned souls, if challenged for putting them thus into hell,
might justify his observation by paraphrasing a line from Christopher
Marlowe: "Why, this is hell, nor are they out of it."

In view of the complaint that Eliot sighs after vanished glories, sentimentalizes the past, and hates the present, one must insist on Eliot's ability to dramatize the urban reality with honesty and sensitivity. If the world about which we must write has lost the rhythm of the seasons, then the poet must be open to the new rhythms so that he can relate them to the old. Eliot once wrote that the poet must be able to use the rhythms of the gasoline engine:

> At the violet hour, when the eyes and back
> Turn upward from the desk, when the human engine waits
> Like a taxi throbbing waiting. . . .

If the modern world has lost its sense of community, the poet must present that loss not as a generalization but as a dramatic rendition, not as observed from the outside but as felt from the inside. He has done so not only in the nightmare passages of *The Waste Land*—

> There is not even solitude in the mountains
> But red sullen faces sneer and snarl
> From doors of mudcracked houses—

but also in the realistic passages:

> 'My nerves are bad to-night. Yes, bad. Stay with me.
> 'Speak to me. Why do you never speak. Speak.
>   'What are you thinking of? What thinking? What?
> 'I never know what you are thinking. Think.'

But he has also on occasion rendered the sense of community in positive terms—not as something lost but as a present reality:

> O City city, I can sometimes hear
> Beside a public bar in Lower Thames Street,
> The pleasant whining of a mandoline
> And a clatter and a chatter from within
> Where fishmen lounge at noon. . . .

As for the sense of loss of purpose, that loss is never merely asserted but always rendered concretely. It occurs so frequently in Eliot's poetry that it hardly needs illustration. Indeed, it may be best in this instance to take the illustration from Joseph Conrad's *Heart of Darkness*, a story that lies behind so much of Eliot's early poetry. Marlow, the character who relates the story, finds many of his experiences tinged with unreality. As he makes his way to the African coast and then on up the Congo to try to locate Kurtz, his sense of unreality is magnified—not merely because the jungle seems fantastic, but because the civilized characters he meets are disoriented, obsessed, and thus absurd. One object stands out sharply from this miasma of unreality. Marlow finds in an abandoned hut "an old tattered book, entitled *An Inquiry into Some Points of Seamanship*, by a man Tower, Towson—some such name. . . . Not a very enthralling book; but at the first glance you could see there a singleness of inten- tion . . . which made these humble pages . . . luminous with another than a professional light. . . . [The book] made me forget the jungle and the [ivory-seeking] pilgrims in a delicious sensation of having come upon something unmistakably real." It seems so because it is instinct with purpose—because, to use Marlow's words, you could see in it "an honest concern for the right way of going to work." This is why the book shines with the light of reality.

The sense of unreality is also associated with the vision of a world that is disintegrating. In *The Waste Land*, the cities of a disintegrating civilization seem unreal as if they were part of a mirage. The parched traveler asks:

> What is the city over the mountains
> Cracks and reforms and bursts in the violet air
> Falling towers—

but these cities are also like a mirage in that they are inverted, are seen as upside-down; and the passage that follows shows everything turned topsy-turvy:

> . . . bats with baby faces in the violet light
> Whistled, and beat their wings
> And crawled head downward down a blackened wall
> And upside down in air were towers
> Tolling reminiscent bells, that kept the hours
> And voices singing out of empty cisterns and exhausted wells.

Eliot also uses the empty whirl in order to suggest the break-up of civi- lization. Toward the end of "Gerontion" we have such a vision, people whose surnames suggest that the disintegration is international and worldwide: De Bailhache, Fresca, and Mrs. Cammel are whirled

> Beyond the circuit of the shuddering Bear
> In fractured atoms.

Though "Gerontion" was written long before the explosion of the first atomic bomb, I suppose there is some temptation nowadays to read into the passage our present unease and to regard the fractured atoms into which humankind has been vaporized as the debris of an atomic war. But I doubt that Mr. Eliot ever changed his opinion about the way the world ends.

"The Hollow Men," who know in their hollow hearts that they are not really "lost/Violent souls," but only "stuffed men," sing

> This is the way the world ends
> This is the way the world ends
> This is the way the world ends
> Not with a bang but a whimper.

The vortex in which De Bailhache, Fresca, and Mrs. Cammel are caught is essentially described in "Burnt Norton":

> Men and bits of paper, whirled by the cold wind
> That blows before and after time. . . .

With the empty whirl, the purposeless moving in a circle, we are back once more to the theme of boredom, and there is a good deal of evidence that Eliot did indeed see in such torpor and apathy the real dying out of a civilization. In 1934, for example, he wrote: "Without religion the whole human race would die, as according to W. H. R. Rivers, some Melanesian tribes have died, solely of boredom." This is a polemical passage out of a polemical essay, but we need not discount the idea merely for that reason. It is an integral part of Eliot's thinking. It is to be found everywhere in his prose and poetry—even in a poem like *Sweeney Agonistes*, where we have the following spoof on the cinematic stereotype of the golden age, life on a South Sea island:

> Where the Gauguin maids
> In the banyan shades
> Wear palmleaf drapery
> Under the bam
> Under the boo
> Under the bamboo tree.

>   Tell me in what part of the wood
> Do you want to flirt with me?
> Under the breadfruit, banyan, palmleaf

Or under the bamboo tree?
Any old tree will do for me
Any old wood is just as good
Any old isle is just my style
Any fresh egg
Any fresh egg
And the sound of the coral sea.

Doris protests that she doesn't like eggs and doesn't like life on "your crocodile isle." And when the singers renew their account of the delights of such a life, Doris replies:

That's not life, that's no life
Why I'd just as soon be dead.

Doris is a young woman who is clearly no better than she should be, but in this essential matter, she shows a great deal more discernment than J. Alfred Prufrock's companions, the ladies who "come and go / Talking of Michelangelo."

I have tried to suggest how the themes and images of Eliot's poetry are related to his convictions about the nature of our present-day civilization. But I shall have badly confused matters if in doing so I have seemed to reduce his poetry to a kind of thin and brittle propaganda for a particular world view. The primary role of poetry is to give us an account of reality, not to argue means for reshaping it. To be more specific: if a culture is sick, the poet's primary task is to provide us with a diagnosis, not to prescribe a specific remedy. For all of his intense interest in the problems of our culture, and in spite of the fact that he himself was deeply committed to a doctrinal religion, Eliot was careful never to confuse poetry with politics or with religion. The loss of a sense of purpose, the conviction that one is simply going round in a circle, is an experience that many of the readers of Eliot's poetry have recognized as their own; but in their decisions as to what to do about it, such readers have differed as much as the Christian differs from the atheistic existentialist. To get out of the circle, to find one's proper end and begin to walk toward it—this is a matter of the highest importance, work for the statesman, the sage, and the saint; but Eliot was too modest ever to claim any of these roles for himself, and he was as well aware as anyone of the confusion of tongues that makes it difficult for men of our century to agree on what the proper goal is. At any rate, he argued the case for what he took to be the true goal, not in his poetry, but in his prose.

In a time of grave disorder, Eliot has moved toward a restoration of order. Not the least important part of this work of restoration has been to clarify the role of poetry, not claiming so much for it that it is transformed into prophecy, or Promethean politics, or an ersatz religion; but at the same time pointing out its unique and irreplaceable function and defending its proper autonomy.

Genuine poetry, seen in its proper role, performing for us what only it can perform, does contribute to the health of a culture. A first step toward the recovery of the health of our culture may well be the writing of a poetry that tells us the truth about ourselves in our present situation, that is capable of dealing with the present world, that does not have to leave out the boredom and the horror of our world in order to discern its true glory. More modestly still, a poetry that can deal with the clutter of language in an age of advertising and propaganda restores to that degree the health of language.

Eliot was well aware of this problem. Advertising and propaganda were for him instruments for "influencing . . . masses of men" by means other than "their intelligence." And he once went so far as to say: "You have only to examine the mass of newspaper leading articles, the mass of political exhortation, to appreciate the fact that good prose cannot be written by a people without convictions."

The difficulty of writing good prose in our era extends to other kinds of writing, including poetry. Of this too, Eliot was aware. In *The Rock*, he has the chorus assert that "The soul of Man must quicken to creation"—not only to create new forms, colors, and music but so that

> Out of the slimy mud of words, out of the sleet and hail of
>   verbal imprecisions,
> Approximate thoughts and feelings, words that have taken
>   the place of thoughts and feelings,
> . . . [may] spring the perfect order of speech, and the beauty
>   of incantation.

In a later and finer poem, he puts this ideal of style more precisely and more memorably still, and he makes this ideal structure of the language a model of that thing which men must try to accomplish in their lives. It is Eliot's description of the relation that obtains among the words that make up a passage luminous with meaning. In it,

> . . . every word is at home,
> Taking its place to support the others,
> The word neither diffident nor ostentatious,

An easy commerce of the old and the new,
The common word exact without vulgarity,
The formal word precise but not pedantic,
The complete consort dancing together. . . .

These beautiful lines celebrate the poet's victory over disorder, the peculiar triumph possible to a master of language. They describe what
Eliot actually achieved many times in his own poetry. They provide an
emblem of the kind of harmony that ought to obtain in wider realms—
in the just society and in the true community.

Religious Poetry in the United States

R. P. BLACKMUR

Originally published in T. S. Eliot's quarterly, the Criterion, *this
essay examines the religious impulse as it has expressed itself in the
work of various American poets. Blackmur describes an American
religious poetry that is unique, much like the splintered denomina-
tions that arose from the nation's Puritan past.*

After meditating off and on for three years about American religious
verse, I find that it seems to reach in different directions and by different
routes than those taken by what is called English or French or Italian religious verse; and it appears to have used, or cultivated, different forces in
the Psyche than those within the specific familiar limits of traditional
Christian feeling and dogma. It is as if religion itself had reached, or is in
the process of reaching, another and different stage in its history than our
regular historical sense would have predicted. Some of our Protestant
theologians—as Reinhold Niebuhr—say this in their own way when they
refer to present times as post-Christian; and they shall have all the rest of
the words on this aspect of the subject, which is American religious verse
and especially the small amount of it which is also poetry; but I want to
keep in mind that unexpected forces of the Psyche are at work in it.

Which is also poetry. Anyone has enough talent to write verse within
a body of recognized conventions, but very few have enough talent to
make their verse poetry. We are all poets in little, else we could not read

it when large; it is a matter, as Croce insisted, of quantity not quality of talent. Most verses written out of love are drivel, and most versifications of the psalms take the poetry out of them and substitute mnemonic rehearsals of doctrine and archetypal images. Hence the morals, like the love, are flagrant, and all the substance of the writer's faith and passion which he would have made public is missing forever. He is not there in front of us, and he has not put his presence into his verse. It is the presence of the human Psyche in words that makes the scandal of poetry as its presence in action makes the scandal of religion.

The distinction is worth insisting on, and I can think of no better language for it than a short passage from George Santayana's preface to *Interpretations of Poetry and Religion* where he outlines the single idea to which his whole book leads. "This idea is that religion and poetry are identical in essence, and differ merely in the way in which they are attached to practical affairs. Poetry is called religion when it intervenes in life, and religion, when it merely supervenes upon life, is seen to be nothing but poetry."[1] It is a matter of choice, chance, and tact or grace, which is which; and religious poetry, I take it, is when the two are taken together. As religion takes new forms and changes the nature and scope of its interventions, so the poetry associated with religion supervenes differently upon our reading lives in manifest presence. There is an area in us where religious poetry at one and the same time both comes among our actions and overcomes them, an ordering together with a ravishing.

The second of the Homeric Hymns to Aphrodite is like that, and the *Pervigilium Veneris,* and perhaps the invocation to Venus in *De Rerum Natura.* They intervene and supervene at once as they persuade us of our occupation. Though the first is a narrative of events, the second an incantation, and the third a part of a philosophical discourse, in each the intervention is religious, the supervention poetic: they touch on behavior fused with aspiration. Reading, we act and breathe and lose the action in our breath. It is the same thing, I think, when we come to the *Cantico delle Creature* of St. Francis where the gap between God and nature is annihilated through the salutation of both in single breath and all our occupation is gone and come at once. Reading St. Francis's Canticle our substance is ravished with all weathers—*onne tempo*—and all the weathers have their own meaning in the being of God. The first three poems we know are not Christian; of the Canticle we know that it is a Christian who wrote it, and one who changed Christianity through the forces that led him to write it. Here are two lines of Iacopone da Todi (of whom it is said that he wrote the *Stabat Mater*) taken from the beginning of his poem on the incarnation of the divine word:

> *Fiorito è Cristo nella carne pura:*
> *or se ralegri l'umana nature*

> Christ has flowered in pure flesh:
> Now let human nature rejoice

and three from the beginning of his poem "That it is the highest wisdom to be thought mad for love of Christ":

> *Senno me pare è cortesia • empazir per lo bel Messia. . . .*
> *Ello me sa sì gran sapere • a chi per Dio vol empazire,*
> *en Parige non se vidde • ancor si gran filoso fia.*[2]

> Sense and nobleness it seems to me to go mad for the fair Messiah.
> . . . It seems to me great wisdom in a man if he wish to go mad for
> God; no philosophy so great as this has yet been seen in Paris.

Iacopone was a Franciscan, too, of the second generation, and a splendid Christian struggle had begun in his poetry, of which St. Francis was free in his simplicity of salutation—the struggle, the wrestling of spirit, to join himself to God. It is a man we know who speaks, as it was in the others a voice we discovered. We hear a voice like this in Donne (in "Batter my heart"), in Crashaw ("The Hymn to St. Teresa"), in George Herbert ("The Pulley"), even in Milton ("Samson Agonistes"). In them all there is a spiritual sensuality behaving like a prodigal mathematics. Religious poetry was for them, as it is somewhat today, a natural technique for the speculative framing and the dramatic solution of the problem of the troubles that beset us when we would play the role of God in our own way. Those who care for the word may say that this was the Baroque spirit at work, and this might be apt from St. John of the Cross to Milton; but it does not help with Iacopone, and helps very little with later poets in the nineteenth and twentieth centuries, like Crane and Eliot and Auden, nor with all those who have read too much St. Augustine and Gerard Manly Hopkins. I would say rather that it is the great wrestling tradition which has inhabited the great majority of religious poets since the Council of Trent, and it makes no difference whether they were Catholic or Protestant or non-juring or simple abstainers. The Reformation and the Counter-Reformation alike put upon us the compulsion to a wrestling (and to an irregular metaphysic to account for the wrestling): a wrestling with God, with the self, with the conscience, and above all in our latter day with our behavior. Pascal stands as a natural monument of one form of this wrestling, Baudelaire as another, and Henry James and James Joyce as a kind of composite for our day.

But the mind roams and needs a point of return which is in Genesis (xxxii, 22–32):

> And Jacob was left alone; and there wrestled a man with him until the breaking of the day.
>
> And when he saw that he prevailed not against him, he touched the hollow of his thigh; and the hollow of Jacob's thigh was out of joint, as he wrestled with him.
>
> And he said, Let me go, for the day breaketh. And he said, I will not let thee go, except thou bless me.
>
> And he said unto him, What is thy name? And he said, Jacob.
>
> And he said, Thy name shall be called no more Jacob, but Israel: for as a prince hast thou power with God and with man, and hast prevailed.
>
> And Jacob asked him, and said, Tell me, I pray thee, thy name. And he said, Wherefore is it that thou dost ask after my name? And he blessed him there.
>
> And Jacob called the name of the place Peniel: for I have seen God face to face, and my life is preserved.
>
> And as he passed over Peniel the sun rose upon him, and he halted upon his thigh.
>
> Therefore the children of Israel eat not of the sinew which shrank, which is upon the hollow of the thigh, unto this day: because he touched the hollow of Jacob's thigh in the sinew that shrank.

It is astonishing that we do not have poems called "The Place Peniel" and "The Sinew that Shrank"; for there is in this adventure of Jacob half the subject-matter of modern poetry—which is why we can fill in so well the bareness of this original account with the muscle and nerve of our own wrestling with God, man, or angel, as it may turn out—at any rate a damaging *and* saving confrontation of the self and the "other" self. What seem to be the beginnings of American religious poetry—Anne Bradstreet and Edward Taylor—illustrate the theme in its simple form as the versification of typical experiences and enthusiasms, of doctrine and behavior, where versification is a kind of rehearsal for an act or a role yet to be undertaken. Mrs. Bradstreet, for example, has a dialogue between Flesh and Spirit which precisely fits this description. Her much lovelier, and more sensuous, poem beginning "As weary pilgrim, now at rest" has a feeling in it of a longing, a wooing, of confrontation; but we do not feel either instance or instant. There is no architecture, and the last line ("Then Come, deare bridgrome, Come away!") seems merely pious where it had struggled to be an act of piety. This, at the furthest imaginable reach, I should like to compare to Henry Adams's "A

Prayer to the Virgin and the Dynamo," a poem which he carried for many years as a kind of amulet in his wallet, and in which there is present both all the architecture of the cathedral at Chartres and all the space in the Hall of Dynamos at the Paris World's Fair. This is, I think, one of those poems in which the poetry ceases to matter—in which, as in Mrs. Bradstreet, the verse does some damage to the moving thought under the words; but there is a great struggle for the confrontation of a vision gone: the vastation in which one still lives. Here is the last stanza:

> Help me to bear! not my own baby load,
>   But yours; who bore the failure of the light,
> The strength, the knowledge and the thought of God,—
>   The futile folly of the Infinite.[3]

One thinks of a Pascal of our days: *Le silence éternel de ces éspaces infinis* . . . and there is a regret only for the *words* of the last line. Under them there is a full act of piety to the numinous power, and Jacob's adventure is very near.

It is near perhaps because, not very good poetry itself, it is in the mode of poetry rather than the mode of religion. Herman Melville left a manuscript poem (which is said to have been much rewritten) that may be taken as evidence as to how these modes may cross—how two prayers may be said at the same time—in the special self-consciousness of American imagination. The poem is called "Art" but it deals also with Jacob. Since it is short it is quoted entire.

> In placid hours well-pleased we dream
> Of many a brave unbodied scheme.
> But form to lend, pulsed life create,
> What unlike things must meet and mate:
> A flame to melt—a wind to freeze;
> Sad patience—joyous energies;
> Humility—yet pride and scorn;
> Instinct and study; love and hate;
> Audacity—reverence. These must mate,
> And fuse with Jacob's mystic heart,
> To wrestle with the angel—Art.[4]

The poetry—the art, the Angel Art—at which these lines are aimed, is, it seems to me, one excellent way to describe what has happened to religious poetry in America, and it is possible to religion herself, too. To keep to the poetry, it has simultaneously insisted on the value of what it can itself create and on the pressure (who knows its value) of the numinous power within us, and the relationship between the two is mutinous; as for God—the intervening power—there is discontent, distrust, and dismay for what he has created, but with a lingering addiction of first and last resort. It is Melville again who put this in the final quatrain of an otherwise undistinguished poem about a picture called "The Coming Storm" by Sandford Gifford. For Melville it was the storm in the lull of which we live.

> No utter surprise can come to him
>   Who reaches Shakespeare's core;
> That which we seek and shun is there—
>   Man's final lore.[5]

Of these lines F. O. Matthiessen observed that they "constitute one of the most profound recognitions of the value of tragedy ever to have been made." I think tragedy an accidental word here, which might have been any other whole word, and especially the word religion; and Shakespeare is another accident. Melville fought the archetypes he sought, and he sought the God he fought. The lines represent many confrontations and many visions, and are therefore always ready to exact from us the details with which to fill them out in what we have done with our own behavior, or in the qualms it has left in us. If it were not so long there is a poem of Melville's called "After the Pleasure Party" which I would quote in illustration at full length; but I content myself with a few lines plus its subtitle, "Lines traced under an Image of Amor Threatening":

> 'Tis Vesta struck with Sappho's smart.
> No fable her delirious leap:
> With more of cause in desperate heart,
> Myself could take it—but to sleep! . . .
>
>   Could I remake me! or set free
> This sexless bound in sex, then plunge
> Deeper than Sappho, in a lunge
> Piercing Pan's paramount mystery!'[6]

These are matters which had been exorcised by Christianity, but they are none the less the very earth of religious concern, and they have been creeping back into the articulations as well as the blood-stream of Christians. Though the argument (since it is the argument of our actual motion) would be worth pursuing for its interest and vitality, for present purposes we can get about as far ahead by thinking of Edward Taylor and Robert Lowell in single context. Both are characteristic New England wrestlers with the spirit. Each has the ghastly sophistication of the Christian Puritan Protestant—a hangnail may be taken as excruciation—and each is aware of the bottomless resources of Enthusiasm and Antinomianism generally. (I remember that T. S. Eliot once in a hot moment reprehended certain addicts of the Inner Voice by saying that it was the eternal voice of Vanity, Fear, and Lust; and he was right.) Lowell wrestles—or behavior wrestles—against the conscience of his faith as revealed to him at the moment. Taylor wrestles against his private conscience. Taylor is full of the *strong lines* of the late metaphysicals, and Lowell writes in strong lines of his own making; each—and I mean the words literally—is obstinate in the spontaneity of his corruption, arrogant in his inadequacy: each is fiercely humble. The chasm between them is like the chasm each saw in himself: upon no razor's edge can this be crossed, and yet one's feet are upon razors. One of Taylor's poems is called "The Souls Groan to Christ for Succour" and it is of such groans that the majority of Lowell's poems are made. Another pair of Taylor's poems make grating accusations of the inner and the outer man where each, so to speak, is stripped into a reversal of role. In each the "other" self confronts the self; and, again, so it is with Lowell, the devil in him wrestles with the man, the angel with the god, in such poems as "To Delmore Schwartz" and "To Speak of Woe that is in Marriage." The difference is that Taylor pushes his sensibility into conceit (almost into formal allegory) and the conceit is the meaning of the sensibility, while Lowell drenches his conceit (the position he has been forced into) with his sensibility and the sensibility, like a road-barrier, is the meaning we are stopped by. Taylor cultivates the numinous or religious force for a purpose already anticipated, Lowell makes the force the purpose itself. For Taylor unity already existed and had to be acknowledged as a mystery that enlightens; for Lowell what unity there is you make yourself and it darkens you forever.

One can imagine Lowell repeating the remark in Gide: God woos us by his calamities, and that is how He shows His love for us; but we cannot imagine Lowell repeating what Taylor heard as "Christ's Reply" to "The Souls Groan to Christ for Succour," for it would have done this latter-day or post-Christian Christian no good. Taylor can write at the end of "Upon a Wasp Chilled with Cold":

> Till I enravisht climb into
> The Godhead on this ladder doe:

> Where all my pipes inspir'de upraise
> An Heavenly musick, furr'd with praise.[7]

Lowell writes at the end of his "Memories of West Street and Lepke":

> Flabby, bald, lobotomized,
> He drifted in a sheepish calm,
> where no agonizing reappraisal
> jarred his concentration on the electric chair—
> hanging like an oasis in his air
> of lost connections . . .[8]

The difference is absolute, and we have come again full circle to Iacopone:

> *Fiorito è Cristo nella carne pura:*
> *or se ralegri l'umana natura.*

That is, we can speak of Whitman, for he could have written the Italian lines with only the substitution, to him simple and natural, of himself for Christ: All of me has flowered in my flesh, so let us rejoice in human nature. Indeed it is not in his naive barbarism (in which the artists and intellectuals of the last century found such companionship) but in his direct and deeply civilized piety, which is precisely where he resembles Iacopone, that his poetry endures. Since it is more familiar to more people than most of his poems, we can let "When Lilacs Last in the Dooryard Bloom'd" stand for the rest, the more especially because in this poem it is very clear how he met his archetypes—his governing and vitalizing images—the symbols that made him fruitful in words—both in the open road and in the thicket of the Psyche: in what man does and in what he finds doing in himself, in which is included what man has in the past done with his poetry. Whitman, says Northrop Frye in his *Anatomy of Criticism,* was "perfectly right in feeling that the *content* of poetry is normally an immediate and contemporary environment. He was right, being the kind of poet he was, in making the content of his own 'When Lilacs Last in the Dooryard Bloomed' an elegy on Lincoln and not a conventional Adonis lament. Yet his elegy is, in its *form,* as conventional as *Lycidas,* complete with purple flowers thrown on coffins, a great star drooping in the west, imagery of 'everreturning spring' and all the rest of it. Poetry organizes the content of the world as it passes before the poet, but the forms in which that content is organized come out of the structure of poetry itself."[9]

This is very fine; but I should like to add for present purposes that this is how *religious* poetry operates—when poetry comes nearest to positive intervention in the actions of the soul. As Mr. Frye says, it is not only the Adonis material; there is also the sprig of lilac with its mastering odor, the hidden bird and the secluded swamp, and the "tallying chant" in which all come together: "Lilac and star and bird twined with the chant of my soul." There are two progresses in the poem, of Lincoln's body and of the images, which join in the sacred knowledge of death. Lincoln, Lilac, and Thrush are merged in a full act of piety.

It is a difference of half a century as much as a difference of sensibility in the particular poets that strikes us when we look into the thicket of Robert Frost: in which there are obstinate possibilities and obstinate forces, not human themselves, that yet—as they are cultivated into the sensibility—change the human dimension and alter, a little, the reticulation of the elements of the human Psyche. To acknowledge this is a religious action: a momentary conversion. The consuming or purifying fire is always at hand in such acknowledgments, and the more so if, as in Frost, the individual is held on to, nevertheless and because. But one does not wish to exaggerate. Here is an example in the poem "Come In."

> As I came to the edge of the woods,
> Thrush music—hark!
> Now if it was dusk outside,
> Inside it was dark.
>
> Too dark in the woods for a bird
> By sleight of wing
> To better its perch for the night,
> Though it still could sing.
>
> The last of the light of the sun
> That had died in the west
> Still lived for one song more
> In a thrush's breast.
>
> Far in the pillared dark
> Thrush music went—
> Almost like a call to come in
> To the dark and lament.

But no, I was out for stars:
I would not come in.
I meant not even if asked;
And I hadn't been.[10]

Frost exposed himself to the thrush in the wood—the *selva oscura*—the thicket where perceptions not one's own become a part of one, and found himself confronted with himself. There is no doctrine here and no dogma, but there is the perception out of which many doctrines have sprung and the kind of grasping imagination which has made dogma vital. Those who have need of doctrine and dogma first, before they risk perception, may bring what they will and it will work. Let us say only that there are two remotenesses here: of what is dark and at hand and of what is light (the little that is known of it) and afar; and there is a double invitation to loneliness. Intimations spring from one to the other through the man between, changing and remaining in the graininess of his voice. This is Frost's way, I hazard it, of recording the light in the dark and the dark in the light and the coiling movement between them of the self confronting the self.

It is perhaps unfair to make a foil for Frost's poem of Edwin Markham's "The Man with the Hoe"—once so famous for its perception of man's lot and man's need; but I can think of nothing that shows so well the difference between poetry and good will as to think of the two poems together. Let us put it baldly. Millet's painting was in natural piety to the land and the man with the hoe was very close to being a part of the land which was his life, which it takes deep knowledge to perceive. To my mind Frost's poem and Millet's painting are two versions of the same perception of the human condition, which it is damnation to ignore and a strange redemption to accept. Markham made of the painting a poem of social protest and flagrantly righteous indignation. Out of a false naïveté he saw a false archetype and constructed a faulty iconography. It is the condition in which every perception disappears and hope is thereby hollow. In Frost's poem, not Markham's, the dumb Terror replies to God.

For the other type of foil to Frost, the type that sustains and protects, there is the poetry of Emily Dickinson, which puts the hand upon the quick within her and sings hymns to the actuality of every illusion, and every crowding hope, that struck her. In her, religion supervenes and poetry intervenes upon her secular life without discrimination. Faith, she thought, was the experiment of our Lord.

The auctioneer of parting,
His "Going, going, gone,"
Shouts even from the crucifix
And brings the hammer down.

He only sells the wilderness.
The prices of despair
Range from a single human heart
To two—not any more."[11]

The variety is sufficient, but I should not like to stop lest it be thought I would set up categories into which religious poetry should, or must, fall. I think of Hart Crane's "Voyages," of Wallace Stevens's "Sunday Morning," of Archibald MacLeish's play about Job, and of the new Catholic poets such as Daniel Berrigan, Thomas Merton, and Ned O'Gorman. All of these poets, and no doubt many more, write poetry which can be understood only if it is taken as religious; and yet the variety varies more than the winds. To repeat, since there is no seal upon us in this post-Christian time, our religious like our other emotions come out of Pandora's box; or, to repeat more precisely, as religion takes new forms and changes the nature and scope of its interventions, so the poetry associated with religion supervenes differently upon our reading lives. If there is anything in common not only with itself but with the past, aside from its impulse, I do not know what it is, but it is possible to make a few unaligned suggestions. We are likely to be concerned with the excruciation (as Jacob was not); with Jacob's wrestling with Angel, Man, or God; with the dark night of the soul that never ends since it was a darkness we ourselves made; with the nightmares of the numen or the night-life of the spirit rather than its waking wide safety; and altogether with the great sweep of rival creation since, like Ivan in *The Brothers Karamazov*, we can accept God but not His Creation. We are lost, as Eliot seems to suggest (in his essay on Dante), in our new immersion in our lower dreams, with the higher dreams gone by the board or unavailing; and indeed only Eliot seems to see the place where the two dreams cross, and it may be only his language that sees that, for he himself calls it "The unread vision in the higher dream" and "the brief transit where the dreams cross." These are the hardships we come by in our daily life, and our poetry reflects them since they are actual.

What is actual, when we would be religious, invades us like a nightmare of our own behavior suddenly seen, and it is our own monsters that keep us from God, and no mere scholarship of the dark will save us, only acknowledgment. We must remove the obstacles, as Pascal saw, that keep us from falling into the abyss; and the obstacles are of our own invention. I think of Allen Tate and his poem "The Wolves," of W. H. Auden and his poem "Petition," and of Eliot's "Little Gidding." Each of these poems, by way of those intrusive monsters anthropology, psychology, and behavior, finds it time for human nature to rejoice, each tries to construct something, as Eliot says, upon which to rejoice, but each is left impaled upon the nature of man. Each therefore is the prayer of what is terrible in human nature (which is nature herself) addressed to the "honor of man," to "a change of heart," and to the "refining fire."

What then are they doing? As one reorganizes one's life one sees that one has been religious all along in the poetry one has made of it. Religious poetry has to do with the modes of power and powerlessness, of glory and misery. These it asserts. With these it wrestles and argues; to them submits; on them rises; in them dies. These are the terms of the poem's relation with the numinous force; the force within the self, other than the self, greater than the self, which, as one cultivates it, moves one beyond the self. Poetry is one of the ways of cultivation; and the harvest is vision. One would see God and die—so Petrarch put it. In any case there is a confrontation, and in the confrontation a flowing of force ending in an access or filling of being, else in a vastation or desolation; and the two are much the same: in calm of mind all passion spent, or *In la sua voluntade è nostra pace.* Who can say which is which?

> And courage never to submit or yield
> And what is else not to be overcome . . .

O dark, dark, dark, amid the blaze of noon . . .

Sunt lacrimae rerum et mentem mortalia tangunt . . .

Myself, my Sepulcher, a moving Grave . . .

or se ralegri l'umana natura.

1. *Interpretations of Poetry and Religion*, New York, 1922, p. v.

2. *The Penguin Book of Italian Verse*, George Kay, ed., Bungay, Suffolk, 1958, pp. 13, 17.

3. "Prayer to the Virgin of Chartres," in *Letters to a Niece*, Boston and New York, 1920, p. 134.

4. *Collected Poems of Herman Melville*, Howard P. Vincent, ed., Chicago, 1947, p. 231.

5. Ibid., p. 94.

6. *Poets of the English Language*, W. H. Auden and Norman H. Pearson, eds., New York, 1950, V, 310, 312.

7. T. H. Johnson, "Edward Taylor Gleanings," *NEQ*, XVI, June 1943, p. 283.

8. *Life Studies*, New York, 1959, p. 86.

9. *Anatomy of Criticism*, Princeton, 1957, p. 102.

10. *A Witness Tree*, New York, 1942, p. 16.

11. *Poets of the English Language*, W. H. Auden and Norman H. Pearson, eds., New York, 1950, V, 396.

Towards a Post-Kantian Verbal Music

KENNETH BURKE

Originally published in the Kenyon Review *in 1958, this book review of French poet Paul Valéry's* The Art of Poetry *is actually a kind of "close reading" of Valéry's ideas regarding the origins of poetic inspiration. This is a fine example of the searching eclecticism of Burke's prose.*

Since Paul Valéry's theory of poetry[1] in general is so closely associated with his speculations on the genesis of his own poems, we could properly begin by quoting a passage in which he sums up his own ways of developing a poem:

> If I am questioned; if anyone wonders . . . what I "wanted to say" in a certain poem, I reply that I did not *want to say* but *wanted to make*, and that it was the intention of *making* which *wanted* what I said. . . .
>
> As for the *Cimetière marin*, this intention was first no more than a rhythmic figure, empty, or filled with meaningless syllables, which obsessed me for some time. . . . It suggested a certain stanza of six lines, and the idea of a *composition* founded on the number of these stanzas and strengthened by a diversity of tones and functions to be assigned to them. Between the stanzas, contrasts or correspondences would be set up. This last condition soon required the potential poem to be a monologue of "self," in which the simplest and most enduring themes of my affective and intellectual life, as they had imposed themselves upon my adolescence, associated with the sea and the light of a particular spot on the Mediterranean coast, were called up, woven together, opposed. . . . All this led to the theme of death and suggested the theme of pure thought. (The chosen line of ten syllables bears some relation to the Dantesque line.)
>
> My line had to be solid and strongly rhythmical. I knew I was tending toward a monologue as personal, but also as universal, as I could make it. The type of line chosen, and the form adopted for stanzas, set me conditions that favored certain "movements," permitted certain changes of tone, called up a certain style. . . . The *Cimetière marin* was conceived. A rather long period of gestation ensued.

And again:

> Whenever I think of the art of writing (in verse or in prose), the same "ideal" presents itself to my mind. The myth of "creation" lures me into wanting to make something from nothing. So I imagine that I discover my work little by little, beginning with pure conditions of form, more and more considered, defined to the point where they propose, or almost impose, a *subject*—or at least kinds of subject.

Our present job is to use this quotation as "generating principle," and to try deriving all other characteristic aspects of Valéry's theory from it.

The notion of starting from a rhythmic figure rather from a theme or plot or situation in the usual sense of such well indicates Valéry's position with regard to "ideas" in poetry. He is not by any means against them (he has said "My memory retains almost nothing but ideas and a few sensations," and his poem ends on "the theme of pure thought"); but thoughts must be subordinated to a kind of motive that is either vaguer or more inclusive, depending on the way you look at it. Whereas Aristotle lists "Thought" (*dianoia*) as one of tragedy's six primary elements, a resource necessary to the portraying of character, Valéry says: "I made up my mind that thought is only an accessory poetry, and that the chief thing in a work in verse, a thing proclaimed by the very use of verse, is the whole, the power resulting from effects compounded of all attributes of language." These attributes, in sum, are: "sound, sense, the real and the imaginary, logic, syntax, and the double invention of content and form," all requiring the use of a "medium essentially practical, perpetually changing, soiled, a maid of all work, *everyday language*, from which we must draw a pure, ideal Voice, capable of communicating without weakness, without apparent effort, without offense to the ear, and without breaking the ephemeral sphere of the poetic universe." Thoughts are used not for their own sake, but like gestures, to indicate something, as when he says that in his poem he "corrupted" some "images from Zeno" as a way "to express the rebellion against the length and painfulness of a meditation that makes too cruelly felt the gap between *being* and *knowing* that is developed by the consciousness of consciousness."

Since the poem must embody all these "attributes," the principle from which it originates cannot be any one of them. It begins in the "poetic state or emotion" which consists "in a dawning perception, a tendency toward perceiving a *world*, or complete system of relations." Just previously he has referred to "that *sense of a universe* which is characteristic of poetry." And on this same page he says that whereas "the beings, things, events, and acts" resemble "those which fill and form the tangible world," they also stand "in an indefinable, but wonderfully accurate, relationship to the modes and laws of our general sensibility."

All told, then, though the words that a poem uses have a relation to the entities of our extra-poetic experience, there are also their purely internal relations that abide by the laws of our "general sensibility." The "self" to which the poem appeals is not the individual self, but is "miraculously superior to Myself," a universal consciousness of the kind he considered when inquiring into "the general conditions of all thought, regardless of its content."

With regard to the poet's discovery of internal relationships (the "contrasts or correspondences" mentioned in our opening quotation), Valéry has many ways of coming upon this subject. When referring to a poem, "La Pythie," which "first appeared as an eight-syllable line whose sound came of its own accord," he adds: "But this line implied a sentence, of which it was a part, and this sentence, if it existed, implied many other sentences." The important word for our purposes is "implied," since his remark is tantamount to saying that the many sentences which the poem finally contained were somehow implicit in the part of a sentence with which he began.

Again, he refers to poems which had as starting point "impulses of the 'formative' sensibility which are anterior to any finite, expressible idea." And he goes on to say that "*La Jeune Parque* was, literally speaking, an endless research into the possibility of attempting in poetry something analogous to what in music is called 'modulation.'" Another synonym he uses here is "transitions," and elsewhere he calls them "transformations." He is apparently dealing with the same subject from a slightly different angle when he says that "At a certain point in my mental processes, all ideas, rhythms, and memories or inventions were merely equivalents," adding that such equivalence "is certainly one of the principal resources of the mind, offering it the most valuable substitutions" (whereupon "substitutions" can be added to our list). At another point they are called "word combinations." And in connection with thoughts on "that whole domain of sensibility which is governed by language," he refers to "the effects resulting from the relations between words, or rather the relations of the overtones of words among themselves." And pure poetry, he says, would deal only with relations which "were themselves perpetually similar to harmonic relations, *in which the transmutation of thoughts into each other appeared more important than any thought.*" Here "transmutations" would be our word.

In sum, the notion seems to involve these three propositions: The materials used by the poet have reference to things outside the poem; but they are put together in accordance with laws that underlie the "poetic state"; and with the underlying poetic state to guide him, the poet can meditate upon single details or "fragments" of his subject until, by going from one to another, or rather, by letting each lead him into the next when each is found to imply the others, he makes a whole that somehow possesses internal consistency. This internal consistency is ultimately referable to consciousness in general. It is a "poetic universe" that he frequently likens to music. Or its wholeness is said to be like a dream in the sense that, when we are dreaming, "our consciousness can be invaded, filled, made up by an assembly of productions remarkably different from the mind's ordinary reactions and perceptions. It gives us the familiar example of a *closed world* where *real* things can be represented, but where everything appears and is modified solely by the fluctuations of our deepest sensibility." By contrast, such an exacting cult of poetic wholeness makes Valéry resentful of words that "have grown up independently and unaware of each other, like English measurements, which have no common divisor."

Valéry's insistence that poetry should start not from prose but "from song" served to re-enforce his stress upon the distinction between poetic diction and practical everyday speech, a point about which Mr. Eliot complains in the introduction:

> The farther the idiom, vocabulary, and syntax of poetry depart from those of prose, the more artificial the language of poetry. . . . And the *norm* for a poet's language is the way his contemporaries talk. In assimilating poetry to music, Valéry has, it seems to me, failed to insist upon its relation to speech. The poet can improve, indeed it is his duty to improve, the language that he speaks and hears. . . . But neither the poem nor the play can afford to ignore the necessity of persuading us that this is the language we should ourselves speak, if we spoke as well as we should like to speak.

Valéry had such a non-dramatic view of lyric contemplation, this argument would probably have had little weight with him. His stress on the importance of artifice could naturally expand to include artificiality, as with his hospitality to inversions, which he says are resented "for reasons that come down to this unacceptable formula: poetry is prose." Inversions would not embarrass him, since they were of a piece with his plea for a special poetic language (a "language within a language"). He says the poet is "a *deviation*, a maker of *deviations*." And it is precisely such deviations that "foreshadow, as it were, a world of relationships distinct from the purely practical world," whereby we can conceive "the possibility of enlarging this exceptional domain," and thus can have the "sensation of grasping a fragment of a noble and living substance."

Though I personally prefer Mr. Eliot's policy here to Valéry's, I do not see how it could be made into an iron law. "Fortunately, in the realm of poetry there is *no recognized means of prescribing or forbidding anything to anyone*," Valéry says, though this view does not keep him from an opposing kind of legislation whereby he would forbid any failure to make a categorical distinction between the language of poetry and the "statistical" language of prose, which he identifies with the practical.

Since he treats musical sound as categorically distinct from non-musical noise (a view more persuasive before the days of *musique concrète*), he can contrast music with words. For whereas the musician has a medium that we recognize as distinct, the poet's medium (words) must also serve for crude practical purposes. Hence, the nearest the poet can come to his desired condition is by a deliberate cult of "deviations" in language.

Music also served Valéry's purposes because the nature of the medium frees the artist from an overstress upon "thought" or "idea" in the strictly verbal sense. The same possibility seemed to him inherent in such rhythmic patterns as attained their complete embodiment in the dance. There is a sense in which his use of the dance as a model for "absolute" poetry could have been embarrassing to his argument. For his whole point about the dance is that dancing is to poetry as walking is to prose. Dancing, in brief, is tainted with practical purpose. Mr. Eliot points out that a war dance can be as purposive as walking. One might also point out that dancing is like language in the sense that in using his body, the dancer is in the same condition as the poet; for, like language, the body is thus used *both* aesthetically *and* practically. Mr. Eliot sums up the issue thus:

> I have never yet come across a final, comprehensive, and satisfactory account of the difference between poetry and prose. We can distinguish between prose and verse, and between verse and poetry; but the moment the intermediate term *verse* is suppressed, I do not believe that any distinction between prose and poetry is meaningful.

Valéry's view, treating "poetry" and "verse" as synonyms (in contrast with prose, which he equates with practical purposiveness and a corresponding disinterest in verbal sound and rhythm for their own sakes) is highly questionable in the case of great prose stylists; but one can readily understand why the attempt to establish the distinction is implicit in the passage we have selected as his "generating principle."

But whatever embarrassments Valéry's position may encounter along the way, we should not overlook the essential symmetry in which it begins. Tonality and rhythm ("music" and "dance") are intrinsic aspects of the spoken word. They are "accidents" of words only when words are considered sheerly as conventions for the conveying of information ("ideas" in the narrowest sense of the term). Thus, while subscribing wholeheartedly to Mallarmé's dictum, "One does not make poetry with ideas, but with words," he also says in a chapter on the speaking of verse, "Refrain for as long as possible from emphasizing words; so far there are no *words*, only syllables and rhythms."

This all comes to a focus in what Valéry calls "verbal materialism." His favorite analogy on this subject involves a pendulum that begins on the side of sound, then swings to the side of meaning. If you stopped here, merely going from sound to sense, you would have simply departed from the realm of what he calls "our dear old body." But what you must do next is reverse the order, thereby getting "the illusion of an indissoluble compound of *sound* and *sense*, although there exists no rational relationship between these two constituents of language." The dialectic is analogous to the orthodox Christian promise that the believer will regain his material body in heaven, though its materiality will have been spiritualized. Valéry's scheme here seems to involve these three steps, or moments: (1) Reception of the sounds, in their sheer materiality; (2) translation of the material sounds into their corresponding sense, or spirit; (3) return to the sounds, which are loved for their own sake, but are inspirited with the experience of stage 2, yet without the loss we should have suffered had we stopped at stage 2 (the truncated stage which Valéry associates with the sheerly "practical" language of prose).

Again, since the tonal and rhythmic aspects of language are so elusive ideologically, it follows that "*there is no true meaning to a text*," or that his verses have whatever meaning the reader attributes to them. ("The one I give them suits only myself and does not contradict anyone else"), or "To speak of a poem in itself, to judge of a poem in itself, has no real or precise meaning. It is to speak of a potentiality."[2]

There is another notable aspect of this ambiguity with regard to "form." Though we are told that the only test of a poem is whether "it sings," Keats and Shelley combine to remind us that there are sweeter unheard melodies which vibrate in the memory. We can more readily imagine such a silent song in terms of rhythm alone, unless by silent song we mean an actual melody specifically imagined, note by note, as one might recite a poem "in his head." Such a sheerly formal aspect of words as rhythm conceived in abstraction from all words would come to fruition in Valéry's notion of the dance which, except for such varieties as tap-dancing and for musical or percussive accompaniments, is heard only in its unwanted accidents, as with the feverish scuffling that disturbs one's attention at times if he is too near the stage.

In contrast with a sheer rhythmic pattern, from the standpoint of pure silence even the purest Mozartian melody is as obtrusive as a laundry list or a political oration. Yet if the "poetic state" is in its essence silent, there must be a kind of reticence which is best suggested by the idea of sheer rhythm, though this rhythm in turn should doubtless be approached from within, with one's eyes closed, and without beats or intervals. For a truly absolute rhythm would have to transcend even the terms of silent bodily movement. (It all depends on how "pure" your germinal principle must be.)

"The aim . . . is to create a kind of silence to which the beautiful responds." As regards the necessities imposed upon the poet by the impurities of language, the nearest viable approximate to this condition involves a kind of pudency whereby suggestion must take the place of definition or explicit labeling. "One is taught: 'Say it is raining if you mean that it is raining!' But a poet's object is not and never can be to tell us that it is raining." Reticence, as so conceived, sometimes brings poets close to a kind of literary charades, in accordance with the formula of the *chef d'école*, Mallarmé: "To name an object is to suppress three-quarters of the enjoyment of the poem which consists in the pleasure of guessing little by little. To suggest, that is to dream." And at times poets err in trying to get the feel of the dream by the simple deflective device of not calling a spade a spade.

Like all silence, the silence of the "poetic state" impinges upon motives of privacy, secrecy, and mystery so basic to problems of morality that this aspect of Valéry's poetics would carry us far into questions of guilt and purgation not directly relevant to our present concerns. Suffice it to note how, if poetic reticence at its worst makes for the morbidities of self-deception, at its best it helps the reader to collaborate in the making of the poem. And the art of the confidence man teaches us that collaboration is of the essence; for invariably, when such a practitioner would delude Mr. X, he sets up the situation by making Mr. X think that the two of them are conspiring to delude Mr. Y. Yet much would be lost if we rid poetry of riddles, "the *not saying* 'it is raining.'" Valéry touches upon the matter pejoratively when he refers to the "subtle relations" between "stupidity and poetry." But on the favorable side he observes: "Thought must be hidden in verse like the nutritive essence in fruit. It is nourishing but seems merely delicious." There is obviously a gain in building up a fog, that readers may break through into the sunlight. That's one way to get the precious sense of revelation, which is a variant of wonder. Besides, there *is* revelation. But we'll get to that later, meanwhile noting that the most radical statement of his principle is in his advice, italicized: *"Hide your God."*[3]

The relation between verse and musicality can be viewed in various ways. We may have in mind verses that can be readily set to music. Or maybe even words and music were conceived simultaneously. (Many Negro spirituals seem beautifully musical in this sense.) Or the words may be thought of as designed for recitation, though with a musical background, as with Valéry's reference to Ronsard "who sang his verses while accompanying himself on the lute."

But the typical lyric poet of our day does not seem much interested in musicality of such sorts. In fact, like Yeats, he may not even have much feeling for music as such. While writing, Yeats apparently had in the back of his mind a kind of incantation which would be intrinsic to the words as he conceived them; thus, along with Valéry, he categorically differentiated this effect from the diction of prose, however "natural" his lines may seem in their approximations to prose word-order.

There's room for everybody. But we should at least pause to note this paradox (the kind of paradox one is wholly entitled to introduce when on the subject of a critic who asks us most of all to think about "absolute" poetry: If a language truly incorporated the *principle* of music, then *actual* music would be a redundancy, and thus an artistic sin. For instance, to shift from sound to sight: In movie versions of Shakespeare's plays the camera sometimes makes you see so literally on the screen various things that the dramatic poet had brought to light solely in your imagination by the sound of his words, the result is that lines which were marvelously *functional* (when used in their original medium) become in their cinematic translation not much better than *flowery talk.*

"Pure" poetry would also presumably drop out all lines that have the merely businesslike quality of stage directions. Many passages in narrative presumably have for him this drawback. Putting a story into verse seems to him "the most antipoetic operation there is." For "In poetry everything which *must* be said is almost impossible to say well." However, he welcomes constraints in such matters as fixed forms, rhymes, and the like: "The gods in their graciousness give us an occasional first line for *nothing*; but it is for us to fashion a second, which must chime with the first and not be unworthy of its supernatural elder." (However, when translating Virgil's *Eclogues*, he avoided rhyming because "This would undoubtedly have led me to make too free with the text.")

Valéry's sympathy with the tendency "to isolate Poetry once for all from every other essence than itself" leads naturally to a corresponding stress upon the value of "working for work's sake." He says that he considers "*work itself* as having its own value, generally much superior to that which the crowd attaches only to the *product.*" He celebrates a "sense of control" which sometimes makes the process of poetic gestation seem like the jealous brooding of a bird warming its eggs. And though he admonishes that the term "pure poetry" should not be confused with "the thought of moral purity," he does much to celebrate the "Ethic of Form."

All told, with constant talk of elegance, perfection, grace, mystery, magic, sensitiveness, perceptiveness, intelligence and the like, and with the steady pressure of such expressions as "infinite labor," "holily," "from a great height," "innocent creative awareness," "innocent state of poetry," "almost religious," "supernatural food," "universal dignity," "language of the gods" (that should be "as distinct as possible from the language of men"), poetry as "the Paradise of Language" designed "to prolong the happiness of a moment," "the soul's assent to exquisite constraints, and the perpetual triumph of sacrifice"—thanks to the persuasive way in which matters of speculation and analysis are seasoned by a heavy sprinkling of such terms, the "special emotive state" that is poetry, with its typical "combination of asceticism and play," is here presented in ways quite appealing to any reader who particularly enjoys hearing poetry done honor to. Such a reader is invited to join in a benign conspiracy, and to love himself the more to the extent that he can identify himself with this Grand Cause. And though, ordinarily, Valéry presents poetry as a realm apart from the language of the tribe, on one occasion he shows how, under the pressure of special conditions, his theory can be made more generally palatable, too. I refer to a piece done in wartime when, speaking to a patriotic French audience assembled to hear readings from French poetry, he first observes that the poet "is inseparable from the speech of his nation," next conceives of all French poetry since its beginnings as having been written by one "immense poet," and finally discloses that this "greatest poet" is none other than France herself. Under less exacting conditions, he would be more likely to speak of the "poet's language" as "*an effort by one man* to create an artificial and ideal order by means of a material of vulgar origin."

In the introduction, Mr. Eliot says that Valéry's essays on poetry are "a kind of substitute for the poems he did not write," and "a kind of defense and vindication of his own poems." Mr. Eliot judges that the essays are not "fully intelligible" unless the reader "has read Valéry's most important poems." Also, it seems to me, the reader would profit greatly by considering the two essays on Da Vinci that are printed in *Variety*. For in the discussion of Da Vinci's "unity of method," one sees the emergence of the previously mentioned concern with "equivalent variations of a common substance," involving inquiries into the ways in which some things "imply" others, an interest that comes to a focus in this passage (in the Da Vinci essay entitled "Note and Digression"):

Color and grief, memories, the expected and the unexpected, this tree, and the fluttering of its foliage, its annual variation and its shadow as well as its substance, the accidents of its shape and position, the remote thoughts which it brings to the edge of my wandering attention—they are equivalents. Any one can be substituted for any other. Is not this perhaps the definition of *things*?

Surely this notion, regarding the way in which things "imply" one another, is the core of Valéry's theories. It explains why the Symbolists could say, in effect: Produce a presence by its absence, by introducing contributory elements which, since they all point in the same direction, implicitly evoke the element deliberately left out. But in ending, I'd like to discuss one more aspect of this concern with "implications" (or "equivalences," "substitutions," "modulations," "universe of reciprocal relations," or whatever other words Valéry uses when approaching this subject from various angles).

The matter has to do with what I have called elsewhere a "Tautological Cycle of Terms" (as per my pages on "The First Three Chapters of Genesis," in *Daedalus*, Summer 1958). There I build around the fact that words mutually imply one another (as the idea of "order" implies the idea of "disorder"; or the idea of "order" implies possibilities of either "obedience" or "disobedience" to an order; then farther afield there is need for a term to designate the attitude of "humility" that inclines one towards "obedience," or a term to designate the attitude of "pride" that inclines one towards "disobedience," etc., in ever-widening circles). Further, while showing that there is no one sequence to be followed in tracing the reciprocal relations among such terms, I discussed how, in narrative forms such as the story of the creation and the fall in the opening chapters of Genesis, there is one fixed, irreversible sequence.

There seems to be a similar consideration at the roots of Valéry's concerns. For note that his search for equivalences involves two kinds of unfolding. First, there is the gradual emergence of the work itself, as the poet, in the course of expressing his thought, must "pass from an *impure* form, a mixture of all the resources of the mind, to a *pure* form, that is, one solely verbal and organized, amounting to a system of arranged acts or contrasts" (a sentence, by the way, that also would have fitted well in our discussions about the dialectics of "form" and "matter"). Here would gradually emerge a body of images, situations, thoughts that seem to possess the quality of the originating germ (elements involving "transverse relations," as he says of a poem that grew from two rhythms). And this gradual emergence of articulacy (by progress from one implication to the next) would not by any means be identical with the irreversible sequence of the poem itself, as presented to readers in its finished, or "abandoned" form. Yet behind either of such unfoldings (the poet's or the reader's), there lies a directionless reticulation of interrelationships that can be traced in any order (quite as a drama proceeds irreversibly although the interrelationships among its *dramatis personae* "just are," and can be traced in many directions).

Sometimes, in his Da Vinci essays, Valéry seems to mean by "unity of method" simply a particular trick or knack on the part of the artist whereby he can turn everything to his purposes, thereby making everything all of one piece. But that's only a "first rough approximate." Essentially, I think, he is concerned there with this vexingly ambiguous relation between a motionless, directionless kind of internal relationship in a poem and the irreversible order of the poem itself, the genesis of the poem having taken place in an area somewhere in between these two realms.

Thus in *The Art of Poetry* he says of the "non-representational arts" that in them "the sequence of our feelings has no longer a chronological order, but a kind of intrinsic, instantaneous order, which is revealed step by step." Here, I take it, he is concerned with the difference between the irreversibility of the presentation and the non-directional aspect of the poetic universe which the terms in their totality imply. And surely he is on the subject of irreversible narrative sequence (as contrasted with his search for the directionless internality of "equivalents") when he writes: "In short, situations, groupings of characters, and the subjects of stories and dramas find nothing in me in which to take root and develop in a single direction." And here is a passage which does not make sense to me unless it is read in line with the distinction I have been proposing:

> In the most famous lyrics I find almost nothing but developments that are purely linear, or . . . delirious—that is, which proceed bit by bit with no more sustained organization than is shown by a flame following a trail of powder. (I am not speaking of poems dominated by a story, where the chronology of events intervenes: these are mixed works—operas, not sonatas or symphonies.)

Valéry contrasts with such lyrics his attempts "to *compose* in the lyric order":

> The fact is that each detail is here essential at each moment, and the cleverest and most beautiful scheme must come to terms with the uncertainty of discoveries. In the lyric universe each moment must consummate an indefinable alliance between the perceptible and the significant. The result is that, in some way, composition is

continuous and can hardly withdraw into another time than that of execution. There is not one time for the "content" and another for the "form"; and composition in this *genre* is not only opposed to disorder or disproportion but also to *decomposition*.

All told, there would be the interrelationships among the parts of the work (interrelationships that have no one direction); there would be the gradual discovery or invention of these relationships on the part of the poet in his progress from the "impure form" of his first inklings, the germ frequently not even verbal that heralded the onset of the "poetic state"; and there would be the quite different series of unfoldings, or revelations, presented in the sequence of the poem's lines and stanzas, a sequence that *implies* the fixed interrelationships among its parts.

Let us illustrate by a parable. The lady artist planned to paint a picture of Pan and a Nymph sitting on a rock. The Nymph did not object to posing in the nude—but she refused to do so when Pan was present. So a compromise was worked out whereby Pan and the Nymph posed on alternate days. One day Pan would come, and pipe his lewd but silent song in the direction of the spot where the Nymph was absent. The next day, the Nymph would serve as model, listening enwrapt in the direction of the absent Pan. But despite this series of alternations as regards the narrative sequence of the painting's genesis, lo! when it was finished, there sit Pan and the Nymph in unalterable mutual interrelationship, "eternity clapped into a single stride."

A serious instance of something similar is Peter Blume's painting, *South of Scranton* (now owned by the Museum of Modern Art in New York City). The main details stem, I believe, from an actual trip taken by the artist. They are modified selections from the many things witnessed on this trip. Such selection was obviously made on the basis of intrinsic relationships that the artist felt them to have towards one another—and these relationships are disclosed in a kind of spatial fixity that has no irreversible temporal sequence such as figured in the extra-artistic experiences that formed its beginnings, though the observer can give it many sequences, depending upon the direction in which he chooses to let his eye rove about the canvas.

I take this sort of consideration to be involved in Valéry's statement that the poem is a "closed cycle . . . the cycle of an act which has, as it were, aroused and given external form to a poetic power." And when a poem had been made, "in completing itself the cycle left something behind." However, Valéry was trying to claim for poetry alone a set of conditions that will prevail in any well-constructed "universe of discourse." His exceptional interest in the genesis of a poem, even at the time when he was writing it, obviously made him more sensitive to this particular aspect of poetic consistency. And apparently he was more aware of reciprocal relations in poems which the reader, approaching "from outside," is more likely to experience as a succession of disclosures, a "linear" unfolding. A poem, to have consistency enough, must have consistency to burn. And what it has poetically (as a self-sustained "universe") need not be identical with what it has rhetorically (what Valéry calls "a kind of machine for producing the poetic state of mind by means of words").

In closing, I might say that the book is excellently translated. (My only complaint might be that once in a while a slight transposition seems needed. For instance, in the sentence, "And composition in this *genre* is not only opposed to disorder or disproportion but also to *decomposition*," the "not only" should come *after* "opposed." But otherwise all is perfect fluency.) Mr. Eliot's characterization, along with his balance sheet of agreements and disagreements, seems to me quite final. Indeed, its judiciousness is the best argument I can offer for trying to approach the material from this other angle; otherwise, I don't see much else to say. All told, the book (including its appearance as a piece of manufacture) makes one feel good. It is done in the spirit of this formula which Valéry applies to La Fontaine's "Adonis": "drawing out by a silken thread the sweetness of each moment."

1. *The Art of Poetry*, by Paul Valéry. Translated by Denise Folliot, with an introduction by T. S. Eliot. Pantheon Books. $3.50.

2. This statement alone could stand a long discussion. First, we should note that there is a sense in which we can properly "speak of a poem in itself," as when we discuss it without relation to its authorship, background, and the like. Valéry's remark obviously does not concern this issue. Second, we might recall his admonition: "What is 'form' for anyone else is 'content' for me." Problems arise here because we may speak of a poem as "taking form," but when the poem is finished (or, as Valéry would say, "abandoned") this final form is said to be but a "potentiality" (that is, "matter" rather than "form") with regard to future readers of it. This ambiguity is better understood when, in connection with a poem which, beginning "merely with the hint of a rhythm," *gradually acquired a meaning*, he explains: "This production developed, as it were, from 'form' to 'content.'" Or see: "I discover my work little by little, beginning with pure conditions of form, more and more considered, defined to the points where they propose, or almost impose, a *subject*—or at least kinds of subject." The sad dialectical fact is that what looks like "form" from one angle is, from another, the *unformed*, the first dawning of a form. But this ever-shifting terminology gets a semblance of solidity in the proposition: "The conception of pure poetry is that of an inaccessible type, an ideal boundary of the poet's desires, efforts, and powers." Among the conditions that make "absolute" poetry "impossible" is this sheerly dialectical shiftiness whereby we can mean by "form" two states as different as the finished product and the first vague inkling which the "poetic state" settles on as likely material for further development.

3. However, there is one point at which we are clearly entitled to complain. Valéry has chosen as his particular critical task the problem of making clear to us the genesis of poetry, as revealed to him first of all through his own experience with the writing of poetry. Yet here are some remarks that I consider scandalous:

I knew, moreover, from a chance early experience, that the magic of literature necessarily derives from "some misunderstanding," owing to the very nature of language, which often enables one to give more than one possesses; and sometimes to give a good deal less.

I was so afraid of being caught in this trap myself that for several years I placed a ban on the use in my notes, which were for myself alone, of a number of *words* . . . I shall not say which. If they came into my head, I tried to substitute an expression which said no more than I wanted to say. If I could not find one, I gave the words a symbol, to show that they were only temporary. To me they were *for external use* only.

Often, while reading Valéry's account of poetic genesis, I was disappointed at the thought that he sometimes let talk of precision do the work of precision (a device that is unintentionally burlesqued in a tendency to speak of a "certain" this or that, when leaving things uncertain). I granted that the subject was difficult, and I chided myself for perhaps violating Aristotle's sound injunction not to demand more exactitude than the nature of the subject-matter permits. But here, where the critic could have been thoroughly explicit, instead we get "I shall not say." Why shouldn't a critic, who has chosen to explain the genesis of his poems, say what words he deliberately dodged in the course of producing these poems? He could have told us such important facts about his methods, while still abiding by the rule he set for himself in his essays on Da Vinci: "No mistresses, no creditors, no anecdotes, no love-affairs."

CODA

Lord Tennyson's Scissors: 1912–1950

R. P. BLACKMUR

Originally published in the Kenyon Review *in 1951, Blackmur's essay remains a sublime overview of modernist poetry. Though we might quibble with some of his judgments (such as the secondary places accorded Auden and Lowell), Blackmur displays here his gift for phrasing magnificently—as when he defines* prosody *as "the loving care for the motion of meaning in language."*

I hope these reflections on the mother tongue of poetry during the last forty years may be, like their subject, inescapably frivolous and indestructibly serious. Poetry is a game we play with reality; and it is the game and the play—the game by history and training, the play by instinct and need—which make it possible to catch hold of the reality at all. Thus there is intimacy and irresponsibility, menace and caress, escape and aspiration, indigestion and sudden death: all this is in the play. I suppose Eliot meant something like this when he called poetry a superior form of amusement; Yeats something like this when he hoped his poems would wither into the truth; and I am sure that Falstaff had no less a message in mind when, in his dying, he babbled of green fields. Poetry is as near as words can get us to our behavior: near enough so that the words sing, for it is when words sing that they give that absolute moving attention which is beyond their prose powers. It is behavior, getting into our words, that sings. It may be only barely song as in Eliot's lines in "The Dry Salvages":

> The salt is on the briar rose,
> The fog is in the fir trees.

Here is the salt of death and of truth and of savor, the salt in our souls of that which is not ours, moving there. The salt is on the wild and thorny rose grappling in the granite at sea's edge, grappling and in bloom, almost ever-blooming; and it is the rose which was before, and may yet be after, the rose of the Court of Love, or the rose of the Virgin. It is the

rose out of the garden which includes the rose in the garden. There is
in Eliot's line (alien but known to our line that we read) also all the
roses that have been in his life, as in the next line is all the fog. The fog
is another salt as the fir trees are another rose. It is all there is in fog that
lowers, covers, silences, imperils, menaces and caresses; but in it, as it
is in them; there is the slowed apparition, coming up under an island,
of evergreen struggling, tenacious life. The two together make an
image, and in their pairing reveal, by self-symbol declare, by verse and
position unite, two halves of a tragic gesture.

> The salt is on the briar rose,
> The fog is in the fir trees.

I do not see that any other illustration is needed of how behavior gets
into the words of the full mind, and how, a little beyond the time that
it is there, it sings. It may have only a brusque lilt:

> I sing because I like to sing
> And not to hurt a living thing.

So the old song says, and it is enough till memory brings another song
which shows that nothing is ever quite enough, either to say or sing. It
may sing music not its own.

> Sweetheart, do not love too long:
> I loved long and long,
> And grew to be out of fashion
> Like an old song.

The author of those lines thought half the time that the poet had to
choose between life and work, but when he looked at verse itself the
occasion and the need for *that* choice had evaporated—true but gone—
like a water-stain on stone; or had disappeared—true but changed—a
snowflake in the river. This author—it was of course Yeats—sometimes
resumed that self which is beyond choice by quoting lines made by a
friend from the Irish: in song of a lifetime.

> When I was young,
> Who now am young no more,
> I did not eat things picked up from the shore:
> The periwinkle, and the tough dog-fish
> At even-tide have got into my dish.

At other times he found that unchoosable self as near at hand as the nearest door, or the clock's tick: in the song of the gathered moment.

> My fiftieth year had come and gone,
> I sat, a solitary man,
> In a crowded London shop,
> An open book and empty cup
> On the marble table-top.
>
> While on the shop and street I gazed
> My body of a sudden blazed;
> And twenty minutes more or less
> It seemed, so great my happiness,
> That I was blessèd and could bless.

The truth of such a man—he is dead; and we may say it—is that neither his vices nor his poetry ever quitted him;[1] and when we say that I think we have touched the quick and very membrane of style; or at any rate we have the gasp and thrill with which we respond to such penetrations: that is, with added song.

> Shakespearean fish swam the sea, far away from land;
> Romantic fish swam in nets coming to the hand;
> What are all those fish that lie gasping on the strand?

Style is the quality of the act of perception but it is mere play and cannot move us much unless married in rhythm to the urgency of the thing perceived: or until—to say it again—behavior gets into the words and sings. Style, if you like, is how that kind of song is read; and it is sometimes, as a shudder may become a blush and a blush may drift into vertigo, by this sort of reading that the urgency of substance is found. There is a zero quality in style by which it seems to project, as it contains, the infinity of numbers. For example: Pound's "Medallion": a song of syllables.

> Luini in porcelain!
> The grand piano
> Utters a profane
> Protest with her clear soprano.
>
> The sleek head emerges
> From the gold-yellow frock

As Anadyomene in the opening
Pages of Reinach.

The name of Reinach's book was Apollo, and Apollo was Lord of the Lyre and Lord of the Light's Edge; in fact, Leader of the Muses, Apollo Musagete. Pound was not worried by all this; he grew up with Reinach, and by that and other hard training got to play a very complicated stylistic game by ear. Whatever words themselves can woo into being is wooed in his words. So to speak, he settled for what came from the conjugation of the spontaneous and the arbitrary through the mind's last mode of beautiful sound. I suppose this was one of the reasons why Eliot made Pound *il miglior fabbro*. "O brother," the lines go in Dante, "this one whom I distinguish to you with my finger, was a better craftsman of the mother tongue." This is too much to say of Pound (as it was not of Arnaut Daniel)—too much to say of anyone except in those moods when the mere movement of words in pattern turns the shudder of recognition into a blush and the blush into vertigo. Vertigo is one of the conditions in which we recognize our behavior. This is what Baudelaire only reminds us of when he says he was forever haunted by vertigo. Let it be, then; there is a true vertigo to be found through the exercise of the craft of the mother tongue. It is the naked voice that sings:

What are all those fish that lie gasping on the strand?

II

Forty years of poetry took their rise in Eliot, Yeats, and Pound. Each of them in his own way understands what Tennyson meant when he said he knew the quantity of every English vowel except those in the word scissors—where each vowel is enclosed and made of uncertain quantity by two consonants. Most of their successors do not understand what Tennyson meant and many of them would repudiate the statement not for its arrogance but for its irrelevant nonsense. W. H. Auden would be an exception, and the knowledge is patent in some of his verse. There are other exceptions but they do not seem to me able to get their knowledge into their verse as a regular thing. This is the chief indictment against that aspect of our poetry which we call verse. Syllable and stress are not enough to make a metric into a style, although they are quite enough to make a doggerel. It only strengthens the indictment when we remember that between 1912 and 1922 Yeats, Pound, and Eliot won their own battle against doggerel and deliquescence and reached their heights of style and idiom. 1922 seems the great year of our time—especially if you let the months run a little both ways—for it holds a good many of Yeats's Tower poems, Pound's first eight Cantos, and Eliot's *The Waste Land,* not to mention *Ulysses,* the finishing of *The Magic Mountain,* and the beginning of *The Counterfeiters.* The year 1922 is almost inexhaustible in all the arts. But here we are concerned directly only with the triumphant style and idiom in our three poets: with their victory, finally achieved, in the revolution of 1912. In their different ways, "Prufrock," "The Second Coming," and *Hugh Selwyn Mauberley* released the expressive burden of sensibility into forms which were suddenly available for everybody for the whole period between the wars of 1914 and 1939. These poems are now the commonplace of our meeting and are known like afterthoughts in the bloodstream. At the time they were thought "new" and were mistaken, like any instinct in the process of formation; they assaulted the sensibility, either investing it or sacking it. As a result there came into print and gradually into reading and meaning many other poets new, and difficult, and damned, and denied who are now blessed and used, if they have not been forgotten. This is what is meant by the triumph of style and idiom; and it is almost as useful to say that this is what is meant by the defeat— temporary and precarious—of doggerel.

The history of any period of poetry seen from the point of view of its verse is the history of its struggle to prevent Language from becoming a new form of doggerel or—equally a hard job—to prevent an older form of language from relapsing into the basic doggerel of the mother tongue; just as, from a social point of view, it is the history of readers catching on to new rhythms or new relations between rhythm and meter. This is not a superficial but a primary interest. The business of rhythm is to move perception into meaning, and so to move meaning into words. The business of meter (the quantitative or numerical measure of words prescribed by laws only partly known) is to keep meaning in motion by giving the rhythm foot and hand holds on the up and down (the up *or* down) of the rock-face to be climbed or descended to reach the theoretic form of life we call poetry. Prosody—the precise and loving care of the motion of meaning in language—is of first but not necessarily conscious importance.

The general prosody of the 'teens and 'twenties had equally little to do with the practice of Yeats, Pound, and Eliot (which as I say understood Tennyson on scissors) and with the practice of the old conservatives. The general prosody was perhaps the weakest and least conscious in English since the dead poetry of the mid-sixteenth century. It ran, under various guises and doctrines, toward a combination of absolute doggerel and absolute expressionism. Ezra Pound was as responsible as anyone for this condition, not by the progress of his own work but by the procession of manifestoes which he promulgated by letter and print. His doctrine, however it may have promoted the incentive of writing, only got in the way of full work and when it got stronger, deeply damaged, though it never destroyed, his expressive powers. We see this if we trace the connection (it would be worth somebody's study in detail) between the Imagism of 1912, which was a mere lively heresy of the visual in the verbal, and the full doctrine of the Ideograph which seems to have undermined the structure of the later Cantos. The ideograph is actual picture-writing in verbal signs and although it has an attractive rationale in languages built upon it, it becomes an irrational agent in the languages of the West. In English, unless taken only as analogy like any other material of poetry, the ideograph destroys the composing power of the rational imagination because it can neither grasp nor replace the rational needs of the language. The procedure is very tempting, always, to get rid of what is behind one and what is ahead of one, neither by capitulation nor by mastery, but by declaring an arbitrary substitute. Then expression becomes immediate, which is good, and spontaneous, which is not; for spontaneity is the curse of poetry to at least the same degree that neologism is the curse of language. But the temptation is very deep; Art, as Maritain says, Art bitten by poetry longs to be freed from reason, but so long as nothing is substituted for reason the longing is not fatal and may indeed promote a fresh and rejoicing sense of disorder, as *The Waste Land* did, or a new underground for reason, as the work of Valéry and Mallarmé did.

Nor should Pound be blamed too much; the heresiarchs were everywhere; all that is known as semantics, semasiology, and semiotics was in the air, and it did no good but worse harm to replace these with Basic English, as Ogden and Richards did, for Basic English makes reading as well as writing an unbearable bore. What, should we get rid of our ignorance, of the very substance of our lives, merely in order to understand one another?

The poets did not think so either. They took both the ideograph and the semiotics (in the guise of free verse and the vade mecum of deliberate ambiguity, which is sometimes called irony or paradox) and made out of them a defense of absolute self-expressionism. The idea was that of absolute style (identity or abolition of form and content), which is all very well in a sacred book, after it has been made sacred, but which otherwise runs the risk of becoming absolute doggerel. *What are all those fish that lie gasping on the strand?*

What they did was to make just enough of a prosody to heroize the sensibility and not quite enough to make a heroic statement. Just enough meter to make a patter, just enough rhyme to make a noise, just enough reason to make an argument; never enough of anything to bind together what came out of the reservoir of their extraordinary sensibility into possible poetry. I refer, of course, to the bad poetry of the time and to the bad poetry which is called modern: to what Yeats meant when he said that the bad poet does with no trouble at all what the good poet does with great difficulty: that is to say, by prosody, by expertness, conscious or not. This bad poetry is not worth reference in itself; it is here only to represent the condition of the language and the state of ambition in which an unusually large amount of good—or partly good—poetry got written. It is here because, outside Yeats who had other wounds, hardly a good poet or a good poem but shows the permanent and somewhat crippling scars of these diseases. To heroize the sensibility is to heroize the very spontaneity which is the enemy of poetry.

Pound (out of Ford Madox Ford) had the cure for this heroism: in his notion of the Prose Tradition in Verse, where the edict was that verse ought to be at least as well-written as prose. But the cure was either unacceptable because of ignorant superstitions about inspiration or because, being by nature allergic to it, the patient would die of the cure. For the most part the bottle was bought but never used after the first gagging dose. Besides, it was seldom taken as it should always have been, along with another of Pound's prescriptions, and without which it could never do anything but harm. Verse should be written, said Pound, not to the metronome but in the sequence of the musical phrase. The prose tradition alone produces flatness, inhibits song, and excludes behavior; and I see no sense in welcoming these disorders, as Eliot has done in parts of the Quartets and as Schwartz has done in all but his earliest work, as other and desirable forms of order. I do not refer to careless writing but to deliberate flatness: which is only the contemporary form of Georgian deliquescence. Pound was right; never mind the metronome, which is the measure of doggerel; the necessity is absolute to compose in the sequence of the musical phrase. That is the difference between writing verse with only the care that goes with prose and writing verse better than prose. What is better is that words written in the prose tradition *and* composed in the sequence of the musical phrase become their own meaning: the meaning which, as Eliot says in prose, persists after the words have stopped; that very meaning of which he says in the better writing of verse: "you are the music while the music lasts." What could be better than that?

Who knows? It is always interesting to consult the two geneses of poetry in prose and in doggerel. In the prose lies the sensibility, in the doggerel the hope, of poetry. The curious may consult Yeats's *Autobiographies* and the versions of "Sailing to Byzantium" printed since his death; both the doggerel and the prose for many poems are there. So with Pound, there is the *ABC of Economics* and the Canto on Usury; and with Eliot there are the deep parallels between the series of essays and the series of poems. In each case the poems are better than the prose because in each the doggerel whether of the verse or of the mind has been lifted into composition in the sequence of the musical phrase; and in each the sensibility has been freed from the heroism of the spontaneous—the merely self-expressed, or the merely argued—and become in some sense an incarnation of actual behavior: so that you are the music while the music lasts.

Of course we have been talking about the history of poetry, not about the history of sensibility except as it affects poetry. Perhaps only because it is our own age and we have a kind of disadvantageous intimacy with it, it seems to have been an age when the sensibility took over much of the task of poetry. That is why we have created so many private worlds each claiming ascendancy over the real world about which nothing, or nearly nothing got said. That is why, too, Yeats and Eliot (though not Pound, except rarely) were almost alone able to express a version—an actual form—of the real world. In each the sensibility had other grounds than itself; the ground of beseeching, history, faith or momentum and the other ground, no less important to poetry, of prosody. To combine words of each poet in a single question, in

> A woman drew her long black hair out tight
> And fiddled whisper music on those strings—
>
> O body swayed to music, O brightening glance,
> How can we know the dancer from the dance?

I submit that in these lines the sensibility has disappeared into the words and the words have disappeared into what is sung, and nothing forgot. *Nothing forgot* because the meter is so united with the rhythm that the quality of the act of perception is united with the urgency of the thing perceived.

III

I suppose that all these words so far make up to an odd way of following Arnold step by step on his touchstones, but I hope the pace is lighter and comes out in another world than his, though I do not know what world because I trust it is the world in which we live. They are meant to give us, these stepping stones, points of perilous vantage from which to estimate the work of other poets *as poets*, and not only the poets who worked under their influence but also those who worked under the influence of other and as some say older parts of the traditions of poetry in English. If we think of Yeats, Pound, and Eliot—each with his pair of Lord Tennyson's scissors—it becomes easy to cut our way through the whole field. We see at once, for a rather lumped-up example, that only at a relatively low level did meter and rhythm unite in Housman, De la Mare, and Masefield; only at rough and uneven levels in Frost and Robinson; only at difficult and precarious levels in Empson and Auden; at faltering and ragged levels in Graves and Marianne Moore; at a chastened level in H. D. Similarly, in the metric of Sturge Moore there is a kind of woolly desperation, in Herbert Read, a brittle desperation, and a mechanical, relaxed desperation, striking idly on under-water objects, in Hardy. Desperation is the quality of action at some critical point unsuccessful because the right equipment is lacking. None of these poets in the bulk of their verse—though all of them by exception—took enough stock in the music of the muse. Hence there is not often enough the steady pressure of cohesion, speed, and exigence. But all of them are better than the flannel-mouthed inflation in the metric of Robinson Jeffers with his rugged rock-garden violence.

None of these men are bad poets; all of them require reading. I only say that what impedes full reading is a faulty relation between language and sensibility, between meter and rhythm. Their engines are inefficient; and they should have been either Keatsed or Vergilianized; where to Keats means to blush at language found and not to blush until it is found, and where to Vergilianize means so to see things bound together in words that they build into permanent structures of the mind, that is, into statement: into reason that sings in the nerves because built into the body of the language.

But think—still with the scissors for hand-run reading—of the parallel Old-Timers' school, what we might call the school of Chaucer and the Ballad; think of Hardy, Housman, Robinson, and Frost: Frost with his close piety to experience; Robinson with his combination of Browning and New England; Housman with the movement of Herbert and the temperament of Hardy; Hardy with his country piety, emotional distrust, and Comtean positivism: each with his view and sense of nature, man, and God. The scissors tell us that the reputation of these men may improve, if not absolutely then relatively to Yeats and Eliot. Reading them, we see why Pound does not occupy a first position, but a position on one side. The superlative metric of Pound may be a clue to their weakness but it would never furnish an understanding of their imperfect strength. Their work stands ready to infect the work of young men who have not yet found a form for their ambition and who can no longer, since they apprehend what has happened to it, heroize their sensibility. At least I should suppose there might be a coming race of poets who would want to reverse Maritain's phrase and say Art, bitten by reason, longs to be freed from poetry: from the spontaneous and the private and the calculated public worlds. There might be a race of poets, that is, who would woo the excited miracles of absolute statement, not as a refuge, but to get their work done. For such a race, Hardy, Housman, Robinson, and Frost would be not masters but the nearest exemplars of the line of work into which the work, itself superior to theirs, of Yeats, Eliot, and Pound would disappear. It is with such an attitude in mind that the work of Lorca becomes important; it permits access without overestimation into the late school of Chaucer.

These young men—the next thing that happens, whatever it may be—would gain little but reaction from the works of the Apocalyptic or Violent school: a school that seemed so lively, so menacing to others, and so destructive of themselves, only twenty years ago—a school that now seems dead, with two exceptions. Here is where we find the remains of Vachel Lindsay, the evangel of enthusiastic rebirth; Robinson Jeffers, the classical Freudian; Roy Campbell the animal, authoritarian evangel of anti-culture; Carl Sandburg, the bard of demagogic anti-culture; and of course others. Perhaps they have partial heirs in Kenneth Patchen who has a kind of *ex cathedra* automatism, Kenneth Fearing who envisages a city without a polity, and Kenneth Rexroth who sees anarchy as the form of culture. All of these stem poetically and emotionally from Whitman-Yates: and all are marked by ignorance, good will, solipsism, and evangelism. Lord Tennyson's scissors can find nothing but cloth in them to cut; nor should we think of them even so briefly as more than false alarms if it were not for the two extraordinary talents that must be grouped with them. With modifications because of their extreme eccentricity of vision or genius, their self-willed marvels of craft, and because of their absolute flair for meaning by rhythm, D. H. Lawrence and Hart Crane belong here. Each is a blow in the face but neither can hit you twice. Both left lasting poems naked as the sensibility itself, dark as their own rebirths in the darkness of blood. But it is Lord Tennyson's scissors, and not any other instruments of insight, that tell us sadly both Lawrence and Crane were outside the tradition they enriched. They stood at the edge of the precipice which yawns to those who lift too hard at their bootstraps.

Besides the Apocalyptic school, and related to it closely, there was another school of anti-intelligence (pro-culture and self-verbal varieties) who filled the little magazines of the 'twenties and early 'thirties, together with the attics and bars, with their random spontaneity and arbitrary rites on words. They got rid of too much of their reason, and as a result they effervesced rather then expressed, and what is left is flat. Nameless they shall be here; they belonged only to their principal journal *transition*. What was wrong with them is clear when you see how weak is their imitation of Apollinaire, Aragon, Cocteau, Soupault, and how great their misunderstanding of Mallarmé, Rilke, Joyce, Kafka, and Pirandello: all men who longing to be freed from reason had a kind of bottom supply of it. Neither the English nor the Americans have ever been very good at this sort of thing. Let us say that we have not so much of reason that we can afford to lose any of it; we need it to make our nonsense real as well as genuine; and one would say that in this respect prosody was a form of reason.

Prosody as reason is what the central school of the time characteristically has over and above our two anti-intelligence schools. This is the school of Donne into which the largest number of individual writers of good verse fall when shaken up and let settle. If we generalize them, they are difficult in style, violent in their constructed emotions, private with actual secrecy in meaning. There is in their work a wrestling struggle toward statement, a struggle through paradox and irony (forms of arrogance and self-distrust), and the detritus of convictions. The statements are therefore impossible to make, but the effort to make them is exciting because genuine and because, in the best poems, there is an emotion created in parallel to the undeclarable intent. Their language has flesh and nerves and is recurrently on the verge of voice.

One does what one can. John Ransom and Allen Tate, for example, around the gaps of the unstateable tremendous, are models of the uncontrollable in pseudo-control. John Wheelwright had again and again the frightening stroke of direct wit on the thing itself unsaid, just as Empson can press his meters on the unsayable until it almost bursts into being. Hugh MacDiarmid is another, in his non-political poems, who has the force of immanent statement. Anybody can make his own list, or consult the anthologies; for it is at this point we see the great tide of talent whirl up individual after individual till the unlike is lost in the like.

What are all those fish that lie gasping on the strand?

The school of Donne; we call it that as a counter in exchange, and a counter of only generally determined value. Like any counter it tells a lie; but it would be a worse lie if we called it the school of Blake. We must tell two lies together. Both intellectually and prosodically we have the right. The general poetry at the center of our time takes the compact and studiable conceit of Donne with the direct eccentricity, vision, and private symbolism of Blake; takes from Hopkins the incalculable and unreliable freedom (which cost him so much, too) of sprung rhythm, and the concentration camp of the single word; and from Emily Dickinson takes spontaneous snatched idiom and wooed accidental inductableness. It is a Court poetry, learned at its fingertips and full of a decorous willfulness called ambiguity. It is, in a mass society, a court poetry without a court. There were some of course who believed there was a court, but they produced very little poetry, or at least very little with the infectiousness of authority. I mean poets like Robert Bridges, Yvor Winters, and Howard Baker. It is not authority one gets from their work but strictures: the impossible effort of the bootstrap-will to remake one's time in accord with one's sense of its defects of sensibility and form. This is the heresy as ancient as that of direct inspiration or (as Winters named it) expressive form: the notion of *a priori* correct form.

Not so much the opposed as the counterpart heresy is William Carlos Williams's notion, which rises from his intense conviction that the only value of sound or sense is in direct perception, that forms are themselves incorrect when they are not unique. To him beauty is absolute and falls like the rain, like the dream of rain in a dry year. He is, if you like, the imagism of 1912 self-transcended. He is contact without tact; he is objectivism without objective; *l'anima semplicetta* run wild, with all the gain in the zest of immediate wonder, with all the loss that strikes when memory and expectation, the double burden of the true music, are both gone. The neo-classicist and the neo-barbarian are alike in this: their vitality is without choice or purpose. *Wind shrieked, and where are they?*

The aghast cry is from Yeats; but the scissors of Eliot or of Pound could have shorn as close. There is in poetry no shearing power so great as the living twist of things called idiom caught on to that qualifying act of perception called style. This, as we hear it, is the music of Lord Tennyson's scissors.

It is a music involved here so that we may remind ourselves how differently, and in what varied voices, it may be heard at one time: all modes being approximations of truth. There are Wallace Stevens, Marianne Moore, and E. E. Cummings, to be invoked here so that we may more richly hear Yeats, Eliot, and Pound. Each, so to speak, is full of syllables where the others are full of words. Each is a kind of dandy, or connoisseur, a true mountebank of behavior made song. I do not know that there is precedence among them; let us say they make an equilateral triangle of three styles hung like a pendant from the three major styles. Each is much interested in prosody at the executive rather than the constructive level: each decorates and expands existing prosody. So with words, each is interested in refinements, recollections, and modifications of major meanings. None of them could ever so penetrate either their prosody or their words that their poems become their own music or their own meaning. It is always a haunting "other" music that you are while the music lasts. That is why each of them has so often been an immediate influence on younger poets and why none of them has ever been a permanent or protracted influence. Each is too remote from the urgency of perception.

Wallace Stevens is a dandy and Platonist, he darlings the syllables of his ideas: it is the stroke of platonism on prosody that produces Euphues, wit with a secret, ornament on beauty. You need an old dictionary and an old ear to get his beauty: as if he had to find an unfamiliar *name* before the beauty of his perception could emerge; and it is along these lines that you have to think of the French symbolists' influence upon him. They taught Eliot the antipoetic and the conversational style; Stevens they taught the archaic and the rhetorical; that is, Eliot and Stevens saw the one prosody running in opposite directions. But Stevens is in essence of a very old tradition, French and Platonic, working on a modern substance. He is a troubadour, a poet of the Court of Love, and his badge is *Trobar Clus*; he has a bias for the hermetic, for the complex and ornamented protection of complex and violent perception—which is his way of heroizing the sensibility. I would think that he has all his life wanted to make supreme statements discreetly, so that their beauty would show before their force. He should have lived in the age of Pope; with his sensibility and his syllables he could have made rational statements with more beauty than that age was capable of. But as it is, he is "the tranquil jewel in this confusion."

Marianne Moore is a syllabist too, for she has written the most complex syllabic verse of our time: as if she brought French numbers to English rhythms with no principle of equivalence. But she is not the syllabist as dandy but a connoisseur; she is the syllabist of the actual, the metrist of the immediate marvel—the small animal, the close perception, the fragment of phrase; and at her best all these small things move in a momentum, like the El Greco "brimming with inner light" of which one of her poems speaks. But almost everywhere she finds, chooses, refines sophisticated *forms* of simple perceptions which return upon their simplicity and their limits. There is a correspondence here to the coerced heightened perception (the forced close observation) in the painting of still-life. Poetry is to her, as she says, an imaginary garden with real toads in it. She knows all about the toads because she has imagined the garden; as you look suddenly everywhere there is the disengaged leap of a green or a brown toad, all warts, all soft, all leaping, all real. If there is not much other reality there, and there seldom is in a connoisseur's garden, you bring her, or ignore, the life she hasn't got just because what she has got is so real: you bring or ignore as with a shut-in whom you love. While you are with her reading, you wonder what reality can be when her remote refinement of it is so genuine in plain American that cats and dogs can read. You wonder, stop wondering, and are for the moment content with the game and the play that are there.

Perhaps this is the best thing that can be said of E. E. Cummings, too. Certainly when you want to read him for what is there you can neither argue with him nor about him; his emotions, feelings, attitudes have all the direct indignation, the natural blasphemy, the lyric purity, and all the sporadic high jinks of a serious child. He is Dante's *anima semplicetta* running into difficulties, but still running and still singing. He is the child turning poet, the child with *that* terrifying and incomplete dimension. Otherwise put, Cummings is the traditionalist who insists on the literal content of his tradition without re-understanding its sources: this is, of course, the easiest form of eccentricity and the most human form of fanaticism. He is St. Francis turned Unitarian and "candid-shot" honest. Nobody could be more direct and more conventional—and for purity of motive more admirable—in his basic perceptions than he. He has too little a developed self ever to escape from it except waywardly, when you want either to console him or beat him. His verse, oddly, is less direct and even more conventional than his perceptions. He was educated by Edmund Spenser, the English sonneteers, Keats, Swinburne, the funny-papers, and John Bunyan; but perhaps he was most educated by the things that were left out that would have gone to make a structured mind. All he knows is by enthusiasm, habit, and aversion. He refuses the job of the full intelligence, preferring intimacy with what he loves and contempt for what he hates; and he accepts what love and hatred give as if they made the music of a full mind. The gifts are great but they beat as well as console each other; and if he were not part of a going concern larger than he, he would be nothing. Here again is a case where prosody is an instrument of reason. Like the wilder currencies in the age of Veluta (or like the seried marks of Hitler) Cummings's experimental typography depends on the constant presence of the standard it departs from and would be worthless if not measured against it. Indeed it is precisely in the lyric quality which is his highest worth that the old meters break through. Like a roller coaster his thrill lets you drop. It is the mountebank in him that makes the vulgar motions, but it is also the mountebank that plays—the child turned poet—the most serious game in the world.

IV

It is thinking of these others under the aegis of Yeats, Eliot, and Pound that makes us realize the everlasting need of keeping Lord Tennyson's scissors sharp. *What are all those fish that lie gasping on the strand?* No doubt they all came out of a common pool, but it is just to observe the order of their apparition, and it is rewarding to guess at those still far from land. The general absence of decorum in metrics and syntax and the general presence of heroized sensibility and private symbolisms only make it plainer (I mean because of the conscious struggle against them) that the work of Yeats, Eliot, and Pound belongs in the full tradition of literature. It is they who stand between the Victorians and Romantics and whatever it is that comes after them. They made form and substance possible. They made possible the further development and release, still inchoate to these observations, of the doomed school of Auden about 1930. The deliberate approach to doggerel through Skelton, the Ballads, the immediate situation, and the multi-valenced distrust of self combined to produce the new flat style on the one hand (as in Auden) and on the other hand (as in Dylan Thomas) what you might call the yelling, swinging style. In between lie many possibilities, not so far satisfied, or if so not so far seen.

Auden alone has all the interest and variety and learning that go with being a true poet, and it would seem that it is something in the age rather than something in himself or the condition of poetry that has kept him from proving the truth. It is as if his crankinesses, his ups and downs, were not what he ate when young but what he picked up on the shore.

> The periwinkle, and the tough dog-fish
> At even-tide have got into my dish.

Auden is not yet through; he has had his first rushes, indeed several of them, his rallies and relapses, and his ventures into taxonomies of all sorts. But he remains quick and perceptive even in the flaccid verse of the *Age of Anxiety*; he has an ear as true as any, the beginnings of a style and the earmarks of an idiom. He has the capacities but not yet the achievements of a great poet. But he is in his middle forties: the climacteric is not yet.

It is all the more reason to think so when we look at the generation born between 1913 and 1918: Shapiro, Barker, Schwartz, Thomas, Berryman, Manifold, Lowell, Betjeman, Meredith, and Reed. I would not say that any of these men have managed the full creation, but they have the enormous advantage over their predecessors that there is an idiom ready for them to develop according to their own needs.

> The salt is on the briar rose,
> The fog is on the fir trees.

They have more than a chance—it is half done for them—to develop out of personality the most objective of all creations, the least arbitrary and spontaneous, a style. This they are aware of. They are more open, more freed, nearer both statement and song than their predecessors. They began nearer the prose tradition and the sequence of the musical phrase. We might have a great age out of them yet. What more do you want? Only that it is by prosody alone—by the loving care for the motion of meaning in language—that a poet may prove that he "was blessèd and could bless." That thought is the music of Lord Tennyson's scissors.

1. Eliot, thinking of Yeats, once cited La Rochefoucauld's aphorism: If you say of a man that he has quitted his vices, watch out! the vices may have only quitted him.

APPENDIX
Selected Biographies and Bibliographies

R. P. BLACKMUR (1904–1965)

Born and raised in Springfield, Massachusetts, Richard Palmer Blackmur was an exemplar of that most American of types: the self-made man. After graduating from Cambridge High and Latin School, Blackmur went to work at a local bookstore while auditing courses at Harvard University. He never enrolled as a student, and never received a degree from any college. Instead, he studied as he saw fit, read what he wanted, and wrote about what mattered to him. This rather bohemian academic record did not keep Blackmur from becoming one of the most honored and influential university professors of his day—a situation that would be, unfortunately, almost impossible today.

When a new student magazine, the *Hound & Horn*, was started by the undergraduate Lincoln Kirstein at Harvard in 1927, Blackmur was made the magazine's first managing editor. Though he served in this position only two years, Blackmur's name has always been tied to the magazine where many of his early essays were first published. (Yvor Winters also served on the staff as a regional editor.) One of the best little magazines of the modernist era, the *Hound & Horn* ceased publication in 1934.

In 1935, Blackmur's first book of criticism, *The Double Agent*, appeared. His first book of poetry, *From Jordan's Delight*, appeared two years later. Though his poetry was respected in its day, Blackmur was never considered an important poet-critic in the same category as John Crowe Ransom or Allen Tate. His criticism, however, was recognized immediately as singularly elegant and bewitching; influenced by Henry Adams and Henry James, Blackmur wrote prose that was as syntactically formidable as his masters' before him. He was not a propagator of new ideas, but rather a critic whose persuasiveness usually rested on a paradox or poetic analogy. Particularly in the later essays, he reached for a sophistication that some found impenetrable; Yvor Winters, for one, found that Blackmur "neglected the arts of syntax and of organization to the point that it is almost impossible to understand him."

Allen Tate helped secure a position for Blackmur at Princeton University in 1940. He was made a resident fellow, and taught creative writing until 1948, when he was made a professor. In 1949, he founded the university's Christian Gauss Seminars in Criticism, a program that became rightly famous for the quality of both its guest lecturers (such as W. H. Auden and Randall Jarrell) and its semiprivate audience.

Blackmur was the first man of letters to hold the Pitt Professorship of American History and Institutions at Cambridge University; he also served as the vice president of the National Institute of Arts and Letters, and as a Fellow in American Letters at the Library of Congress.

R. P. Blackmur died in 1965.

Selected Bibliography

By the author:

The Double Agent: Essays in Craft and Elucidation. Arrow Editions, 1935.
The Expense of Greatness. Arrow Editions, 1940.
Form and Value in Modern Poetry. Doubleday, 1952.
Language as Gesture: Essays in Poetry. Harcourt, Brace, 1952.
The Lion and the Honeycomb: Essays in Solicitude and Critique. Harcourt, Brace, 1955.
A Primer of Ignorance, edited by Joseph Frank. Harcourt, Brace and World, 1967.
The Poems of R. P. Blackmur. Princeton University Press, 1977.
Henry Adams, edited by Veronica A. Makowsky. Harcourt, Brace Jovanovich, 1980.
Selected Essays of R. P. Blackmur, edited by Denis Donoghue. Ecco, 1986.
Outsider at the Heart of Things: Essays by R. P. Blackmur, edited by James T. Jones. University of Illinois Press, 1989.

About the author:

A Mingled Yarn: The Life of R. P. Blackmur, by Russell A. Fraser. Harcourt, Brace Jovanovich, 1981.

Criticism of the author and his works:

The Function of Criticism, by Yvor Winters. Swallow, 1957. ("Problems for the Modern Critic of Literature")
Selected Essays of Delmore Schwartz, edited by Donald A. Dike and David H. Zucker. University of Chicago Press, 1970. ("The Critical Method of R. P. Blackmur")
R. P. Blackmur, Poet-Critic: Toward a View of Poetic Objects, by Robert Boyers. University of Missouri Press, 1980.

Wayward Skeptic: The Theories of R. P. Blackmur, by James T. Jones. University of Illinois Press, 1986.

The Legacy of R. P. Blackmur, edited by Edward T. Cone, Joseph Frank, and Edmund Keeley. Ecco, 1987.

Note:

R. P. Blackmur's prose has not been collected in a definitive edition yet. *Form and Value in Modern Poetry* is available as a paperback, and it gathers the famous early essays on poetry from *Language as Gesture*, along with several items originally published in various little magazines. The interested reader should begin with it. Both recent selections of essays are valuable, as some of the early books are hard to find. Blackmur's later and more mandarin style is available in *A Primer of Ignorance*. His poetry is little read now, and of limited interest. All of his critical prose, including the book on Henry Adams, is worth reading.

CLEANTH BROOKS (1906–1994)

One of the most influential of the New Critics and its chief pedagogist, Cleanth Brooks was born in Kentucky. Brooks's father was a Methodist minister, and so the gift of examining and explaining texts was for the young man almost a family inheritance. As an undergraduate at Vanderbilt University, he became friends with Robert Penn Warren, and knew many of the poets and intellectuals associated with the *Fugitive*; though he was not officially a member of the Southern Agrarians, he read and admired their work as well.

After obtaining degrees at Tulane and Oxford universities, Brooks began his teaching career at Louisiana State University in 1932. Two years later, Robert Penn Warren arrived there as well and, together, the pair coedited the *Southern Review* (1935–1942) and coauthored the most influential college textbooks of their day: *Understanding Poetry* (1938) and *Understanding Fiction* (1943). It is hard to overestimate how successful these guides were in teaching a generation of students how to read literature closely. Indeed, these books enshrined and popularized the New Criticism as an academic movement in the American universities; Cleanth Brooks, more than anyone, is widely credited for this revolution. Perhaps the best compliment paid to him was from his mentor John Crowe Ransom, who regarded him as "the most forceful and influential critic of poetry that we have."

Brooks was also instrumental in defining New Critical practices: his usual term for the new movement was *formalist* (referring to its emphasis on the formal characteristics of literature, such as meter and rhyme). Brooks's most important individual collections of criticism are *Modern Poetry and the Tradition* (1939) and *The Well Wrought Urn* (1947). The latter, in particular, was important in summarizing Brooks's interest in *irony*, *ambiguity*, and *paradox* as vital attributes of the best poetry. Among his other books of chief interest, the brilliant four-volume survey *Literary Criticism* (coauthored with William K. Wimsatt) examined the critical arts from Plato to the scholarship of the mid-twentieth century.

An outstanding Faulkner scholar, Brooks also wrote four books on his fellow Southerner; many scholars considered him the highest authority on the literature of the American South. In 1947, Brooks was appointed professor of English at Yale University; he taught there until his retirement in 1975.

Cleanth Brooks died in New Haven, Connecticut, in 1994.

Selected Bibliography

By the author:

Modern Poetry and the Tradition. University of North Carolina Press, 1939.

Understanding Poetry: An Anthology for College Students (with Robert Penn Warren). Henry Holt, 1939.

The Well Wrought Urn: Studies in the Structure of Poetry. Harcourt, Brace, 1947.

Literary Criticism: A Short History (with W. K. Wimsatt). Knopf, 1957.

The Hidden God: Studies in Hemingway, Faulkner, Yeats, Eliot, and Warren. Yale University Press, 1963.

A Shaping Joy: Studies in the Writer's Craft. Harcourt, Brace, Jovanovich, 1971.

American Literature: The Makers and the Making (with Robert Penn Warren and R. W. B. Lewis). Macmillan, 1973.

Historical Evidence and the Reading of Seventeenth-Century Poetry. University of Missouri Press, 1991.

Community, Religion, and Literature: Essays. University of Missouri Press, 1995.

About the author:

Cleanth Brooks: An Annotated Bibliography, by John M. Walsh. Routledge, 1990.

Cleanth Brooks and Allen Tate: Collected Letters, 1933–1976, edited by Alphonse Vinh. University of Missouri Press, 1998.

Cleanth Brooks and Robert Penn Warren: A Literary Correspondence, edited by James A. Grimshaw Jr. University of Missouri Press, 1998.

Criticism of the author and his works:

Critics and Criticism, edited by Ronald S. Crane. University of Chicago Press, 1952. ("Cleanth Brooks; Or the Bankruptcy of Critical Monism," by Ronald S. Crane.)

The Possibilities of Order: Cleanth Brooks and His Work, edited by Lewis P. Simpson. Louisiana State University Press, 1976.

Parnassus on the Mississippi: The Southern Review *and the Baton Rouge Literary Community, 1935–1942*, by Thomas W. Cutrer. Louisiana State University Press, 1984.

Cleanth Brooks and the Rise of Modern Criticism, by Mark Royden Winchell. University Press of Virginia, 1996.

Note:

Cleanth Brooks's prose has not been collected in a definitive edition as yet, and most of his miscellaneous essays and reviews are hard to find. The best place to begin is with *The Well Wrought Urn*. One should also read *Modern Poetry and the Tradition*, while *Literary Criticism: A Short History* is a major work of scholarship that is too little known today.

KENNETH BURKE (1897–1993)

One of the most interesting and peripatetic theoretical critics that America has ever produced, Kenneth Duva Burke was born in Pittsburgh, Pennsylvania. Like R. P. Blackmur, Burke was an autodidact; he never held a degree higher than a high school diploma, though he briefly studied at Ohio State University (for one semester) and Columbia University (for a year or so). He dropped out of college in order to live in Greenwich Village and keep company with fellow Bohemian intellectuals such as Hart Crane and Malcolm Cowley (a friend since their days together in high school).

Burke was not, however, a café lounger or a literary poseur. In fact, his energy was profound and protean. Poetry, short stories, translations from French and German, reviews on music and history, at least one novel, and a popular song—Burke wrote in many genres on many subjects. He published the first English translation of Thomas Mann's *Death in Venice* in 1924. Three years later, he became the music critic for the *Dial*, one of the most important little magazines of that era. He earned his living as a critic, and also as a researcher for the Bureau of Social Hygiene during these years. His first major critical work, *Counter-Statement*, appeared in 1931 and was warmly received by the New Critics.

After winning a Guggenheim Fellowship in 1935, Burke used the money to build a tiny house on farmland in Andover, New Jersey. Without gas heat or electricity, he lived the life of a rustic sage in the mold of Henry David Thoreau, growing his own vegetables and chopping his own firewood. He was also producing important works on rhetoric and literary theory: *Attitudes toward History* (1937), *Philosophy of Literary Form* (1941), and *A Grammar of Motives* (1945) were works that both entranced and mystified his contemporaries.

Burke's growing reputation allowed him to teach at the University of Chicago, and later at Bennington College, without an academic degree. Meanwhile, over the years, Burke's writings moved from the close analysis of literary works (his New Critical phase) to rhetorical and grammatical speculations and, finally, to abstract theories of language—or what would now be called "communication studies." This wide span of interests mirrors Burke's catholic intellectual appetites. Though early in life he was sympathetic to Marxism, psychoanalysis, and other radical intellectual trends of the era, Burke was also friendly with the Southern New Critics and the neo-Aristotelian scholars (some of whom taught at the University of Chicago). His books fit into none of these categories well: some claim that Burke was the first to create "cultural studies" (criticism that incorporates various intellectual disciplines) while others consider him the greatest theorist of rhetoric since Aristotle.

Kenneth Burke died in 1993 in Andover, New Jersey.

Selected Bibliography

By the author:

Counter-Statement. Harcourt, Brace, 1931.

Permanence and Change: An Anatomy of Purpose. New Republic, 1935.

Attitudes toward History. New Republic, 1937.

Philosophy of Literary Form: Studies in Symbolic Action. Louisiana State University Press, 1941.

A Grammar of Motives. Prentice Hall, 1945.

A Rhetoric of Motives. Prentice Hall, 1950.

The Rhetoric of Religion. Beacon, 1961.

Perspectives by Incongruity, edited by Stanley Edgar Hyman. Indiana University Press, 1964.

Terms for Order, edited by Stanley Edgar Hyman. Indiana University Press, 1964.

Language as Symbolic Action: Essays on Life, Literature, and Method. University of California Press, 1966.

Collected Poems, 1915–1967. University of California Press, 1968.

About the author:

The Selected Correspondence of Kenneth Burke and Malcolm Cowley, 1915–1981, edited by Paul Jay. Viking, 1988.

Kenneth Burke in Greenwich Village: Conversing with the Moderns, 1915–1931, by Jack Selzer. University of Wisconsin Press, 1997.

Criticism of the author and his works:

Encounters with Kenneth Burke, by William H. Rueckert. University of Illinois Press, 1994.

Kenneth Burke and the 21st Century, edited by Bernard L. Brock. State University of New York Press, 1998.

Unending Conversations: New Writings by and about Kenneth Burke, edited by Greig E. Henderson and David Cratis Williams. Southern Illinois University Press, 2001.

Note:

There are three Kenneth Burkes. The critical realist who was associated with the New Critics is to be found in his first four books. The second phase of Burke's career—which centers on his critique of rhetoric—begins with *A Grammar of Motives* and ends with *Language as Symbolic Action.* The third phase—when he elaborated on his "Logology" (an attempt at a "unified field theory" of rhetoric and language)—begins with his 1968 essay on "Dramatism" and continues through all the later books until his death. The interested reader should start with the first four books; the two selections of essays edited by Stanley Edgar Hyman are also good introductions. The University of California Press keeps Burke's major works in print. Burke's poetry, alas, is best avoided.

J. V. CUNNINGHAM (1911–1985)

The greatest American epigrammatist and an important Renaissance scholar, James Vincent Cunningham was born in Cumberland, Maryland. His family moved to Montana and then to Colorado, where Cunningham studied Latin and Greek at a Jesuit high school in Denver. The young man even began to correspond with a graduate student at Stanford, Yvor Winters, about their favorite subject: poetry. The decisive event in the young Cunningham's life was tragic: his father (a steam shovel operator) died in an accident at work, the family's finances became precarious, and so the young Cunningham found it difficult to complete his university education.

Instead, he was forced to take a number of odd jobs, including working for local newspapers. During the Depression, Cunningham wandered through the American Southwest looking for work; often, he was homeless and virtually destitute. In 1931, Cunningham wrote again to

Winters, asking for help to enter Stanford University. Winters graciously allowed the young man to live in a shed in his backyard, and ensured that he was enrolled in classes. Though Cunningham was never formally Winters's pupil, he has always been considered his favorite and protégé. Cunningham graduated from Stanford with a degree in classics in 1934; he received his doctorate in English there in 1945.

Cunningham's poetry, which seems so classical in its formal elegance, is like nothing else written in the last century. Much like the shorter poems of Walter Savage Landor or Martial (a poet whom Cunningham translated), the marmoreal finish of the work balances against the poet's wit and ribaldry—often to stunning effect. Cunningham's prose displays many of the same qualities as his verse: precise sentences and compact arguments betray the rhetorical skill of the Jesuit-trained. Like his mentor Winters, Cunningham wrote prose with a clarity and logical force that is unusual. His individual volumes of poetry and prose are hard to find today, but recent editions of his *Collected Poems* (1997) and *Collected Essays* (1976) have attracted renewed critical interest in his unfairly neglected work.

He held teaching posts at the University of Chicago, the University of Hawaii, Harvard University, the University of Virginia, and Washington University before settling at Brandeis University in 1953, from which he retired in 1980.

J. V. Cunningham died in Waltham, Massachusetts, in 1985.

Selected Bibliography

By the author:

Woe or Wonder: The Emotional Effect of Shakespearean Tragedy. University of Denver Press, 1951.
Tradition and Poetic Structure. Swallow, 1960.
The Collected Poems and Epigrams of J. V. Cunningham. Swallow, 1971.
The Collected Essays of J. V. Cunningham. Swallow, 1976.
The Poems of J. V. Cunningham, edited by Timothy Steele. Swallow, 1997.

Criticism of the author and his works:

The Poetry of J. V. Cunningham, by Yvor Winters. Swallow, 1961.

Note:

Cunningham's individual volumes of poetry are hard to find; his entire *oeuvre* consists of fewer than two hundred poems. The interested reader should seek out Timothy Steele's recent edition of the collected poems. The *Collected Essays* is harder to find, and generally expensive, but worth the effort. That leaves the two early volumes of criticism, which are rare and best obtained at a research library.

T. S. ELIOT (1888–1965)

The most influential poet-critic of the twentieth century, Thomas Stearns Eliot was born in St. Louis, Missouri. At Harvard University, he studied with Irving Babbitt, encountered George Santayana, and wrote "The Love Song of J. Alfred Prufrock" before earning his master's degree. In Europe on a fellowship, Eliot found himself diverted to Oxford University by the opening salvos of the First World War. By 1915, he had met his lifelong friend and literary colleague Ezra Pound, abandoned a looming career as a philosophy professor, and married an Englishwoman—these latter two incidents, particularly, led to an estrangement from his parents. A life as a poet, and as an American among the English, beckoned.

His first book of poetry, *Prufrock and Other Observations*, appeared in 1917. *The Sacred Wood*, his first collection of essays, was published three years later—a volume that inaugurated, and embodied, the New Criticism (a label not used widely until John Crowe Ransom's 1941 book by that title). Between 1917 and 1921, Eliot wrote more than seventy essays—in these five years, he "carried out what must be the most arduous, the most concentrated critical labor of which detailed record exists: nothing less than a rethinking, in the specific terms exacted by conscientious book-reviewing, of the traditional heritage of English letters" as Hugh Kenner has written. Though he was trying to earn money quickly, by writing reviews almost weekly at times, Eliot also managed to systematically examine the writers of certain periods of literature, such as the Elizabethan and Jacobean dramatists. From these early essays also derive a startling number of the New Critical ideas that were most influential: the impersonality of art, the individual artist's relation to tradition, the objective correlative, and the dissociation of sensibility—to name a few.

While "writing essays on Marvell, reading the later chapters of *Ulysses*, attending Stravinsky's *Le Sacre du Printemps*, and visiting seances presided over by P. D. Ouspensky," Eliot, perhaps unsurprisingly, began to have terrible headaches. He was prescribed the rest treatment, and went to a sanitarium in Lausanne, where he finished *The Waste Land*. It was printed, without notes, in the first issue of the *Criterion*, a little magazine launched in 1922 with Eliot as the editor—though he kept this fact quiet for fear of losing his position at Lloyds Bank. (Richard

Aldington was paid to serve as assistant editor and the public face of the quarterly.) Until its demise in 1939, Eliot's magazine was one of the finest quarterlies published in Europe.

In 1925, Eliot left the bank to become an editor at the publishing firm of Faber and Gwyer (later known as Faber and Faber). Universally acknowledged as the central figure of the New Criticism, he was also one of the most famous poets in the world (his lectures and readings often were sold-out events overflowing with admirers). His fellow critics and poets were also reverential. To William Empson, Eliot's example was profound: "I did not know for certain how much of my own mind he invented, let alone how much of it is a reaction against him or indeed a consequence of misreading him. He has a penetrating influence, perhaps not unlike an east wind." Today, when we take for granted the influence of Dante, of Donne and the metaphysicals, of such French poets as Baudelaire and Laforgue on modernism, it is because we forget that Eliot, along with Pound, created—in the words again of Hugh Kenner—"that view of the literature of the past which the twentieth century recognizes as peculiarly its own."

T. S. Eliot died in London in 1965.

Selected Bibliography

By the author:

The Use of Poetry and the Use of Criticism. Harvard University Press, 1933.
Selected Essays. 3rd ed. Faber and Faber, 1951.
The Three Voices of Poetry. Cambridge University Press, 1954.
On Poetry and Poets. Farrar, Straus and Cudahy, 1957.
To Criticize the Critic and Other Writings. Farrar, Straus and Giroux, 1965.
The Complete Poems and Plays. Faber, 1969.
Selected Prose of T. S. Eliot, edited by Frank Kermode. Faber and Faber, 1975.

About the author:

T. S. Eliot: The Man and His Work, edited by Allen Tate. Delacorte/Dell, 1966.
Eliot's Early Years, by Lyndall Gordon. Oxford University Press, 1977.
Eliot's New Life, by Lyndall Gordon. Oxford University Press, 1988.

Criticism of the author and his works:

The New Criticism, by John Crowe Ransom. New Directions, 1941.
The Anatomy of Nonsense, by Yvor Winters. New Directions, 1943.
T. S. Eliot: The Design of His Poetry, by Elizabeth Drew. Charles Scribner's Sons, 1949.
The Art of T. S. Eliot, by Helen Gardner. E. P. Dutton, 1950.

The Achievement of T. S. Eliot: An Essay on the Nature of Poetry, by F. O.
   Matthiessen. 3rd ed., with a chapter on Eliot's later work by C. L. Barber.
   Oxford University Press, 1959.
The Invisible Poet: T. S. Eliot, by Hugh Kenner. McDowell, Obolensky, 1959.
Thomas Stearns Eliot, Poet, by A. David Moody. 2nd ed. Cambridge University
   Press, 1994.

Note:

The critical books and secondary sources on T. S. Eliot number in the
hundreds and constitute a cottage industry. Therefore, I have been severe in my accounting and named only a few of the most famous from
the multitude. After beginning with the last edition of the *Selected Essays*, the interested reader must choose between several of Eliot's later
essay collections to sample the views of his maturity. Probably *The Use
of Poetry and the Use of Criticism* and *To Criticize the Critic* are the
finest selections here. (A collected edition of Eliot's critical prose will be
published in 2008.) As for the critical literature on Eliot, the books by
Matthiessen and Kenner are essential; while the essays by Yvor Winters
in *The Anatomy of Nonsense* and John Crowe Ransom in *The New Criticism* must be considered the best (and almost the only) pieces of severe
criticism on Eliot's critical ideas that we have.

RANDALL JARRELL (1914–1965)

The most influential poetry critic of the last thirty years in America,
Randall Jarrell was born in Nashville, Tennessee. At Vanderbilt University, he was immediately recognized as one of the most brilliant students
that his teachers, John Crowe Ransom and Robert Penn Warren, had
come across. Jarrell was not a fresh recruit for Southern Agrarianism,
however; he was interested in Marx, Freud, and all the contemporary
intellectual trends that his famously conservative teachers abhorred.
Nevertheless, Jarrell was encouraged to publish poems, and review
books, in the little magazines of the Southern New Critics—this latter assignment, in particular, was one that suited his talent exception-
ally well.
   Jarrell followed John Crowe Ransom when he left Vanderbilt for
Kenyon College; there, he met and became close friends with fellow
student Robert Lowell. Jarrell was a beloved, and magnetic, teacher. As
the college's tennis coach, Jarrell was apparently not above reciting
verse to his team—one colleague recalled seeing student players like
Don Budge reading poetry books between games.

In 1942, Jarrell enlisted in the army, and served in the air corps. Some of his finest early poems come from his wartime experience. Returning home, he taught at several universities before settling at the Women's College at the University of North Carolina at Greensboro.

As a critic, Randall Jarrell was the exact opposite of Yvor Winters: he erected no critical system, and embraced no general principle or theory of literature. Instead, he embodied such faultless taste that subsequent generations have amended none of his judgments regarding his fellow poets. He was so often right that, as one friend admitted, people thought he was always right. That is a verdict reached only with hindsight; at the time that Jarrell was writing, his literary criticism was often daring and unconventional. He championed the work of Walt Whitman and Robert Frost when they were out of fashion; he attacked the later works of W. H. Auden fearlessly at a time when many critics considered Auden the greatest living poet in the English language. And he did so in charming and witty prose that had none of the scholar's terminology and none of the specialist's narrow rigor—Jarrell always wrote for the common reader without a hint of condescension. This perhaps explains why his prose is so highly regarded today; certainly, he has been the decisive influence on the current generation of poetry critics.

Randall Jarrell died in 1965, after he was struck by a car while walking on a road in Chapel Hill, North Carolina.

Selected Bibliography

By the author:

Poetry and the Age. Knopf, 1953.

Pictures from an Institution. Knopf, 1954.

A Sad Heart at the Supermarket: Essays and Fables. Atheneum, 1962.

The Third Book of Criticism. Farrar, Straus and Giroux, 1969.

The Complete Poems. Farrar, Straus and Giroux, 1969.

Kipling, Auden & Co.: Essays and Reviews, 1935–1964. Farrar, Straus and Giroux, 1980.

Selected Poems, edited by William H. Pritchard. Farrar, Straus and Giroux, 1990.

No Other Book: Selected Essays of Randall Jarrell, edited by Brad Leithauser. HarperCollins, 1999.

Randall Jarrell on W. H. Auden, edited by Stephen Burt, with Hannah Brooks-Motl. Columbia University Press, 2005.

About the author:

Randall Jarrell, 1914–1965, edited by Robert Lowell, Peter Taylor, and Robert Penn Warren. Farrar, Straus and Giroux, 1967.

Randall Jarrell's Letters, edited by Mary Jarrell, assisted by Stuart Wright. Houghton Mifflin, 1985.

Randall Jarrell: A Descriptive Bibliography, 1929–1983, edited by Stuart Wright. University Press of Virginia, 1986.

Randall Jarrell: A Literary Life, by William H. Pritchard. Farrar, Straus and Giroux, 1990.

Remembering Randall: A Memoir of Poet, Critic, and Teacher Randall Jarrell, by Mary von Schrader Jarrell. HarperCollins, 2000.

Criticism of the author and his works:

Randall Jarrell, by Karl Shapiro. Library of Congress Press, 1967.

Understanding Randall Jarrell, by J. A. Bryant Jr. University of South Carolina Press, 1986.

Randall Jarrell and His Age, by Stephen Burt. Columbia University Press, 2002.

Note:

There are very few readers of critical prose who are unfamiliar with Randall Jarrell. Those who don't know his work should start with *No Other Book*; all of Jarrell's critical prose is worth reading, however, and the individual books should be sought out. *A Sad Heart at the Supermarket*, for example, has been unfairly neglected. *The Third Book of Criticism* contains Jarrell's important essays on W. H. Auden. Stephen Burt's reconstruction of Jarrell's lectures on Auden is the book-length treatment that Jarrell never finished on his favorite poet. Jarrell's poetry is very good generally, and he has left a dozen or so poems of permanent value to American literature. Finally, his one novel, *Pictures from an Institution*, is a comic masterpiece on the absurdities of academic life.

HUGH KENNER (1923–2003)

Probably the greatest scholar of literary modernism, Hugh Kenner was born in Peterborough, Ontario; his father was a local schoolteacher of Latin and Greek. Kenner graduated from the University of Toronto, where he was one of the favorite pupils of Marshall McLuhan, the eminent communications theorist and literary critic. It was McLuhan who introduced his young student to Ezra Pound (at that time held at St. Elizabeths Hospital in Washington, D.C.) during a road trip in 1948, and this meeting proved the decisive intellectual influence in Kenner's life.

Kenner went on to Yale University, where he earned his doctorate under Cleanth Brooks in 1950, with a dissertation on Ezra Pound. A year later, it appeared as a book (*The Poetry of Ezra Pound*)—the first to be published on that subject, and still one of the best introductions to that poet's work. Kenner, meanwhile, was appointed to the first of his posts as a professor, at the University of California at Santa Barbara (1950–73). He later taught at Johns Hopkins University (1973–90), followed by the University of Georgia, from which he retired in 1999.

Kenner's witty and learned prose was the envy of his fellow professors, and yet it always remained prose that many outside the academy could understand. (William F. Buckley Jr. even recruited him to serve as the poetry editor for the *National Review*.) Admirably prolific, Kenner wrote more than thirty books, contributed to two hundred more, and wrote almost a thousand articles on subjects as wide-ranging as computer technology, cartoons, and Buster Keaton movies. His teaching style was also virtuosic. Guy Davenport has written admiringly of Kenner: "His command of any subject was such that he could lecture without notes or script. He usually had a folder of blank pages, or letters from friends, that he pretended to be reading from, to assure audiences that he'd written out what he was saying."

Having started with Ezra Pound, Kenner moved on to write on almost every modernist author in Pound's artistic circle: T. S. Eliot, Wyndham Lewis, James Joyce, William Carlos Williams, and Louis Zukofsky. His books on Joyce and Eliot are still considered classics. Kenner's masterpiece on international modernism, *The Pound Era*, appeared in 1971. His surveys of American modernism (*A Homemade World*), Irish modernism (*A Colder Eye*), and English modernism (*A Sinking Island*) are also valuable.

Not content with confining himself to literary studies (much like his mentor Marshall McLuhan), Kenner wrote books on Buckminster Fuller and on geodesic math. He also wrote on mathematics, science, technology, and visual arts. Kenner received honorary doctorates from the University of Chicago and Trent University, was awarded two Guggenheim fellowships (1956, 1963), and was named a Fellow of the Royal Society of Literature (1956).

Hugh Kenner died at his home in Athens, Georgia, in 2003.

Selected Bibliography

By the author:

The Poetry of Ezra Pound. New Directions, 1951.
Wyndham Lewis. New Directions, 1954.
Dublin's Joyce. Indiana University Press, 1956.
Gnomon: Essays on Contemporary Literature. McDowell, Obolensky, 1958.

The Invisible Poet: T. S. Eliot. McDowell, Obolensky, 1959.

Samuel Beckett: A Critical Study. Grove, 1961. Rev. ed., University of California Press, 1968.

Flaubert, Joyce, and Beckett: The Stoic Comedians. Beacon, 1962.

The Pound Era. University of California Press, 1971.

A Homemade World: The American Modernist Writers. Knopf, 1974.

A Colder Eye: The Modern Irish Writers. Knopf, 1983.

A Sinking Island: The Modern English Writers. Knopf, 1988.

Mazes: Essays. North Point, 1989.

Historical Fictions: Essays. North Point, 1990.

About the author:

There Is No End of Things in the Heart: A Celebration of Hugh Kenner in Honor of his 70th Birthday, edited by Carroll F. Terrell. Northern Lights, 1993.

"Hugh Kenner, R.I.P.," by William F. Buckley. *National Review,* December 22, 2003.

"Hugh Kenner, 1923–2003," by Guy Davenport. *New Criterion* 22 (January 2004).

Note:

Hugh Kenner's masterpiece is *The Pound Era,* and it is not too extravagant to say that it is the finest book on literary modernism that we have. Readers should begin with it. Kenner's shorter essays have not been collected as yet: the miscellanies *Gnomon, Mazes,* and *Historical Fictions* are all worth finding. The studies on individual writers are still classic introductions to their subjects, and should not be ignored. Finally, this reader has found even the book on Buckminster Fuller engrossing.

EZRA POUND (1885–1972)

The guiding creative force of literary modernism, Ezra Pound was born in Hailey, Idaho. His father was a local official who assayed gold and registered mining claims; his mother was a relative of Henry Wadsworth Longfellow. The young Pound was a gifted student of foreign languages (he was familiar with at least ten of them) and of the arts of the *impresario:* after meeting William Carlos Williams at the University of Pennsylvania in 1902, and falling in love with Hilda Doolittle (H.D.) a few years later, Pound encouraged both of them to be poets.

Brash and bohemian, Pound tired of America's juvenile culture; his restless energy pushed him to travel abroad. He landed in Europe in 1908, off a cattle boat (after having been dismissed from his first teaching appointment at Wabash College), and *walked* to Italy, where he had a hundred copies of his first poetry collection printed before moving on to London. Within a year, he had met George Bernard Shaw, T. E. Hulme, Ford Madox Ford, Wyndham Lewis, D. H. Lawrence, and the man he regarded as the greatest living poet, William Butler Yeats. Two more collections of his verse were published a few months after his arrival in the city, printed by the most prestigious house in England. They were accepted after Pound walked into the publisher's offices one day, uninvited and unannounced; he simply stormed the city. One critic called him "the most remarkable thing in poetry since Robert Browning." He was twenty-four.

In short order, Pound began editing anthologies, founding literary movements, and contributing to countless literary journals. He launched the careers of T. S. Eliot and Robert Frost. He found publishers for James Joyce and Henry Miller; he supported the work of D. H. Lawrence, Wyndham Lewis, and William Carlos Williams when they were unknown; and he acted as a secretary for W. B. Yeats, in which capacity he edited and influenced the older poet's work. As T. S. Eliot asserted, "It is on his total work for literature that he must be judged: on his poetry, *and* his criticism, *and* his influence on men and on events at a turning point in literature."

Pound's interest in foreign literatures essentially created the international perspective of modernist poetry. His first book of critical prose, *The Spirit of Romance*, examined the troubadours and poets of the early romance languages; along with Pound's translations of these poets, the book focused critical interest on such figures as Arnaut Daniel and Guido Cavalcanti. The imagist movement that he initiated in 1912 was the starting point for the free verse revolution in modern poetry. Likewise, Pound's later interest in Chinese poetry birthed the still-flourishing scholarship on Asian literature in English. If today we read Arnaut Daniel, Guido Cavalcanti, Bertrand de Born, the author of *The Seafarer*, Li Po, and Japanese *Noh* plays, it is because of Pound.

Together with T. S. Eliot, Pound was responsible not only for the revolution of taste in English-language poetry that we now call modernism but also for the New Criticism. As Eliot has written: "I think that Pound was original in insisting that poetry was an art, an art which demands the most arduous application and study; and in seeing that in our own time it had to be a highly conscious art." His early critical prose, in particular, had a decisive influence on American and English literature. As for the brash and often elliptical style of his essays, the critic Marshall McLuhan has said: "If there is any critical prose more exact, more pointed, more weighted with perception it may be found in the last essays of Mallarmé, but nowhere else in English."

Ezra Pound died in Venice in 1972.

Selected Bibliography

By the author:

The Spirit of Romance. Dent, 1910.
ABC of Reading. New Directions, 1934.
Personae: The Shorter Poems of Ezra Pound. New Directions, 1949; rev. ed., prepared by Lea Baechler and A. Walton Litz, New Directions, 1990.
The Translations of Ezra Pound. New Directions, 1953.
Literary Essays of Ezra Pound, edited by T. S. Eliot. New Directions, 1954.
Selected Prose, 1909–1965, edited by William Cookson. New Directions, 1973.
The Cantos. 4th collected ed. Faber and Faber, 1987.

About the author:

A Serious Character: The Life of Ezra Pound, by Humphrey Carpenter. Houghton Mifflin, 1988.

Criticism of the author and his works:

The Poetry of Ezra Pound, by Hugh Kenner. New Directions, 1951.
Ezra Pound: The Poet as Sculptor, by Donald Davie. Oxford University Press, New York, 1964.
The Pound Era, by Hugh Kenner. University of California Press, 1971.

Note:

Like his friend Eliot, Pound has enjoyed (and occasionally suffered from) a cottage industry of unusually devoted scholars. Therefore, I have mentioned only a few of the most important books. The best critical books on Pound are the two by Hugh Kenner. Pound's poetry and prose should be read concurrently, in order to see his mind at work: his first critical prose, *The Spirit of Romance,* alongside the early poetry and translations, followed by Pound's imagist and Chinese work with their attendant essays, and so forth. This requires a great deal of time and study, but no American poet (with the possible exception of Eliot) rewards the reader's effort like Pound—almost the entire history of poetry is captured by following the arc of Pound's interests through Anglo-Saxon, Provençal, Italian, Chinese, Japanese, French, and Greek models.

JOHN CROWE RANSOM (1888–1974)

Probably the most influential literature professor of the last century, the poet and critic John Crowe Ransom was born in Pulaski, Tennessee.

Only fifteen when he entered Vanderbilt University, Ransom earned a degree there before attending Oxford University as a Rhodes Scholar. In 1914, he started teaching at Vanderbilt, where he stayed until 1937. His tenure there was interrupted only by his service as an artillery officer in World War I.

At Vanderbilt, a small group began meeting on Saturday evenings to discuss philosophy, aesthetics, and poetry; the members of this group included Ransom, his fellow professor Donald Davidson, and two students, Robert Penn Warren and Allen Tate. By 1922, the group had firmly established its identity by founding a magazine, the *Fugitive*. Much of Ransom's best poetry was written and published during the brief life of this publication, which ended in 1925.

He did not reserve all his energy for verse. In fact, with Ransom as the leader, a clique from the *Fugitive* group (including Warren and Tate) joined with like-minded intellectuals to form the Southern Agrarians. Its members took a great interest in defending traditional Southern culture against the encroachments of the modern industrial society. Their defense of Southern agrarian society became the group's most famous book—*I'll Take My Stand* (1930). (Ransom later distanced himself from the movement in various essays.)

In 1941, Ransom published a book that provided the group name for the literary analysis with which he had become associated: *The New Criticism*. The book examined the critical ideas of such important figures as T. S. Eliot and I. A. Richards, and provided Ransom's own definition of what the new ideal should be: "ontological" criticism. Its definition rests on the claim that "the differentia of poetry as discourse is an ontological one. It treats an order of existence, a grade of objectivity, which cannot be treated in scientific discourse." Another of Ransom's basic premises was that a poem consisted of a structure (or argument) and a texture (images or icons) in creative balance. Similarly, "the composition of a poem is an operation in which an argument fights to displace a meter, and the meter fights to displace the argument." From this battle results the ambiguity and indeterminateness of poetry.

Ransom's reputation as a legendary teacher is probably best illustrated by mentioning the names of the three students who followed him when he moved to Kenyon College in 1937: Robert Lowell, Randall Jarrell, and Peter Taylor. Two years later, the *Kenyon Review* was established with Ransom as editor; it remains one of the best little magazines published in America. In 1951, Ransom won the Bollingen Prize for Poetry, and in 1964 he received the National Book Award.

John Crowe Ransom died in 1974 at his home on the Kenyon College campus; his ashes were interred near the library.

Selected Bibliography

By the author:

The World's Body. Charles Scribner's Sons, 1938.
The New Criticism. New Directions, 1941.
Selected Poems. Knopf, 1945; 3rd enl. and rev. ed., New Directions, 1969.
Beating the Bushes: Selected Essays, 1941–1970. New Directions, 1972.
Selected Essays of John Crowe Ransom, edited by Thomas Daniel Young and John J. Hindle. Louisiana State University Press, 1984.

About the author:

Gentleman in a Dustcoat: A Biography of John Crowe Ransom, by Thomas Daniel Young. Louisiana State University Press, 1976.
Selected Letters of John Crowe Ransom, edited by Thomas Daniel Young and George Core. Louisiana State University Press, 1985.

Criticism of the author and his works:

The Anatomy of Nonsense, by Yvor Winters. New Directions, 1943.
The Fugitive Group: A Literary History, by Louise Cowan. Louisiana State University Press, 1959.
The Burden of Time: The Fugitives and Agrarians, by John L. Stewart. Princeton University Press, 1965.
The Equilibrist: A Study of John Crowe Ransom's Poems, 1916–1963, by Robert Buffington. Vanderbilt University Press, 1967.
John Crowe Ransom: Critical Essays and a Bibliography, edited by Thomas Daniel Young. Louisiana State University Press, 1968.
The Poetry of John Crowe Ransom, by Miller Williams. Rutgers, 1972.
The Kenyon Review, 1939–1970: A Critical History, by Marian Janssen. Louisiana State University Press, 1990.

Note:

The World's Body is the place to start with Ransom. *Beating the Bushes* collects a number of his essays on poetry and aesthetics from the *Kenyon Review,* along with the concluding chapter of *The New Criticism,* which is now out of print and rare; the entire book needs to be reprinted. Ransom is the best poet to emerge from the American South, and one of the finest minor poets that this country has produced. Ransom's prose has not been collected and published in a definitive edition.

DELMORE SCHWARTZ (1913–1966)

A poet and critic of great early promise, Delmore Schwartz was born in Brooklyn, New York. He attended the University of Wisconsin and then New York University, where he completed his degree in philosophy in 1935. Enrolled in graduate school at Harvard, Schwartz received the Bowdoin Prize for an essay but never completed an advanced degree.

That cycle of achievement and failure would repeat itself many times in his life. In 1938, New Directions published Schwartz's first book, *In Dreams Begin Responsibilities*, which contained short stories and poems. It was immediately hailed as the debut of an important American poet—and Schwartz found himself in the enviable position of being considered the best poet of his emerging generation. Two years later, he was already an instructor at Harvard, a Guggenheim fellow, and the poetry editor of *Partisan Review*. Yet his next book, a translation of Arthur Rimbaud's "A Season in Hell," was considered mediocre; the same reception was given to his long poem, *Genesis*. A book on T. S. Eliot never made it to publication. In 1947, Schwartz abandoned Cambridge for New York City without warning—Harvard University, for one, was never informed that he would be unavailable, and out of state, for his classes.

Schwartz always enjoyed a reputation as an important critic; as early as 1940, his publisher was preparing a collection of his essays and reviews. It was not, however, until 1970 that a selection of his critical prose finally appeared—a delay no doubt caused by the author himself. In a further irony, it is not improbable that Schwartz might ultimately be considered a better prose writer than a poet, and that some of his critical essays and short stories are permanent contributions to American literature.

Always ambitious and anxious, Schwartz became delusional later in life. His most famous saying remains the dark quip that "even paranoids have real enemies," and he tragically lived out his last years heeding that dictum, living in cheap hotels in Manhattan, a destitute and manic-depressive alcoholic. Though his close friends included John Berryman, Robert Lowell, and Saul Bellow, Schwartz estranged himself from most of his family and acquaintances in his final years. (Bellow, in particular, wrote a moving and thinly fictionalized account of his long relationship with the poet, *Humboldt's Gift*.)

Delmore Schwartz died from a heart attack at the Columbia Hotel in New York City in 1966.

Selected Bibliography

By the author:

Genesis. New Directions, 1943.

Selected Poems (1938–1958): Summer Knowledge. New Directions, 1967.

Selected Essays of Delmore Schwartz, edited by Donald A. Dike and David H. Zucker. University of Chicago Press, 1970.

In Dreams Begin Responsibilities and Other Stories, edited by James Atlas. New Directions, 1978.

About the author:

Letters of Delmore Schwartz, edited by Robert S. Phillips. Ontario Review Press, 1984.

Delmore Schwartz: The Life of an American Poet, by James Atlas. Farrar, Straus and Giroux, 1977; repr., Welcome Rain, 2000.

Note:

No definitive collection of Delmore Schwartz's work has yet appeared. A good selection of his poetry is available, *Summer Knowledge*, and his early verse is still considered to be his best. The *Selected Essays* is hard to find and generally expensive, but well worth the price; it also contains an important introduction by his friend and literary executor, Dwight Macdonald. The best introduction to Schwartz's stories is James Atlas's 1978 selection. Finally, Saul Bellow's novel, *Humboldt's Gift*, is so touching a book about friendship that it should not be missed.

ALLEN TATE (1899–1979)

One of the greatest poet-critics of the twentieth century, Jon Orley Allen Tate was born in Winchester, Kentucky. He entered Vanderbilt University in 1918, where his roommate was Robert Penn Warren; the two undergraduates were soon attending an informal meeting of poets that included professors John Crowe Ransom and Donald Davidson. In time, the group called itself the Fugitives, and produced a famous but short-lived magazine bearing that name. Tate was also a member of the Southern Agrarians, who defended traditional Southern culture against the encroachments of the modern industrial society in their manifesto, *I'll Take My Stand* (1930).

After graduating from college, Tate married the novelist Caroline Gordon; the pair moved to New York City and befriended a number of important writers, including Hart Crane. Throughout his life, Tate provided valuable aid and encouragement to his fellow writers: he wrote the foreword to Hart Crane's first book of poems (*White Buildings*, 1926) and even allowed Crane to stay in his house for several months. He edited the poems of John Peale Bishop, after that poet's death, and helped R. P. Blackmur secure a teaching position at Princeton University. When the young Robert Lowell came to visit the Tates, pitching a tent in the yard so that he could stay longer, the Tates did not object to their houseguest's presumption.

A Southern Agrarian, an excommunicated Catholic thrice married, a modernist poet, an editor of the *Sewanee Review*—Tate was a brilliant and complex man. The contradictions, or perhaps the violent tensions, that arose from his social, political, and literary views were not lost on his fellow critics. Randall Jarrell, reviewing *Reason in Madness* in 1941, found Tate (and his fellow Southern New Critics) part of "a distinguished and very forlorn hope; what they are fighting is history. . . . It has been later than they think for four hundred years."

Tate's critical prose often carried an obvious aim (Randall Jarrell described his method simply as "the attack"); his usual objective was to find and destroy elements of positivist philosophy lurking in literary studies. Though Ransom and Eliot were his obvious mentors (in the preface to his collected essays, Tate admitted, "What I owe to T. S. Eliot is pervasive"), Tate was no imitator or simple disseminator of other men's ideas. In truth, there are very few modern critics who can match him for the force of his arguments or the strength of his prose.

Tate was the poet in residence at Princeton University until 1942, and he founded the creative writing program there as well. Though Tate was considered one of the finest American poets during his lifetime, his verse is now less read, and less admired, than it should be.

Allen Tate died in Nashville, Tennessee, in 1979.

Selected Bibliography

By the author:

Reactionary Essays on Poetry and Ideas. Charles Scribner's Sons, 1936.
Reason in Madness: Critical Essays. G. P. Putnam's Sons, 1941.
Poems, 1922–1947. C. Scribner's Sons, 1948.
On the Limits of Poetry: Selected Essays, 1928–1948. Swallow and William Morrow, 1948.
The Hovering Fly and Other Essays. Cummington School of the Arts, 1949.
Collected Essays. Swallow, 1959.
Essays of Four Decades. Swallow, 1968.

Collected Poems, 1919–1976. Farrar, Straus and Giroux, 1977.
The Poetry Reviews of Allen Tate, 1924–1944, edited by Ashley Brown and Frances
   Neel Cheney. Louisiana State University Press, 1983.

About the author:

Allen Tate: Orphan of the South, by Thomas A. Underwood. Princeton University
   Press, 2000.

Criticism of the author and his works:

Allen Tate, by Ferman Bishop. Twayne, 1967.
Allen Tate and His Work: Critical Evaluations, edited by Radcliffe Squires. Uni-
   versity of Minnesota Press, 1972.
Allen Tate and the Augustinian Imagination: A Study of the Poetry, by Robert S.
   Dupree. Louisiana State University Press, 1983.
Hart Crane and Allen Tate: Janus-Faced Modernism, by Langdon Hammer.
   Princeton University Press, 1993.

Note:

Essays of Four Decades is the indispensable one-volume selection of
Tate's critical prose, but there are important essays scattered through all
the other books; his critical prose awaits its definitive edition. The 1983
gathering of his poetry reviews is certainly valuable. Unfortunately, Tate's
poetry is as widely neglected today as it was widely read half a century
ago; he has left us a score of good poems and a few masterpieces like
"Aeneas in Washington" and his translation of the *Pervigilium Veneris.*

ROBERT PENN WARREN (1905–1989)

Probably the most versatile American man of letters in his day, Robert
Penn Warren was born in Guthrie, Kentucky. "Red," as he was called
by his friends (a nickname referring to his hair color), lost sight in one
eye after an adolescent hunting accident, and had to give up on attending the Naval Academy; he went to Vanderbilt University instead, where
he shared a room with fellow student Allen Tate, and had John Crowe
Ransom for a professor. Warren was soon a member of the important intellectual circles at Vanderbilt—he helped edit the *Fugitive* magazine,
and he also contributed to the Southern Agrarian manifesto, *I'll Take
My Stand* (though he later repudiated this work and became involved
in the civil rights movement).

After graduate work at Berkeley and Yale, Warren went to Oxford University on a Rhodes Scholarship. In 1934, he started teaching at Louisiana
State University; his schoolmate from Vanderbilt, Cleanth Brooks, had

joined the faculty there two years before. Together, the two men coedited the important little magazine *Southern Review* (1935–42) and coauthored the most influential college textbooks of their day: *Understanding Poetry* (1938) and *Understanding Fiction* (1943). In 1950, Warren moved to Yale University, where he taught for several decades until retirement.

Already an important poet and critic, Warren enjoyed his greatest success with the publication of his novel *All the King's Men* (1946). The book won the Pulitzer Prize, and the movie version won an Academy Award. A prolific author, Warren would ultimately write a dozen works of fiction in all and sixteen books of poetry, in addition to his criticism and editing work in thirty-odd volumes. That a man of such varied accomplishments should be neglected today seems unthinkable. Yet in none of these genres is Warren's reputation secure and unquestioned — rarely numbered among American critics of the first rank, he is also usually dismissed as a poet (though he won two Pulitzer Prizes in that category). Of his fiction, only *All the King's Men* remains widely read and admired. In an age of specialists, Warren seems to suffer because he never restrained himself to one category of literature.

There have been signs of renewed interest in his work recently. John Burt's *Selected Poems* (2001) focused critical attention on Warren's best verse, written in the last decades of his life. In 2005, the United States Postal Service issued a commemorative stamp to mark the centennial of his birth, while a new film version of *All the King's Men* appeared in 2006. Among the many honors he received during his lifetime, Warren served as the third Consultant in Poetry to the Library of Congress, in 1944; he was again chosen to serve in that post when the title changed to Poet Laureate in 1986.

Robert Penn Warren died in Stratton, Vermont, in 1989.

Selected Bibliography

By the author:

All the King's Men. Harcourt, Brace, 1946
A Robert Penn Warren Reader, edited by Albert Erskine. Random House, 1987.
New and Selected Essays. Random House, 1989.
The Collected Poems of Robert Penn Warren, edited by John Burt. Louisiana State University Press, 1998.
Selected Poems of Robert Penn Warren, edited by John Burt. Louisiana State University Press, 2001.

About the author:

Robert Penn Warren: A Collection of Critical Essays, edited by John Lewis Longley. New York University Press, 1965.

Robert Penn Warren Talking: Interviews (1950–1978), edited by Floyd C. Watkins
and John T. Hiers. Random House, 1980.
Homage to Robert Penn Warren: A Collection of Critical Essays, edited by Frank
Graziano. Logbridge-Rhodes, 1981.
A Southern Renascence Man: Views of Robert Penn Warren, edited by Walter B.
Edgar. Louisiana State University Press, 1984.
Robert Penn Warren: A Biography, by Joseph Blotner. Random House, 1997.

Criticism of the author and his works:

In the Heart's Last Kingdom: Robert Penn Warren's Major Poetry, by Calvin Be-
dient. Harvard University Press, 1984.

Note:

Probably the most wide-ranging littérateur of his day, Robert Penn
Warren is one of the few New Critics whose books have remained consistently in print. His novels are easy to find; his poetry has been collected
and selected recently; and much of his correspondence is also available.
In addition, the secondary literature is remarkably large — biographies,
bibliographies, and studies of his work appear regularly from a small but
devoted group of scholars. Even so, Warren is one of the most difficult
writers to assess in the canon of American literature. His current place
rests almost entirely upon one of his ten novels, *All the King's Men*, and,
though he always considered himself primarily a poet, he has never enjoyed a large following among his fellow versifiers. (Critical opinion on
this vast body of work still varies greatly; the interested reader should find
John Burt's selection of the poems.) He was also a less distinguished literary critic than many of his compatriots. *A Robert Penn Warren Reader*
(1987) usefully samples his many works.

W. K. WIMSATT (1907–1975)

William Kurtz Wimsatt Jr. was born in Washington, D.C. He attended
Georgetown University and, later, Yale University, where he received
his PhD. In 1939, Wimsatt joined the English Department at Yale,
where he taught until his death. His Yale department colleague Cleanth
Brooks soon became his critical collaborator as well.

Along with Monroe C. Beardsley, Wimsatt coauthored two of the
most influential essays of the New Criticism: "The Intentional Fallacy"
and "The Affective Fallacy" (both collected in *The Verbal Icon*). Together, they outlined an "objective criticism" that would minimize the
intentions of the poet and the effect of the poem on the audience as

factors in analyzing poetry. Wimsatt's major essays on poetry are collected in three books: *The Verbal Icon: Studies in the Meaning of Poetry*
(1954), *Hateful Contraries: Studies in Literature and Criticism* (1965),
and *Day of the Leopards: Essays in Defense of Poems* (1976).

Wimsatt also cowrote (with Cleanth Brooks) the brilliant four-volume
survey *Literary Criticism*, which examined the critical arts from Plato
to the scholarship of the mid-twentieth century. His valuable books
of scholarship include *The Prose Style of Samuel Johnson* (1941) and
*Philosophic Words: A Study of Style and Meaning in the Rambler and
Dictionary of Samuel Johnson* (1948). The preeminent Johnson scholar
of his day, Wimsatt edited numerous collections of that writer's poetry
and prose; he also coedited an edition of the private papers of James
Boswell.

Selected Bibliography

By the author:

The Prose Style of Samuel Johnson. Yale University Press, 1941.

*Philosophic Words: A Study of Meaning in the Rambler and Dictionary of
  Samuel Johnson.* Yale University Press, 1948.

The Verbal Icon: Studies in the Meaning of Poetry (with Monroe C. Beardsley).
  University of Kentucky Press, 1954.

Literary Criticism: A Short History (with Cleanth Brooks). Knopf, 1957.

Hateful Contraries: Studies in Literature and Criticism. University of Kentucky
  Press, 1965.

Day of the Leopards: Essays in Defense of Poems. Yale University Press, 1976.

About the author:

Literary Theory and Structure: Essays in Honor of W. K. Wimsatt, edited by
  Frank Brady, John Palmer, and Martin Price. Yale University Press, 1973.

Note:

Like his great subject, Samuel Johnson, W. K. Wimsatt was an editor
of great vitality, so I have not listed the many books that he oversaw.
The reader should begin with *The Verbal Icon*, and continue on to
Hateful Contraries and then *The Day of the Leopards*, which is probably the last book published by a New Critic. With it, the movement
came to its end. By 1976, the new trends of politicized scholarship that
were to be so destructive to traditional literary studies were already in
their infancy.

YVOR WINTERS (1900–1968)

Though born in Chicago, Arthur Yvor Winters lived most of his life in California—the only New Critic (other than his favorite protégé, J. V. Cunningham) to be associated with the American West. Winters led an isolated existence: first as a young poet recovering from tuberculosis in a sanitarium and virtually immobilized for three years; later as a professor of English at Stanford University, espousing neoclassical views at the height of modernism's influence in the academy. Though he was by nature reclusive, and his literary views were highly unorthodox, Winters still drew a coterie of poets to him: J. V. Cunningham, Edgar Bowers, Thom Gunn, and Robert Pinsky were all devoted students.

His first book of criticism, *Primitivism and Decadence*, outlined a theory of moral criticism that remains influential, and controversial, to this day. Though Winters was himself a religious skeptic, he steadfastly held to absolute standards of moral and aesthetic judgment; no New Critic was more independent in his literary opinions. Winters also proved in this first book that he was the best practical critic regarding the stylistic excesses and vices of modernism.

His second book, *Maule's Curse*, discussed the crippling effects of Puritanism on early American writers. Randall Jarrell called it "the best book on American literature I ever read." Winters battled against deterministic philosophies and what he called "Romantic amoralism" in all his major works, but particularly here; his criticism of the writings of Edgar Allan Poe and Ralph Waldo Emerson, to cite two chapters as examples, permanently altered the critical consensus regarding these authors.

Almost alone in being dismissive of T. S. Eliot's poetry and critical of his prose, Winters was the great contrarian of the New Criticism, and the antimodernist *par excellence*. A moralist who insisted on consistency of system above all else, he always wanted to "lay the groundwork for general theories," and so great authors were routinely dismissed, and inferior talents overpraised, to illustrate his precepts. In this, he was our Sainte-Beuve: wrong about many things but extremely interesting to read, principally as an antidote to modernist orthodoxies.

Just as T. S. Eliot revived interest in the metaphysical poets, Winters created an audience for his alternate pantheon of writers. If, today, we read the poems of Jones Very or T. Sturge Moore, it is largely because of Winters's regard for them. He is also credited with almost single-handedly reviving interest in the poetry of the English Renaissance: his essay "The Sixteenth-Century Lyric in England" led to new editions and commentaries for such neglected poets as Fulke Greville and Barnabe Googe.

Yvor Winters died of cancer in Palo Alto in 1968.

Selected Bibliography

By the author:

Primitivism and Decadence: A Study of American Experimental Poetry. Arrow Editions, 1937.

Maule's Curse: Seven Studies in the History of American Obscurantism. New Directions, 1938.

The Anatomy of Nonsense. New Directions, 1943.

Edwin Arlington Robinson. New Directions, 1946.

In Defense of Reason. Swallow, 1947.

The Function of Criticism: Problems and Exercises. Swallow, 1957.

Collected Poems. Swallow, 1960.

Forms of Discovery: Critical and Historical Essays on the Forms of the Short Poem in English. Swallow, 1967.

The Uncollected Essays and Reviews of Yvor Winters, edited by Francis Murphy. Swallow, 1973.

Selected Poems of Yvor Winters, edited by R. L. Barth. Swallow, 1999.

Yvor Winters: Selected Poems, edited by Thom Gunn. Library of America, 2003.

About the author:

Yvor Winters: A Bibliography, by Kenneth A. Lohf and Eugene P. Sheehy. Swallow, 1959.

Selected Letters of Yvor Winters, edited by R. L. Barth. Swallow, 2000.

Criticism of the author and his works:

The New Criticism, by John Crowe Ransom. New Directions, 1941.

An Introduction to the Poetry of Yvor Winters, by Elizabeth Isaacs. Swallow, 1981.

Wisdom and Wilderness: The Achievement of Yvor Winters, by Dick Davis. University of Georgia Press, 1983.

In Defense of Winters: The Poetry and Prose of Yvor Winters, by Terry Comito. University of Wisconsin Press, 1986.

Note:

In Defense of Reason collects Winters's first three books of criticism, and is the essential starting place. *The Function of Criticism* and *Forms of Discovery* collect the important later essays. In his own poetry, Winters moved from an early style of modernist free verse to a highly formal classicism in his later work—he is a minor poet, but there are half a dozen short poems that embody his ideal of neoclassicism (such as "At the San Francisco Airport"). Thom Gunn's selection of Winters's verse is widely available.

SOURCE CREDITS

"Lord Tennyson's Scissors: 1912–1950" by R. P. Blackmur, first published in the *Kenyon Review*, Winter 1952. Reprinted by permission of the *Kenyon Review*.

"Religious Poetry in the United States" by R. P. Blackmur, first published in the *Criterion*. Reprinted by permission of the author's literary executor.

"The Formalist Critics" by Cleanth Brooks, first published in the *Kenyon Review*, Winter 1951. Reprinted by permission of the *Kenyon Review*.

"T. S. Eliot: Thinker and Artist" by Cleanth Brooks. First published in the *Sewanee Review*, vol. 74, no. 1, Winter 1966. Copyright © 1966 by the University of the South. Reprinted with the permission of the editor and the author's agent.

"Towards a Post-Kantian Verbal Music" by Kenneth Burke, first published in the *Kenyon Review*, Autumn 1958. Reprinted by permission of the *Kenyon Review*.

"The Problem of Form" by J. V. Cunningham, from *The Collected Essays of J. V. Cunningham*, copyright © 1976. Reprinted by permission of Ohio University Press.

"Hamlet and His Problems" by T. S. Eliot, from *The Sacred Wood: Essays on Poetry and Criticism* (Methuen & Company, 1920). Rights are in the public domain.

Introduction to *The Sacred Wood* by T. S. Eliot, from *The Sacred Wood: Essays on Poetry and Criticism* (Methuen & Company, 1920). Rights are in the public domain.

"The Metaphysical Poets" by T. S. Eliot, first published in the *Times Literary Supplement* (October 20, 1921). Rights are in the public domain.

"The Perfect Critic" by T. S. Eliot, from *The Sacred Wood: Essays on Poetry and Criticism* (Methuen & Company, 1920). Rights are in the public domain.

"Reflections on *Vers Libre*" by T. S. Eliot, first published in *New Statesman* 8 (March 3, 1917). Rights are in the public domain.

"The End of the Line" by Randall Jarrell, first published in the *Nation*, February 21, 1942 issue.

"Texts from Housman" by Randall Jarrell, first published in the *Kenyon Review*, Summer 1939. Reprinted by permission of the *Kenyon Review*.